THE INCREDIBLE HULK

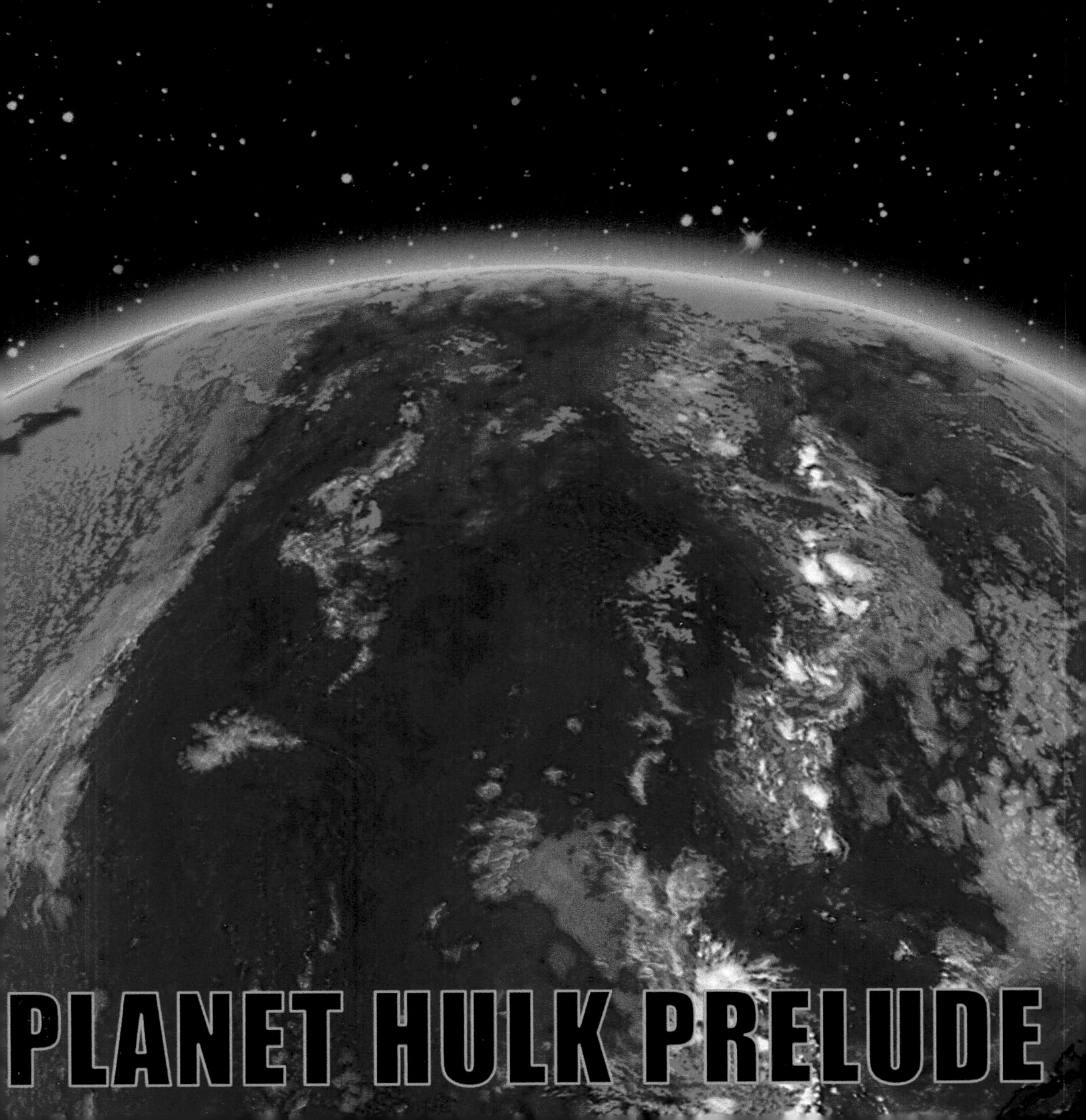

PLANET HULK PRELUDE

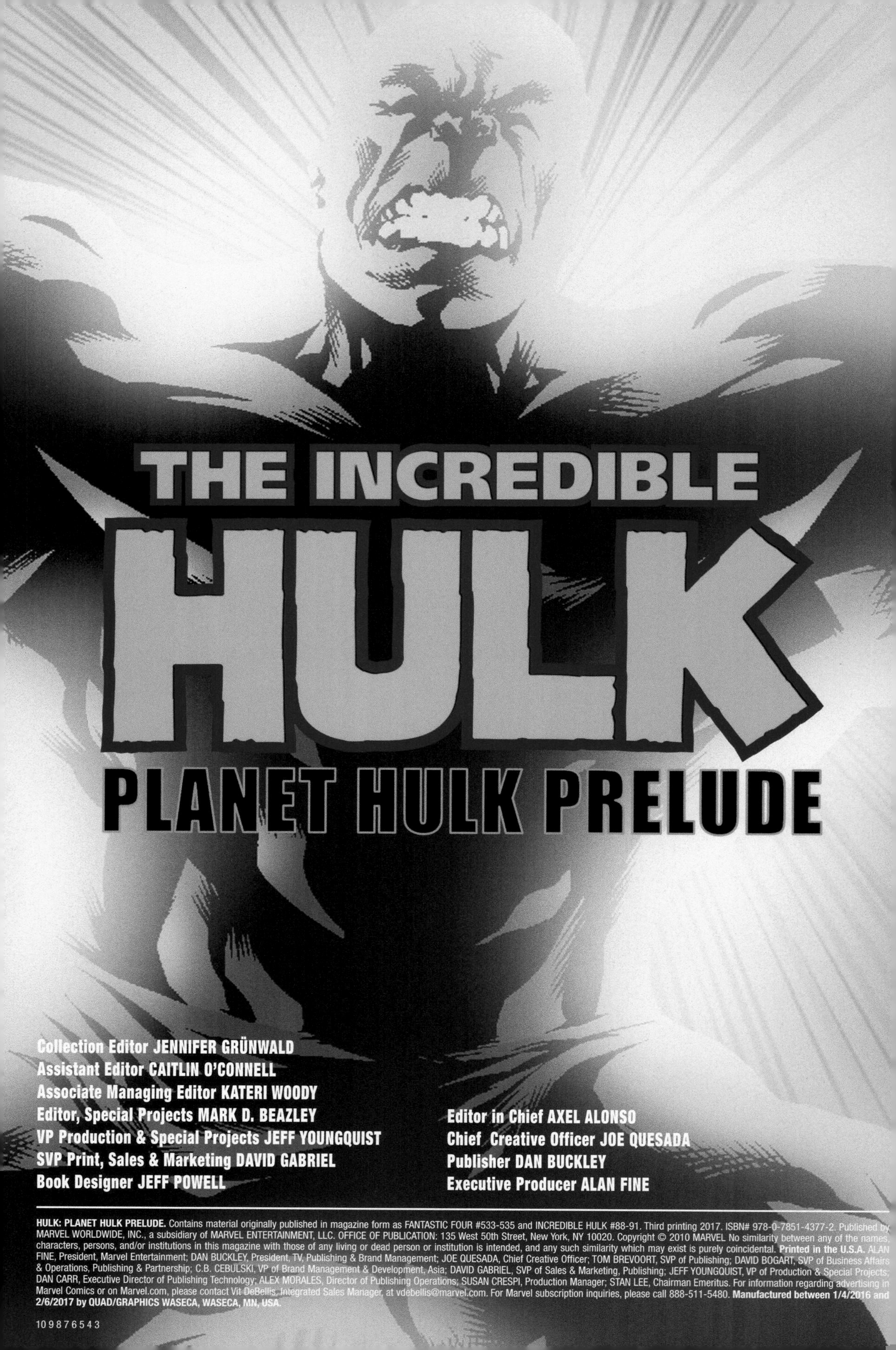

THE INCREDIBLE HULK
PLANET HULK PRELUDE

Collection Editor JENNIFER GRÜNWALD
Assistant Editor CAITLIN O'CONNELL
Associate Managing Editor KATERI WOODY
Editor, Special Projects MARK D. BEAZLEY
VP Production & Special Projects JEFF YOUNGQUIST
SVP Print, Sales & Marketing DAVID GABRIEL
Book Designer JEFF POWELL

Editor in Chief AXEL ALONSO
Chief Creative Officer JOE QUESADA
Publisher DAN BUCKLEY
Executive Producer ALAN FINE

HULK: PLANET HULK PRELUDE. Contains material originally published in magazine form as FANTASTIC FOUR #533-535 and INCREDIBLE HULK #88-91. Third printing 2017. ISBN# 978-0-7851-4377-2. Published by MARVEL WORLDWIDE, INC., a subsidiary of MARVEL ENTERTAINMENT, LLC. OFFICE OF PUBLICATION: 135 West 50th Street, New York, NY 10020. **Printed in the U.S.A.** ALAN FINE, President, Marvel Entertainment; DAN BUCKLEY, President, TV, Publishing & Brand Management; JOE QUESADA, Chief Creative Officer; TOM BREVOORT, SVP of Publishing; DAVID BOGART, SVP of Business Affairs & Operations, Publishing & Partnership; C.B. CEBULSKI, VP of Brand Management & Development, Asia; DAVID GABRIEL, SVP of Sales & Marketing, Publishing; JEFF YOUNGQUIST, VP of Production & Special Projects; DAN CARR, Executive Director of Publishing Technology; ALEX MORALES, Director of Publishing Operations; SUSAN CRESPI, Production Manager; STAN LEE, Chairman Emeritus. For information regarding advertising in Marvel Comics or on Marvel.com, please contact Vit DeBellis, Integrated Sales Manager, at vdebellis@marvel.com. For Marvel subscription inquiries, please call 888-511-5480. **Manufactured between 1/4/2016 and 2/6/2017 by QUAD/GRAPHICS WASECA, WASECA, MN, USA.**

10 9 8 7 6 5 4 3

FANTASTIC FOUR #533-535

WRITER: J. MICHAEL STRACZYNSKI

PENCILER: MIKE MCKONE

INKERS: ANDY LANNING
WITH SIMON COLEBY (#533)
& CAM SMITH (#534)

COLORIST: PAUL MOUNTS

LETTERERS: VIRTUAL CALLIGRAPHY'S
RUS WOOTON & RANDY GENTILE

COVER ART: MIKE MCKONE

ASSISTANT EDITORS: ANDY SCHMIDT,
MOLLY LAZER & AUBREY SITTERSON

EDITOR: TOM BREVOORT

INCREDIBLE HULK #88-91

WRITER: DANIEL WAY

ARTISTS: KEU CHA (#88-89)
& JUAN SANTACRUZ (#90-91)

COLORISTS: JASON KEITH (#88)
& WILLIAM MURAI (#89-91)

LETTERER: VIRTUAL CALLIGRAPHY'S
RANDY GENTILE

COVER ART: BRANDON PETERSON

ASSISTANT EDITOR: NATE COSBY

EDITOR: MARK PANICCIA

SPECIAL THANKS TO AXEL ALONSO
& CORY SEDLMEIER

HULK CREATED BY STAN LEE & JACK KIRBY

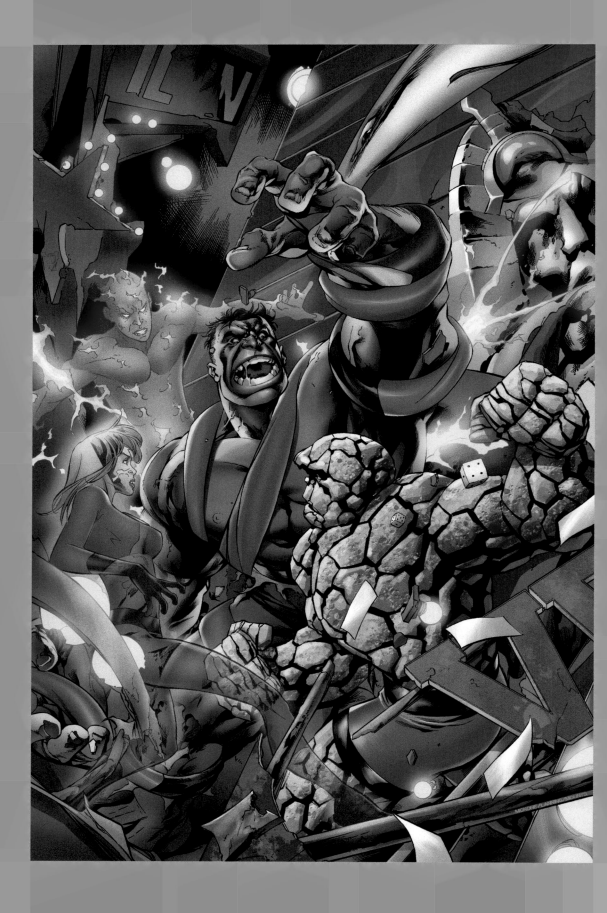

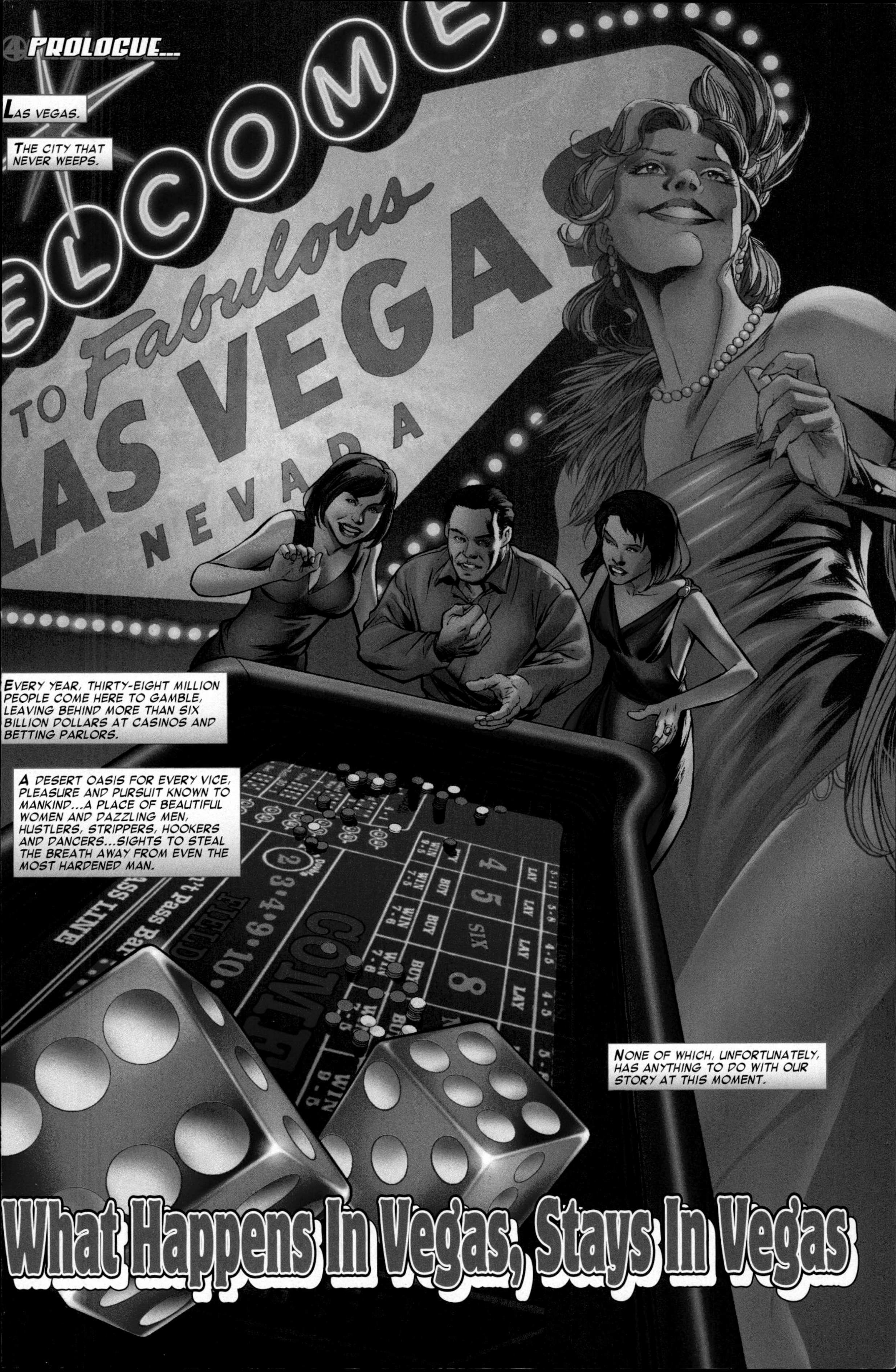
PROLOGUE...
LAS VEGAS.
THE CITY THAT NEVER WEEPS.
WELCOME TO Fabulous LAS VEGA NEVADA
EVERY YEAR, THIRTY-EIGHT MILLION PEOPLE COME HERE TO GAMBLE, LEAVING BEHIND MORE THAN SIX BILLION DOLLARS AT CASINOS AND BETTING PARLORS.
A DESERT OASIS FOR EVERY VICE, PLEASURE AND PURSUIT KNOWN TO MANKIND...A PLACE OF BEAUTIFUL WOMEN AND DAZZLING MEN, HUSTLERS, STRIPPERS, HOOKERS AND DANCERS...SIGHTS TO STEAL THE BREATH AWAY FROM EVEN THE MOST HARDENED MAN.
NONE OF WHICH, UNFORTUNATELY, HAS ANYTHING TO DO WITH OUR STORY AT THIS MOMENT.
What Happens In Vegas, Stays In Vegas

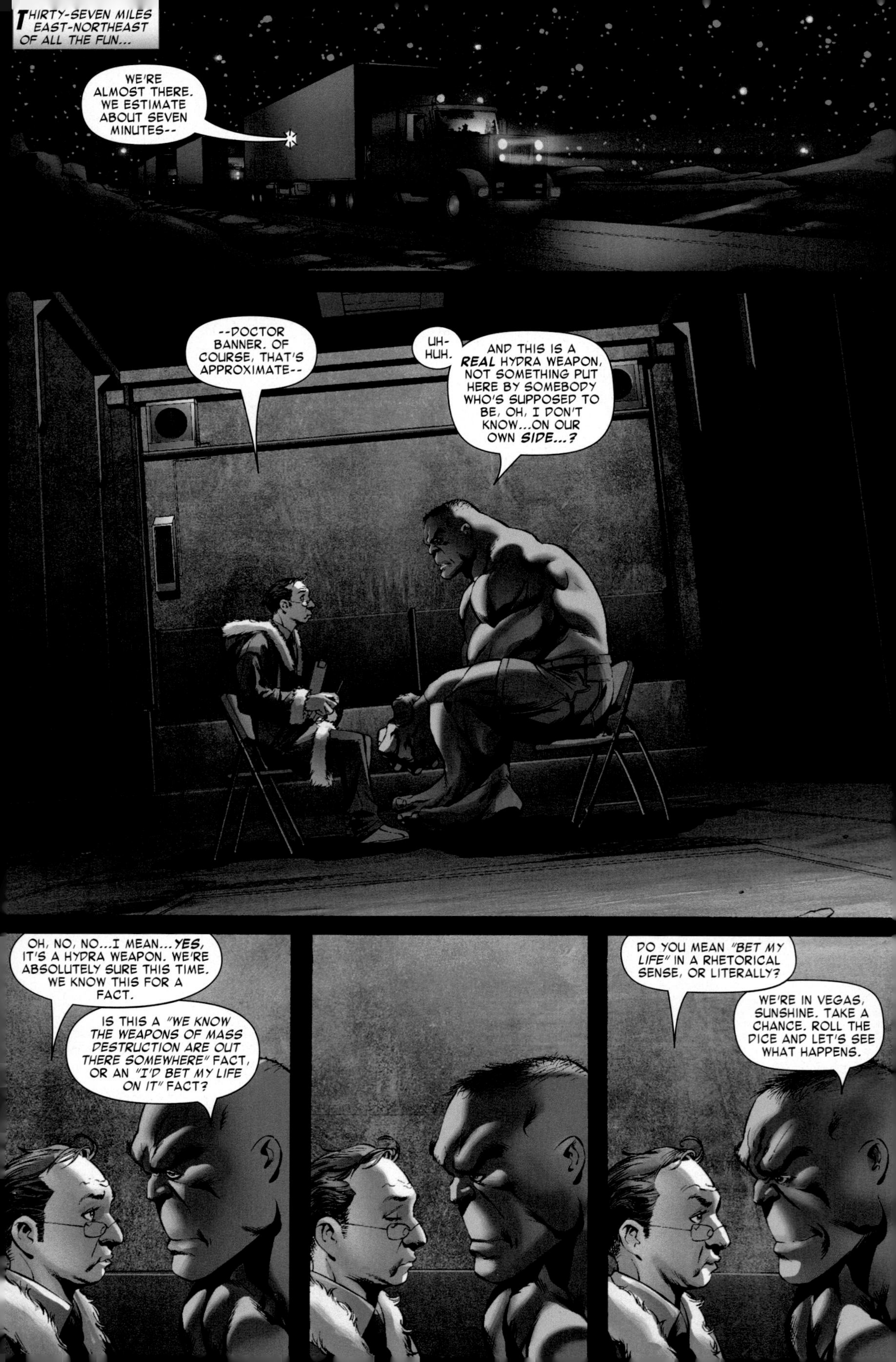
THIRTY-SEVEN MILES EAST-NORTHEAST OF ALL THE FUN...
WE'RE ALMOST THERE. WE ESTIMATE ABOUT SEVEN MINUTES--
--DOCTOR BANNER. OF COURSE, THAT'S APPROXIMATE--
UH-HUH.
AND THIS IS A REAL HYDRA WEAPON, NOT SOMETHING PUT HERE BY SOMEBODY WHO'S SUPPOSED TO BE, OH, I DON'T KNOW...ON OUR OWN SIDE...?
OH, NO, NO...I MEAN...YES, IT'S A HYDRA WEAPON. WE'RE ABSOLUTELY SURE THIS TIME. WE KNOW THIS FOR A FACT.
IS THIS A "WE KNOW THE WEAPONS OF MASS DESTRUCTION ARE OUT THERE SOMEWHERE" FACT, OR AN "I'D BET MY LIFE ON IT" FACT?
DO YOU MEAN "BET MY LIFE" IN A RHETORICAL SENSE, OR LITERALLY?
WE'RE IN VEGAS, SUNSHINE. TAKE A CHANCE. ROLL THE DICE AND LET'S SEE WHAT HAPPENS.

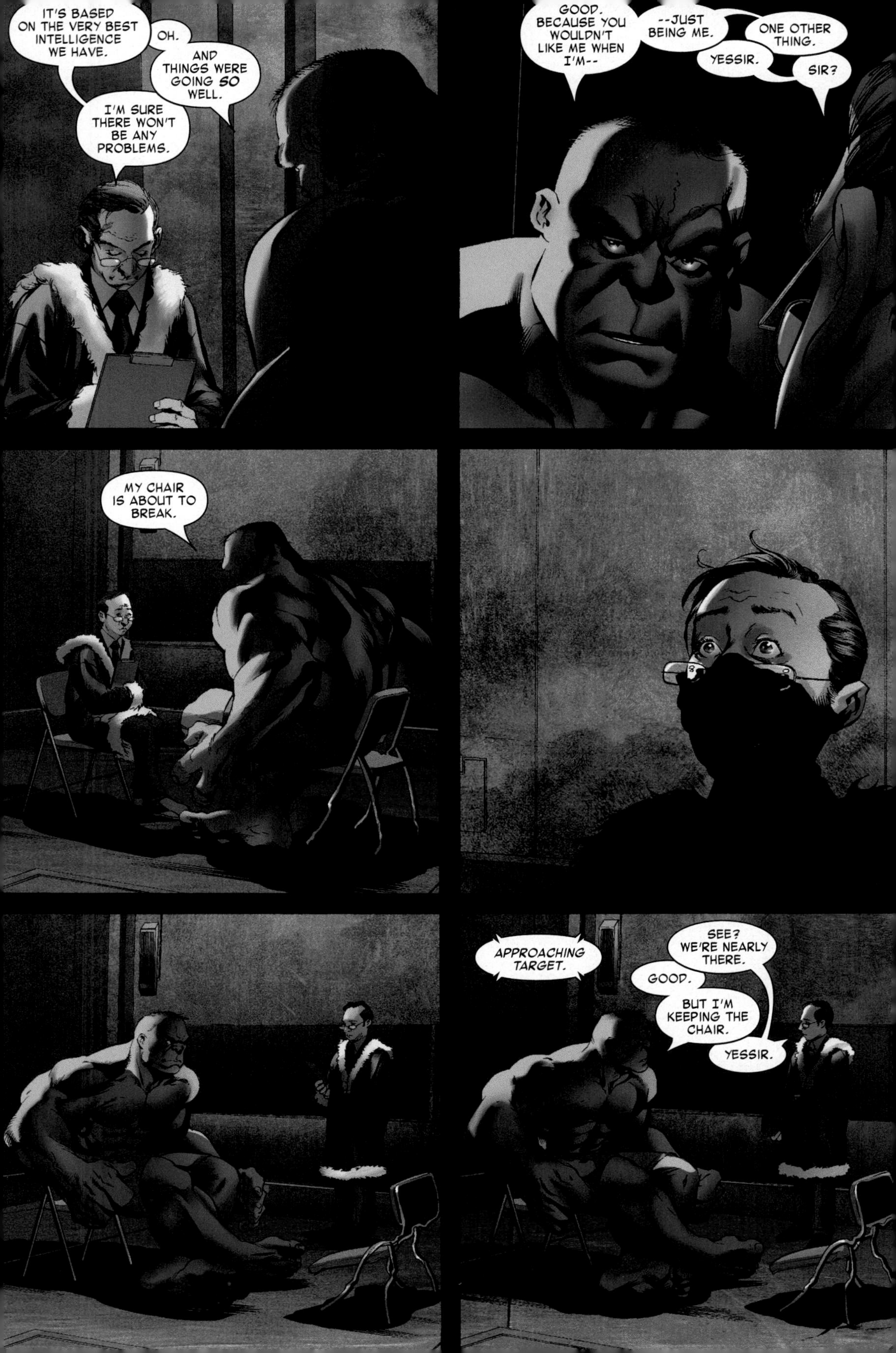
IT'S BASED ON THE VERY BEST INTELLIGENCE WE HAVE.
OH.
AND THINGS WERE GOING SO WELL.
I'M SURE THERE WON'T BE ANY PROBLEMS.
GOOD. BECAUSE YOU WOULDN'T LIKE ME WHEN I'M--
--JUST BEING ME.
YESSIR.
ONE OTHER THING.
SIR?
MY CHAIR IS ABOUT TO BREAK.
APPROACHING TARGET.
SEE? WE'RE NEARLY THERE.
GOOD.
BUT I'M KEEPING THE CHAIR.
YESSIR.

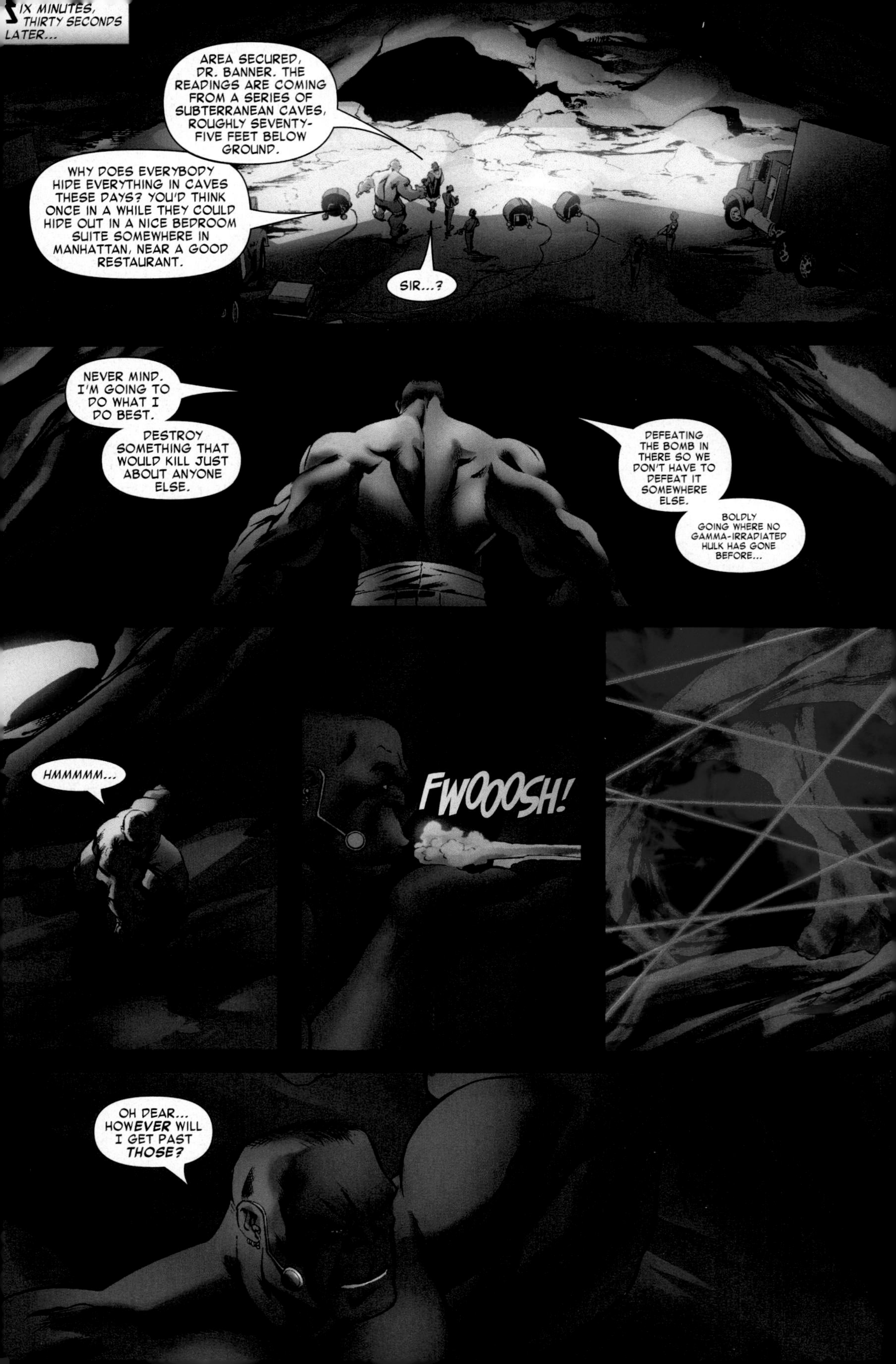
SIX MINUTES, THIRTY SECONDS LATER...
AREA SECURED, DR. BANNER. THE READINGS ARE COMING FROM A SERIES OF SUBTERRANEAN CAVES, ROUGHLY SEVENTY-FIVE FEET BELOW GROUND.
WHY DOES EVERYBODY HIDE EVERYTHING IN CAVES THESE DAYS? YOU'D THINK ONCE IN A WHILE THEY COULD HIDE OUT IN A NICE BEDROOM SUITE SOMEWHERE IN MANHATTAN, NEAR A GOOD RESTAURANT.
SIR...?
NEVER MIND. I'M GOING TO DO WHAT I DO BEST.
DESTROY SOMETHING THAT WOULD KILL JUST ABOUT ANYONE ELSE.
DEFEATING THE BOMB IN THERE SO WE DON'T HAVE TO DEFEAT IT SOMEWHERE ELSE.
BOLDLY GOING WHERE NO GAMMA-IRRADIATED HULK HAS GONE BEFORE...
HMMMMM...
FWOOOSH!
OH DEAR... HOW*EVER* WILL I GET PAST *THOSE?*

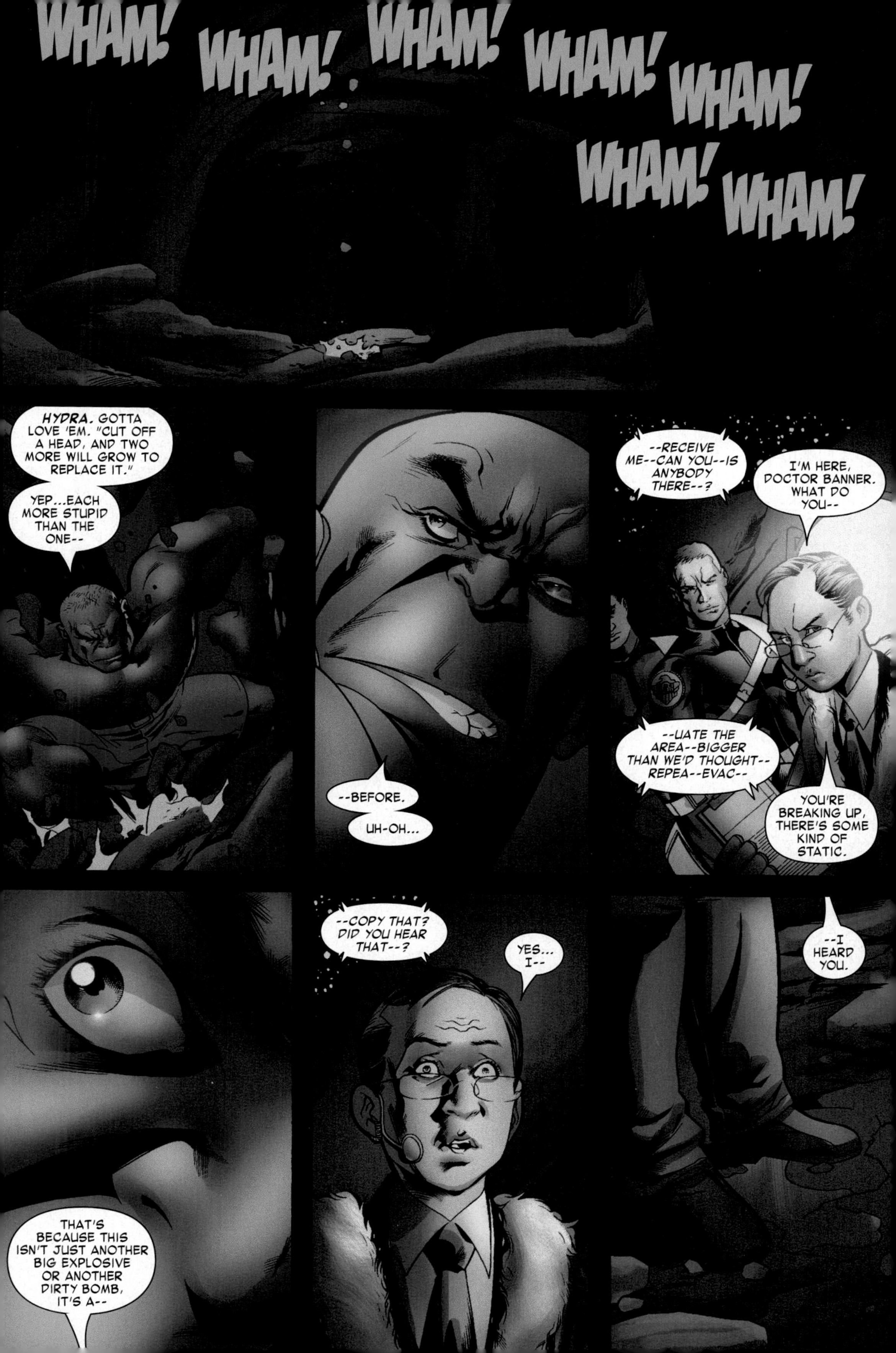
WHAM! WHAM! WHAM! WHAM! WHAM! WHAM! WHAM!
HYDRA. GOTTA LOVE 'EM. "CUT OFF A HEAD, AND TWO MORE WILL GROW TO REPLACE IT."
YEP...EACH MORE STUPID THAN THE ONE--
--BEFORE.
UH-OH...
--RECEIVE ME--CAN YOU--IS ANYBODY THERE--?
I'M HERE, DOCTOR BANNER. WHAT DO YOU--
--UATE THE AREA--BIGGER THAN WE'D THOUGHT--REPEA--EVAC--
YOU'RE BREAKING UP, THERE'S SOME KIND OF STATIC.
THAT'S BECAUSE THIS ISN'T JUST ANOTHER BIG EXPLOSIVE OR ANOTHER DIRTY BOMB, IT'S A--
--COPY THAT? DID YOU HEAR THAT--?
YES... I--
--I HEARD YOU.

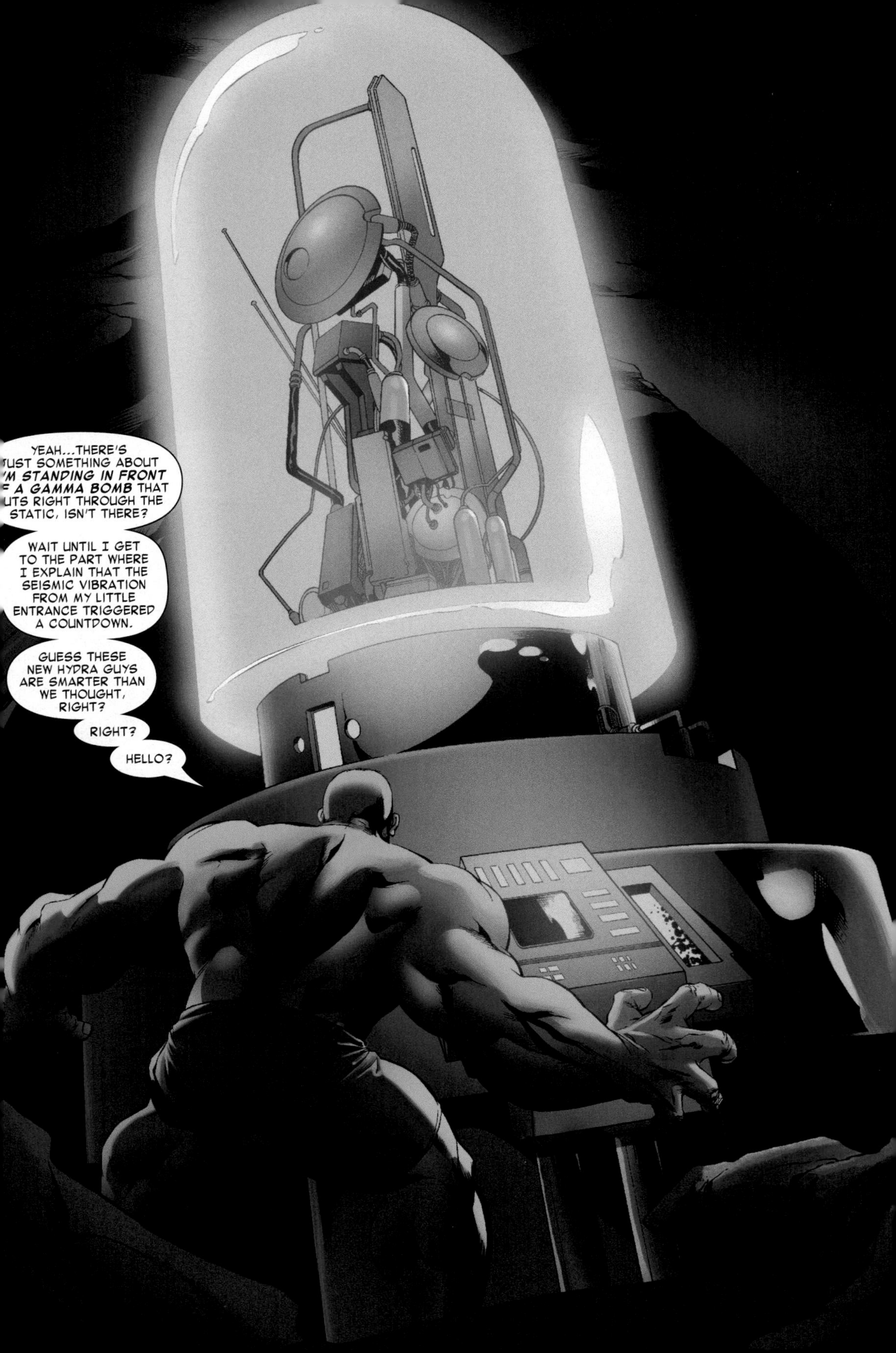
YEAH...THERE'S
UST SOMETHING ABOUT
'M STANDING IN FRONT
A GAMMA BOMB THAT
UTS RIGHT THROUGH THE
STATIC, ISN'T THERE?
WAIT UNTIL I GET TO THE PART WHERE I EXPLAIN THAT THE SEISMIC VIBRATION FROM MY LITTLE ENTRANCE TRIGGERED A COUNTDOWN.
GUESS THESE NEW HYDRA GUYS ARE SMARTER THAN WE THOUGHT, RIGHT?
RIGHT?
HELLO?

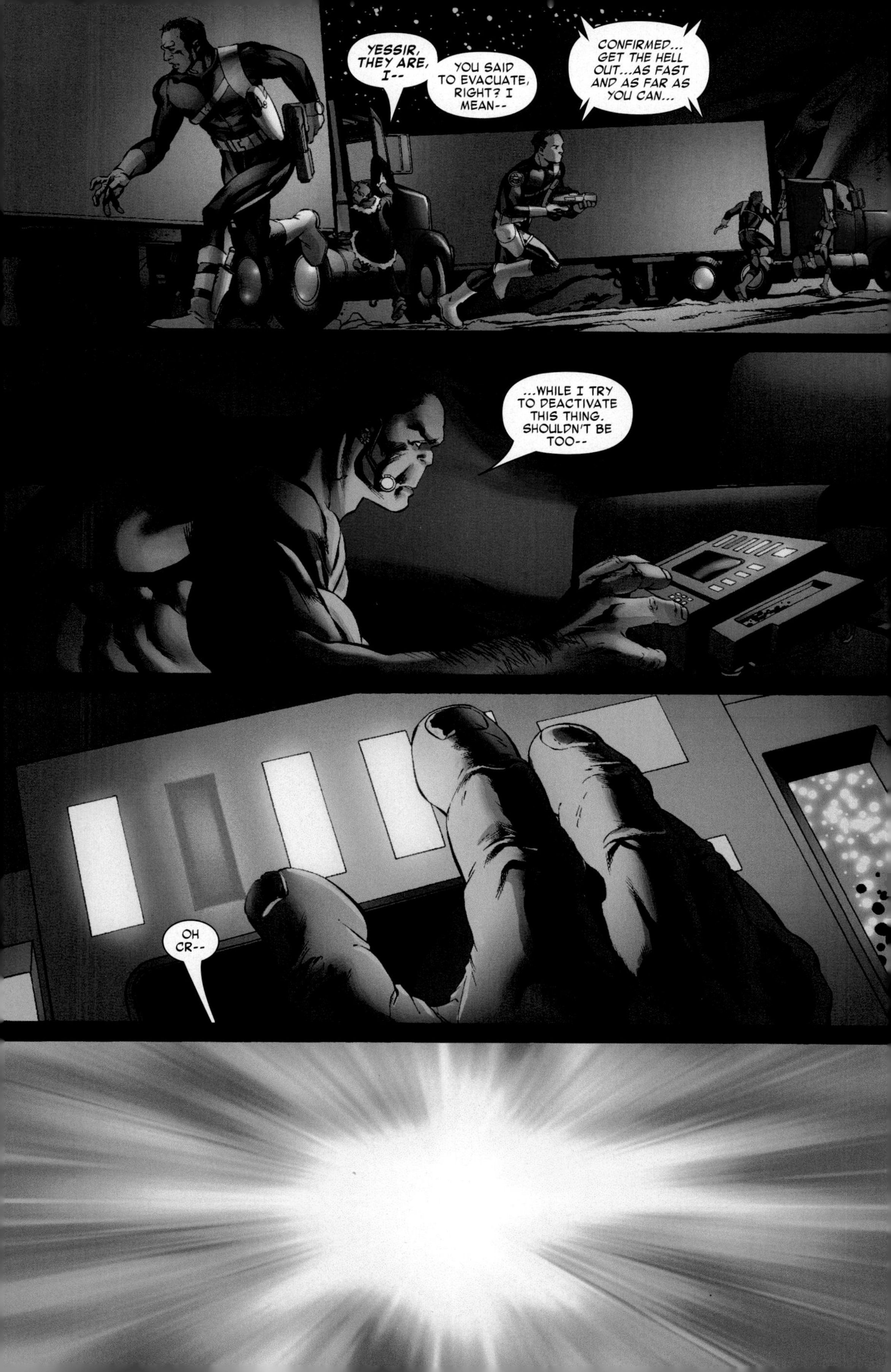
YESSIR, THEY ARE, I--
YOU SAID TO EVACUATE, RIGHT? I MEAN--
CONFIRMED... GET THE HELL OUT...AS FAST AND AS FAR AS YOU CAN...
...WHILE I TRY TO DEACTIVATE THIS THING. SHOULDN'T BE TOO--
OH CR--

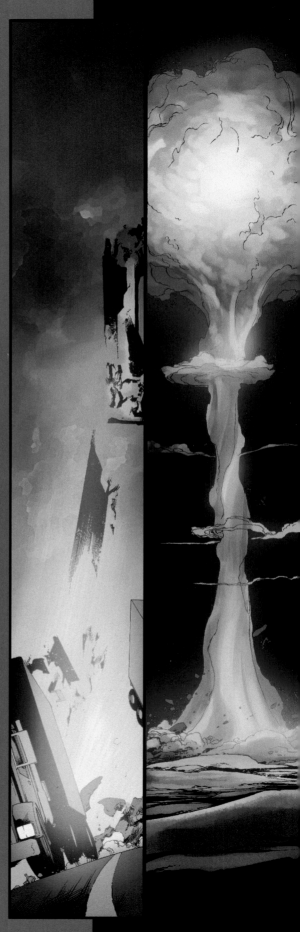

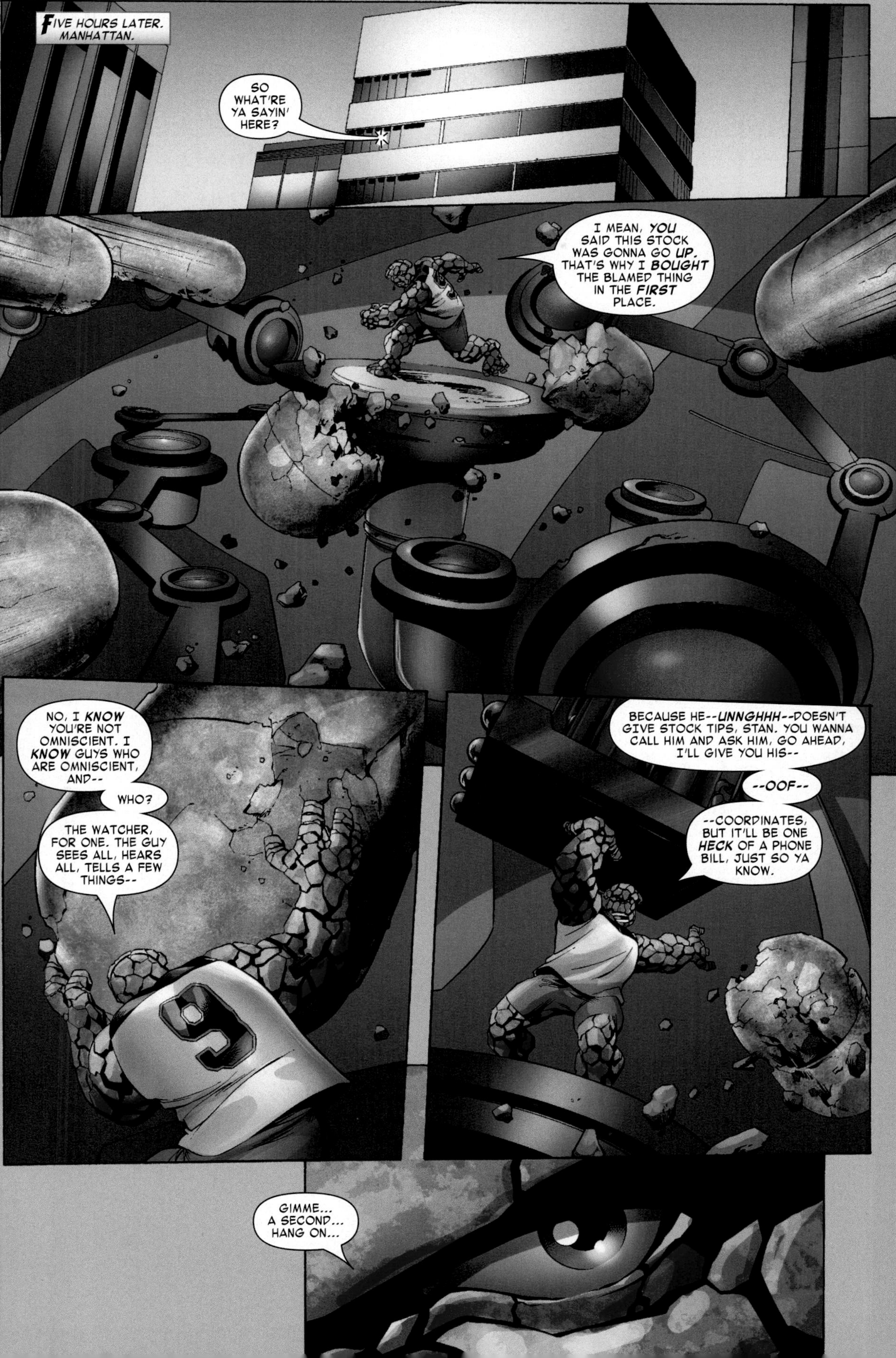
FIVE HOURS LATER. MANHATTAN.
SO WHAT'RE YA SAYIN' HERE?
I MEAN, YOU SAID THIS STOCK WAS GONNA GO UP. THAT'S WHY I BOUGHT THE BLAMED THING IN THE FIRST PLACE.
NO, I KNOW YOU'RE NOT OMNISCIENT. I KNOW GUYS WHO ARE OMNISCIENT, AND--
WHO?
THE WATCHER, FOR ONE. THE GUY SEES ALL, HEARS ALL, TELLS A FEW THINGS--
BECAUSE HE--UNNGHHH--DOESN'T GIVE STOCK TIPS, STAN. YOU WANNA CALL HIM AND ASK HIM, GO AHEAD, I'LL GIVE YOU HIS--
--OOF--
--COORDINATES, BUT IT'LL BE ONE HECK OF A PHONE BILL, JUST SO YA KNOW.
GIMME... A SECOND... HANG ON...

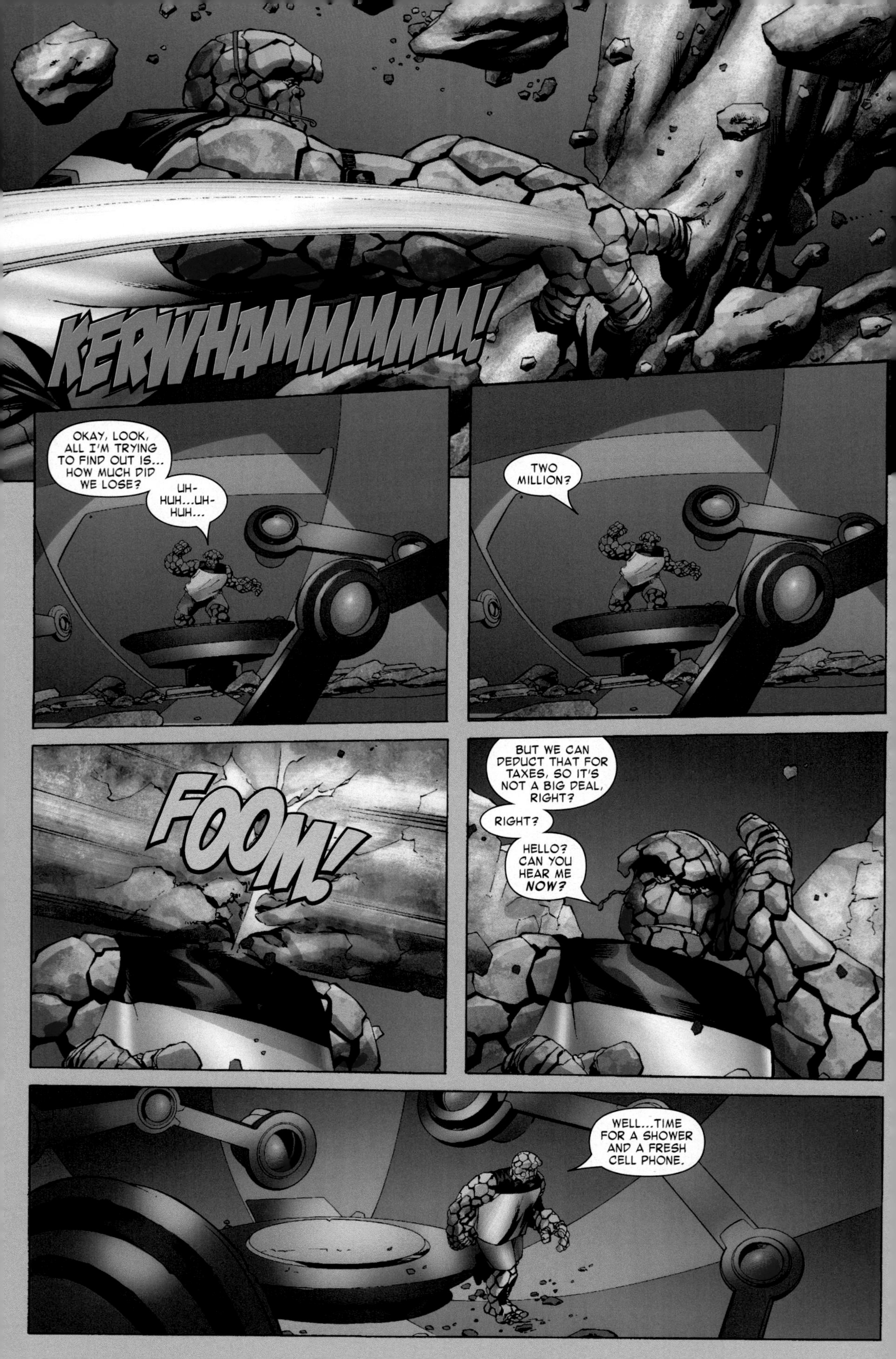
KERWHAMMMMMM!
OKAY, LOOK, ALL I'M TRYING TO FIND OUT IS... HOW MUCH DID WE LOSE?
UH-HUH...UH-HUH...
TWO MILLION?
FOOM!
BUT WE CAN DEDUCT THAT FOR TAXES, SO IT'S NOT A BIG DEAL, RIGHT?
RIGHT?
HELLO? CAN YOU HEAR ME NOW?
WELL...TIME FOR A SHOWER AND A FRESH CELL PHONE.

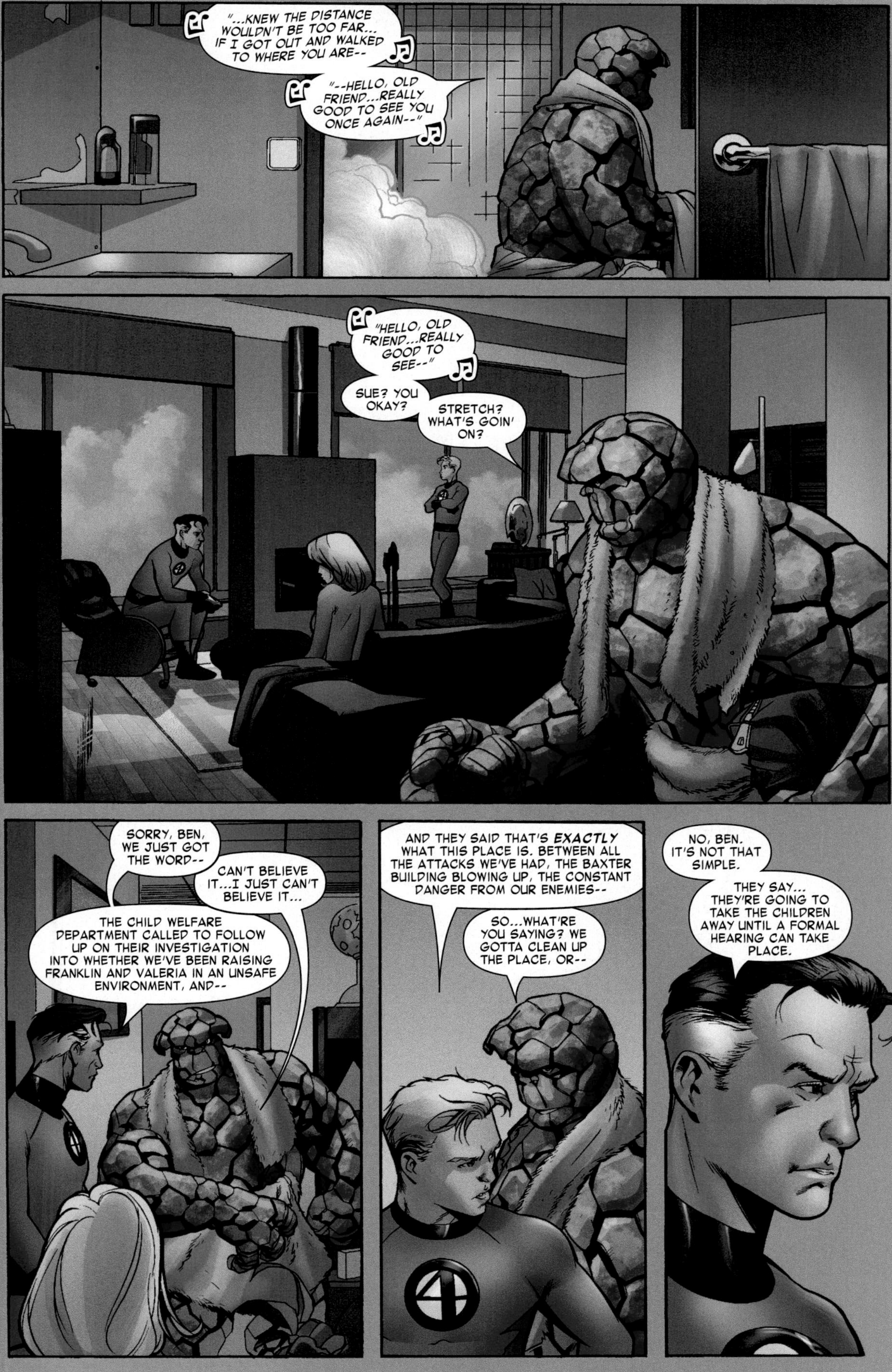
"...KNEW THE DISTANCE WOULDN'T BE TOO FAR... IF I GOT OUT AND WALKED TO WHERE YOU ARE--
"--HELLO, OLD FRIEND...REALLY GOOD TO SEE YOU ONCE AGAIN--"
"HELLO, OLD FRIEND...REALLY GOOD TO SEE--"
SUE? YOU OKAY?
STRETCH? WHAT'S GOIN' ON?
SORRY, BEN, WE JUST GOT THE WORD--
CAN'T BELIEVE IT...I JUST CAN'T BELIEVE IT...
THE CHILD WELFARE DEPARTMENT CALLED TO FOLLOW UP ON THEIR INVESTIGATION INTO WHETHER WE'VE BEEN RAISING FRANKLIN AND VALERIA IN AN UNSAFE ENVIRONMENT, AND--
AND THEY SAID THAT'S EXACTLY WHAT THIS PLACE IS. BETWEEN ALL THE ATTACKS WE'VE HAD, THE BAXTER BUILDING BLOWING UP, THE CONSTANT DANGER FROM OUR ENEMIES--
SO...WHAT'RE YOU SAYING? WE GOTTA CLEAN UP THE PLACE, OR--
NO, BEN. IT'S NOT THAT SIMPLE.
THEY SAY... THEY'RE GOING TO TAKE THE CHILDREN AWAY UNTIL A FORMAL HEARING CAN TAKE PLACE.

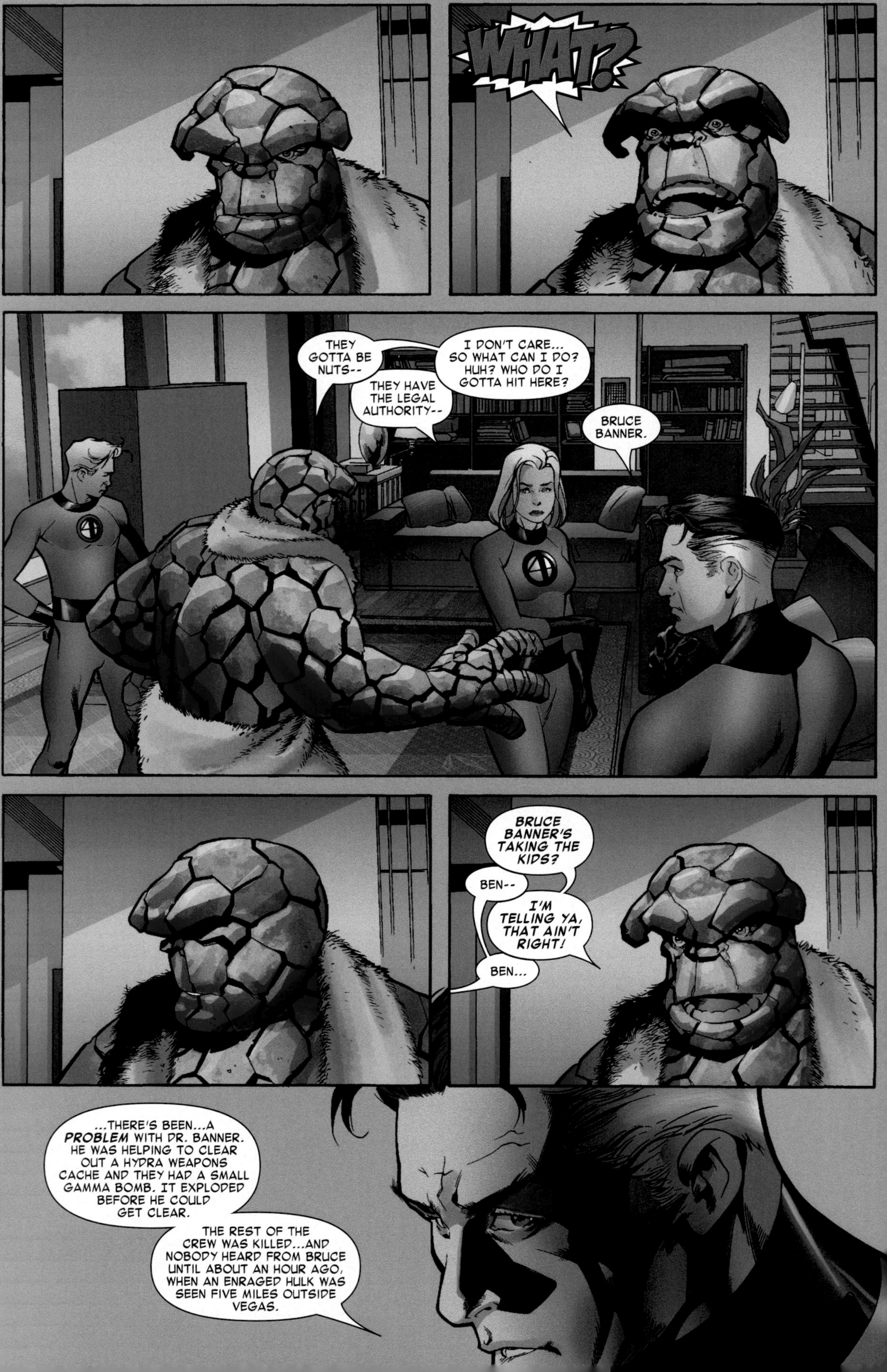
WHAT?
THEY GOTTA BE NUTS--
THEY HAVE THE LEGAL AUTHORITY--
I DON'T CARE... SO WHAT CAN I DO? HUH? WHO DO I GOTTA HIT HERE?
BRUCE BANNER.
BRUCE BANNER'S TAKING THE KIDS?
BEN--
I'M TELLING YA, THAT AIN'T RIGHT!
BEN...
...THERE'S BEEN...A PROBLEM WITH DR. BANNER. HE WAS HELPING TO CLEAR OUT A HYDRA WEAPONS CACHE AND THEY HAD A SMALL GAMMA BOMB. IT EXPLODED BEFORE HE COULD GET CLEAR.
THE REST OF THE CREW WAS KILLED...AND NOBODY HEARD FROM BRUCE UNTIL ABOUT AN HOUR AGO, WHEN AN ENRAGED HULK WAS SEEN FIVE MILES OUTSIDE VEGAS.

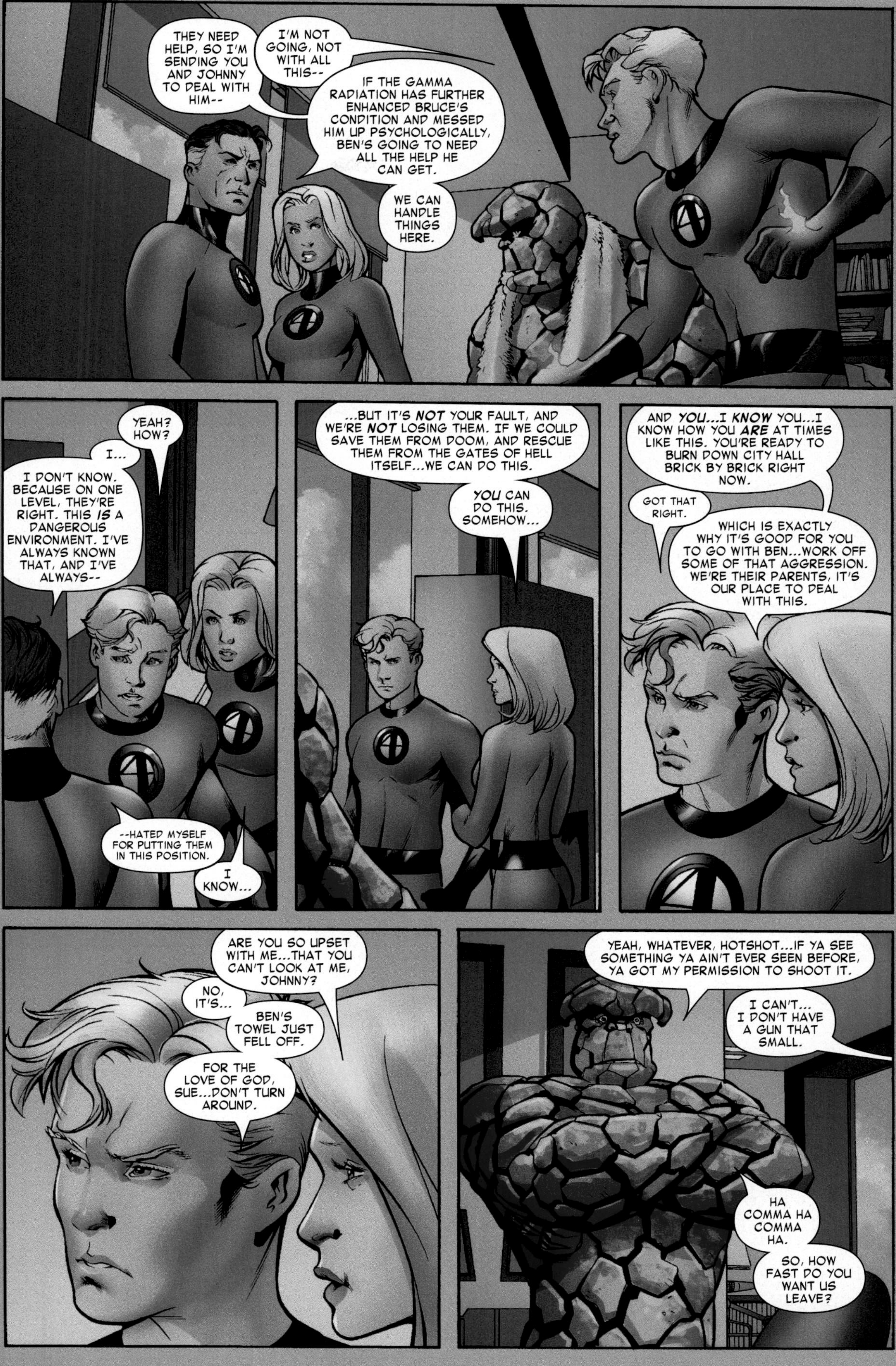
THEY NEED HELP, SO I'M SENDING YOU AND JOHNNY TO DEAL WITH HIM--
I'M NOT GOING, NOT WITH ALL THIS--
IF THE GAMMA RADIATION HAS FURTHER ENHANCED BRUCE'S CONDITION AND MESSED HIM UP PSYCHOLOGICALLY, BEN'S GOING TO NEED ALL THE HELP HE CAN GET.
WE CAN HANDLE THINGS HERE.
YEAH? HOW?
I...
I DON'T KNOW. BECAUSE ON ONE LEVEL, THEY'RE RIGHT. THIS IS A DANGEROUS ENVIRONMENT. I'VE ALWAYS KNOWN THAT, AND I'VE ALWAYS--
--HATED MYSELF FOR PUTTING THEM IN THIS POSITION.
I KNOW...
...BUT IT'S NOT YOUR FAULT, AND WE'RE NOT LOSING THEM. IF WE COULD SAVE THEM FROM DOOM, AND RESCUE THEM FROM THE GATES OF HELL ITSELF...WE CAN DO THIS.
YOU CAN DO THIS. SOMEHOW...
AND YOU...I KNOW YOU...I KNOW HOW YOU ARE AT TIMES LIKE THIS. YOU'RE READY TO BURN DOWN CITY HALL BRICK BY BRICK RIGHT NOW.
GOT THAT RIGHT.
WHICH IS EXACTLY WHY IT'S GOOD FOR YOU TO GO WITH BEN...WORK OFF SOME OF THAT AGGRESSION. WE'RE THEIR PARENTS, IT'S OUR PLACE TO DEAL WITH THIS.
ARE YOU SO UPSET WITH ME...THAT YOU CAN'T LOOK AT ME, JOHNNY?
NO, IT'S...
BEN'S TOWEL JUST FELL OFF.
FOR THE LOVE OF GOD, SUE...DON'T TURN AROUND.
YEAH, WHATEVER, HOTSHOT...IF YA SEE SOMETHING YA AIN'T EVER SEEN BEFORE, YA GOT MY PERMISSION TO SHOOT IT.
I CAN'T... I DON'T HAVE A GUN THAT SMALL.
HA COMMA HA COMMA HA.
SO, HOW FAST DO YOU WANT US LEAVE?

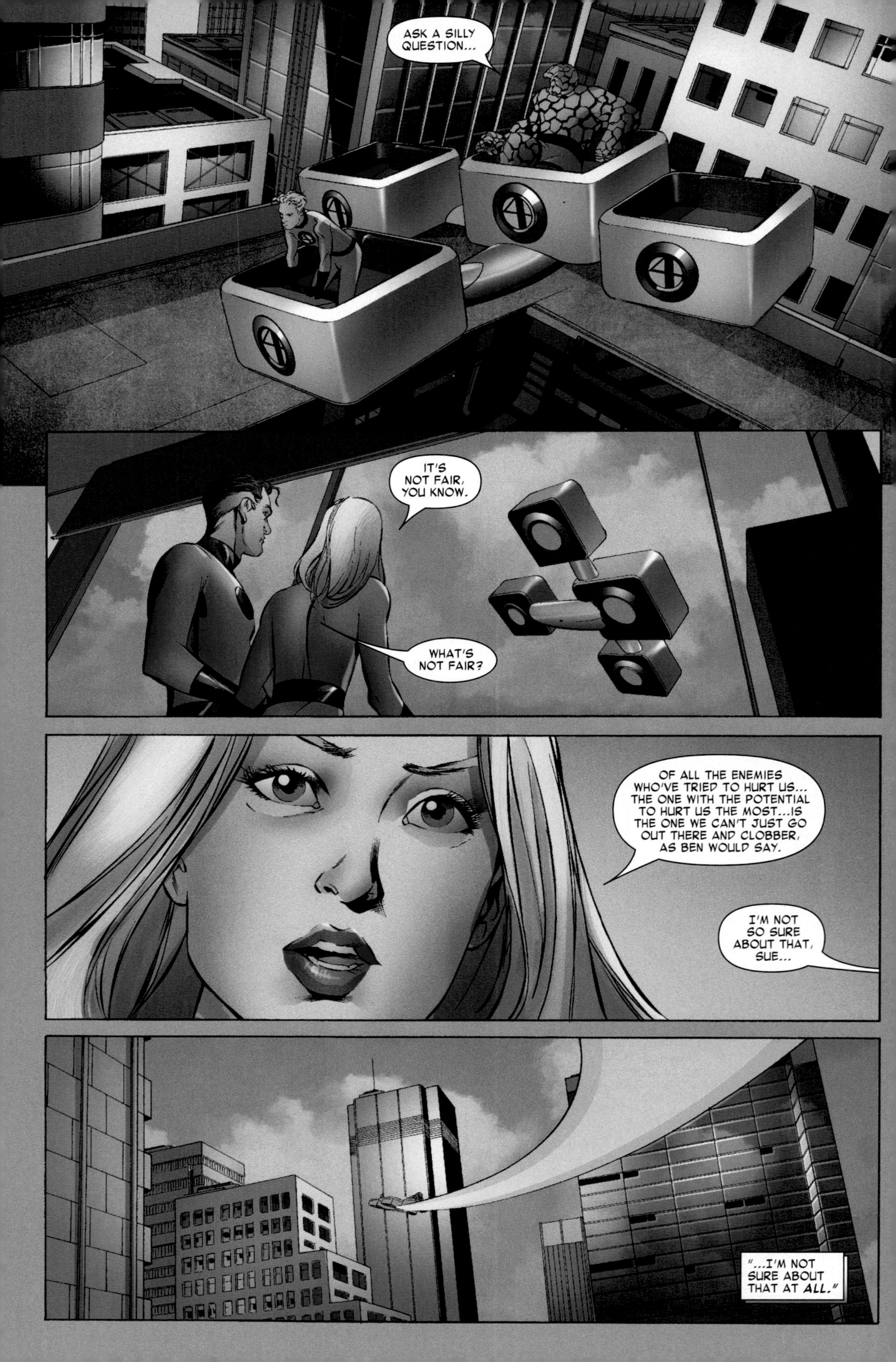
ASK A SILLY QUESTION...
IT'S NOT FAIR, YOU KNOW.
WHAT'S NOT FAIR?
OF ALL THE ENEMIES WHO'VE TRIED TO HURT US... THE ONE WITH THE POTENTIAL TO HURT US THE MOST...IS THE ONE WE CAN'T JUST GO OUT THERE AND CLOBBER, AS BEN WOULD SAY.
I'M NOT SO SURE ABOUT THAT, SUE...
"...I'M NOT SURE ABOUT THAT AT ALL."

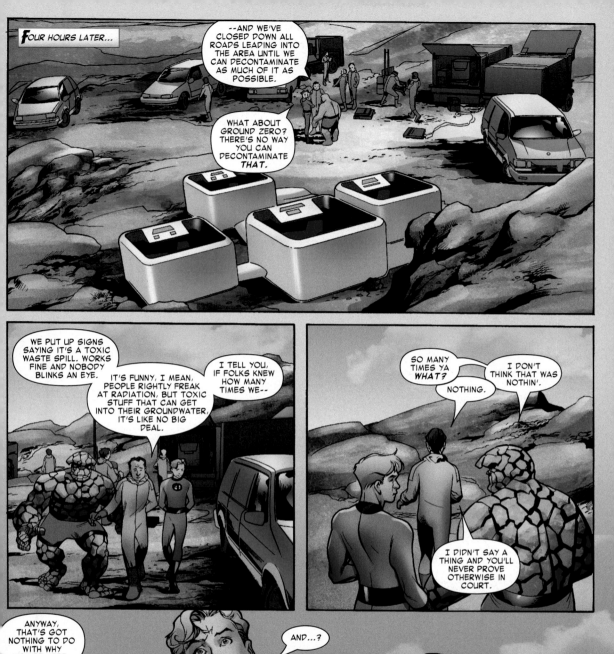

--AND WE'VE CLOSED DOWN ALL ROADS LEADING INTO THE AREA UNTIL WE CAN DECONTAMINATE AS MUCH OF IT AS POSSIBLE.

WHAT ABOUT GROUND ZERO? THERE'S NO WAY YOU CAN DECONTAMINATE *THAT*.

WE PUT UP SIGNS SAYING IT'S A TOXIC WASTE SPILL. WORKS FINE AND NOBODY BLINKS AN EYE.

IT'S FUNNY, I MEAN, PEOPLE RIGHTLY FREAK AT RADIATION, BUT TOXIC STUFF THAT CAN GET INTO THEIR GROUNDWATER, IT'S LIKE NO BIG DEAL.

I TELL YOU, IF FOLKS KNEW HOW MANY TIMES WE--

SO MANY TIMES YA *WHAT?*

NOTHING.

I DON'T THINK THAT WAS NOTHIN'.

I DIDN'T SAY A THING AND YOU'LL NEVER PROVE OTHERWISE IN COURT.

ANYWAY, THAT'S GOT NOTHING TO DO WITH WHY YOU'RE HERE.

AFTER THE BLAST, WE LOST TRACK OF DR. BANNER. BUT A LOW-FLYING CHOPPER SPOTTED A FIGURE BY AN ABANDONED AIRFIELD THAT MIGHT HAVE BEEN HIM. SO THEY WENT TO CHECK IT OUT.

AND...?

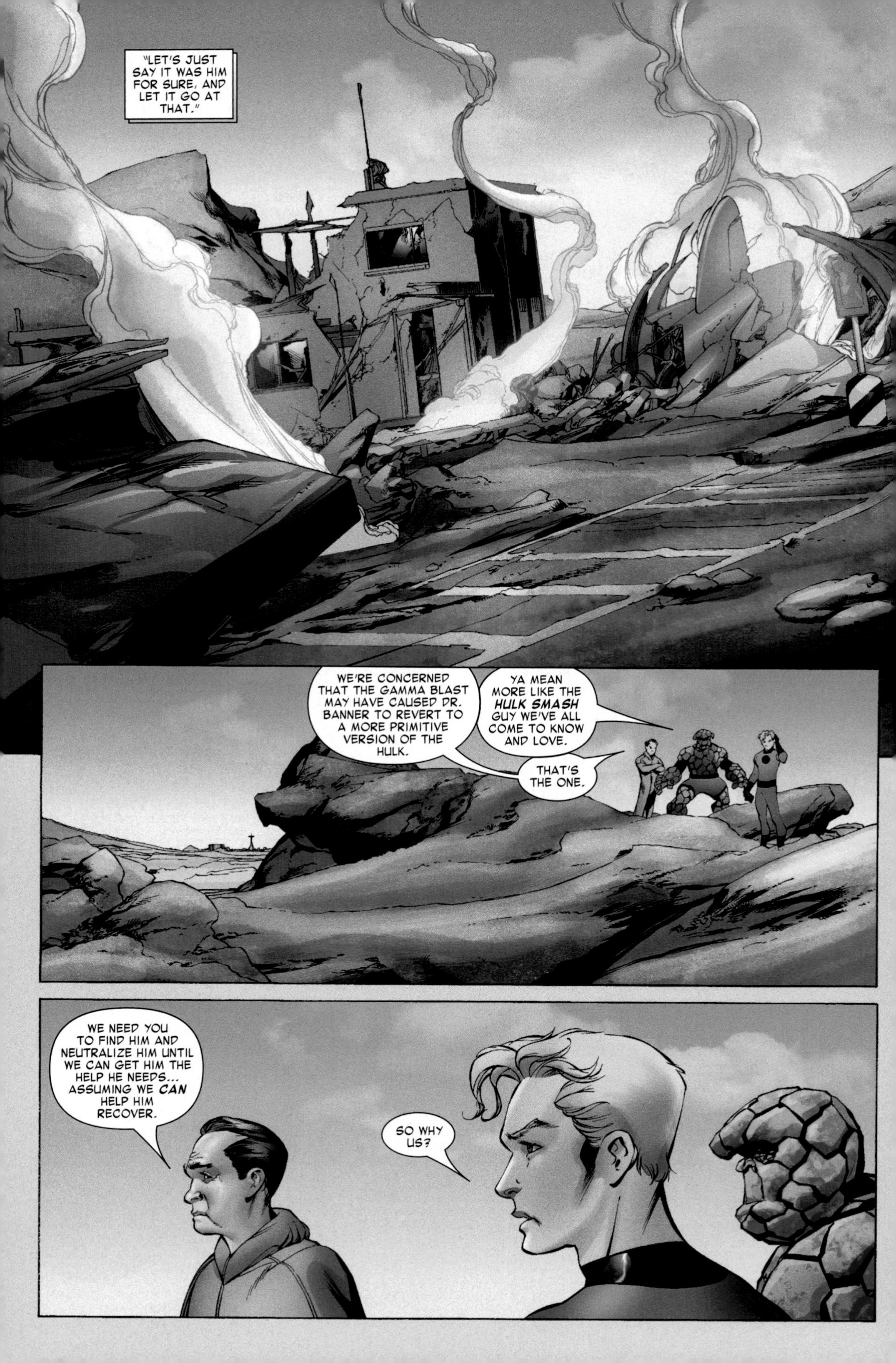
"LET'S JUST SAY IT WAS HIM FOR SURE, AND LET IT GO AT THAT."
WE'RE CONCERNED THAT THE GAMMA BLAST MAY HAVE CAUSED DR. BANNER TO REVERT TO A MORE PRIMITIVE VERSION OF THE HULK.
YA MEAN MORE LIKE THE HULK SMASH GUY WE'VE ALL COME TO KNOW AND LOVE.
THAT'S THE ONE.
WE NEED YOU TO FIND HIM AND NEUTRALIZE HIM UNTIL WE CAN GET HIM THE HELP HE NEEDS... ASSUMING WE CAN HELP HIM RECOVER.
SO WHY US?

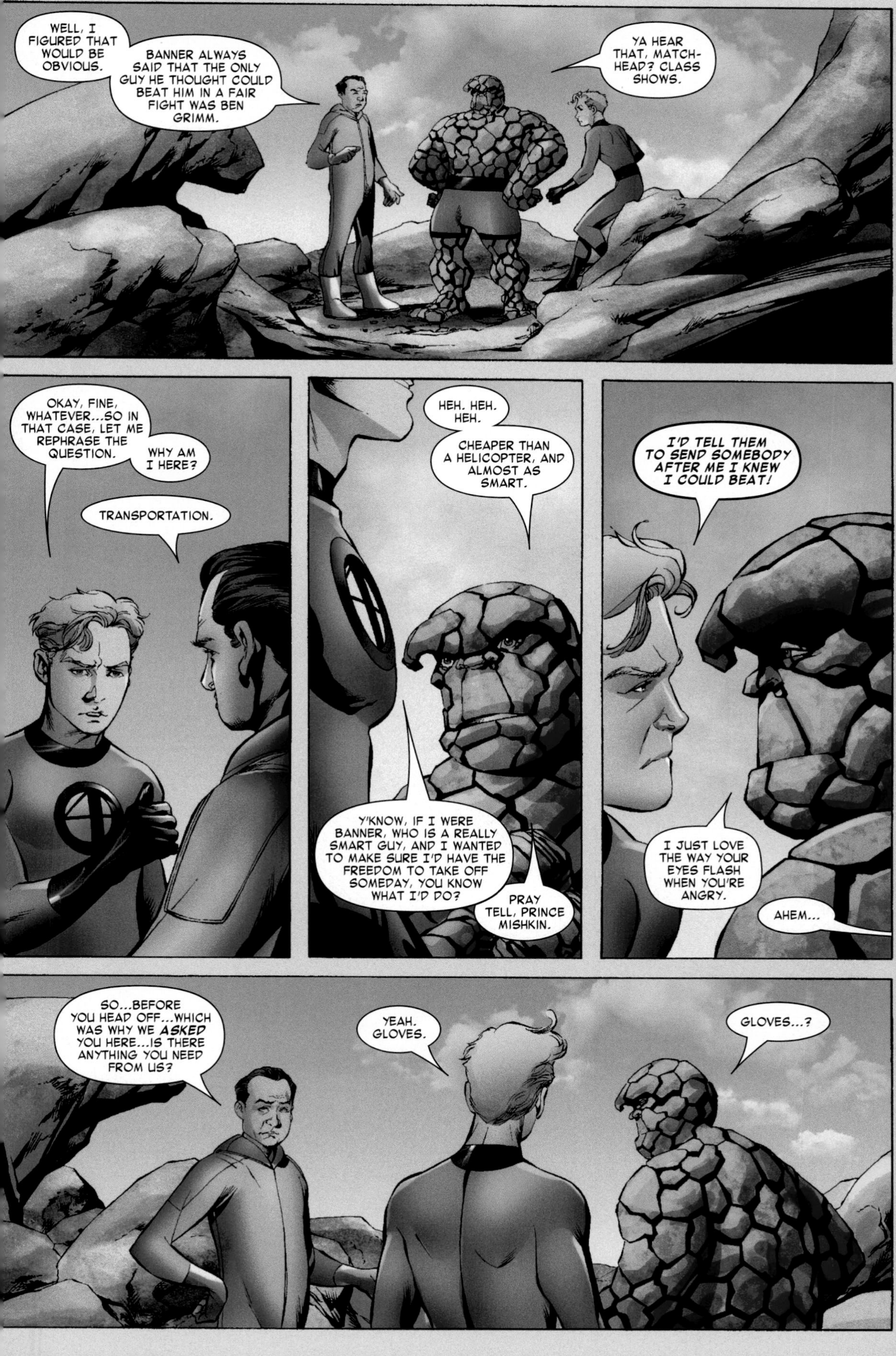

WELL, I FIGURED THAT WOULD BE OBVIOUS.
BANNER ALWAYS SAID THAT THE ONLY GUY HE THOUGHT COULD BEAT HIM IN A FAIR FIGHT WAS BEN GRIMM.
YA HEAR THAT, MATCH-HEAD? CLASS SHOWS.
OKAY, FINE, WHATEVER...SO IN THAT CASE, LET ME REPHRASE THE QUESTION.
WHY AM I HERE?
TRANSPORTATION.
HEH. HEH. HEH.
CHEAPER THAN A HELICOPTER, AND ALMOST AS SMART.
Y'KNOW, IF I WERE BANNER, WHO IS A REALLY SMART GUY, AND I WANTED TO MAKE SURE I'D HAVE THE FREEDOM TO TAKE OFF SOMEDAY, YOU KNOW WHAT I'D DO?
PRAY TELL, PRINCE MISHKIN.
I'D TELL THEM TO SEND SOMEBODY AFTER ME I KNEW I COULD BEAT!
I JUST LOVE THE WAY YOUR EYES FLASH WHEN YOU'RE ANGRY.
AHEM...
SO...BEFORE YOU HEAD OFF...WHICH WAS WHY WE ASKED YOU HERE...IS THERE ANYTHING YOU NEED FROM US?
YEAH. GLOVES.
GLOVES...?

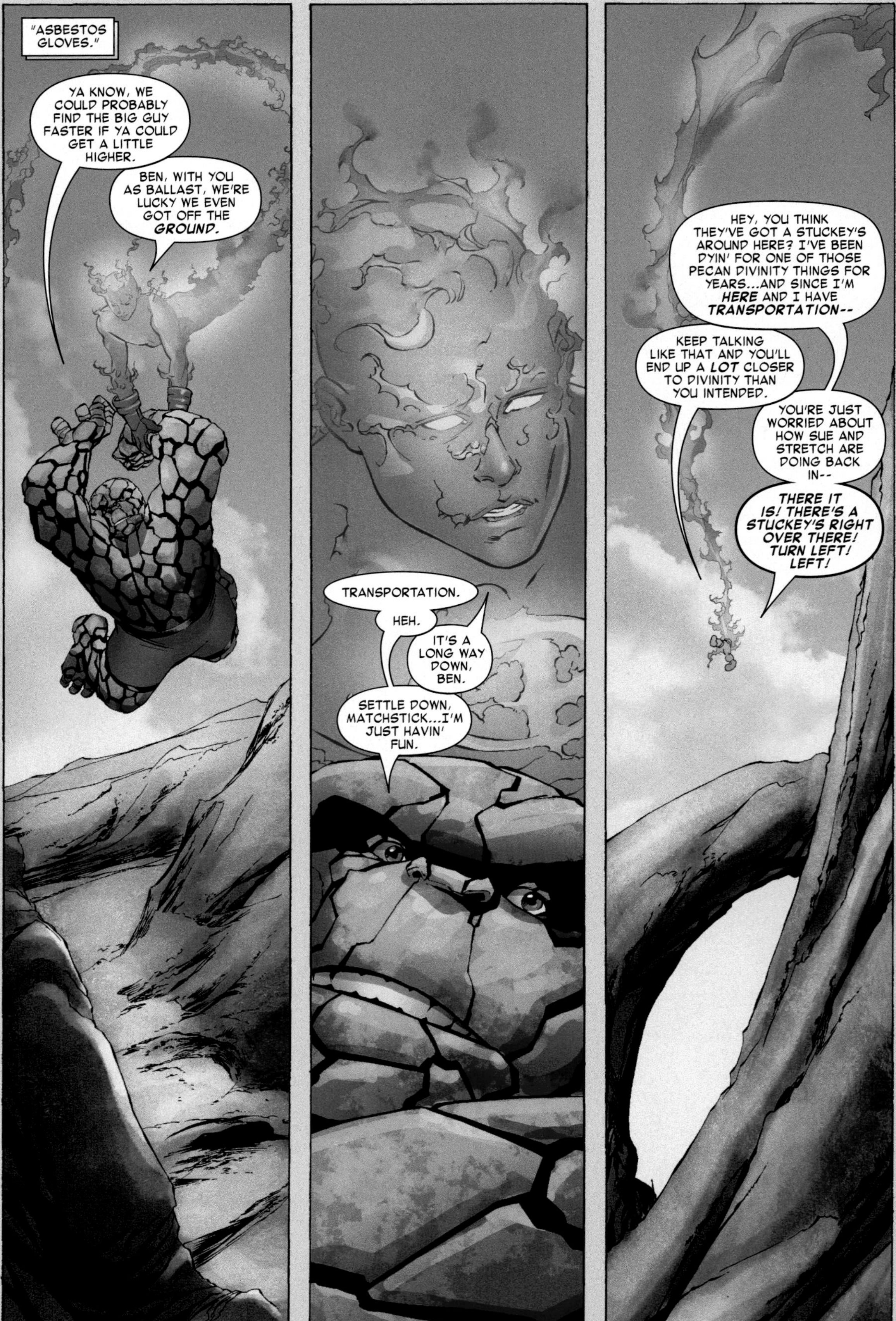
"ASBESTOS GLOVES."
YA KNOW, WE COULD PROBABLY FIND THE BIG GUY FASTER IF YA COULD GET A LITTLE HIGHER.
BEN, WITH YOU AS BALLAST, WE'RE LUCKY WE EVEN GOT OFF THE GROUND.
TRANSPORTATION.
HEH.
IT'S A LONG WAY DOWN, BEN.
SETTLE DOWN, MATCHSTICK...I'M JUST HAVIN' FUN.
HEY, YOU THINK THEY'VE GOT A STUCKEY'S AROUND HERE? I'VE BEEN DYIN' FOR ONE OF THOSE PECAN DIVINITY THINGS FOR YEARS...AND SINCE I'M HERE AND I HAVE TRANSPORTATION--
KEEP TALKING LIKE THAT AND YOU'LL END UP A LOT CLOSER TO DIVINITY THAN YOU INTENDED.
YOU'RE JUST WORRIED ABOUT HOW SUE AND STRETCH ARE DOING BACK IN--
THERE IT IS! THERE'S A STUCKEY'S RIGHT OVER THERE! TURN LEFT! LEFT!

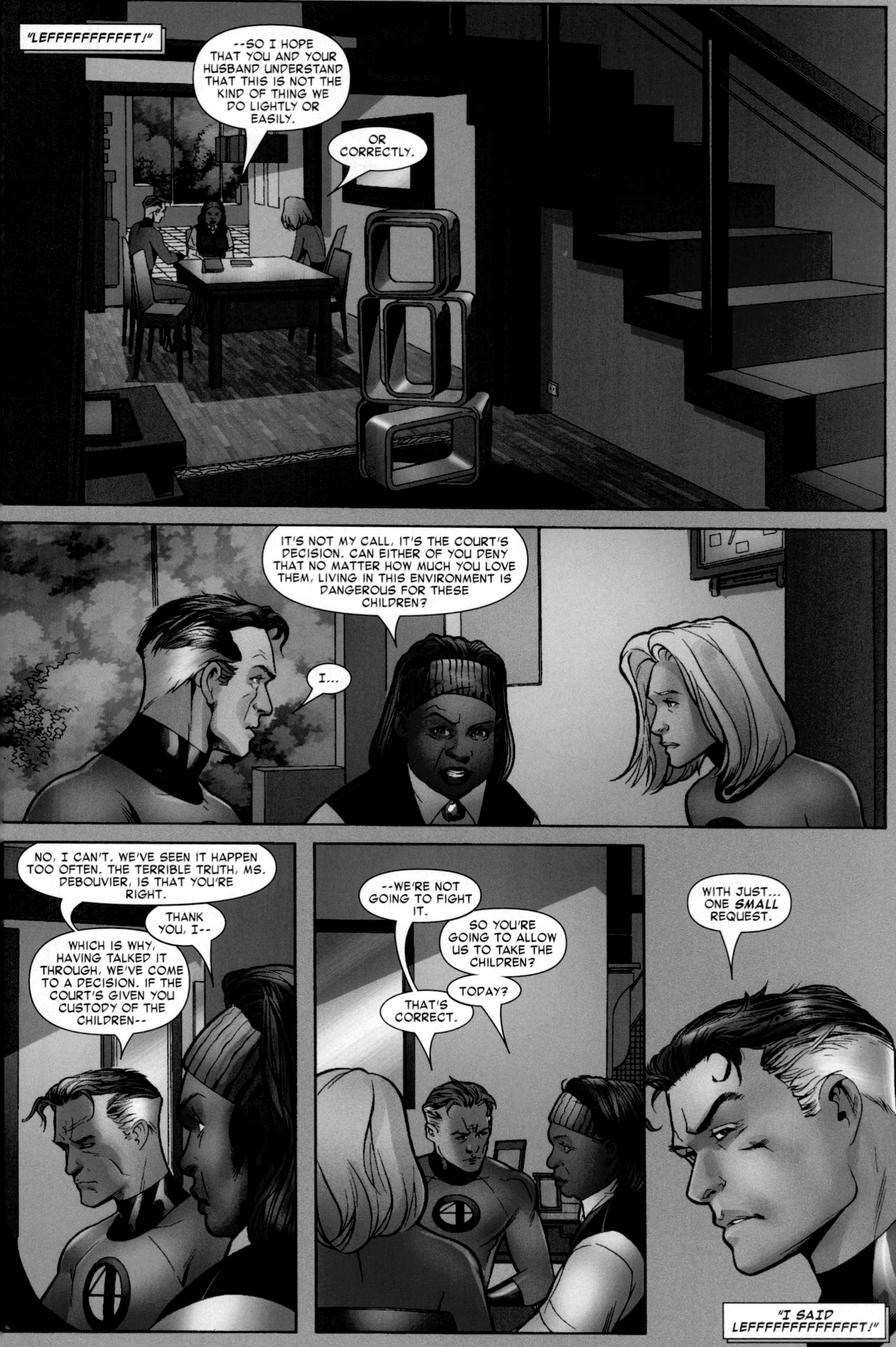
"LEFFFFFFFFFFT!"
--SO I HOPE THAT YOU AND YOUR HUSBAND UNDERSTAND THAT THIS IS NOT THE KIND OF THING WE DO LIGHTLY OR EASILY.
OR CORRECTLY.
IT'S NOT MY CALL, IT'S THE COURT'S DECISION. CAN EITHER OF YOU DENY THAT NO MATTER HOW MUCH YOU LOVE THEM, LIVING IN THIS ENVIRONMENT IS DANGEROUS FOR THESE CHILDREN?
I...
NO, I CAN'T. WE'VE SEEN IT HAPPEN TOO OFTEN. THE TERRIBLE TRUTH, MS. DEBOUVIER, IS THAT YOU'RE RIGHT.
THANK YOU, I--
WHICH IS WHY, HAVING TALKED IT THROUGH, WE'VE COME TO A DECISION. IF THE COURT'S GIVEN YOU CUSTODY OF THE CHILDREN--
--WE'RE NOT GOING TO FIGHT IT.
SO YOU'RE GOING TO ALLOW US TO TAKE THE CHILDREN?
TODAY?
THAT'S CORRECT.
WITH JUST... ONE SMALL REQUEST.
"I SAID LEFFFFFFFFFFFFFT!"

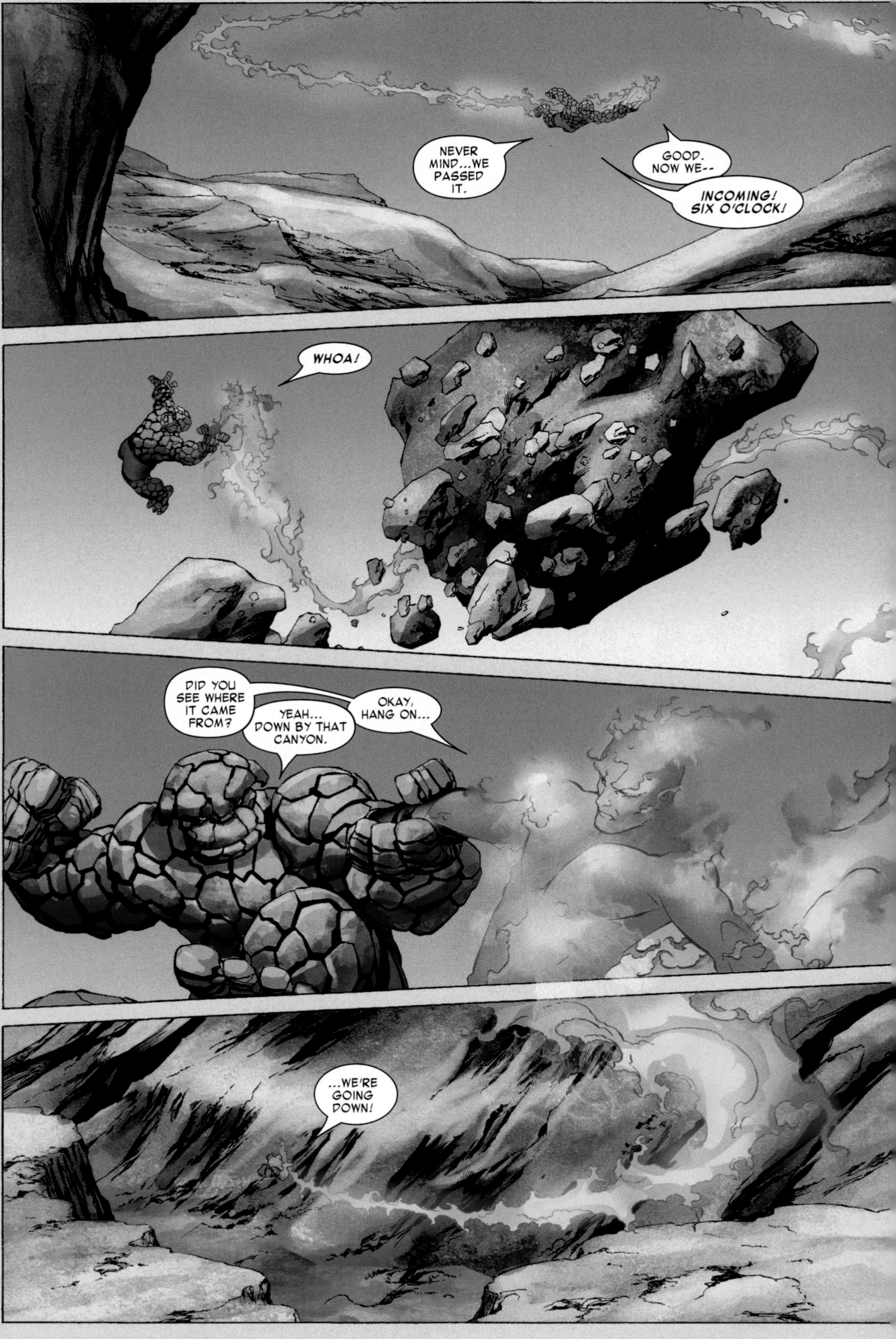
NEVER MIND...WE PASSED IT.
GOOD. NOW WE--
INCOMING! SIX O'CLOCK!
WHOA!
DID YOU SEE WHERE IT CAME FROM?
YEAH... DOWN BY THAT CANYON.
OKAY, HANG ON...
...WE'RE GOING DOWN!

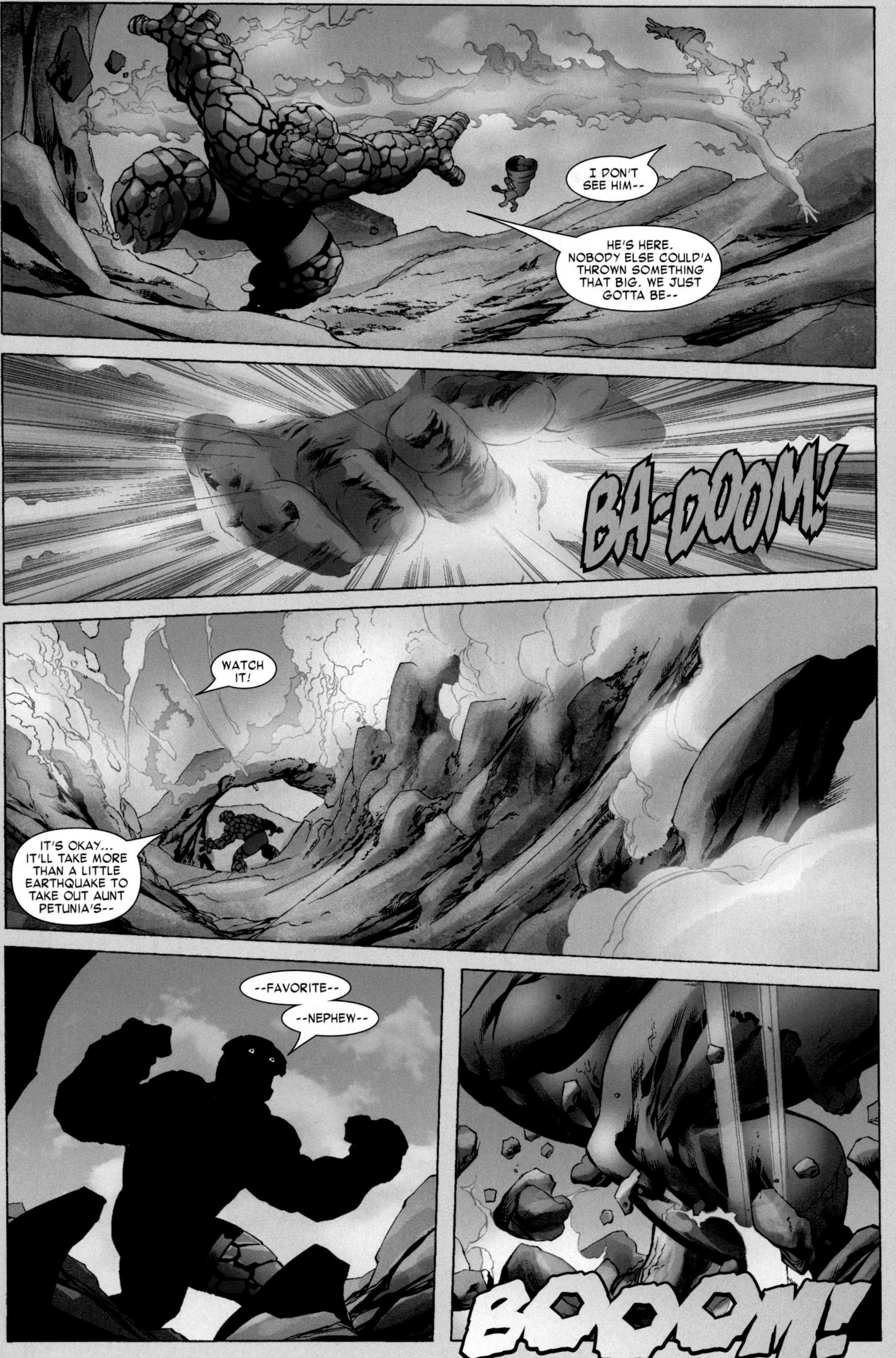
I DON'T SEE HIM--
HE'S HERE. NOBODY ELSE COULD'A THROWN SOMETHING THAT BIG. WE JUST GOTTA BE--
BA-DOOM!
WATCH IT!
IT'S OKAY... IT'LL TAKE MORE THAN A LITTLE EARTHQUAKE TO TAKE OUT AUNT PETUNIA'S--
--FAVORITE--
--NEPHEW--
BOOOM!

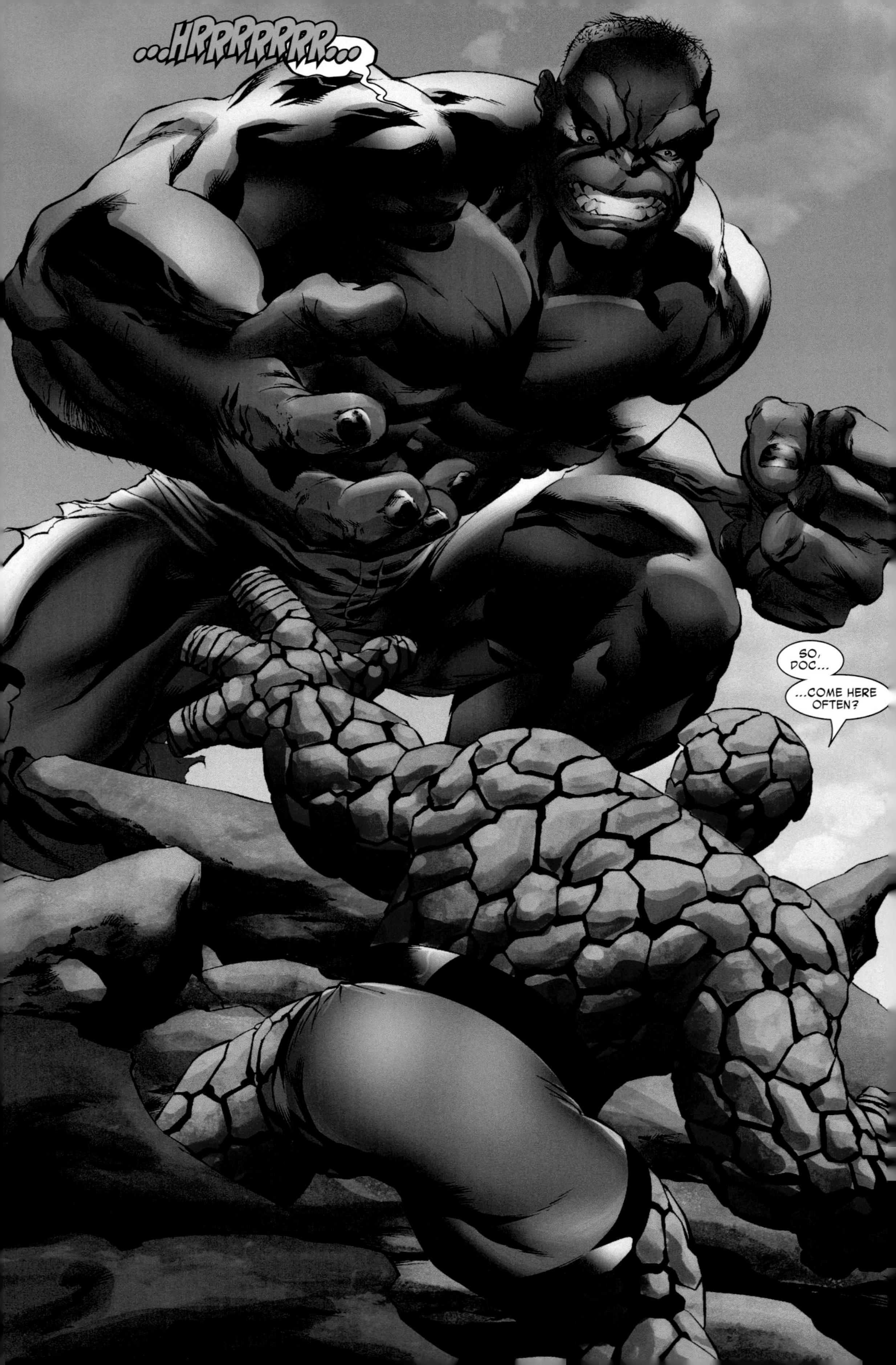
..HRRRRRRR...
SO, DOC...
...COME HERE OFTEN?

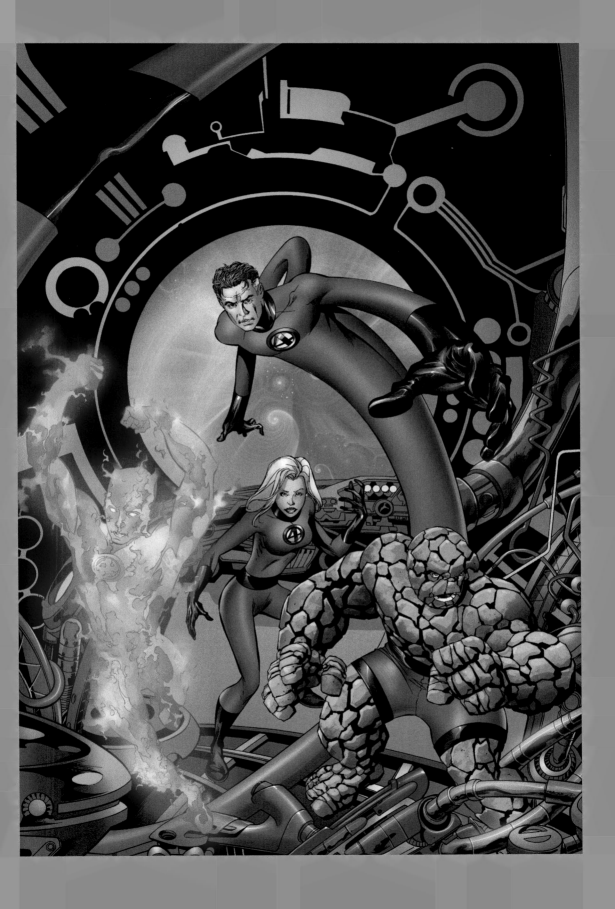

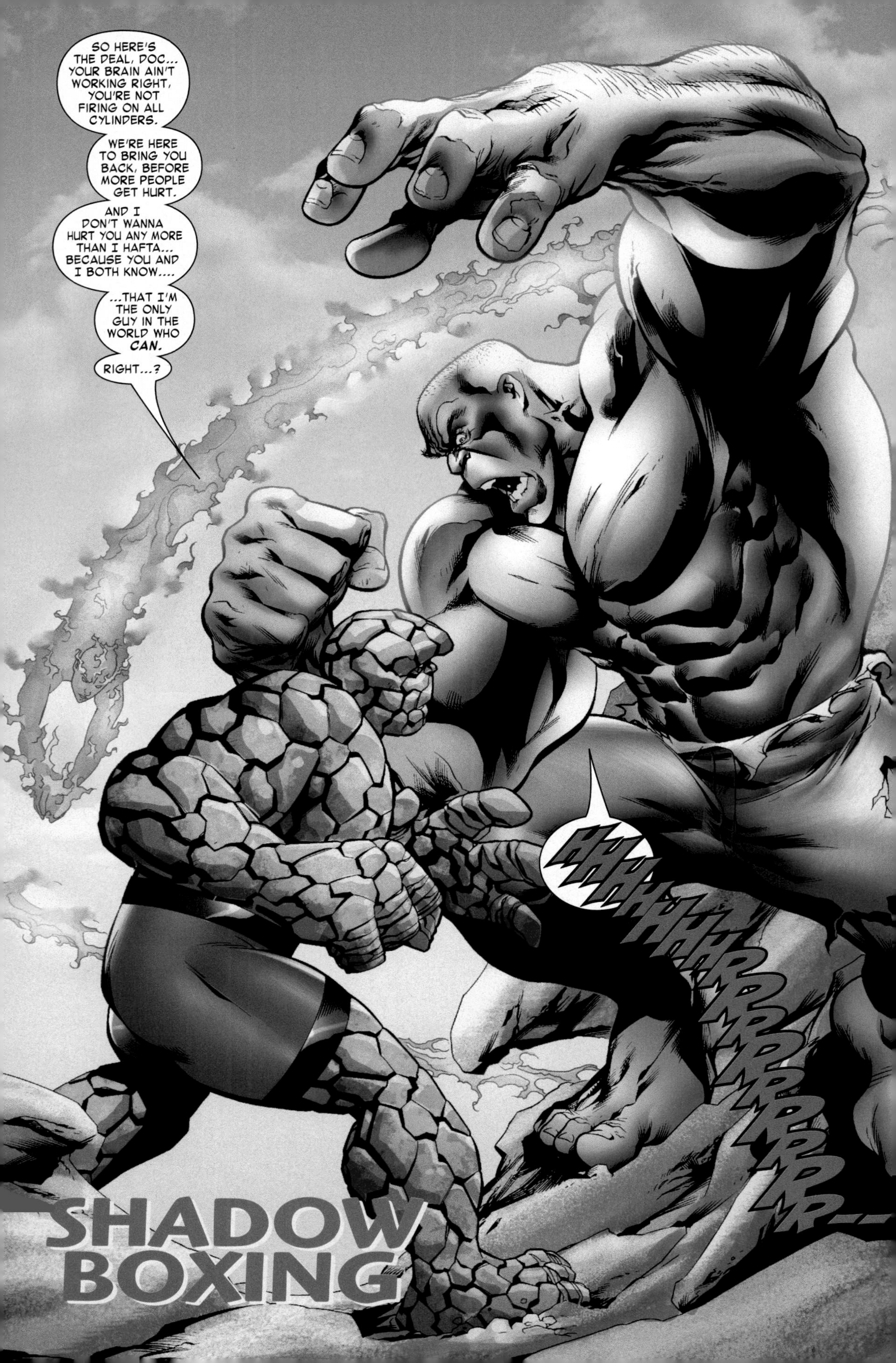
SO HERE'S THE DEAL, DOC... YOUR BRAIN AIN'T WORKING RIGHT, YOU'RE NOT FIRING ON ALL CYLINDERS.
WE'RE HERE TO BRING YOU BACK, BEFORE MORE PEOPLE GET HURT.
AND I DON'T WANNA HURT YOU ANY MORE THAN I HAFTA... BECAUSE YOU AND I BOTH KNOW....
...THAT I'M THE ONLY GUY IN THE WORLD WHO CAN.
RIGHT...?
HHHHHHHRRRRRRRRRRR...
SHADOW BOXING

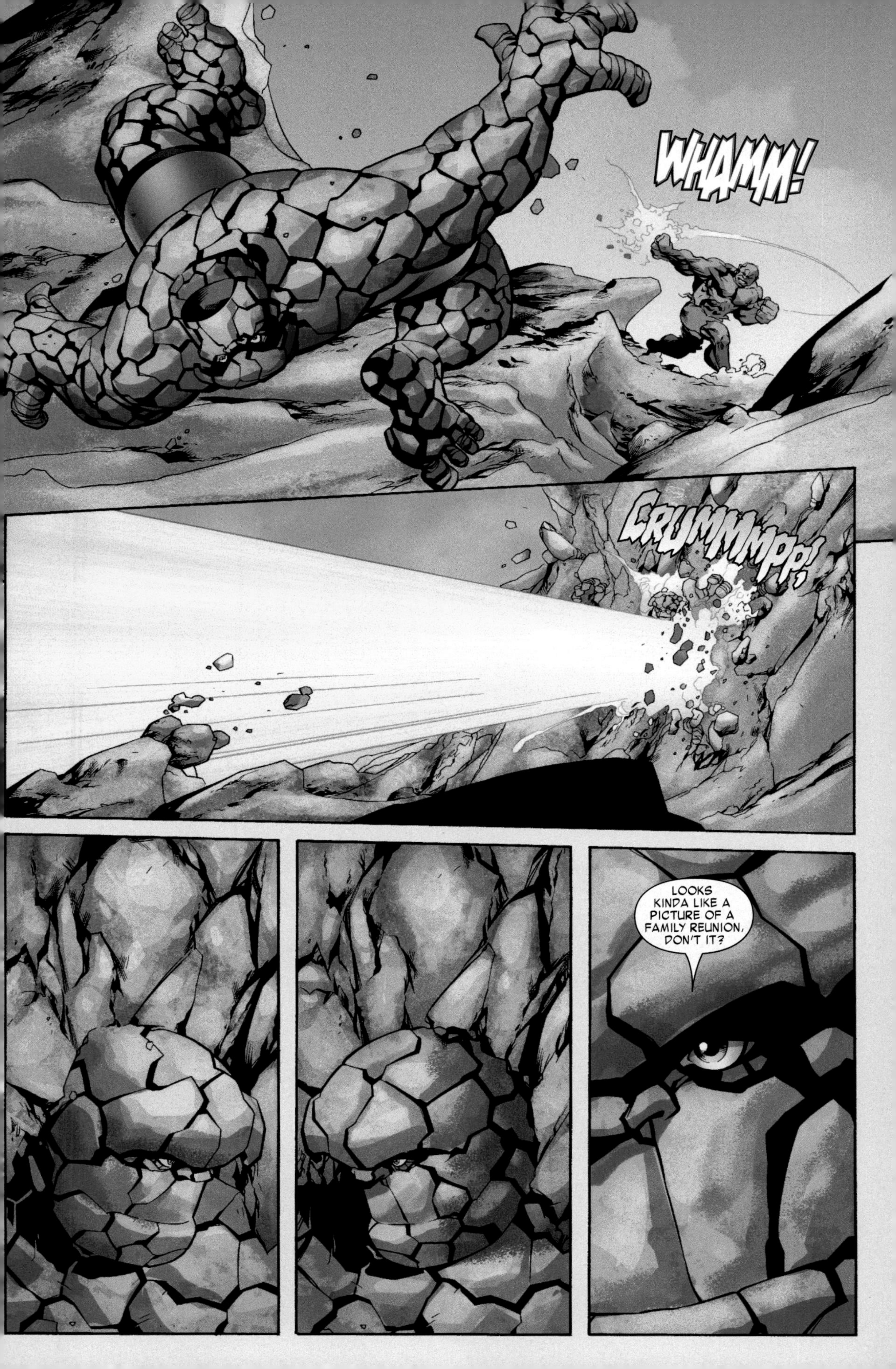
WHAMM!
CRUMMMMPP!
LOOKS KINDA LIKE A PICTURE OF A FAMILY REUNION, DON'T IT?

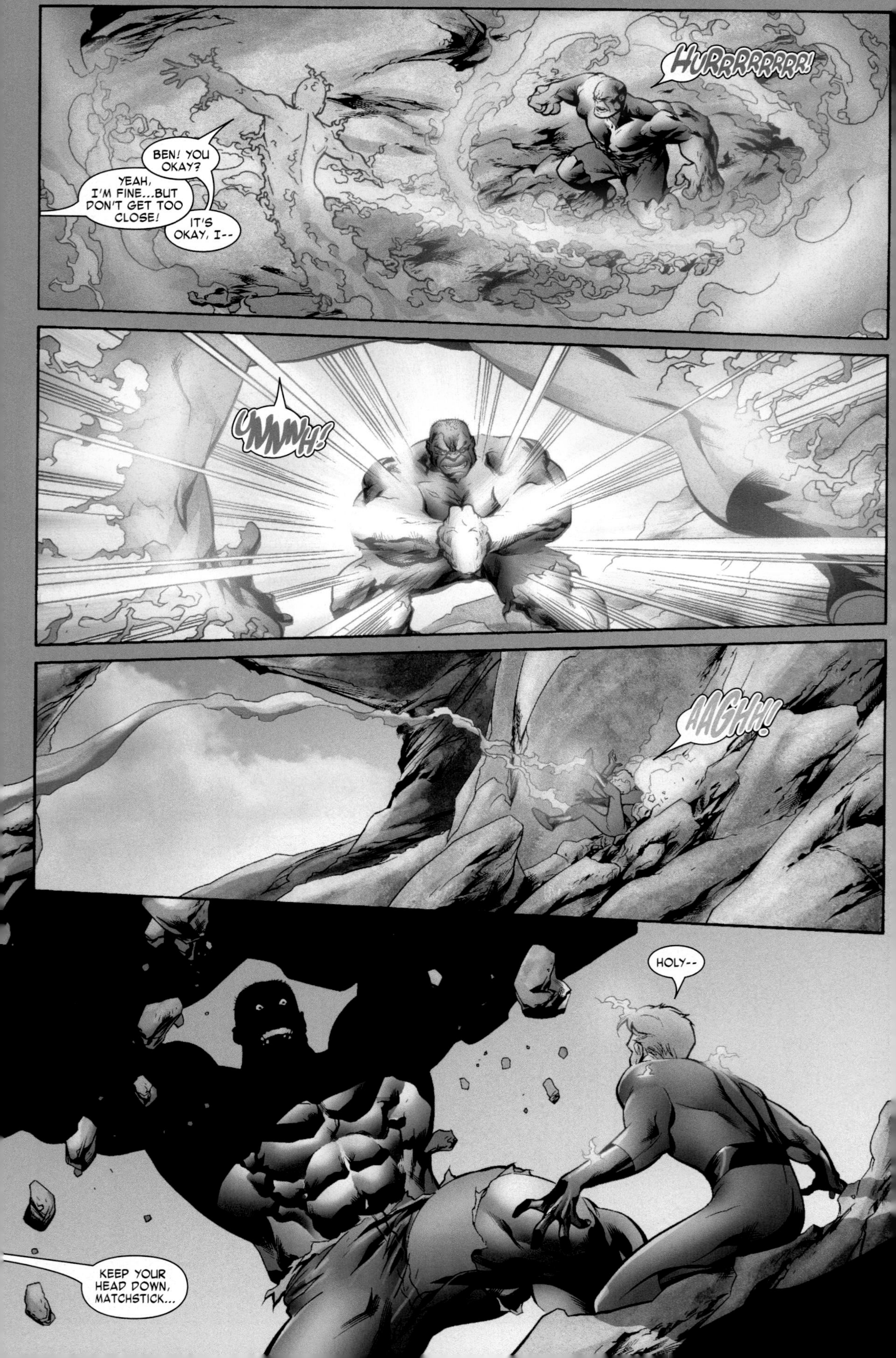
HURRRRRRRR!
BEN! YOU OKAY?
YEAH, I'M FINE...BUT DON'T GET TOO CLOSE!
IT'S OKAY, I--
UNNNH!
AAGHH!
HOLY--
KEEP YOUR HEAD DOWN, MATCHSTICK...

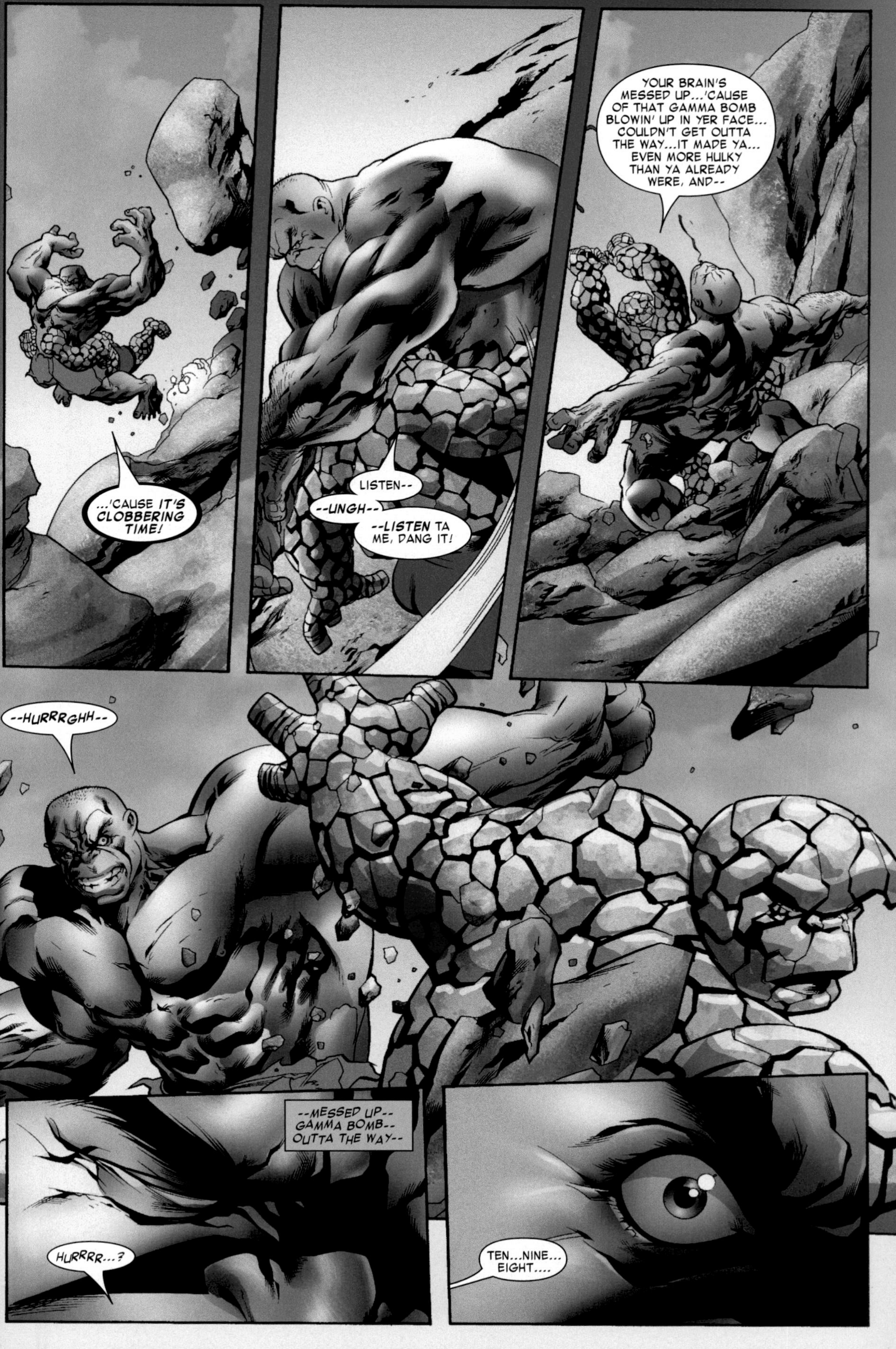
...'CAUSE IT'S CLOBBERING TIME!
LISTEN--
--UNGH--
--LISTEN TA ME, DANG IT!
YOUR BRAIN'S MESSED UP...'CAUSE OF THAT GAMMA BOMB BLOWIN' UP IN YER FACE... COULDN'T GET OUTTA THE WAY...IT MADE YA... EVEN MORE HULKY THAN YA ALREADY WERE, AND--
--HURRRGHH--
--MESSED UP-- GAMMA BOMB-- OUTTA THE WAY--
HURRRR...?
TEN...NINE... EIGHT....

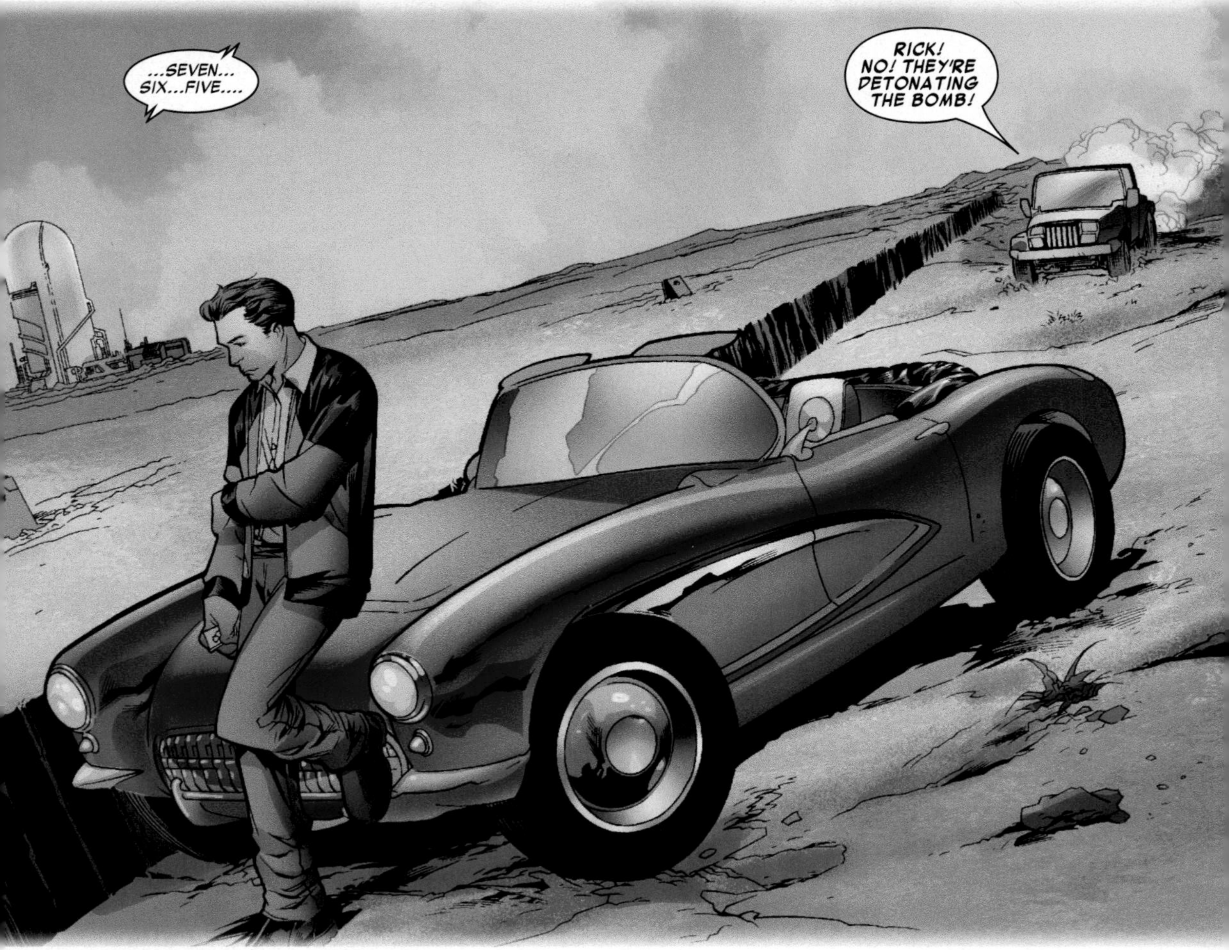
...SEVEN... SIX...FIVE....
RICK! NO! THEY'RE DETONATING THE BOMB!

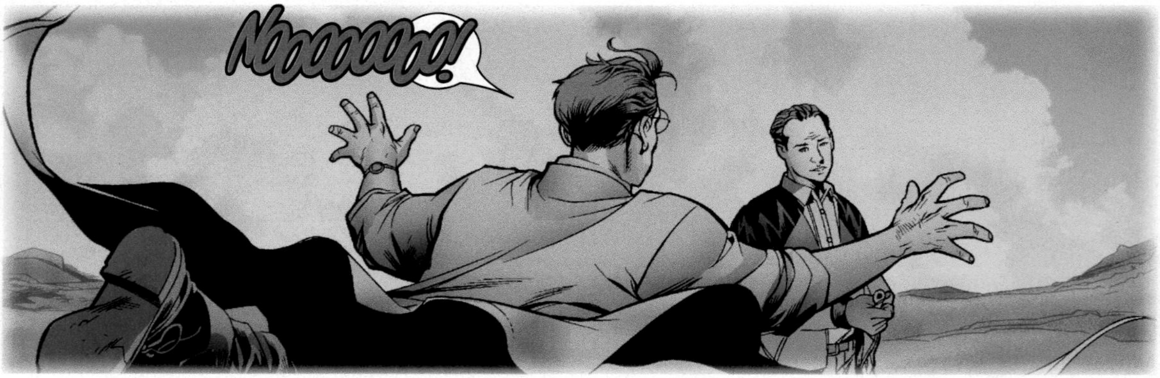
NOOOOOOOO!

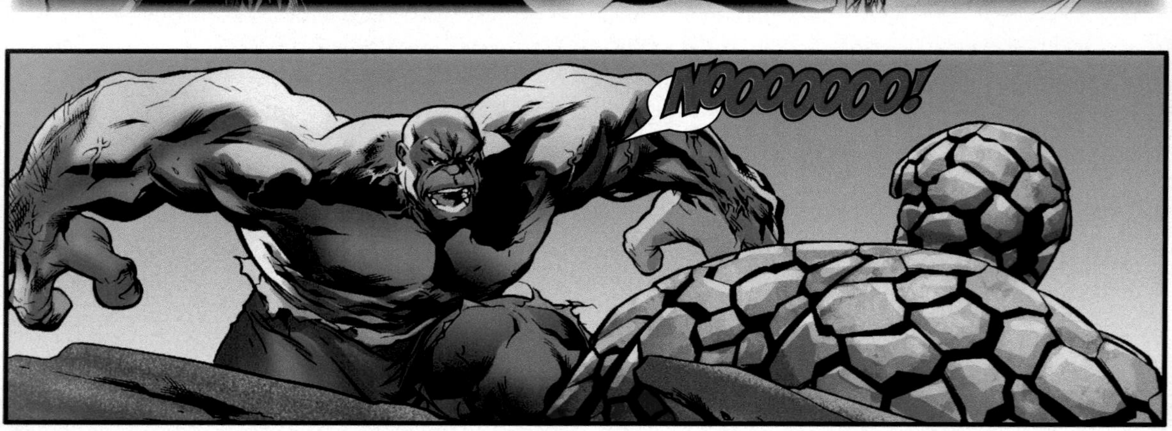
NOOOOOOOO!

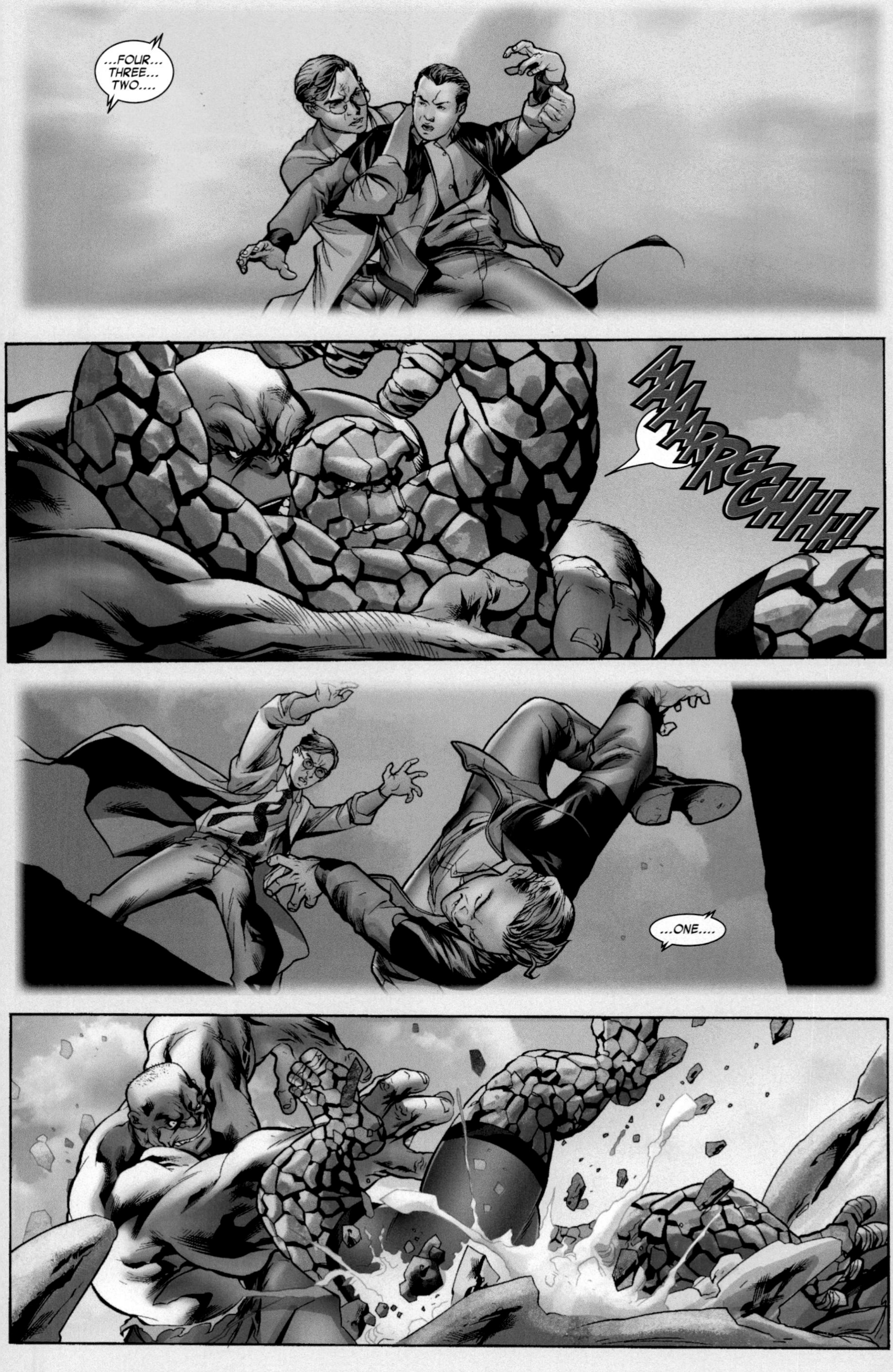
...FOUR... THREE... TWO....
AAAARRGHHHH!
...ONE....

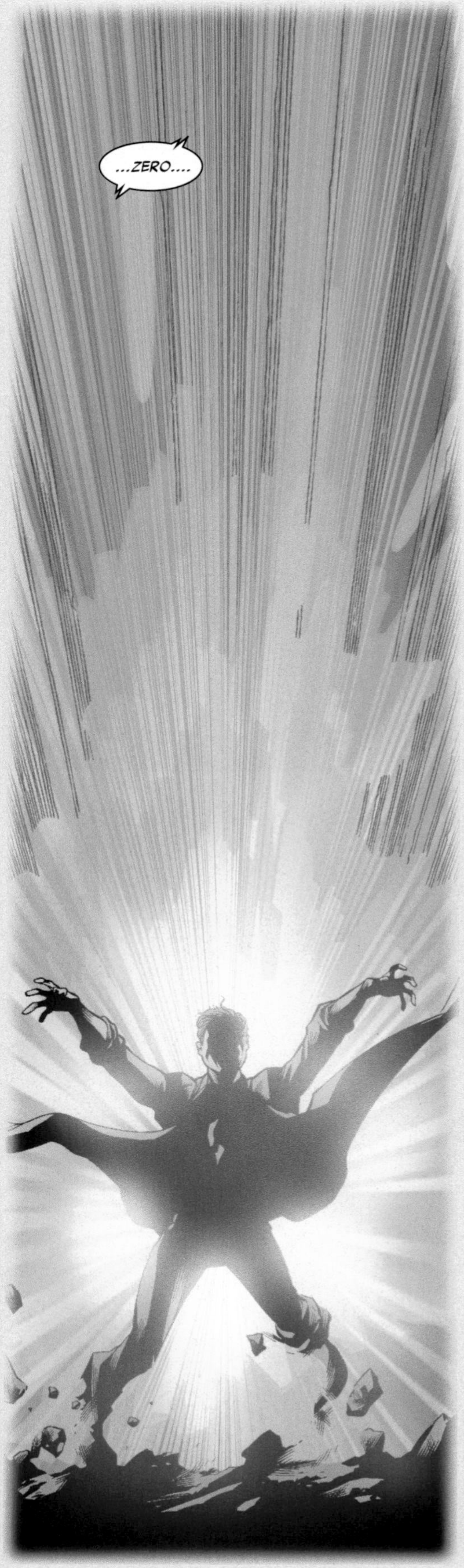
...ZERO....

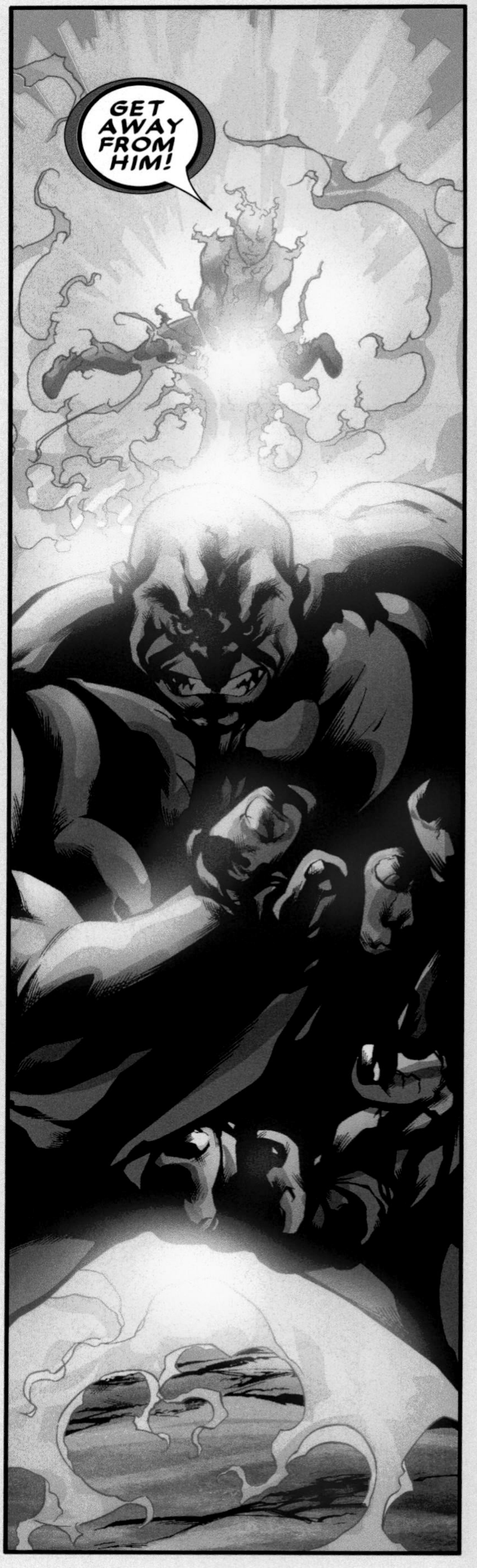
GET AWAY FROM HIM!

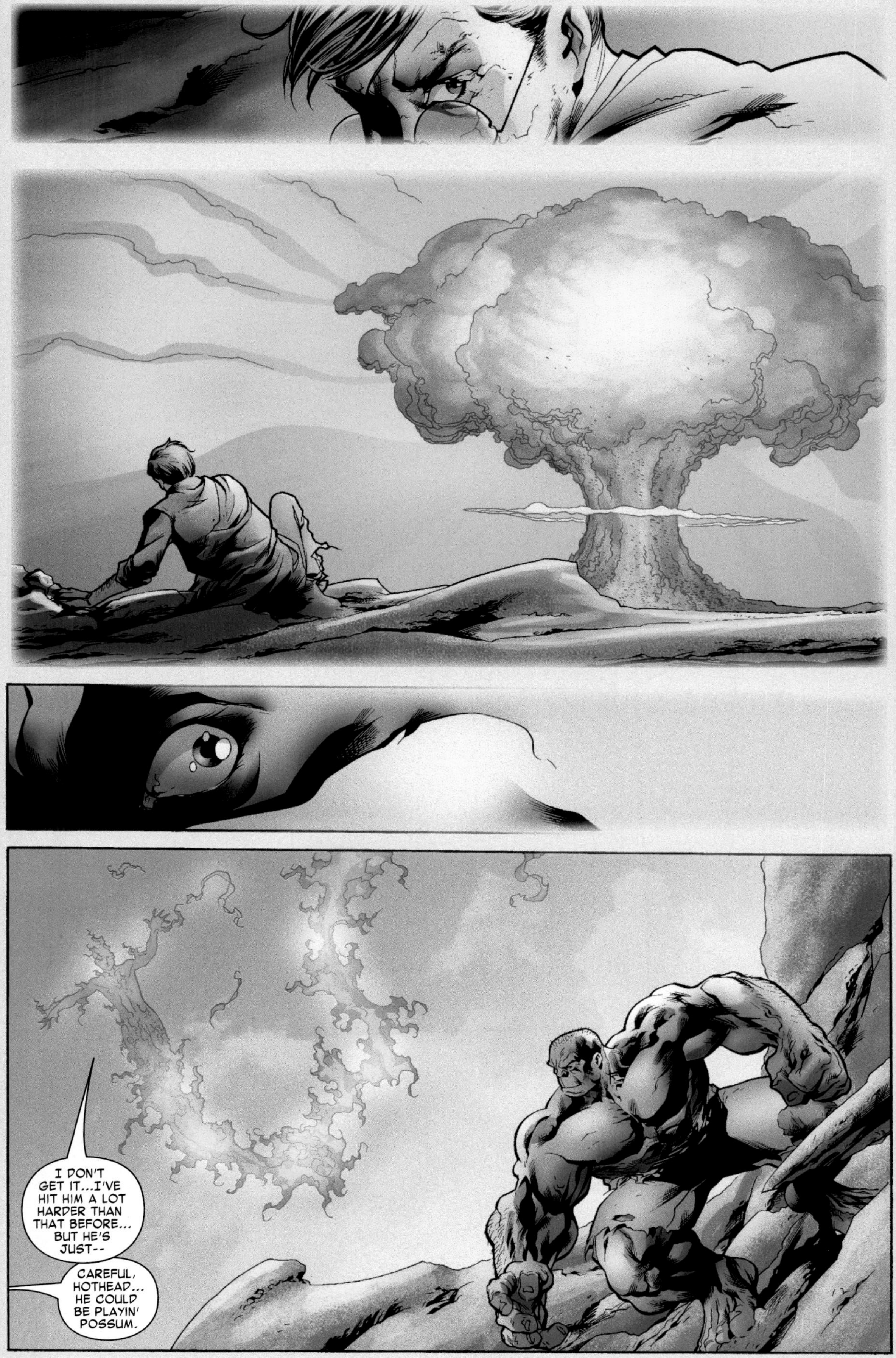

I DON'T GET IT...I'VE HIT HIM A LOT HARDER THAN THAT BEFORE... BUT HE'S JUST--
CAREFUL, HOTHEAD... HE COULD BE PLAYIN' POSSUM.

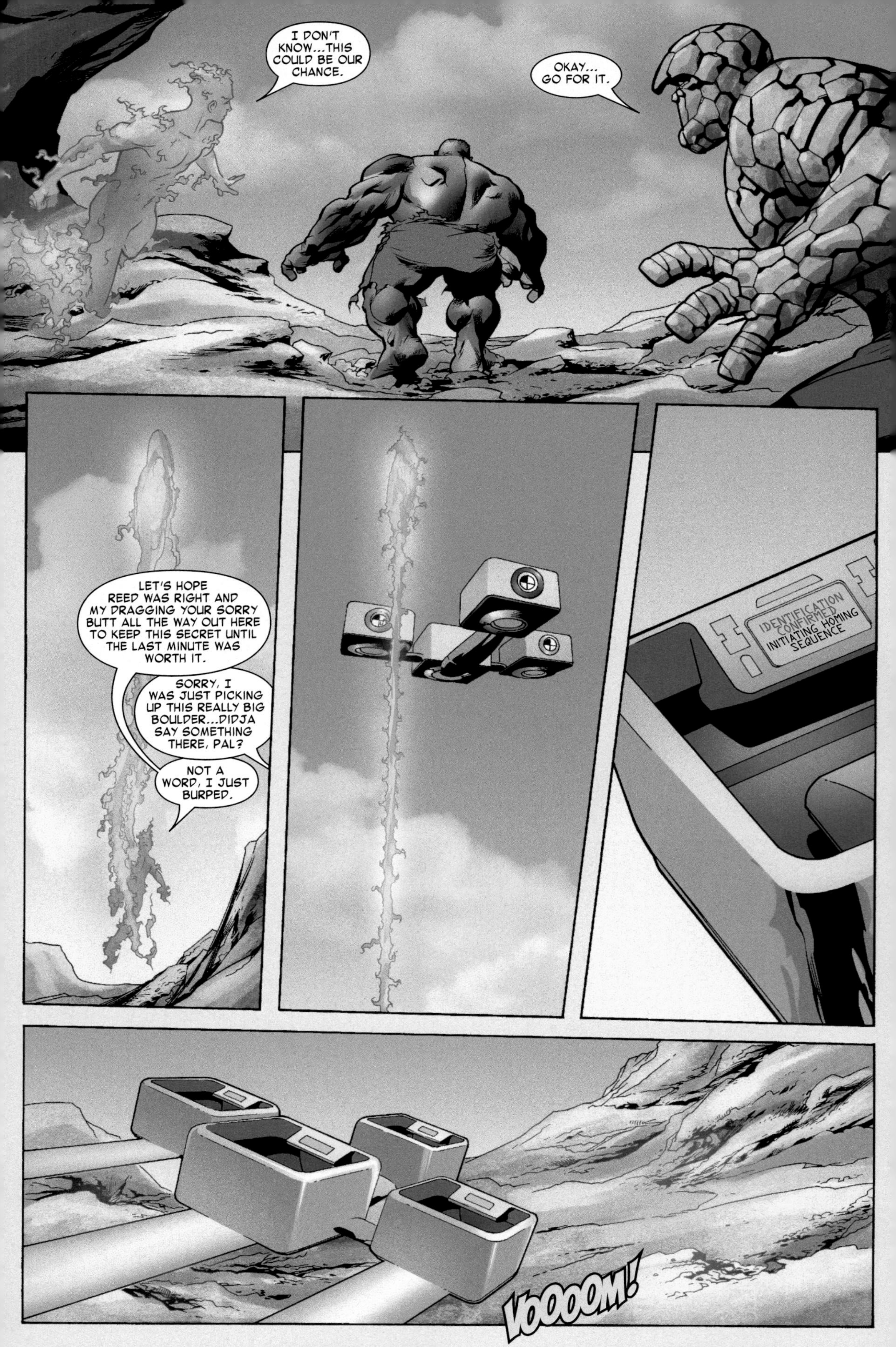
I DON'T KNOW...THIS COULD BE OUR CHANCE.
OKAY... GO FOR IT.
LET'S HOPE REED WAS RIGHT AND MY DRAGGING YOUR SORRY BUTT ALL THE WAY OUT HERE TO KEEP THIS SECRET UNTIL THE LAST MINUTE WAS WORTH IT.
SORRY, I WAS JUST PICKING UP THIS REALLY BIG BOULDER...DIDJA SAY SOMETHING THERE, PAL?
NOT A WORD, I JUST BURPED.
IDENTIFICATION CONFIRMED
INITIATING HOMING SEQUENCE
VOOOOM!

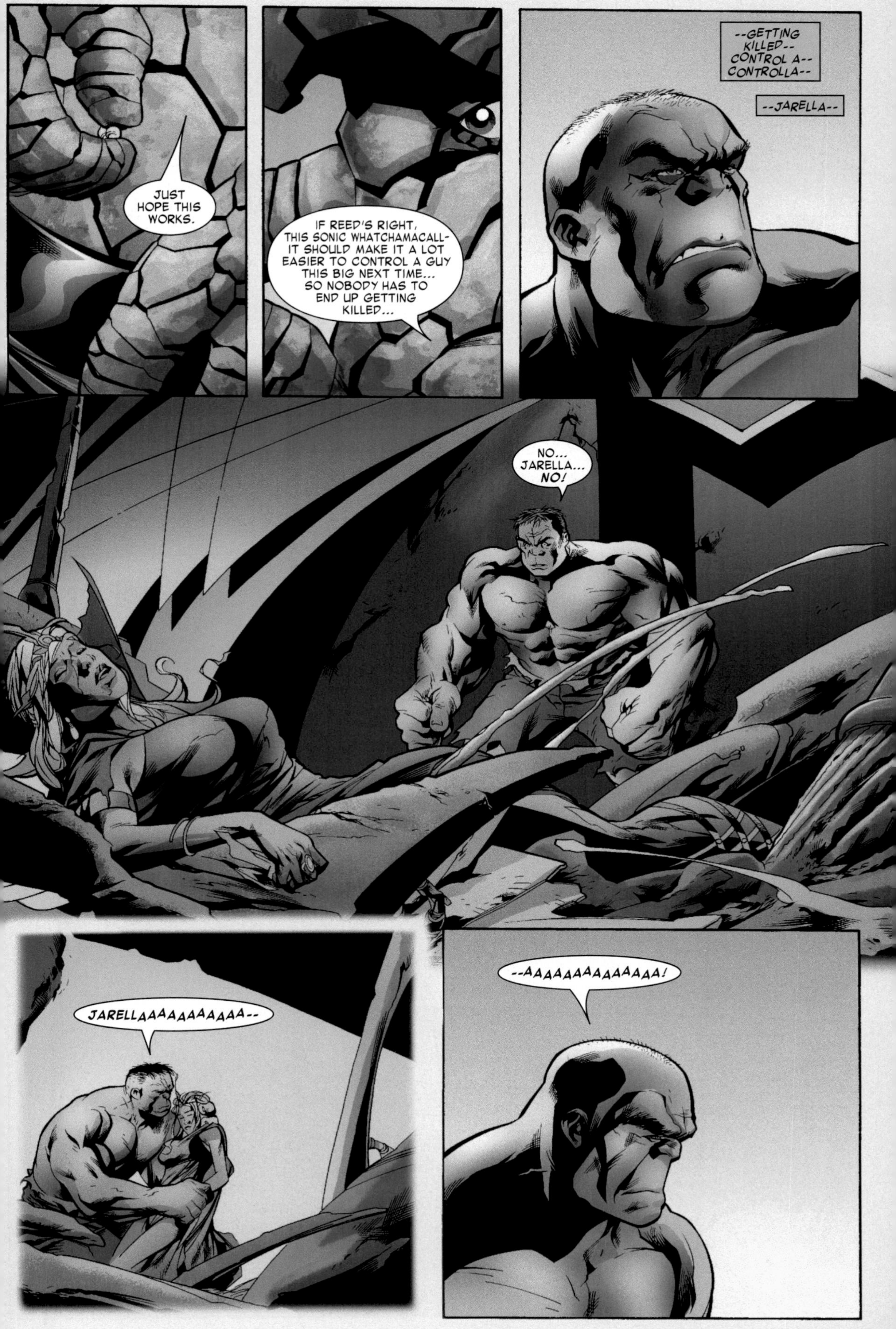
JUST HOPE THIS WORKS.
IF REED'S RIGHT, THIS SONIC WHATCHAMACALL-IT SHOULD MAKE IT A LOT EASIER TO CONTROL A GUY THIS BIG NEXT TIME... SO NOBODY HAS TO END UP GETTING KILLED...
--GETTING KILLED-- CONTROL A-- CONTROLLA--
--JARELLA--
NO... JARELLA... NO!
JARELLAAAAAAAAAAA--
--AAAAAAAAAAAAAA!

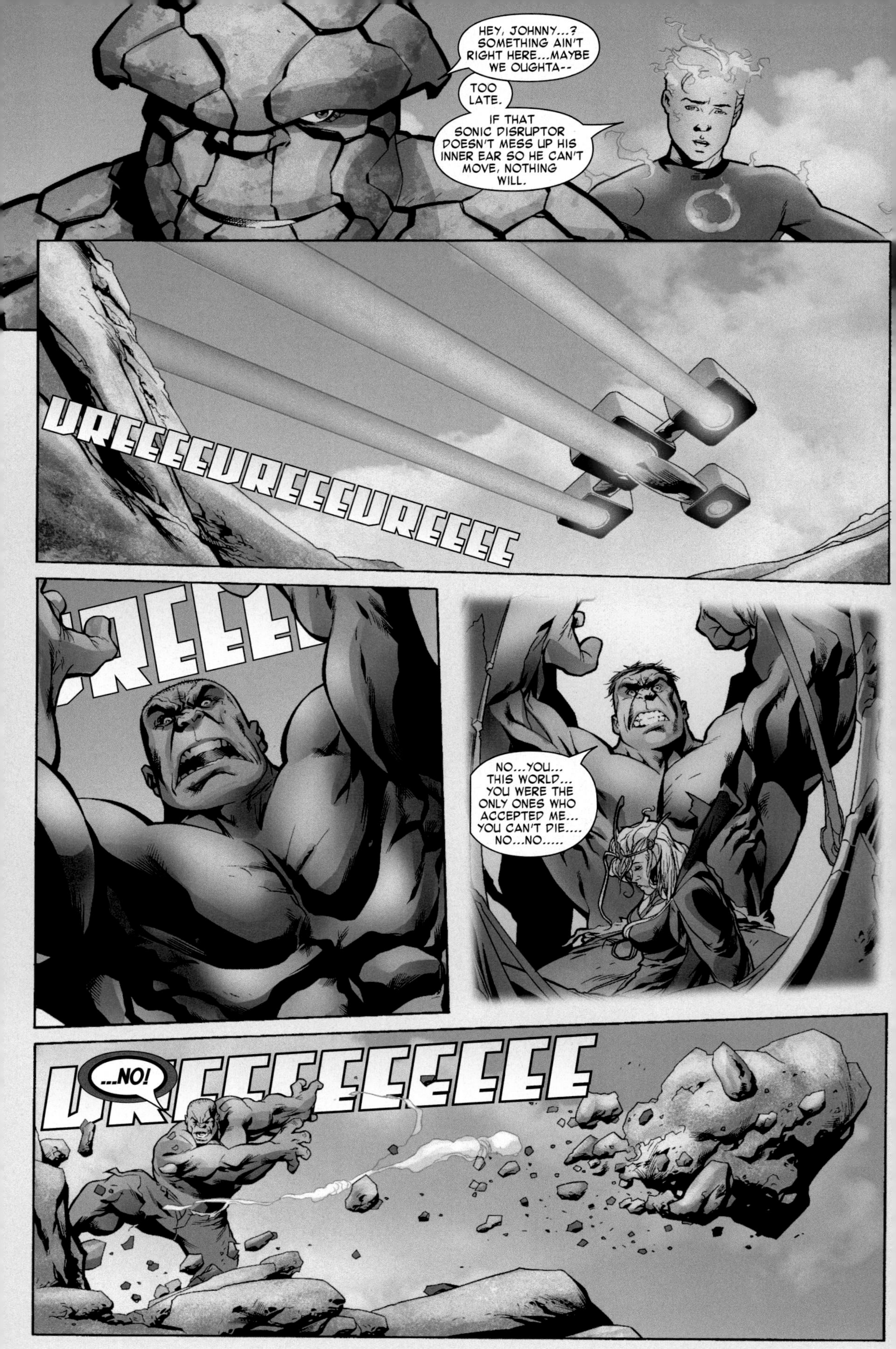

HEY, JOHNNY...? SOMETHING AIN'T RIGHT HERE...MAYBE WE OUGHTA--
TOO LATE.
IF THAT SONIC DISRUPTOR DOESN'T MESS UP HIS INNER EAR SO HE CAN'T MOVE, NOTHING WILL.
VREEEEVREEEEVREEEE
NO...YOU... THIS WORLD... YOU WERE THE ONLY ONES WHO ACCEPTED ME... YOU CAN'T DIE.... NO...NO.....
...NO!
VREEEEEEEEEEE

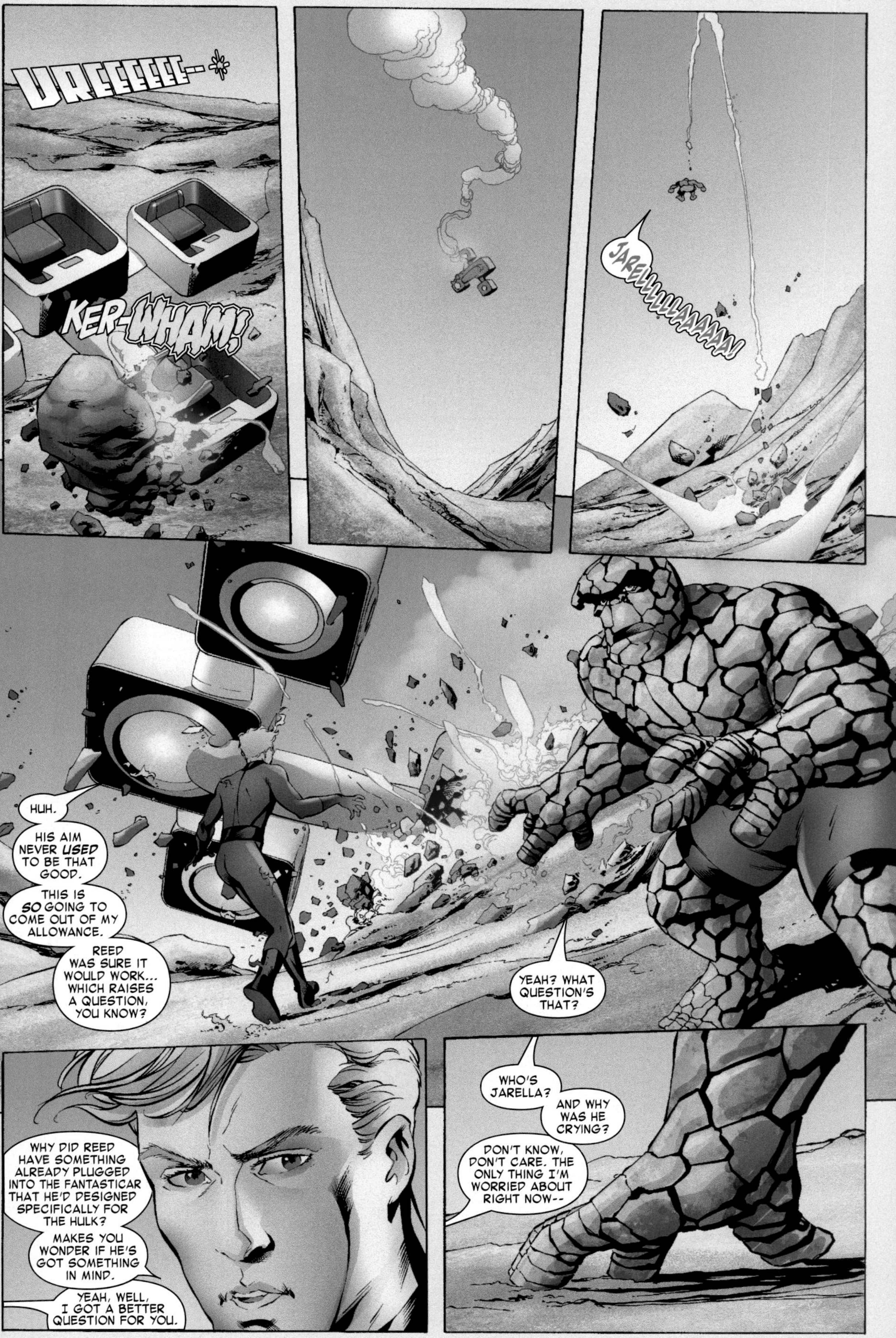
UREEEEEE--
KER-WHAM!
JARELLLLLLAAAAAA!
HUH.
HIS AIM NEVER *USED* TO BE THAT GOOD.
THIS IS *SO* GOING TO COME OUT OF MY ALLOWANCE.
REED WAS SURE IT WOULD WORK... WHICH RAISES A QUESTION, YOU KNOW?
YEAH? WHAT QUESTION'S THAT?
WHY DID REED HAVE SOMETHING ALREADY PLUGGED INTO THE FANTASTICAR THAT HE'D DESIGNED SPECIFICALLY FOR THE HULK?
MAKES YOU WONDER IF HE'S GOT SOMETHING IN MIND.
YEAH, WELL, I GOT A BETTER QUESTION FOR YOU.
WHO'S JARELLA?
AND WHY WAS HE CRYING?
DON'T KNOW, DON'T CARE. THE ONLY THING I'M WORRIED ABOUT RIGHT NOW--

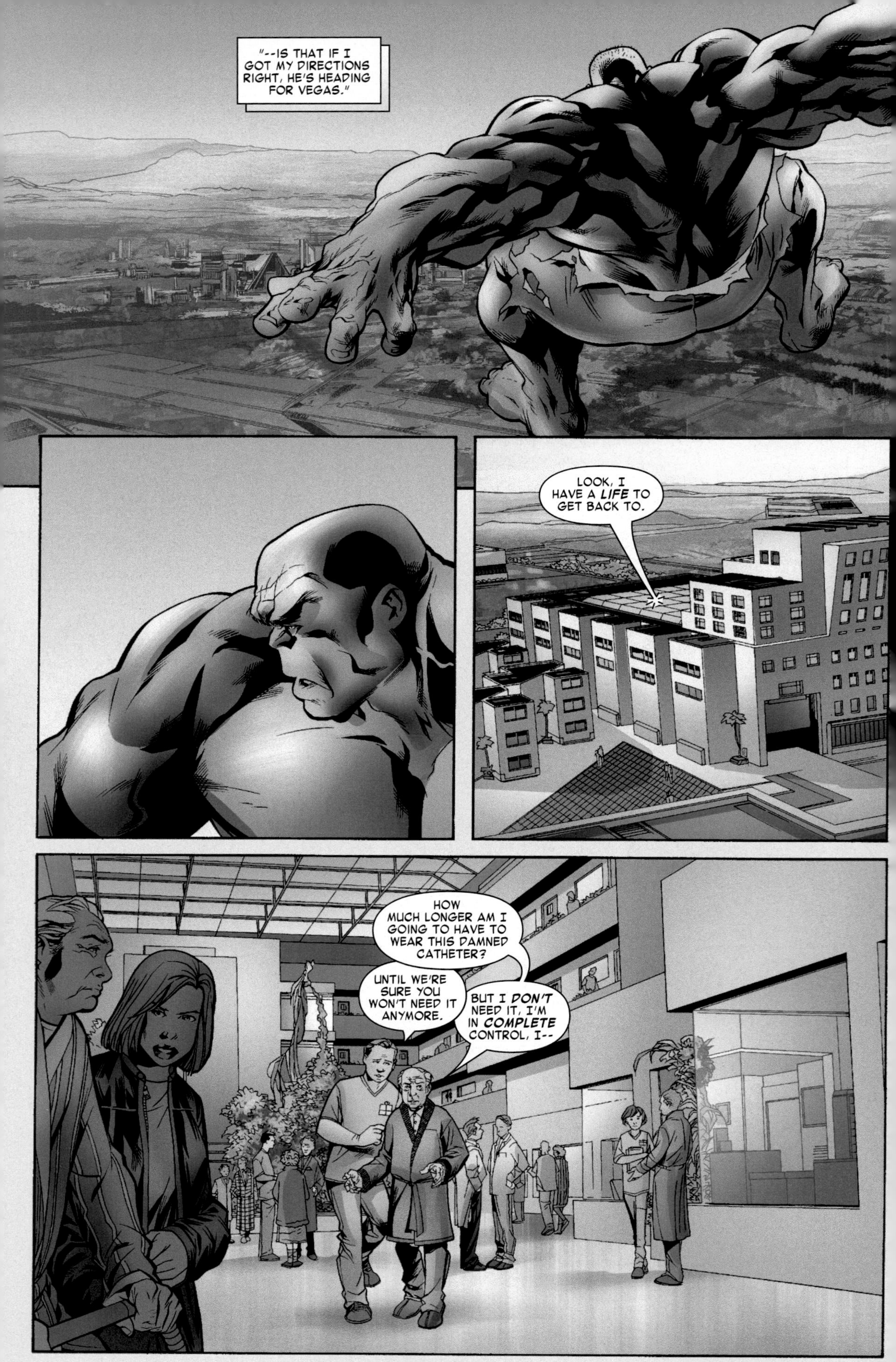
"--IS THAT IF I GOT MY DIRECTIONS RIGHT, HE'S HEADING FOR VEGAS."
LOOK, I HAVE A *LIFE* TO GET BACK TO.
HOW MUCH LONGER AM I GOING TO HAVE TO WEAR THIS DAMNED CATHETER?
UNTIL WE'RE SURE YOU WON'T NEED IT ANYMORE.
BUT I *DON'T* NEED IT, I'M IN *COMPLETE* CONTROL, I--

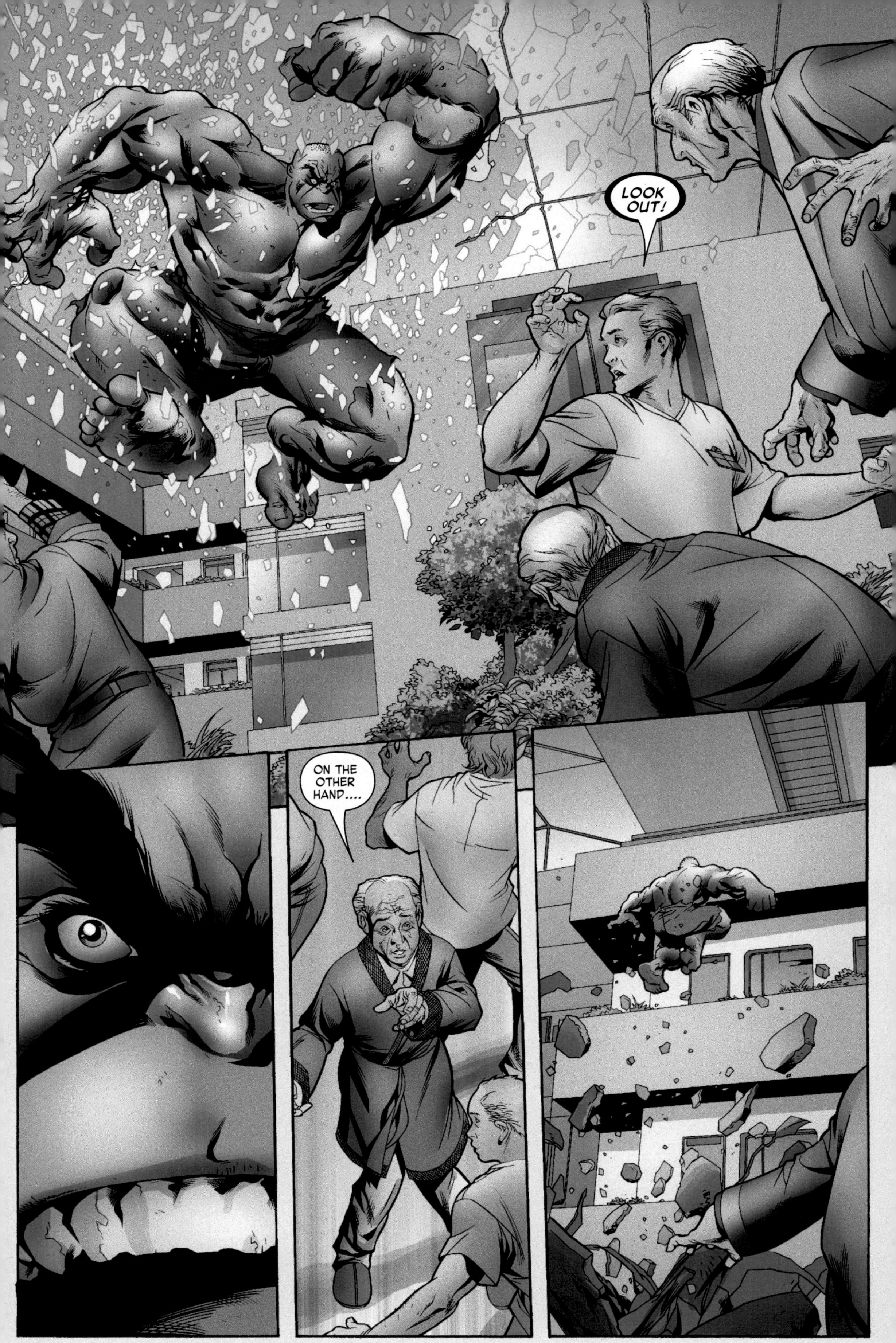
LOOK OUT!
ON THE OTHER HAND....

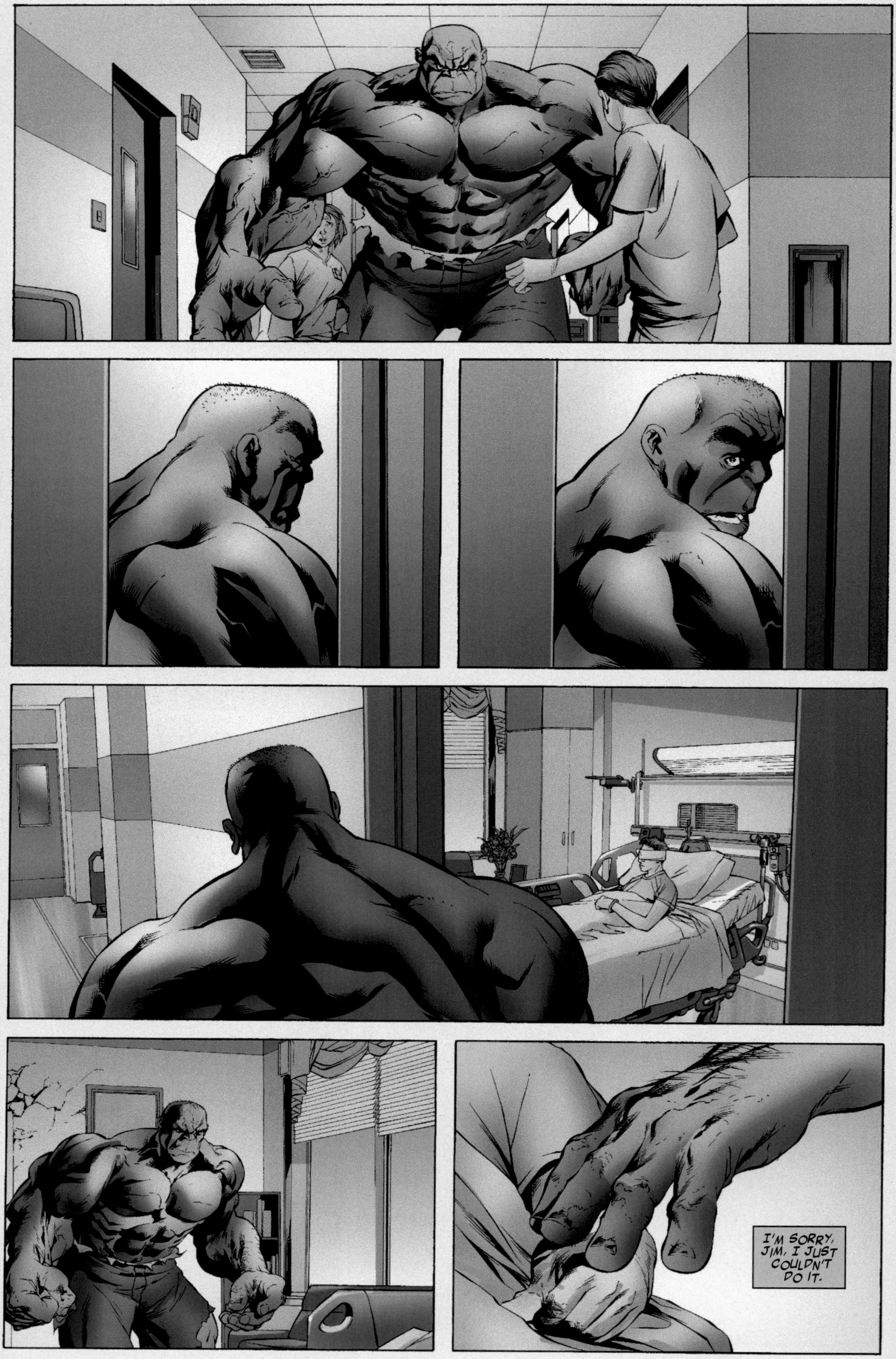
I'M SORRY, JIM, I JUST COULDN'T DO IT.

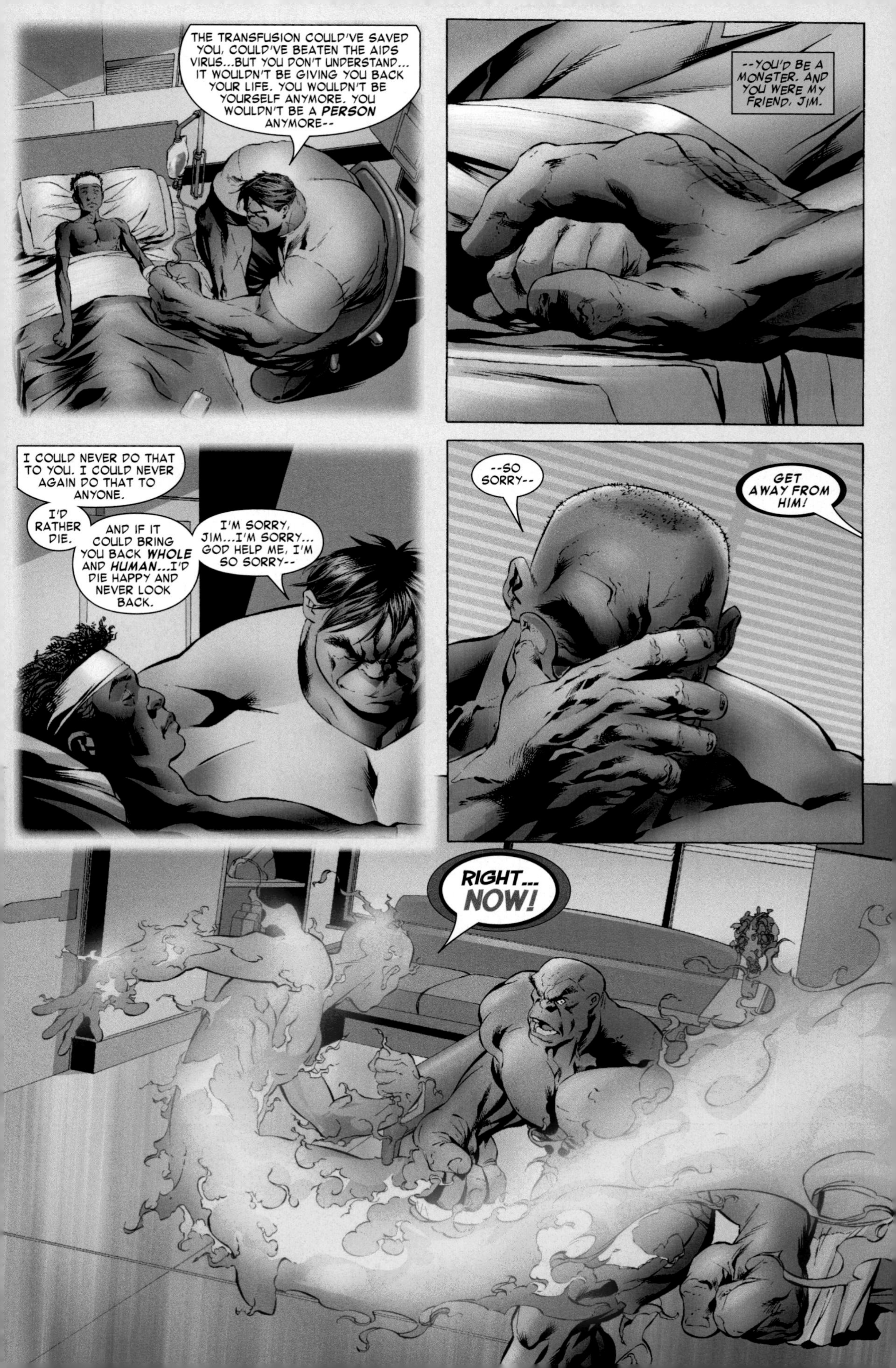
THE TRANSFUSION COULD'VE SAVED YOU, COULD'VE BEATEN THE AIDS VIRUS...BUT YOU DON'T UNDERSTAND... IT WOULDN'T BE GIVING YOU BACK YOUR LIFE. YOU WOULDN'T BE YOURSELF ANYMORE. YOU WOULDN'T BE A PERSON ANYMORE--
--YOU'D BE A MONSTER. AND YOU WERE MY FRIEND, JIM.
I COULD NEVER DO THAT TO YOU. I COULD NEVER AGAIN DO THAT TO ANYONE.
I'D RATHER DIE.
AND IF IT COULD BRING YOU BACK WHOLE AND HUMAN...I'D DIE HAPPY AND NEVER LOOK BACK.
I'M SORRY, JIM...I'M SORRY... GOD HELP ME, I'M SO SORRY--
--SO SORRY--
GET AWAY FROM HIM!
RIGHT... NOW!

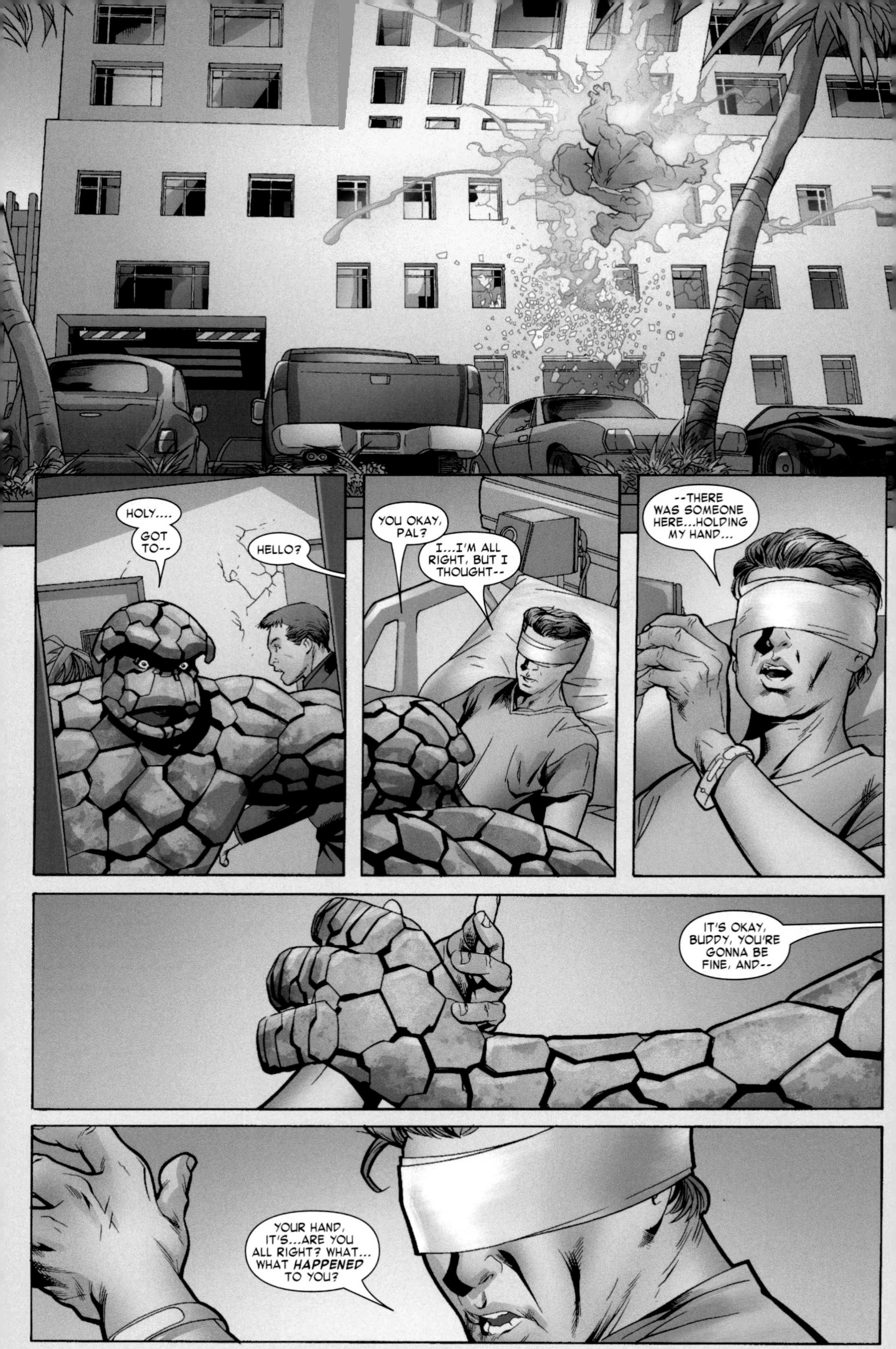
HOLY.... GOT TO--
HELLO?
YOU OKAY, PAL?
I...I'M ALL RIGHT, BUT I THOUGHT--
--THERE WAS SOMEONE HERE...HOLDING MY HAND...
IT'S OKAY, BUDDY, YOU'RE GONNA BE FINE, AND--
YOUR HAND, IT'S...ARE YOU ALL RIGHT? WHAT... WHAT *HAPPENED* TO YOU?

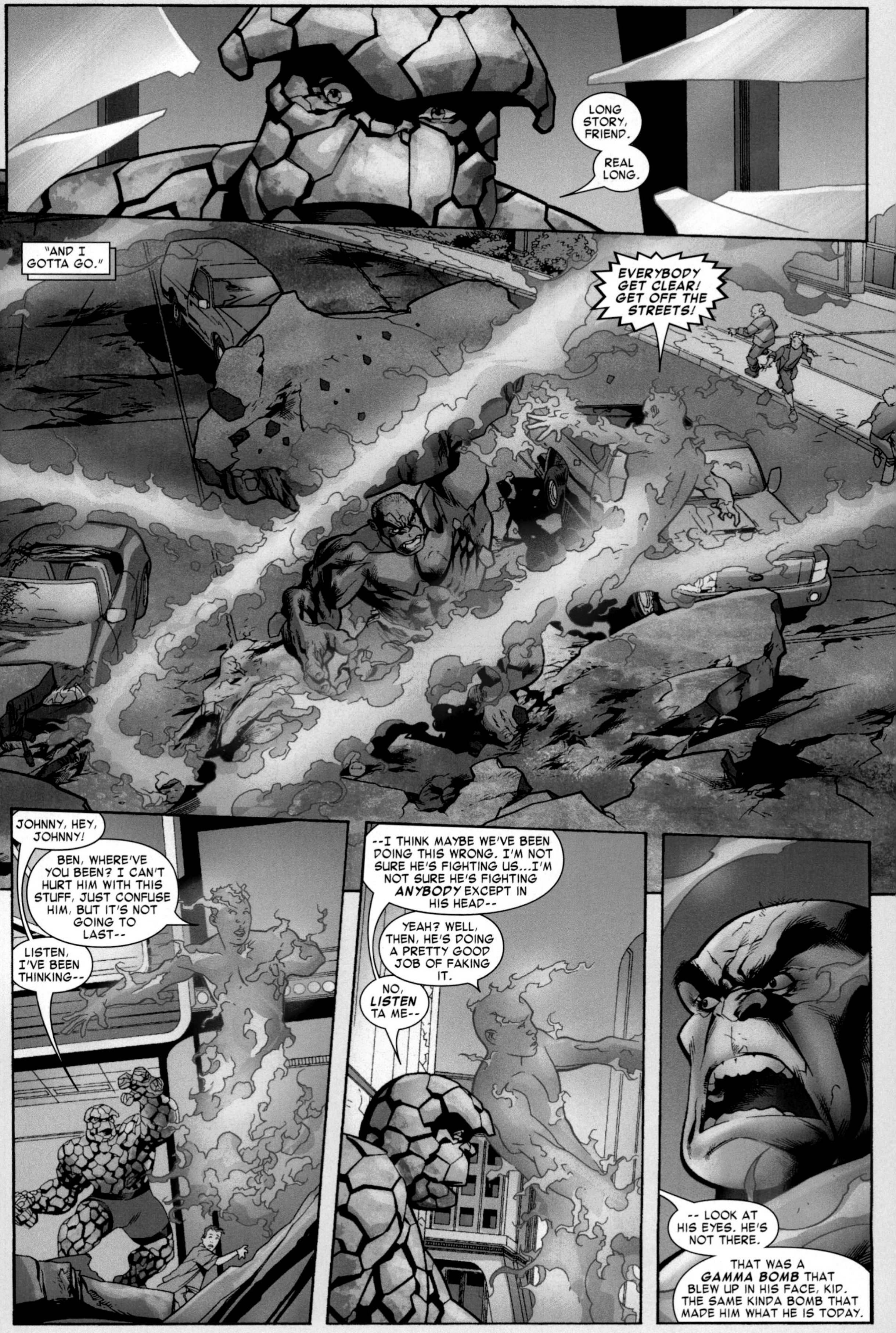
LONG STORY, FRIEND.
REAL LONG.
"AND I GOTTA GO."
EVERYBODY GET CLEAR! GET OFF THE STREETS!
JOHNNY, HEY, JOHNNY!
BEN, WHERE'VE YOU BEEN? I CAN'T HURT HIM WITH THIS STUFF, JUST CONFUSE HIM, BUT IT'S NOT GOING TO LAST--
LISTEN, I'VE BEEN THINKING--
--I THINK MAYBE WE'VE BEEN DOING THIS WRONG. I'M NOT SURE HE'S FIGHTING US...I'M NOT SURE HE'S FIGHTING ANYBODY EXCEPT IN HIS HEAD--
YEAH? WELL, THEN, HE'S DOING A PRETTY GOOD JOB OF FAKING IT.
NO, LISTEN TA ME--
-- LOOK AT HIS EYES. HE'S NOT THERE.
THAT WAS A GAMMA BOMB THAT BLEW UP IN HIS FACE, KID. THE SAME KINDA BOMB THAT MADE HIM WHAT HE IS TODAY.

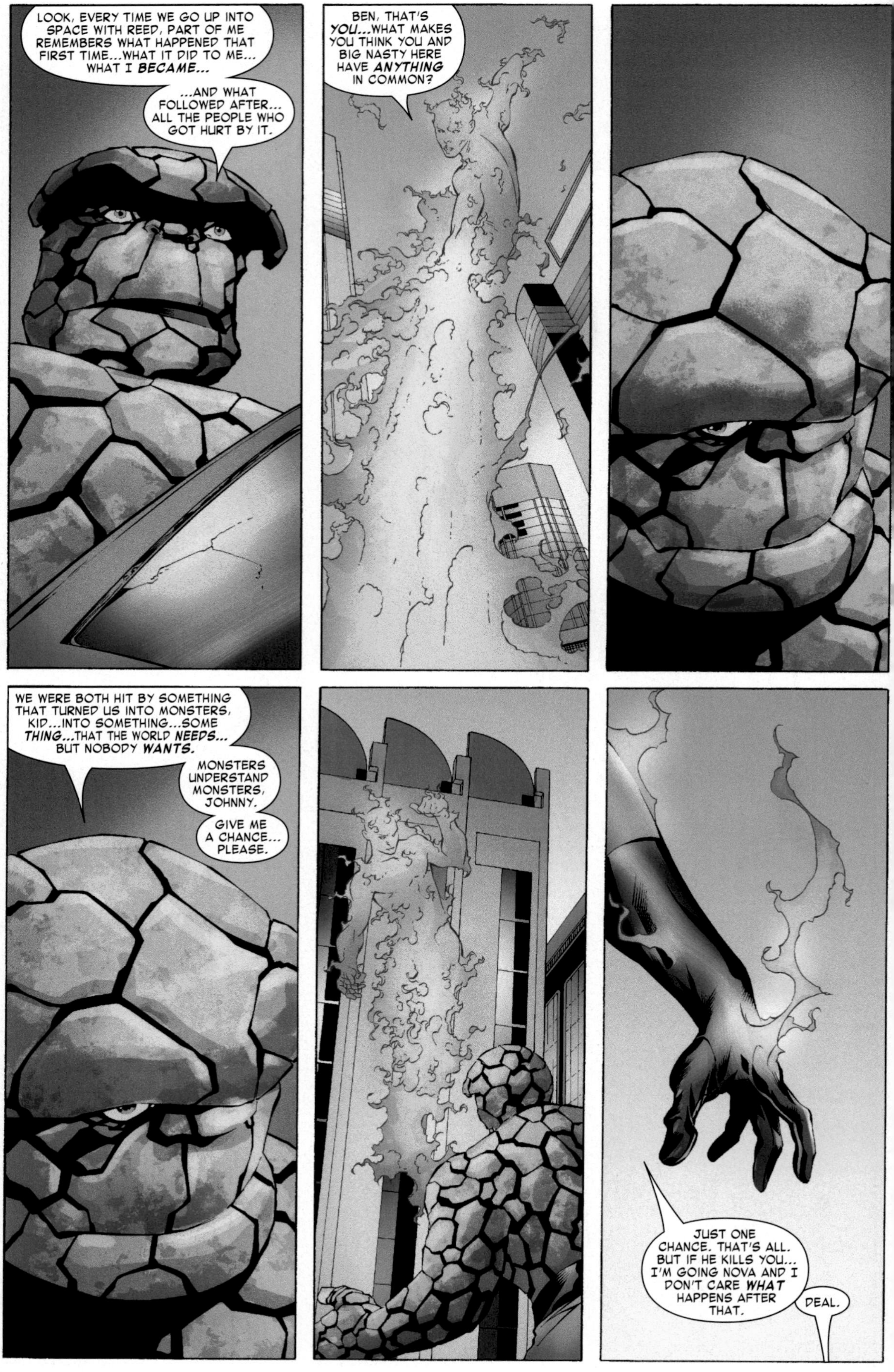
LOOK, EVERY TIME WE GO UP INTO SPACE WITH REED, PART OF ME REMEMBERS WHAT HAPPENED THAT FIRST TIME...WHAT IT DID TO ME... WHAT I *BECAME...*
...AND WHAT FOLLOWED AFTER... ALL THE PEOPLE WHO GOT HURT BY IT.
BEN, THAT'S *YOU...*WHAT MAKES YOU THINK YOU AND BIG NASTY HERE HAVE *ANYTHING* IN COMMON?
WE WERE BOTH HIT BY SOMETHING THAT TURNED US INTO MONSTERS, KID...INTO SOMETHING...SOME *THING*...THAT THE WORLD *NEEDS...* BUT NOBODY *WANTS.*
MONSTERS UNDERSTAND MONSTERS, JOHNNY.
GIVE ME A CHANCE... PLEASE.
JUST ONE CHANCE. THAT'S ALL. BUT IF HE KILLS YOU... I'M GOING NOVA AND I DON'T CARE *WHAT* HAPPENS AFTER THAT.
DEAL.

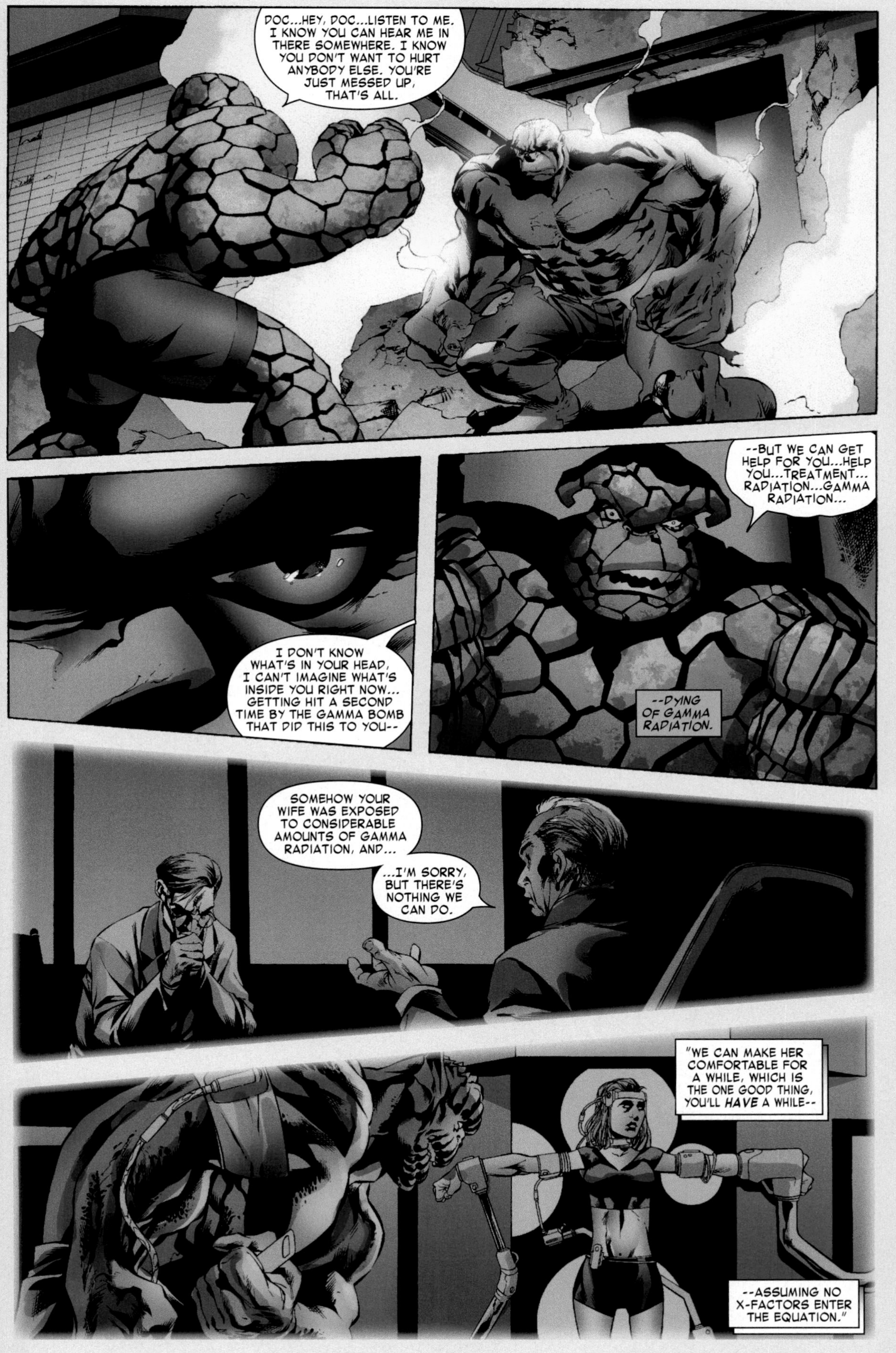
DOC...HEY, DOC...LISTEN TO ME. I KNOW YOU CAN HEAR ME IN THERE SOMEWHERE. I KNOW YOU DON'T WANT TO HURT ANYBODY ELSE. YOU'RE JUST MESSED UP, THAT'S ALL.
I DON'T KNOW WHAT'S IN YOUR HEAD, I CAN'T IMAGINE WHAT'S INSIDE YOU RIGHT NOW... GETTING HIT A SECOND TIME BY THE GAMMA BOMB THAT DID THIS TO YOU--
--BUT WE CAN GET HELP FOR YOU...HELP YOU...TREATMENT... RADIATION...GAMMA RADIATION...
--DYING OF GAMMA RADIATION.
SOMEHOW YOUR WIFE WAS EXPOSED TO CONSIDERABLE AMOUNTS OF GAMMA RADIATION, AND...
...I'M SORRY, BUT THERE'S NOTHING WE CAN DO.
"WE CAN MAKE HER COMFORTABLE FOR A WHILE, WHICH IS THE ONE GOOD THING, YOU'LL *HAVE* A WHILE--
--ASSUMING NO X-FACTORS ENTER THE EQUATION."

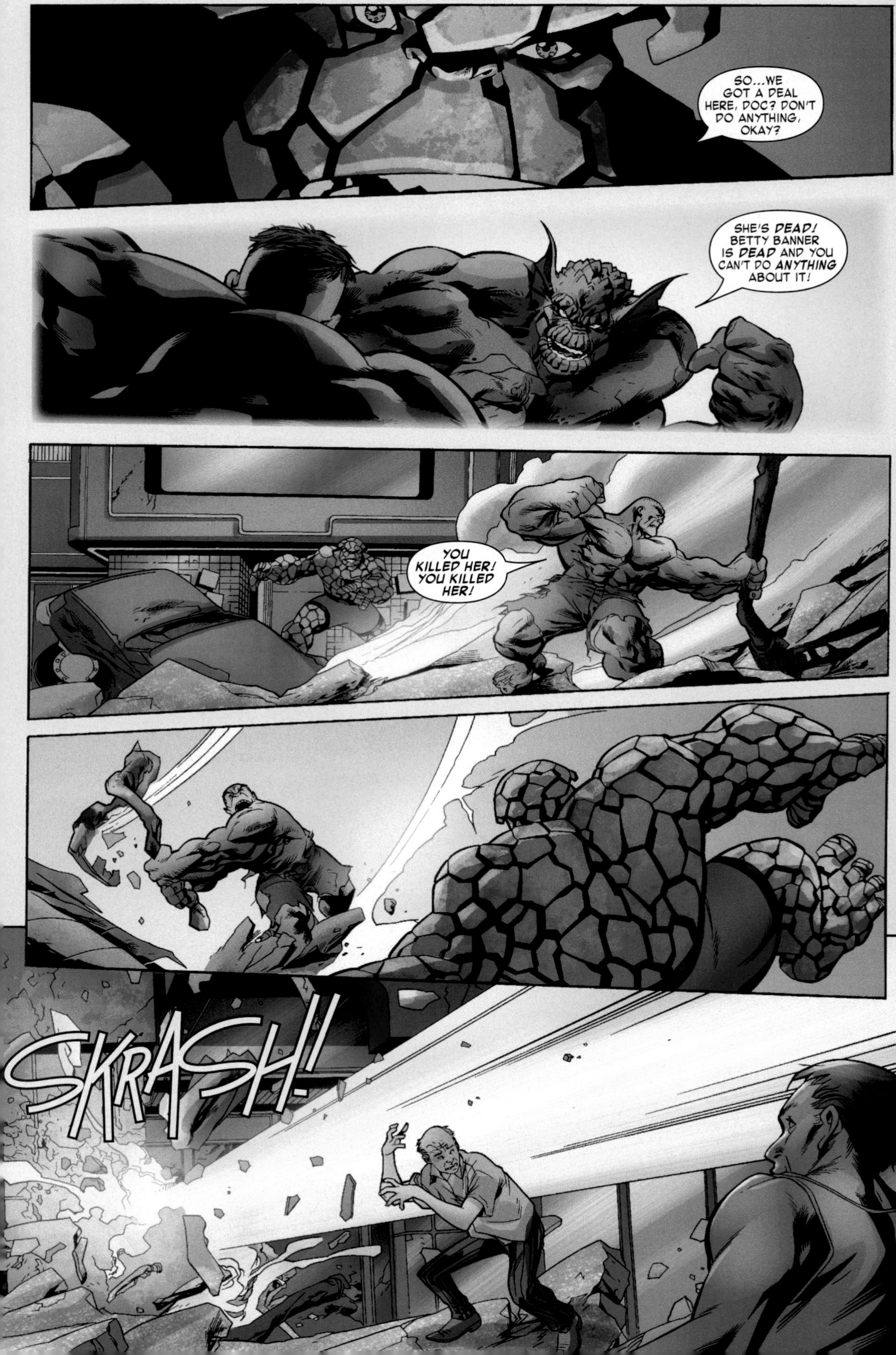
SO...WE GOT A DEAL HERE, DOC? DON'T DO ANYTHING, OKAY?
SHE'S DEAD! BETTY BANNER IS DEAD AND YOU CAN'T DO ANYTHING ABOUT IT!
YOU KILLED HER! YOU KILLED HER!
SKRASH!

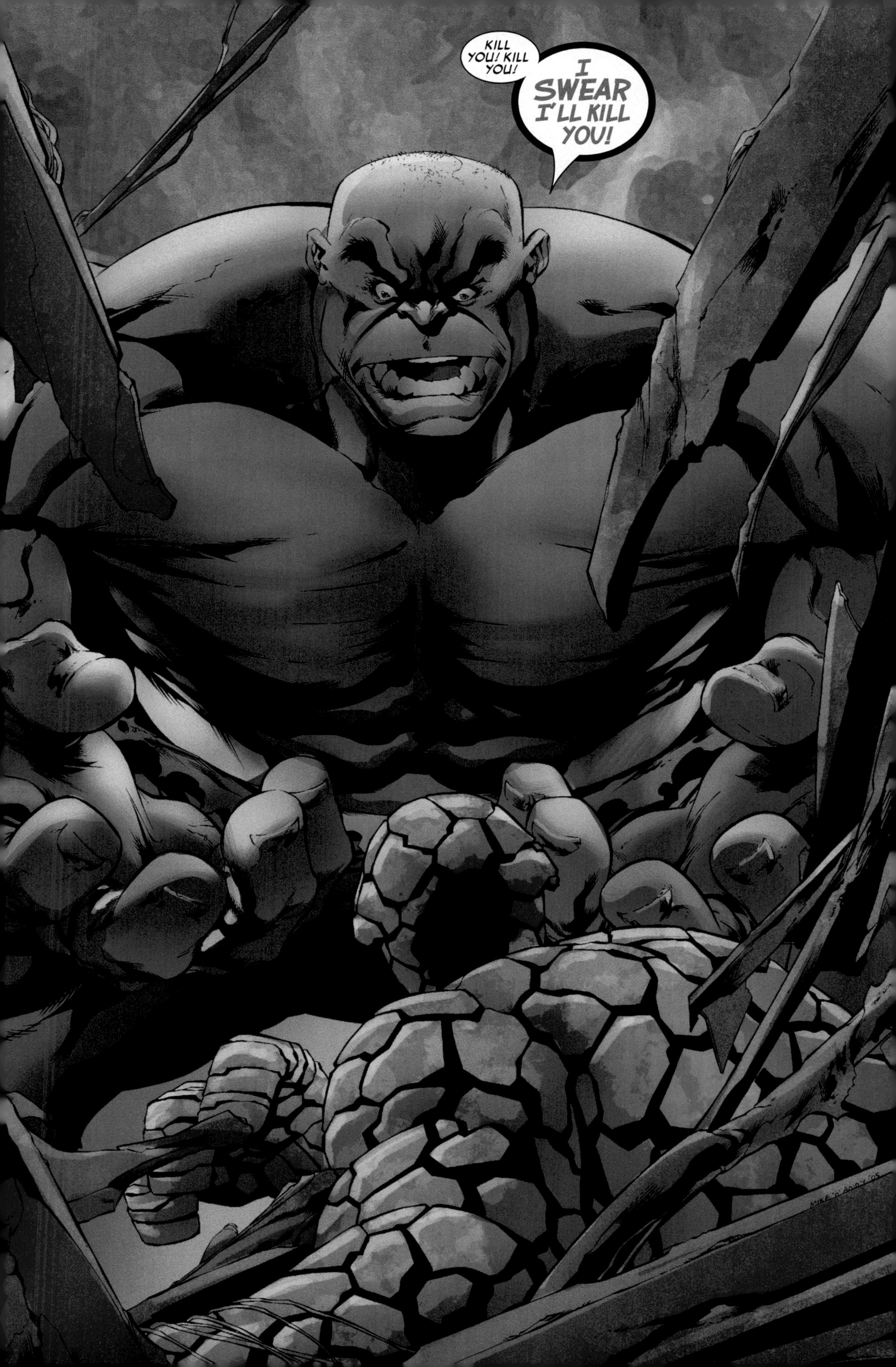
KILL YOU! KILL YOU!
I SWEAR I'LL KILL YOU!

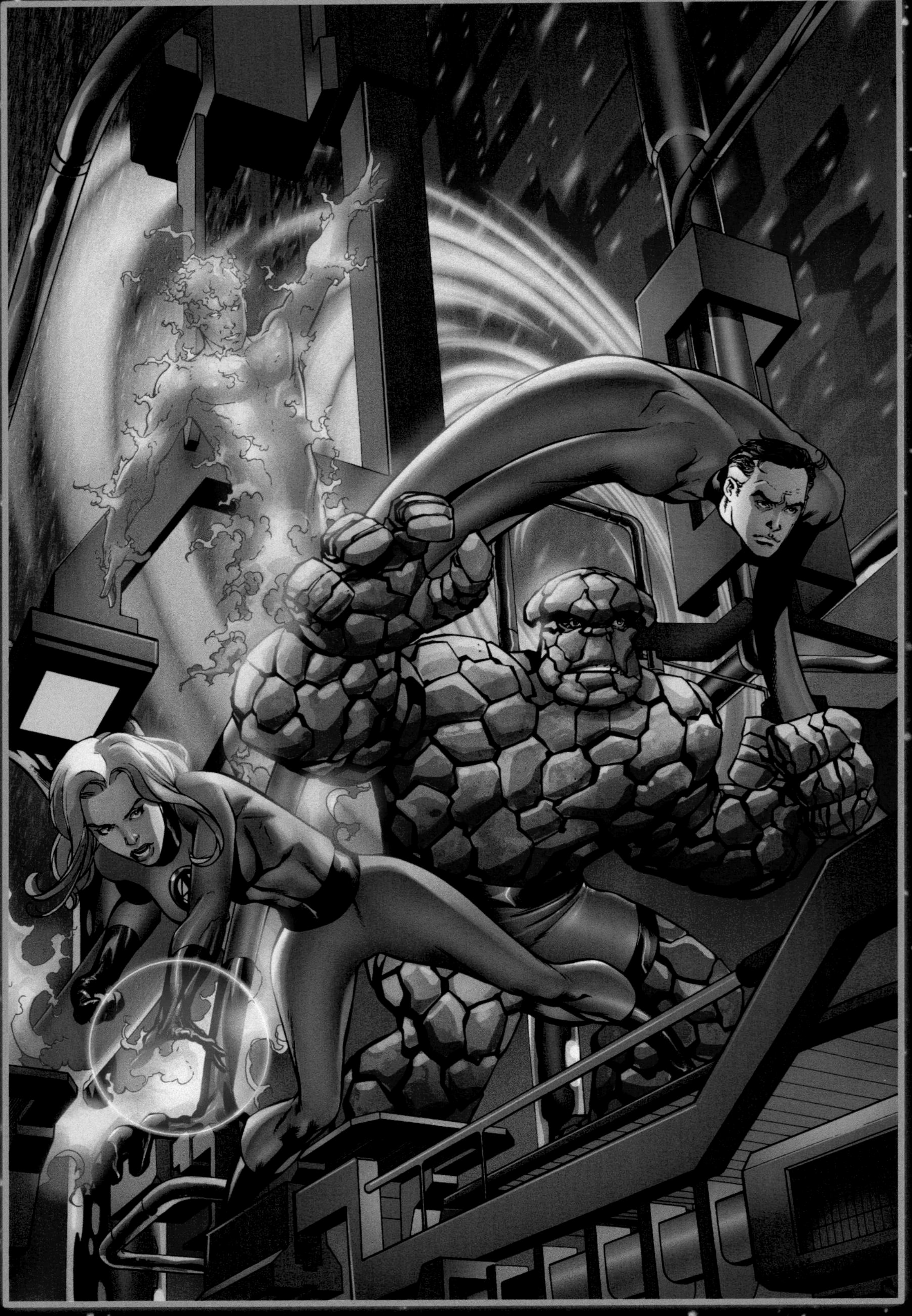

FANTASTIC FOUR #535

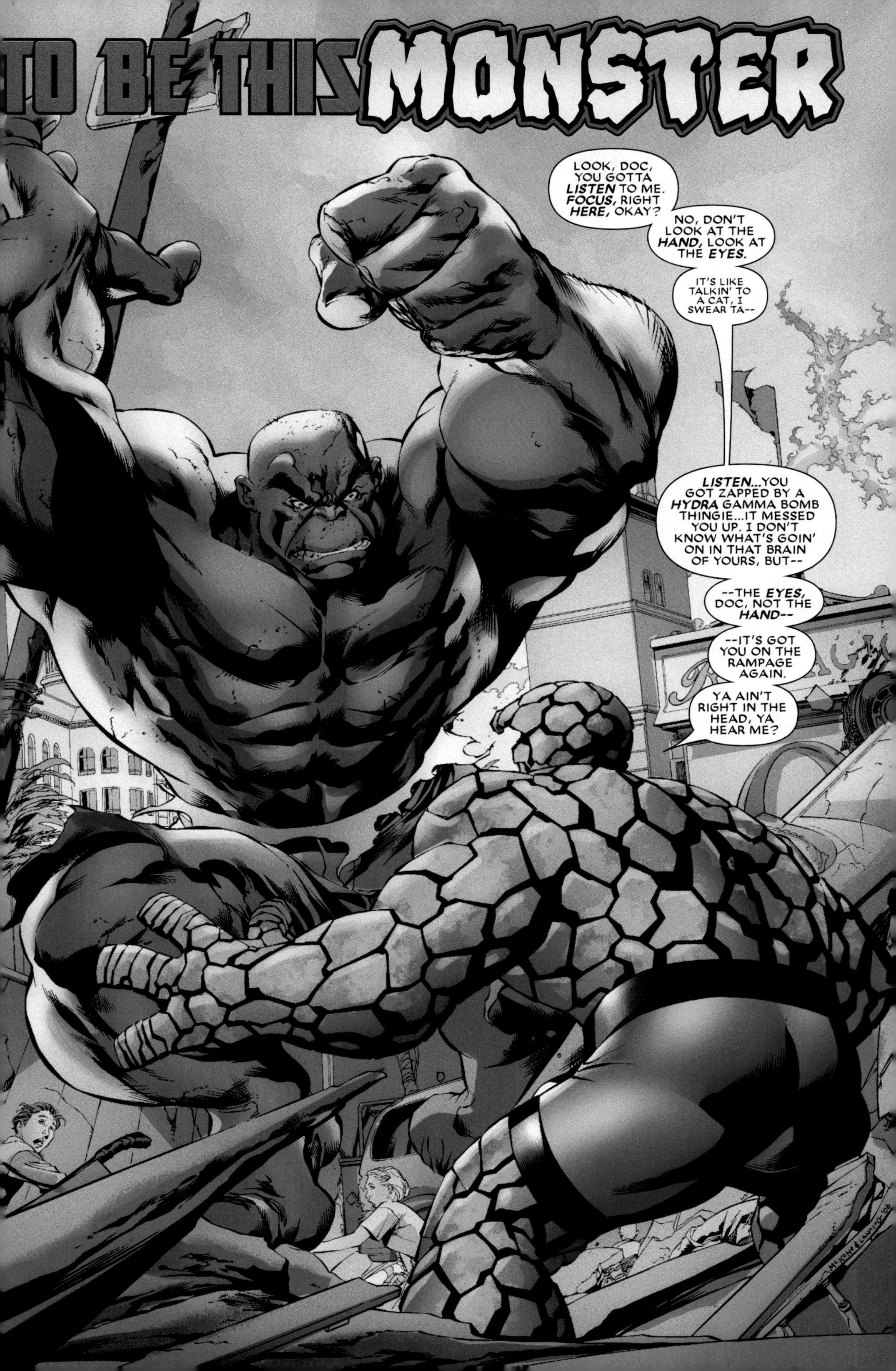
TO BE THIS MONSTER
LOOK, DOC, YOU GOTTA LISTEN TO ME. FOCUS, RIGHT HERE, OKAY?
NO, DON'T LOOK AT THE HAND, LOOK AT THE EYES.
IT'S LIKE TALKIN' TO A CAT, I SWEAR TA--
LISTEN...YOU GOT ZAPPED BY A HYDRA GAMMA BOMB THINGIE...IT MESSED YOU UP. I DON'T KNOW WHAT'S GOIN' ON IN THAT BRAIN OF YOURS, BUT--
--THE EYES, DOC, NOT THE HAND--
--IT'S GOT YOU ON THE RAMPAGE AGAIN.
YA AIN'T RIGHT IN THE HEAD, YA HEAR ME?

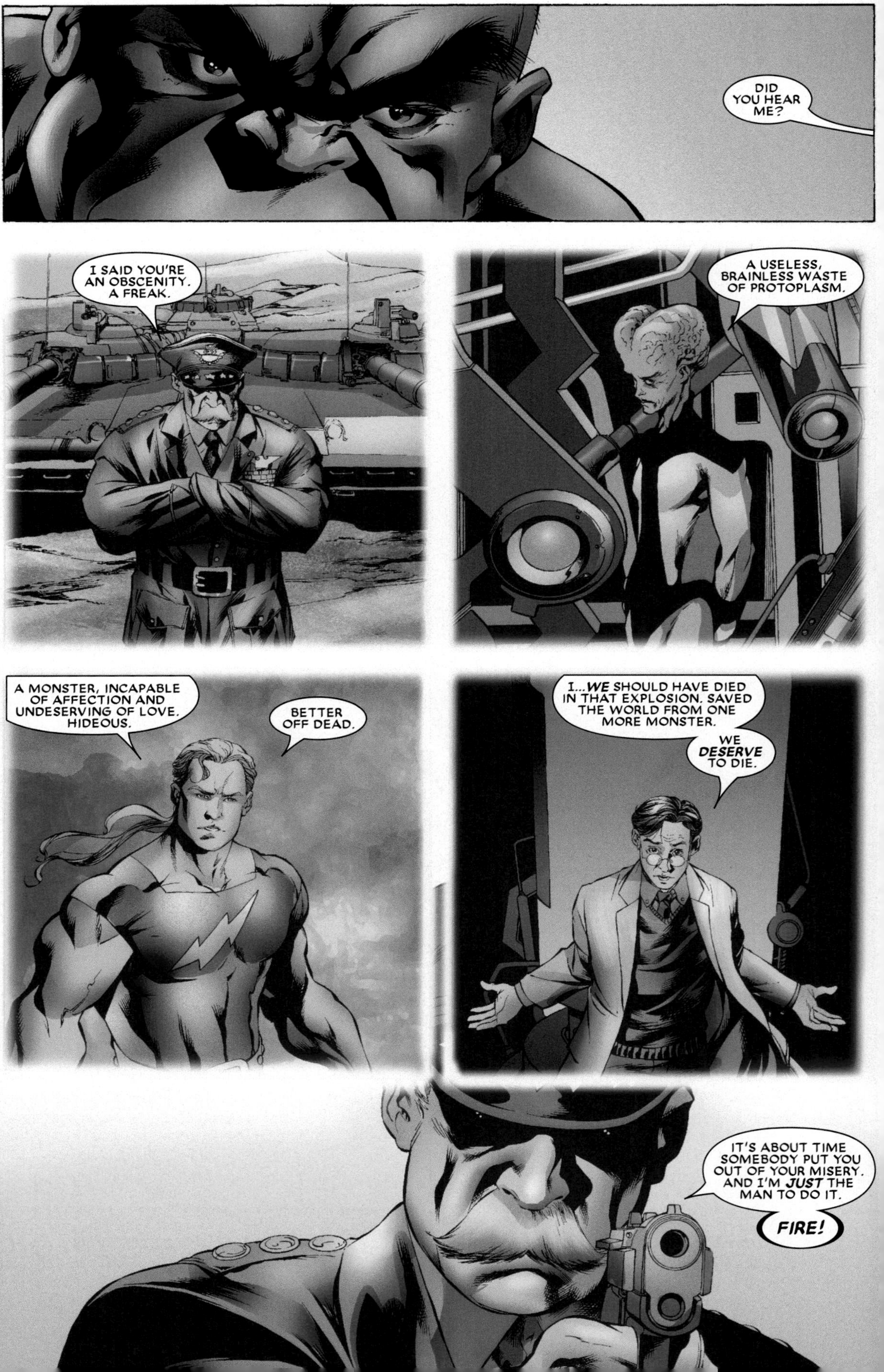
DID YOU HEAR ME?
I SAID YOU'RE AN OBSCENITY. A FREAK.
A USELESS, BRAINLESS WASTE OF PROTOPLASM.
A MONSTER, INCAPABLE OF AFFECTION AND UNDESERVING OF LOVE. HIDEOUS.
BETTER OFF DEAD.
I... *WE* SHOULD HAVE DIED IN THAT EXPLOSION. SAVED THE WORLD FROM ONE MORE MONSTER.
WE *DESERVE* TO DIE.
IT'S ABOUT TIME SOMEBODY PUT YOU OUT OF YOUR MISERY. AND I'M *JUST* THE MAN TO DO IT.
FIRE!

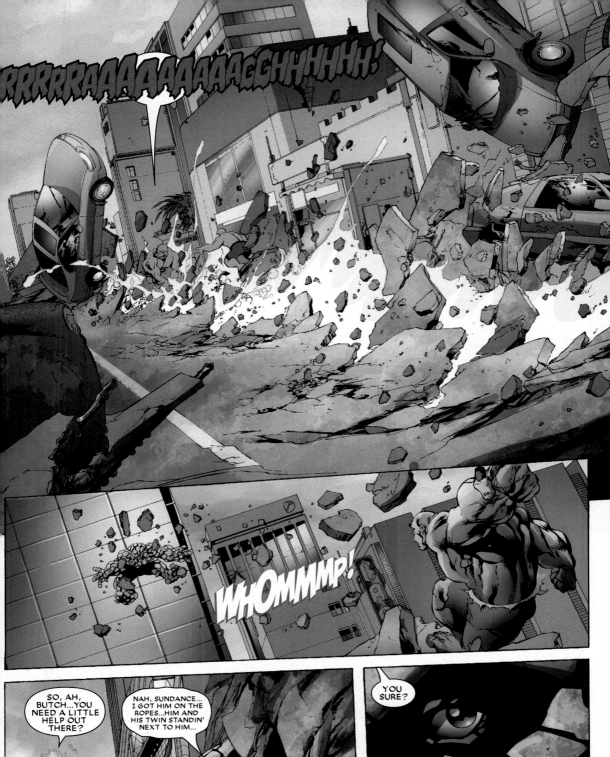

RRRRRAAAAAAAAAGGHHHHH!

WHOMMMP!

SO, AH, BUTCH...YOU NEED A LITTLE HELP OUT THERE?

NAH, SUNDANCE... I GOT HIM ON THE ROPES...HIM AND HIS TWIN STANDIN' NEXT TO HIM...

YOU SURE?

YEAH...HE'S GOT "I'M A MONSTER" IN HIS EYES. I KNOW THAT LOOK. WE GOTTA SETTLE THIS BETWEEN US.

JUST BETWEEN US MONSTERS.

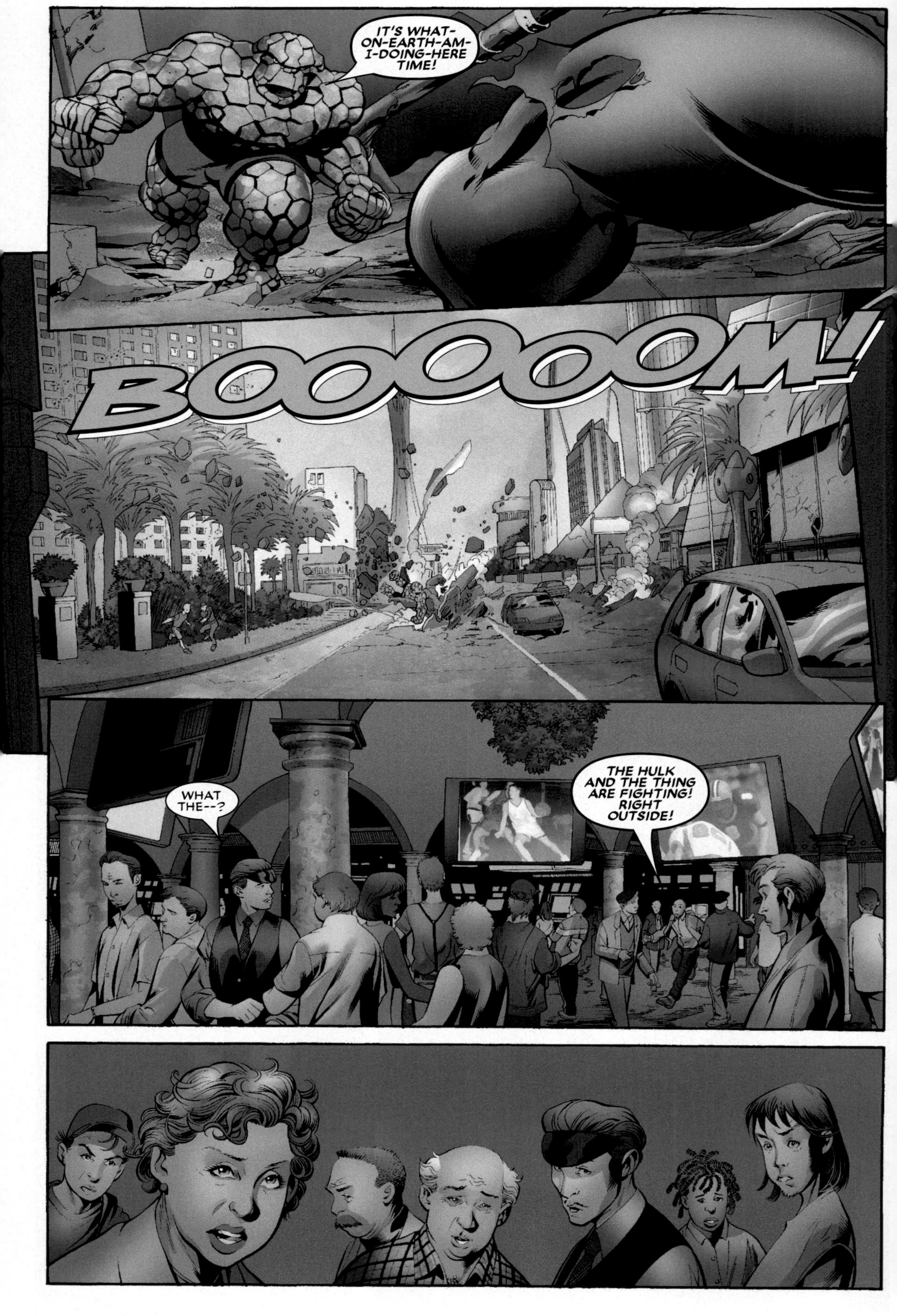
IT'S WHAT-ON-EARTH-AM-I-DOING-HERE TIME!
BOOOOOM!
WHAT THE--?
THE HULK AND THE THING ARE FIGHTING! RIGHT OUTSIDE!

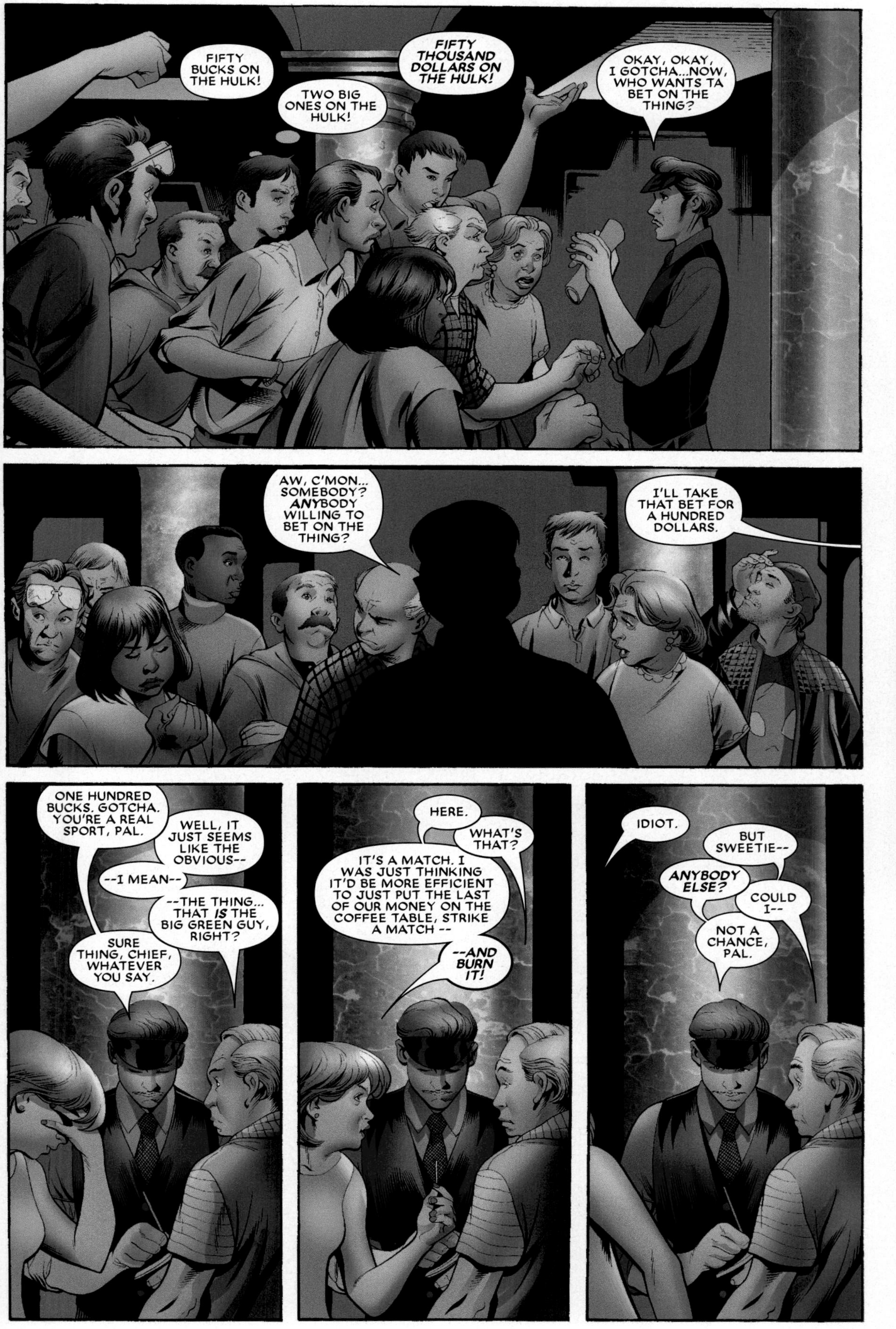
FIFTY BUCKS ON THE HULK!
TWO BIG ONES ON THE HULK!
FIFTY THOUSAND DOLLARS ON THE HULK!
OKAY, OKAY, I GOTCHA...NOW, WHO WANTS TA BET ON THE THING?
AW, C'MON... SOMEBODY? ANYBODY WILLING TO BET ON THE THING?
I'LL TAKE THAT BET FOR A HUNDRED DOLLARS.
ONE HUNDRED BUCKS. GOTCHA. YOU'RE A REAL SPORT, PAL.
WELL, IT JUST SEEMS LIKE THE OBVIOUS--
--I MEAN--
--THE THING... THAT IS THE BIG GREEN GUY, RIGHT?
SURE THING, CHIEF, WHATEVER YOU SAY.
HERE.
WHAT'S THAT?
IT'S A MATCH. I WAS JUST THINKING IT'D BE MORE EFFICIENT TO JUST PUT THE LAST OF OUR MONEY ON THE COFFEE TABLE, STRIKE A MATCH --
--AND BURN IT!
IDIOT.
BUT SWEETIE--
ANYBODY ELSE?
COULD I--
NOT A CHANCE, PAL.

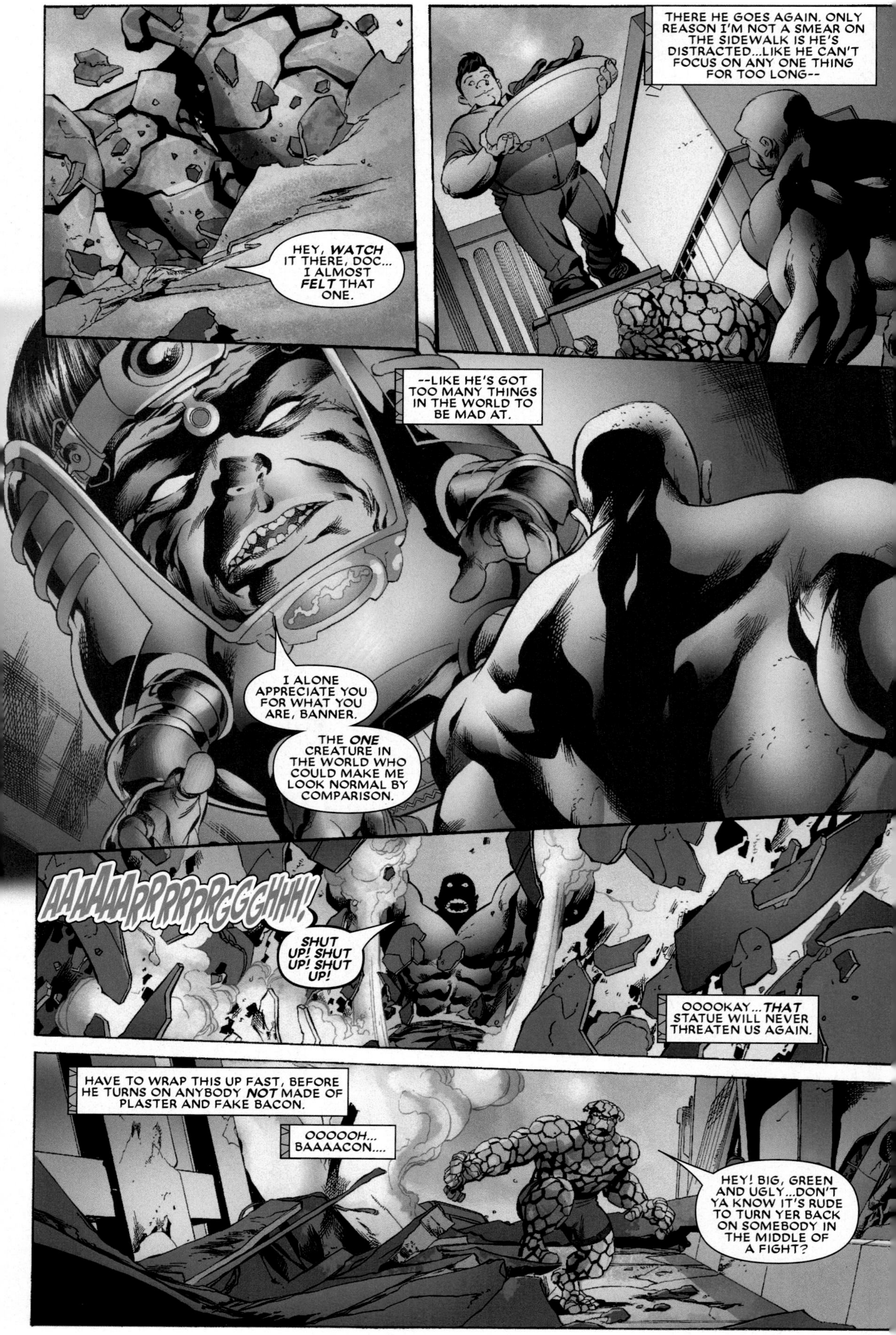
HEY, WATCH IT THERE, DOC... I ALMOST FELT THAT ONE.
THERE HE GOES AGAIN. ONLY REASON I'M NOT A SMEAR ON THE SIDEWALK IS HE'S DISTRACTED...LIKE HE CAN'T FOCUS ON ANY ONE THING FOR TOO LONG--
--LIKE HE'S GOT TOO MANY THINGS IN THE WORLD TO BE MAD AT.
I ALONE APPRECIATE YOU FOR WHAT YOU ARE, BANNER.
THE ONE CREATURE IN THE WORLD WHO COULD MAKE ME LOOK NORMAL BY COMPARISON.
AAAAAARRRRRRGGHHH!
SHUT UP! SHUT UP! SHUT UP!
OOOOKAY...THAT STATUE WILL NEVER THREATEN US AGAIN.
HAVE TO WRAP THIS UP FAST, BEFORE HE TURNS ON ANYBODY NOT MADE OF PLASTER AND FAKE BACON.
OOOOOH... BAAAACON....
HEY! BIG, GREEN AND UGLY...DON'T YA KNOW IT'S RUDE TO TURN YER BACK ON SOMEBODY IN THE MIDDLE OF A FIGHT?

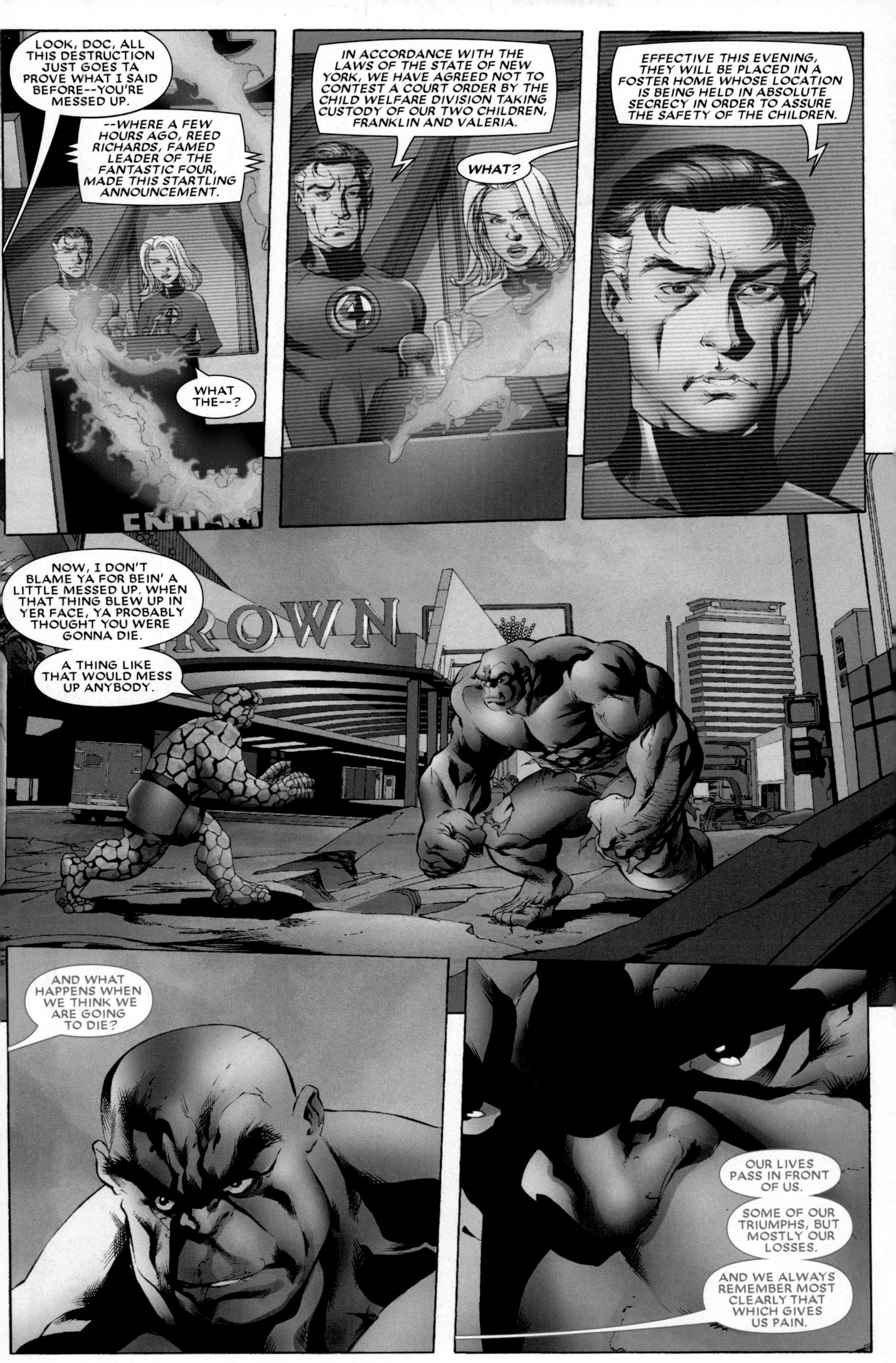

LOOK, DOC, ALL THIS DESTRUCTION JUST GOES TA PROVE WHAT I SAID BEFORE--YOU'RE MESSED UP.
--WHERE A FEW HOURS AGO, REED RICHARDS, FAMED LEADER OF THE FANTASTIC FOUR, MADE THIS STARTLING ANNOUNCEMENT.
WHAT THE--?
IN ACCORDANCE WITH THE LAWS OF THE STATE OF NEW YORK, WE HAVE AGREED NOT TO CONTEST A COURT ORDER BY THE CHILD WELFARE DIVISION TAKING CUSTODY OF OUR TWO CHILDREN, FRANKLIN AND VALERIA.
WHAT?
EFFECTIVE THIS EVENING, THEY WILL BE PLACED IN A FOSTER HOME WHOSE LOCATION IS BEING HELD IN ABSOLUTE SECRECY IN ORDER TO ASSURE THE SAFETY OF THE CHILDREN.
NOW, I DON'T BLAME YA FOR BEIN' A LITTLE MESSED UP. WHEN THAT THING BLEW UP IN YER FACE, YA PROBABLY THOUGHT YOU WERE GONNA DIE.
A THING LIKE THAT WOULD MESS UP ANYBODY.
ROWN
AND WHAT HAPPENS WHEN WE THINK WE ARE GOING TO DIE?
OUR LIVES PASS IN FRONT OF US.
SOME OF OUR TRIUMPHS, BUT MOSTLY OUR LOSSES.
AND WE ALWAYS REMEMBER MOST CLEARLY THAT WHICH GIVES US PAIN.

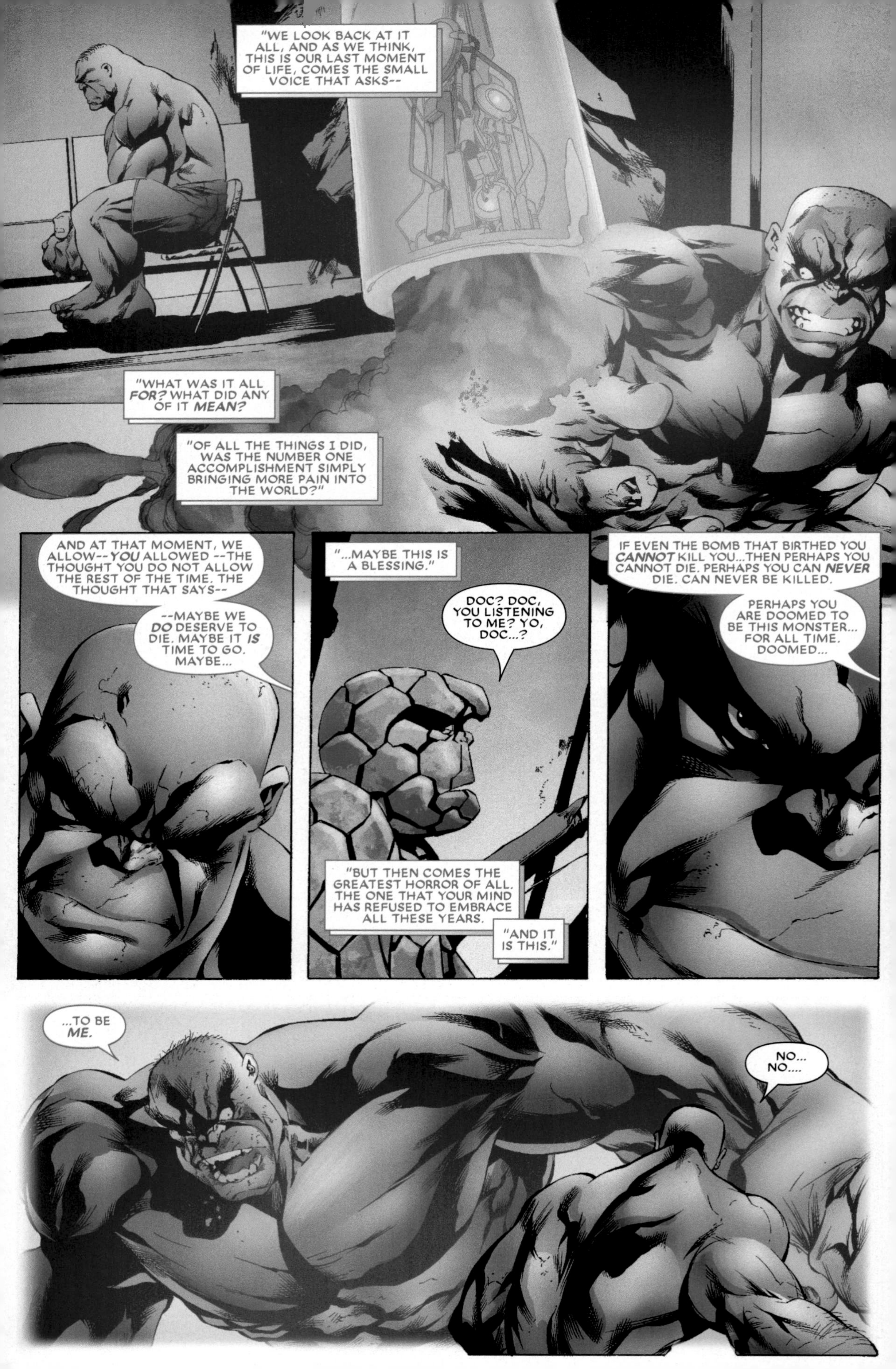
"WE LOOK BACK AT IT ALL, AND AS WE THINK, THIS IS OUR LAST MOMENT OF LIFE, COMES THE SMALL VOICE THAT ASKS--
"WHAT WAS IT ALL *FOR?* WHAT DID ANY OF IT *MEAN?*
"OF ALL THE THINGS I DID, WAS THE NUMBER ONE ACCOMPLISHMENT SIMPLY BRINGING MORE PAIN INTO THE WORLD?"
AND AT THAT MOMENT, WE ALLOW--*YOU* ALLOWED --THE THOUGHT YOU DO NOT ALLOW THE REST OF THE TIME. THE THOUGHT THAT SAYS--
--MAYBE WE *DO* DESERVE TO DIE. MAYBE IT *IS* TIME TO GO. MAYBE...
"...MAYBE THIS IS A BLESSING."
DOC? DOC, YOU LISTENING TO ME? YO, DOC...?
"BUT THEN COMES THE GREATEST HORROR OF ALL. THE ONE THAT YOUR MIND HAS REFUSED TO EMBRACE ALL THESE YEARS.
"AND IT IS THIS."
IF EVEN THE BOMB THAT BIRTHED YOU *CANNOT* KILL YOU...THEN PERHAPS YOU CANNOT DIE. PERHAPS YOU CAN *NEVER* DIE. CAN NEVER BE KILLED.
PERHAPS YOU ARE DOOMED TO BE THIS MONSTER... FOR ALL TIME. DOOMED...
...TO BE *ME.*
NO... NO....

...NOOOOOOOOOOOOOO!

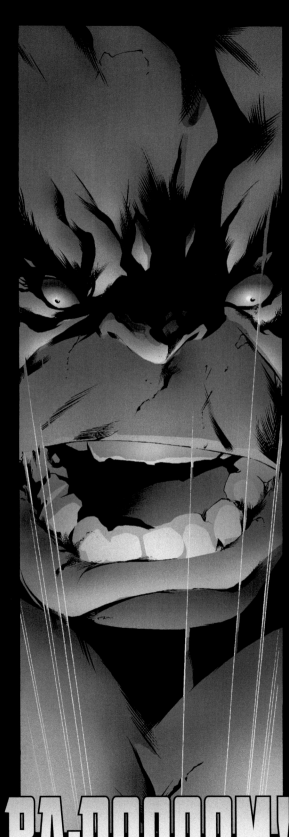

BA-DOOOOM!

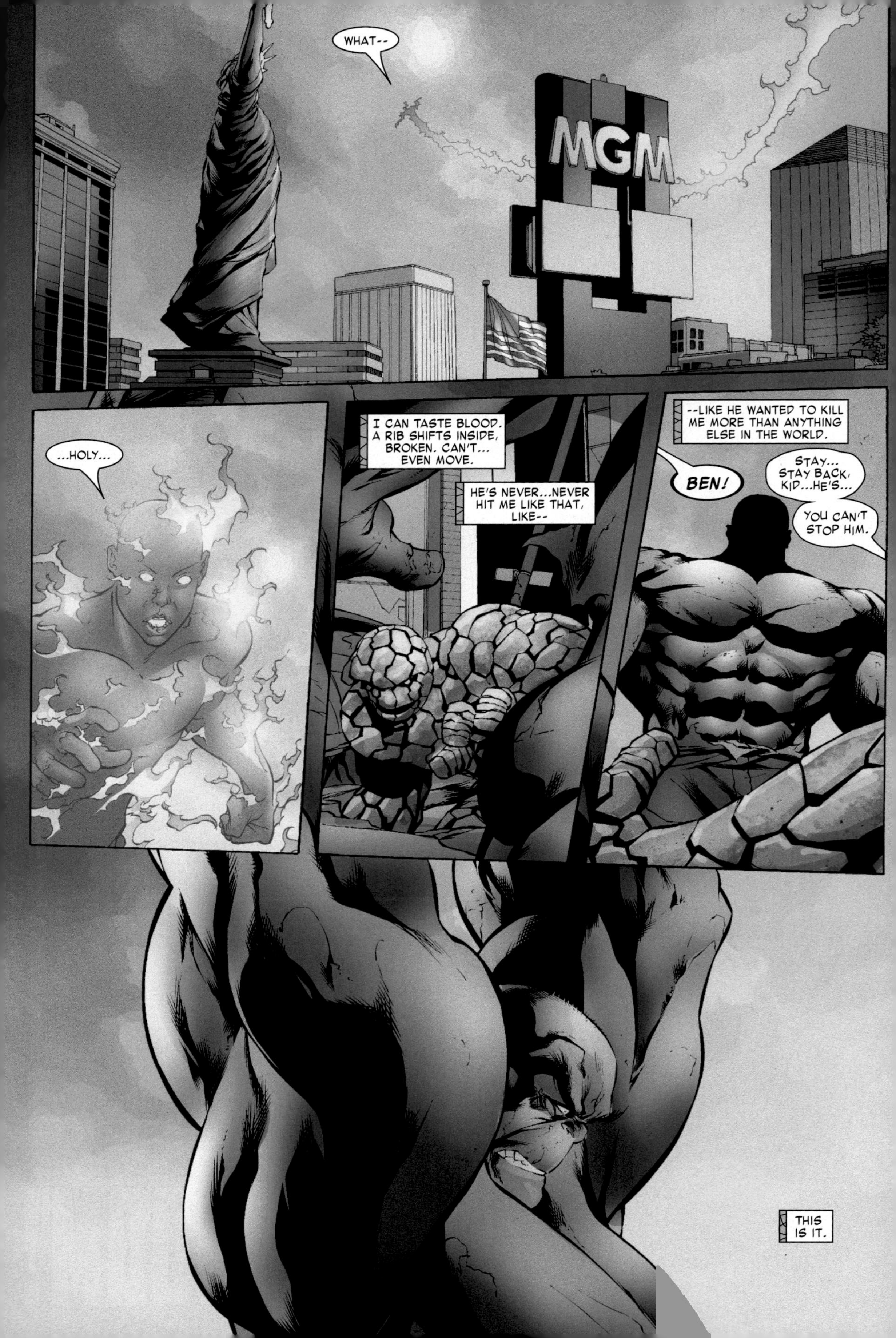
WHAT--
MGM
...HOLY...
I CAN TASTE BLOOD. A RIB SHIFTS INSIDE, BROKEN. CAN'T... EVEN MOVE.
HE'S NEVER...NEVER HIT ME LIKE THAT, LIKE--
--LIKE HE WANTED TO KILL ME MORE THAN ANYTHING ELSE IN THE WORLD.
BEN!
STAY... STAY BACK, KID...HE'S...
YOU CAN'T STOP HIM.
THIS IS IT.

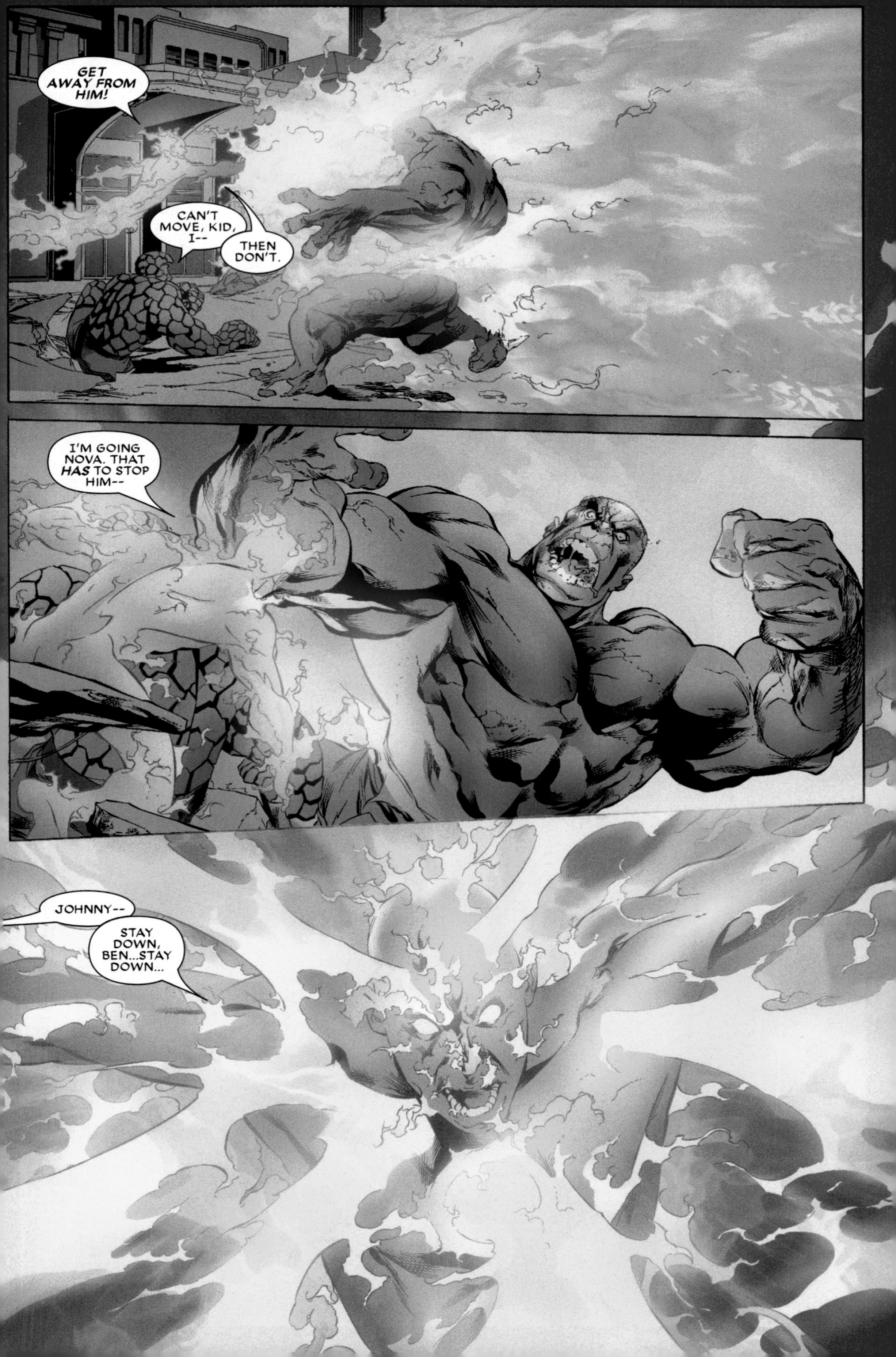
GET AWAY FROM HIM!
CAN'T MOVE, KID, I--
THEN DON'T.
I'M GOING NOVA. THAT HAS TO STOP HIM--
JOHNNY--
STAY DOWN, BEN...STAY DOWN...

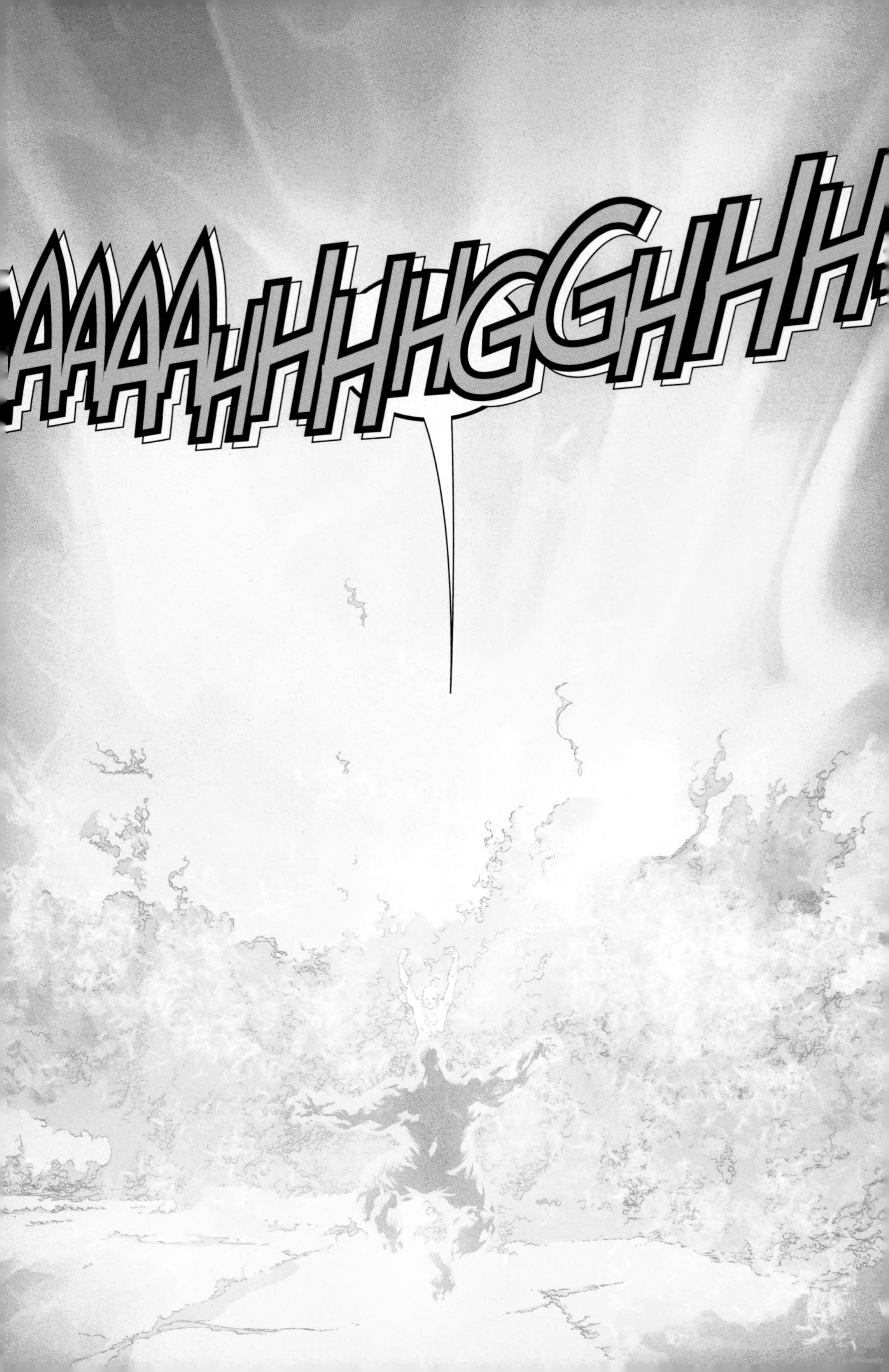
AAAAHHHHGGHHH

HUNH...
HUNH...HUNH

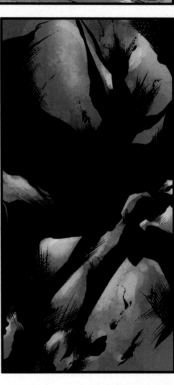

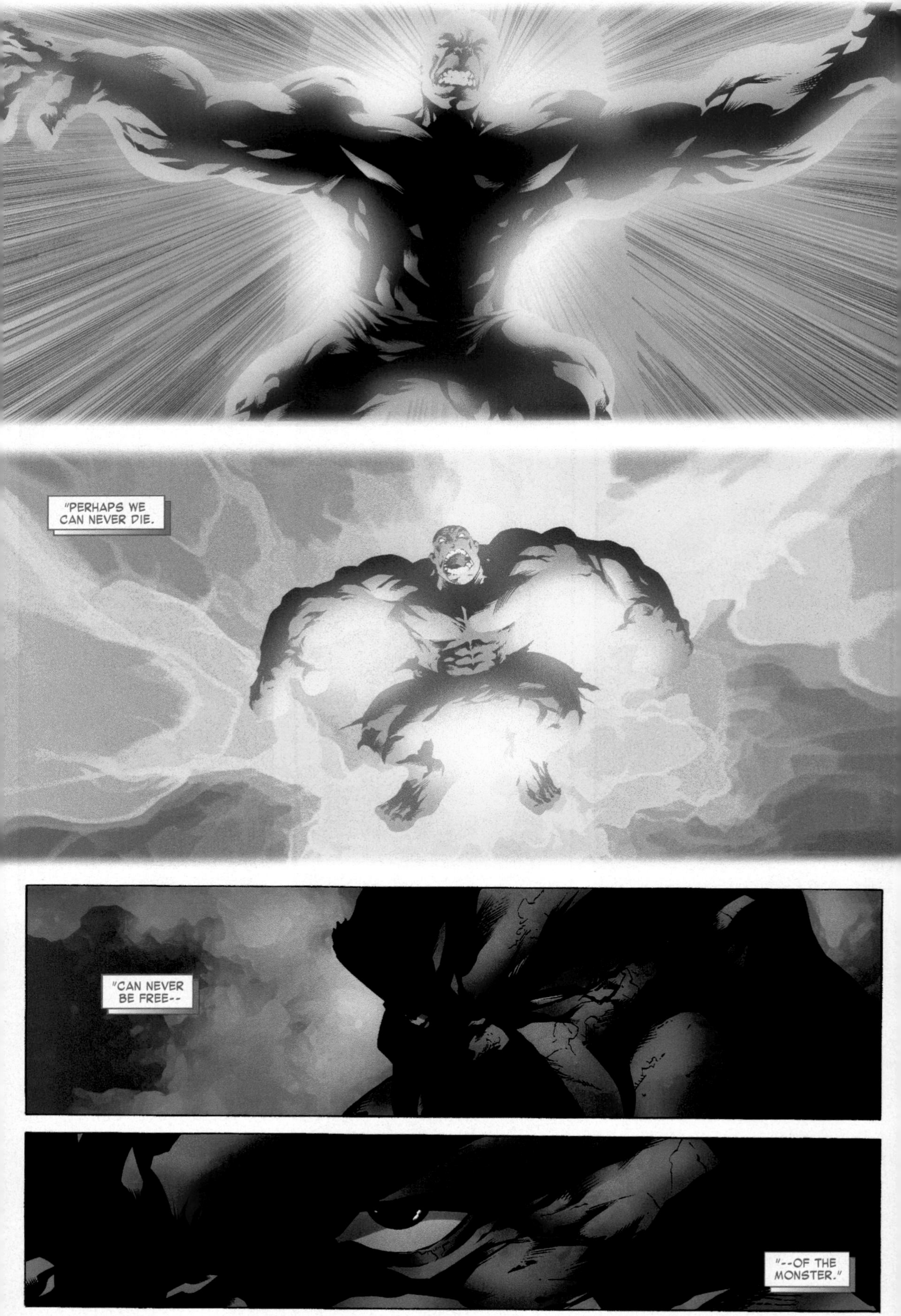
"PERHAPS WE CAN NEVER DIE.
"CAN NEVER BE FREE--
"--OF THE MONSTER."

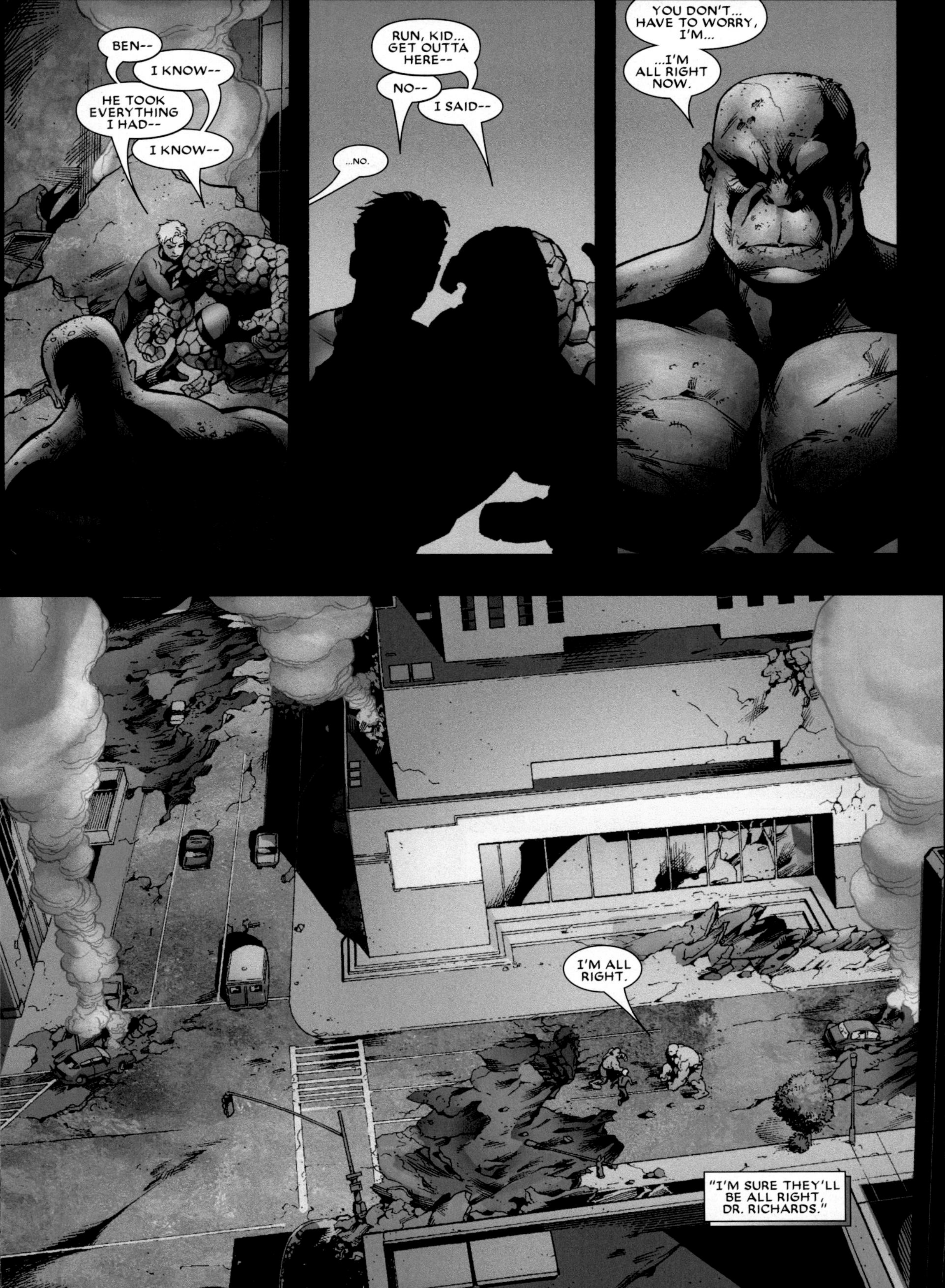
BEN--
I KNOW--
HE TOOK EVERYTHING I HAD--
I KNOW--
RUN, KID... GET OUTTA HERE--
NO--
I SAID--
...NO.
YOU DON'T... HAVE TO WORRY, I'M...
...I'M ALL RIGHT NOW.
I'M ALL RIGHT.
"I'M SURE THEY'LL BE ALL RIGHT, DR. RICHARDS."

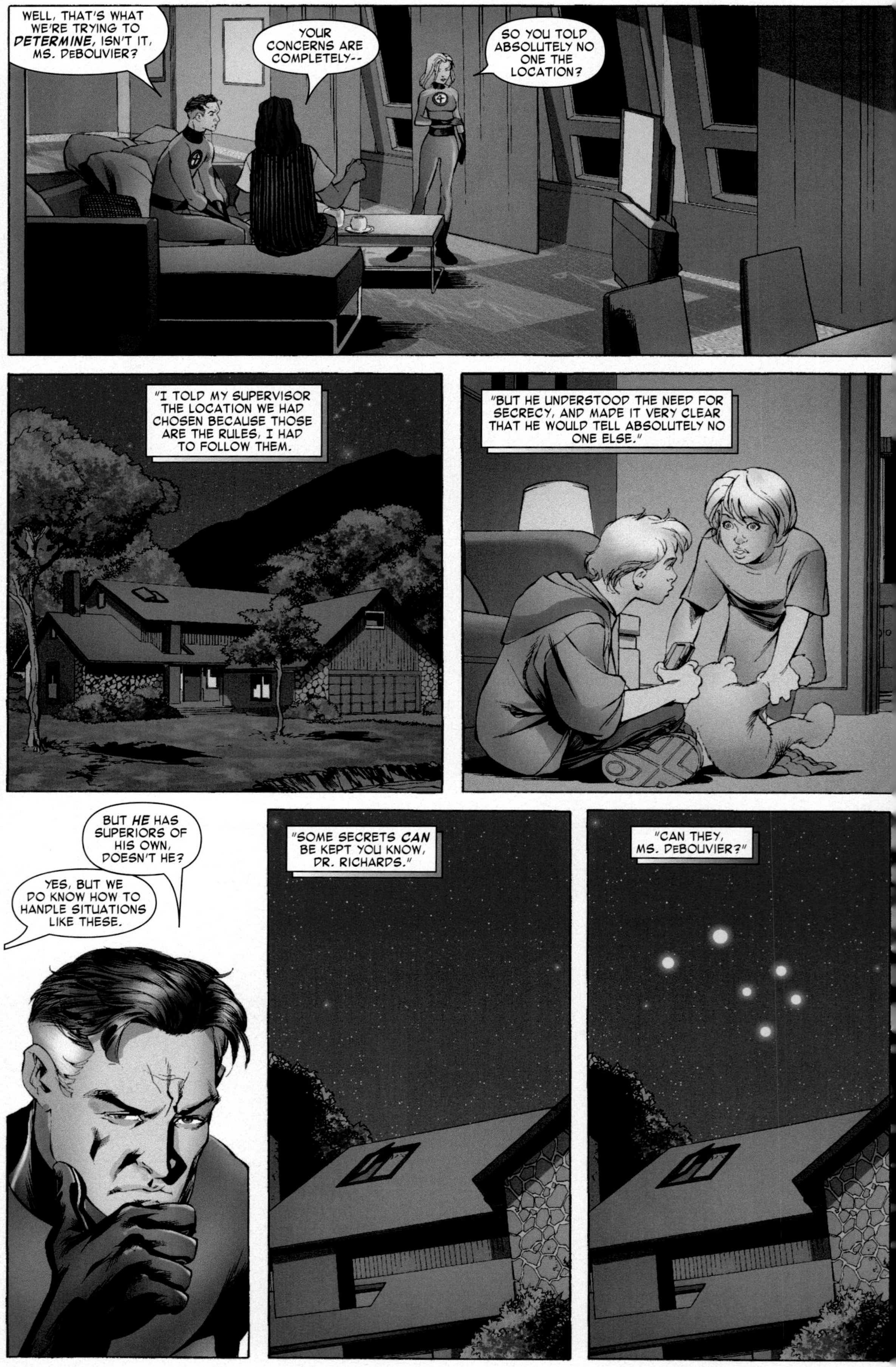
WELL, THAT'S WHAT WE'RE TRYING TO DETERMINE, ISN'T IT, MS. DEBOUVIER?
YOUR CONCERNS ARE COMPLETELY--
SO YOU TOLD ABSOLUTELY NO ONE THE LOCATION?
"I TOLD MY SUPERVISOR THE LOCATION WE HAD CHOSEN BECAUSE THOSE ARE THE RULES, I HAD TO FOLLOW THEM.
"BUT HE UNDERSTOOD THE NEED FOR SECRECY, AND MADE IT VERY CLEAR THAT HE WOULD TELL ABSOLUTELY NO ONE ELSE."
BUT HE HAS SUPERIORS OF HIS OWN, DOESN'T HE?
YES, BUT WE DO KNOW HOW TO HANDLE SITUATIONS LIKE THESE.
"SOME SECRETS CAN BE KEPT YOU KNOW, DR. RICHARDS."
"CAN THEY, MS. DEBOUVIER?"

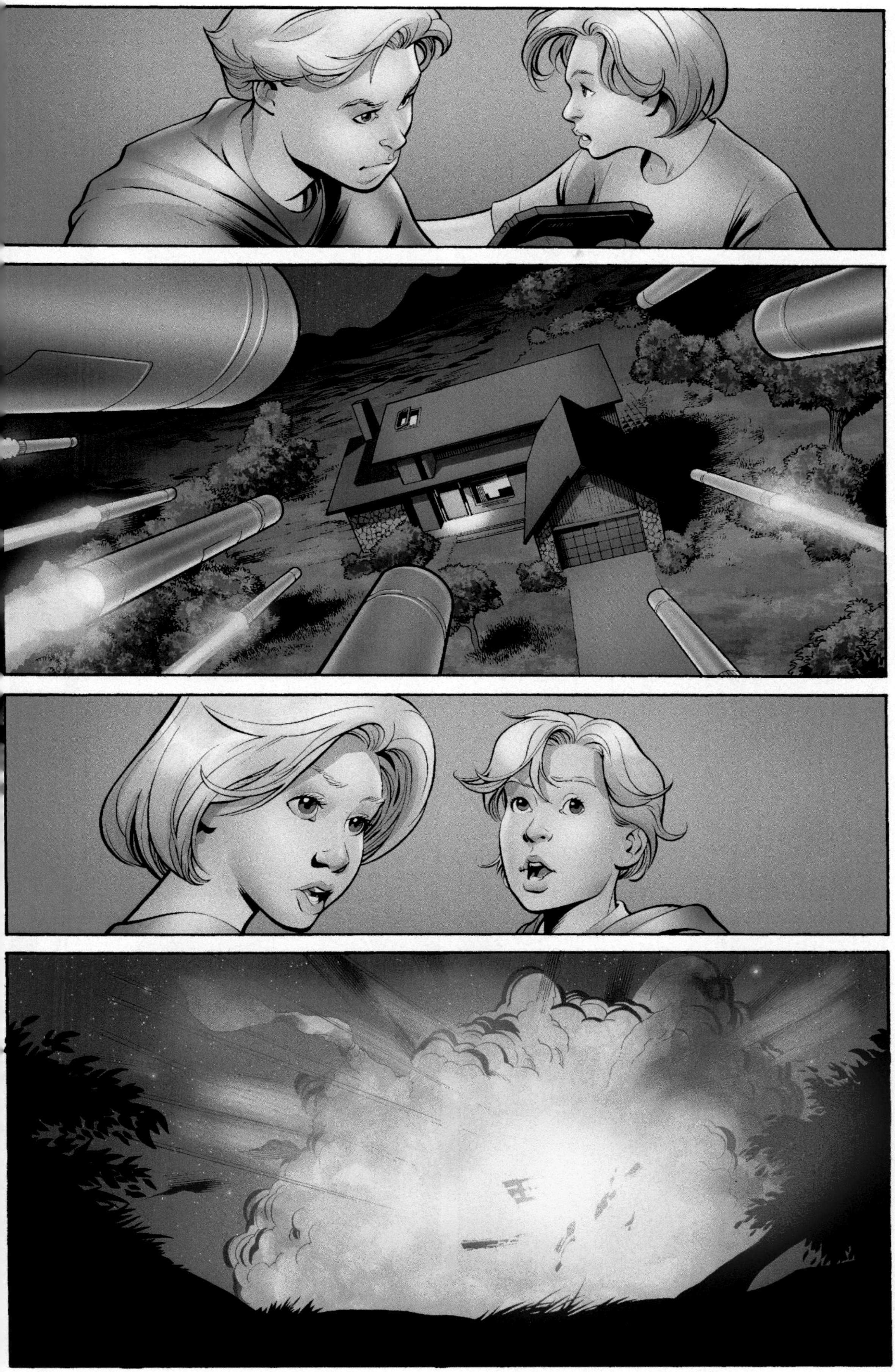

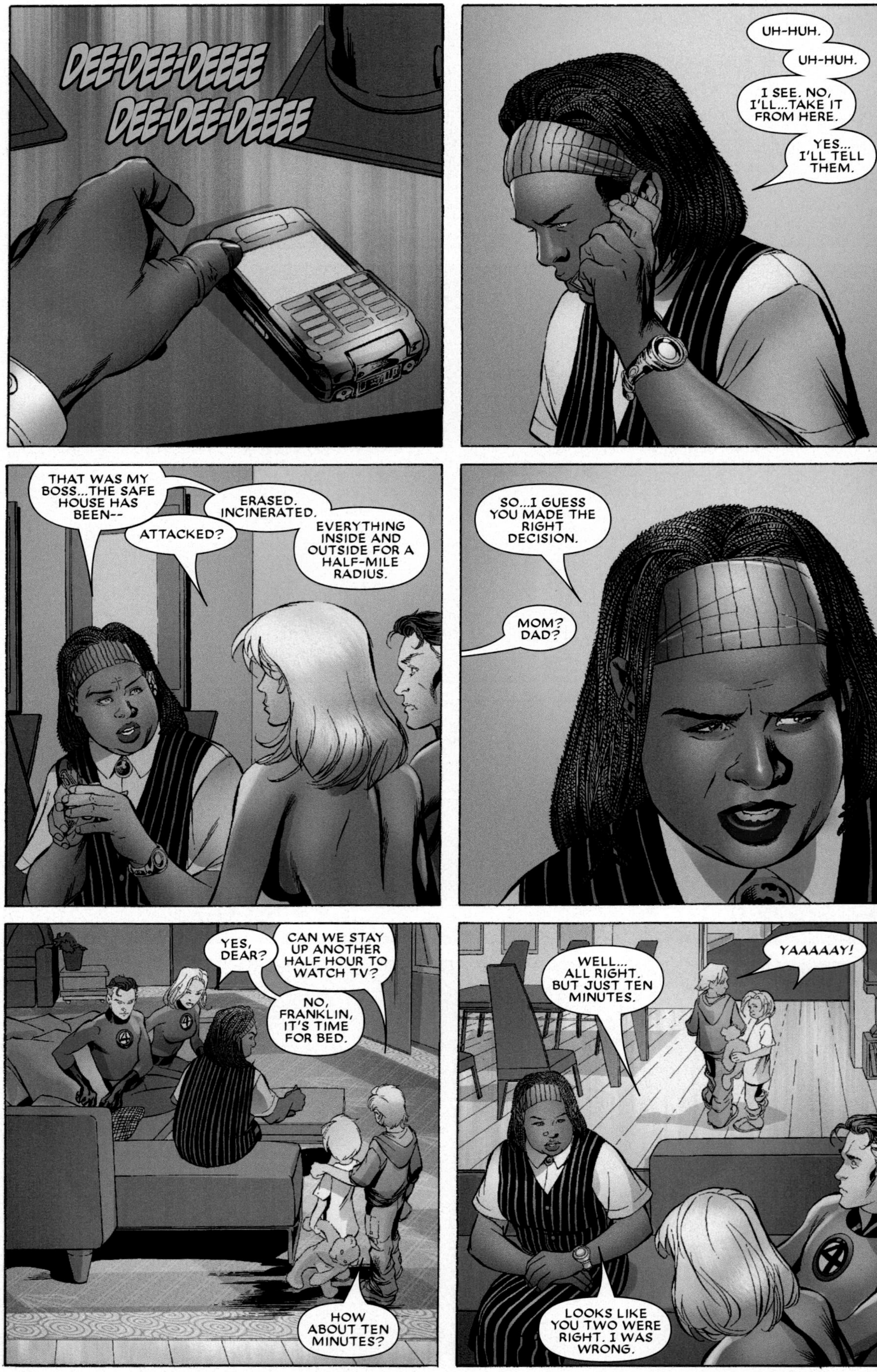
DEE-DEE-DEEEE
DEE-DEE-DEEEE
UH-HUH.
UH-HUH.
I SEE. NO, I'LL...TAKE IT FROM HERE.
YES... I'LL TELL THEM.
THAT WAS MY BOSS...THE SAFE HOUSE HAS BEEN--
ATTACKED?
ERASED. INCINERATED.
EVERYTHING INSIDE AND OUTSIDE FOR A HALF-MILE RADIUS.
SO...I GUESS YOU MADE THE RIGHT DECISION.
MOM? DAD?
YES, DEAR?
CAN WE STAY UP ANOTHER HALF HOUR TO WATCH TV?
NO, FRANKLIN, IT'S TIME FOR BED.
HOW ABOUT TEN MINUTES?
WELL... ALL RIGHT. BUT JUST TEN MINUTES.
YAAAAAY!
LOOKS LIKE YOU TWO WERE RIGHT. I WAS WRONG.

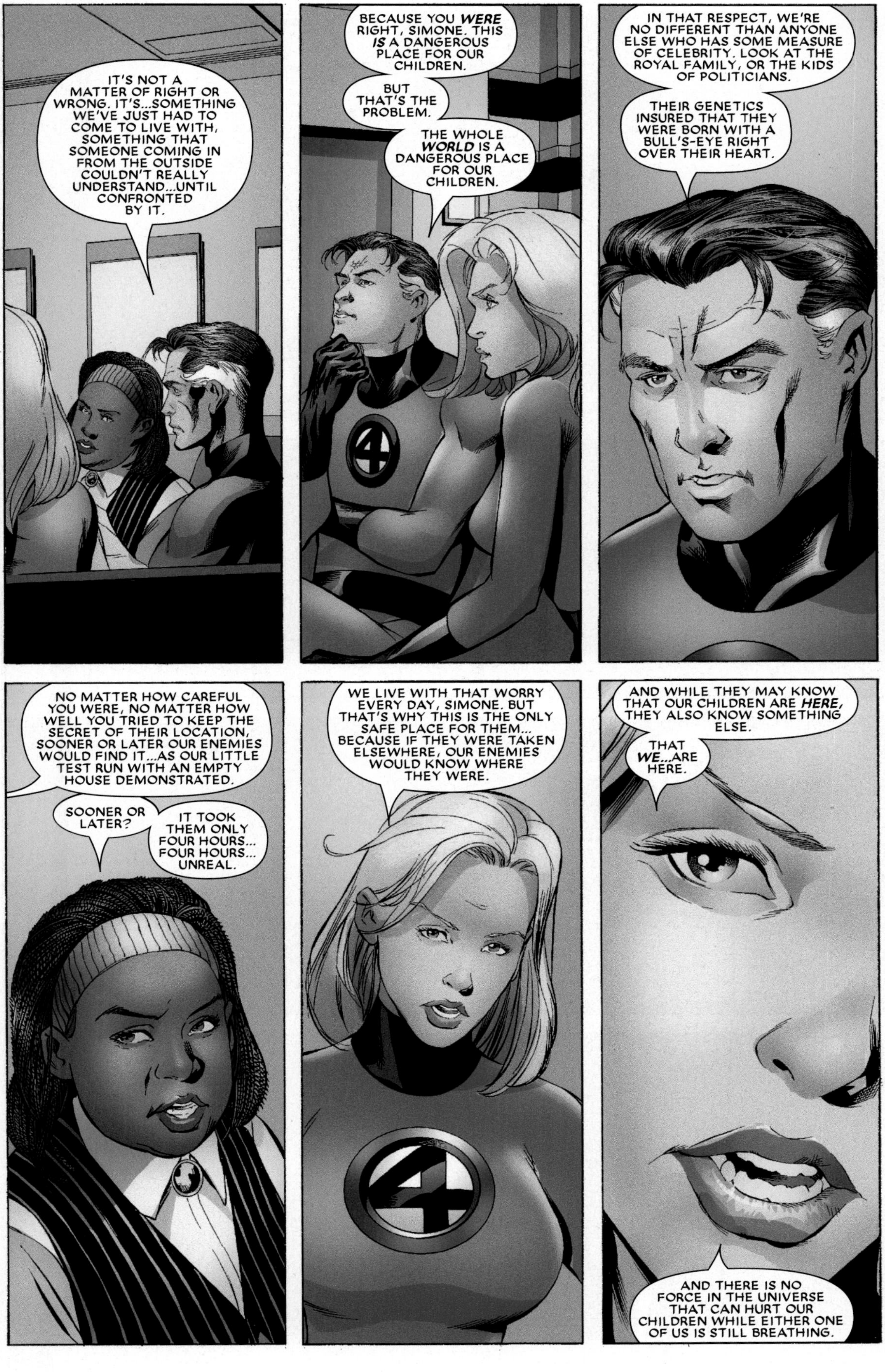
IT'S NOT A MATTER OF RIGHT OR WRONG. IT'S...SOMETHING WE'VE JUST HAD TO COME TO LIVE WITH, SOMETHING THAT SOMEONE COMING IN FROM THE OUTSIDE COULDN'T REALLY UNDERSTAND...UNTIL CONFRONTED BY IT.
BECAUSE YOU WERE RIGHT, SIMONE. THIS IS A DANGEROUS PLACE FOR OUR CHILDREN.
BUT THAT'S THE PROBLEM.
THE WHOLE WORLD IS A DANGEROUS PLACE FOR OUR CHILDREN.
IN THAT RESPECT, WE'RE NO DIFFERENT THAN ANYONE ELSE WHO HAS SOME MEASURE OF CELEBRITY. LOOK AT THE ROYAL FAMILY, OR THE KIDS OF POLITICIANS.
THEIR GENETICS INSURED THAT THEY WERE BORN WITH A BULL'S-EYE RIGHT OVER THEIR HEART.
NO MATTER HOW CAREFUL YOU WERE, NO MATTER HOW WELL YOU TRIED TO KEEP THE SECRET OF THEIR LOCATION, SOONER OR LATER OUR ENEMIES WOULD FIND IT...AS OUR LITTLE TEST RUN WITH AN EMPTY HOUSE DEMONSTRATED.
SOONER OR LATER?
IT TOOK THEM ONLY FOUR HOURS... FOUR HOURS... UNREAL.
WE LIVE WITH THAT WORRY EVERY DAY, SIMONE. BUT THAT'S WHY THIS IS THE ONLY SAFE PLACE FOR THEM... BECAUSE IF THEY WERE TAKEN ELSEWHERE, OUR ENEMIES WOULD KNOW WHERE THEY WERE.
AND WHILE THEY MAY KNOW THAT OUR CHILDREN ARE HERE, THEY ALSO KNOW SOMETHING ELSE.
THAT WE...ARE HERE.
AND THERE IS NO FORCE IN THE UNIVERSE THAT CAN HURT OUR CHILDREN WHILE EITHER ONE OF US IS STILL BREATHING.

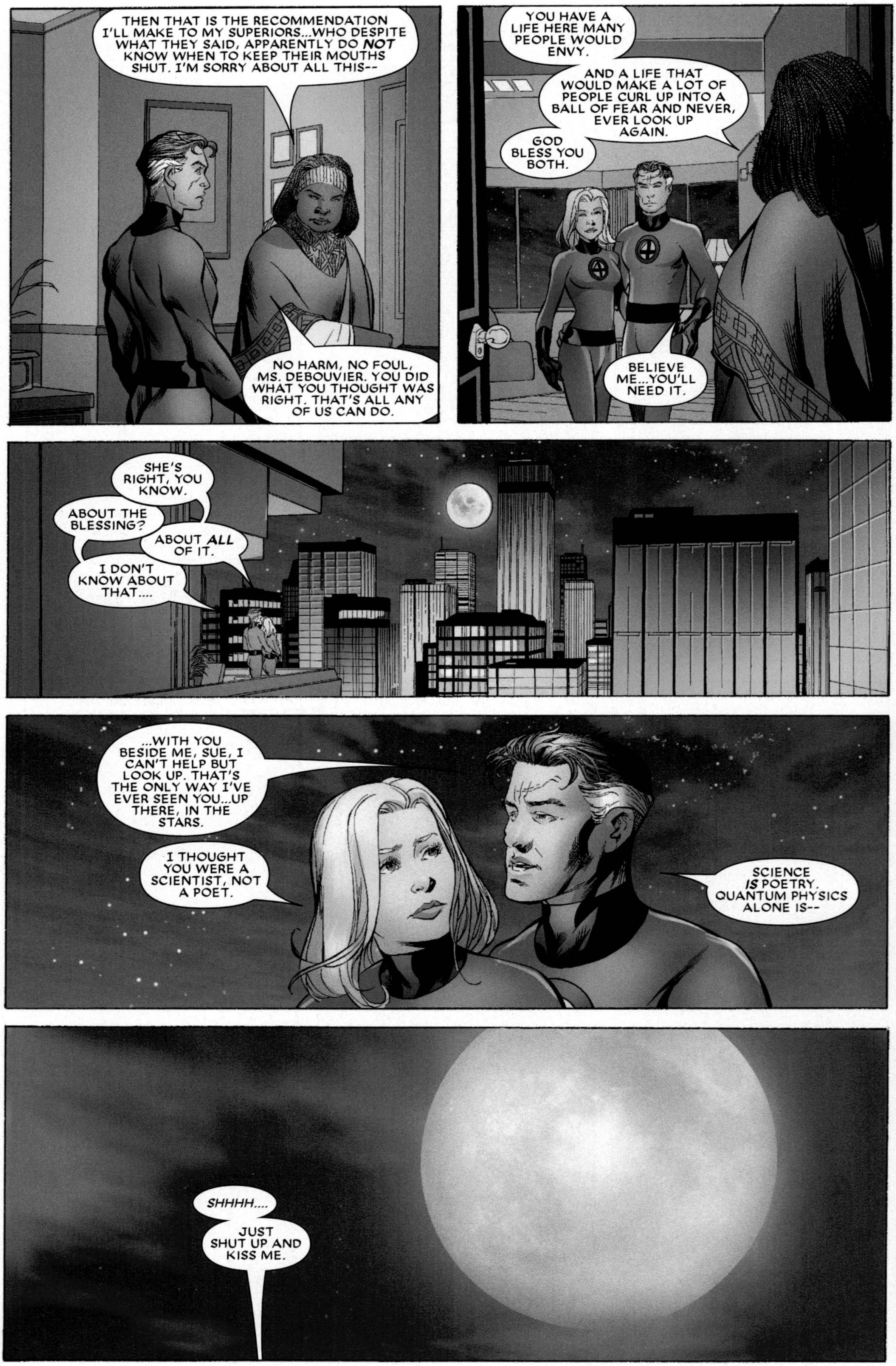
THEN THAT IS THE RECOMMENDATION I'LL MAKE TO MY SUPERIORS...WHO DESPITE WHAT THEY SAID, APPARENTLY DO NOT KNOW WHEN TO KEEP THEIR MOUTHS SHUT. I'M SORRY ABOUT ALL THIS--
NO HARM, NO FOUL, MS. DEBOUVIER. YOU DID WHAT YOU THOUGHT WAS RIGHT. THAT'S ALL ANY OF US CAN DO.
YOU HAVE A LIFE HERE MANY PEOPLE WOULD ENVY.
AND A LIFE THAT WOULD MAKE A LOT OF PEOPLE CURL UP INTO A BALL OF FEAR AND NEVER, EVER LOOK UP AGAIN.
GOD BLESS YOU BOTH.
BELIEVE ME...YOU'LL NEED IT.
SHE'S RIGHT, YOU KNOW.
ABOUT THE BLESSING?
ABOUT ALL OF IT.
I DON'T KNOW ABOUT THAT....
...WITH YOU BESIDE ME, SUE, I CAN'T HELP BUT LOOK UP. THAT'S THE ONLY WAY I'VE EVER SEEN YOU...UP THERE, IN THE STARS.
I THOUGHT YOU WERE A SCIENTIST, NOT A POET.
SCIENCE IS POETRY. QUANTUM PHYSICS ALONE IS--
SHHHH....
JUST SHUT UP AND KISS ME.

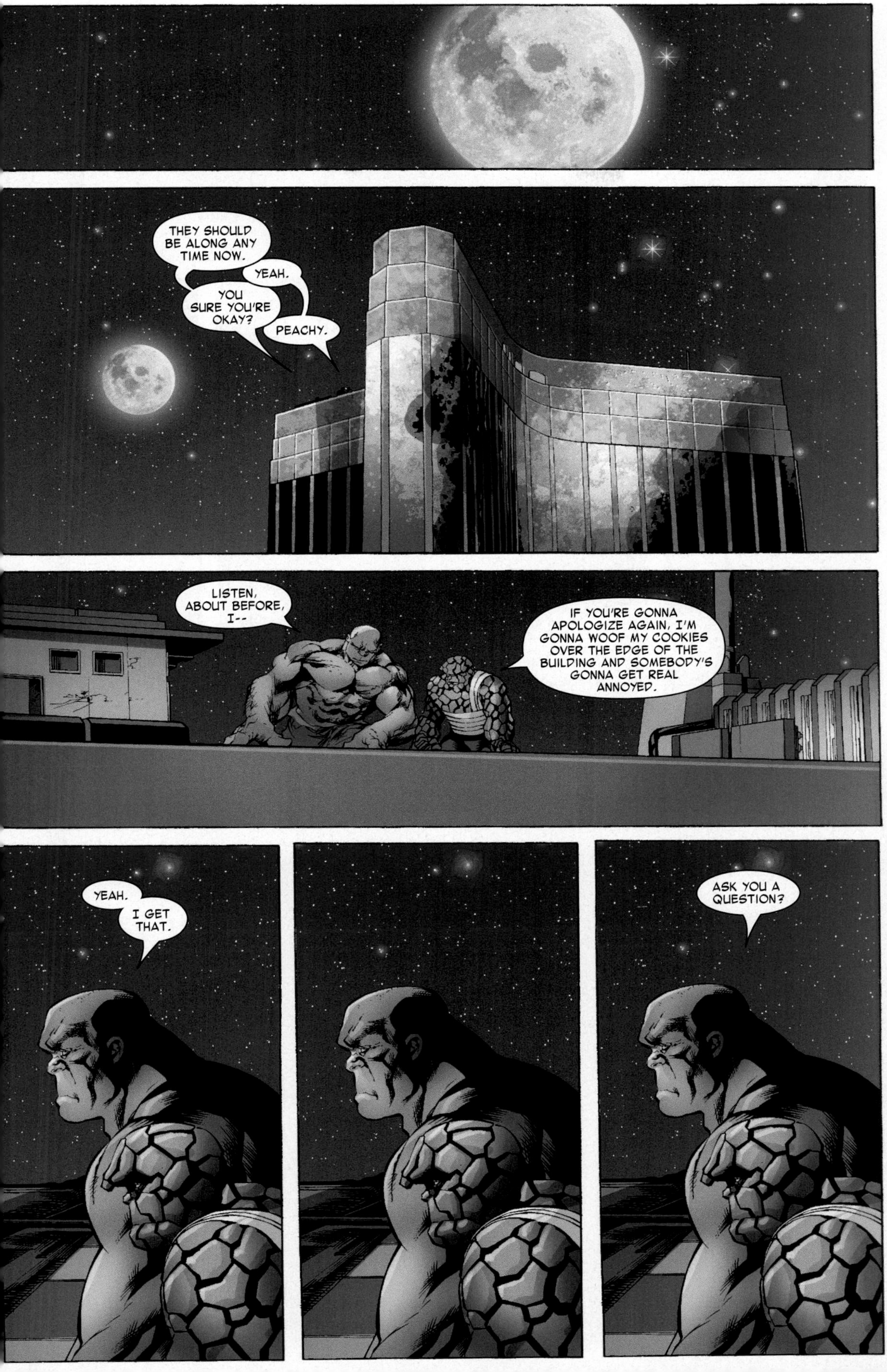
THEY SHOULD BE ALONG ANY TIME NOW.
YEAH.
YOU SURE YOU'RE OKAY?
PEACHY.
LISTEN, ABOUT BEFORE, I--
IF YOU'RE GONNA APOLOGIZE AGAIN, I'M GONNA WOOF MY COOKIES OVER THE EDGE OF THE BUILDING AND SOMEBODY'S GONNA GET REAL ANNOYED.
YEAH.
I GET THAT.
ASK YOU A QUESTION?

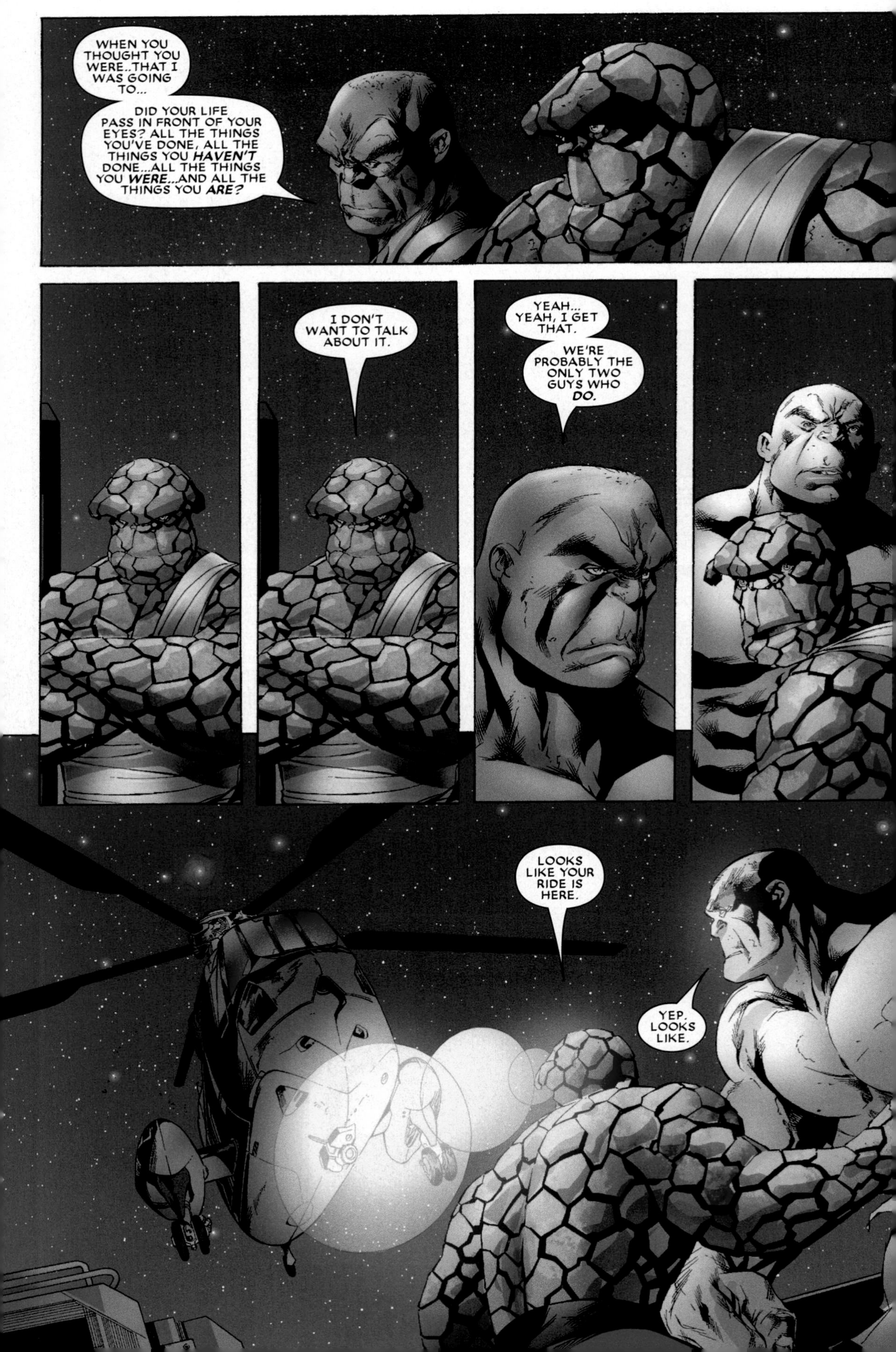
WHEN YOU THOUGHT YOU WERE..THAT I WAS GOING TO...
DID YOUR LIFE PASS IN FRONT OF YOUR EYES? ALL THE THINGS YOU'VE DONE, ALL THE THINGS YOU HAVEN'T DONE...ALL THE THINGS YOU WERE...AND ALL THE THINGS YOU ARE?
I DON'T WANT TO TALK ABOUT IT.
YEAH... YEAH, I GET THAT.
WE'RE PROBABLY THE ONLY TWO GUYS WHO DO.
LOOKS LIKE YOUR RIDE IS HERE.
YEP. LOOKS LIKE.

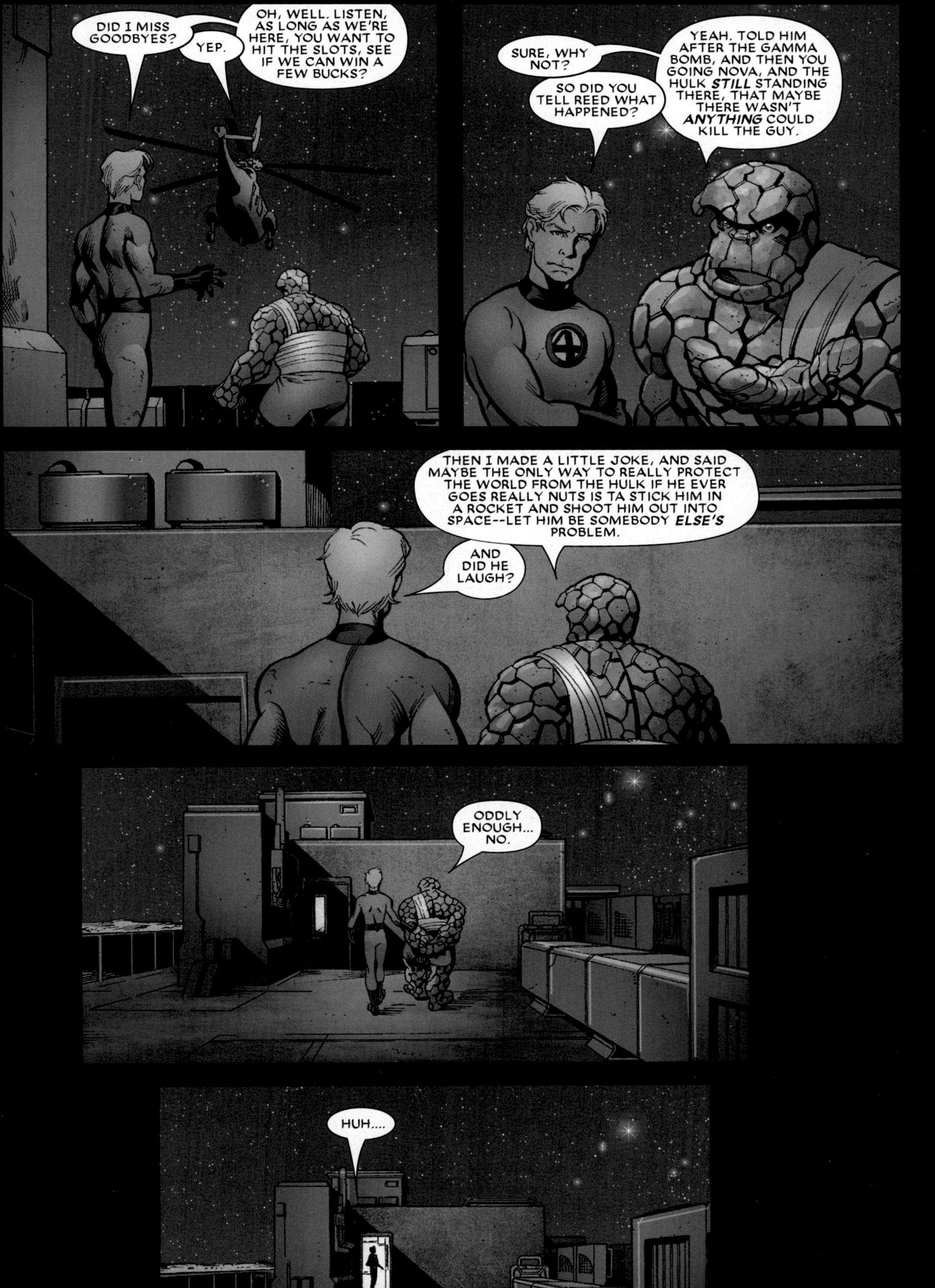

DID I MISS GOODBYES?
YEP.
OH, WELL. LISTEN, AS LONG AS WE'RE HERE, YOU WANT TO HIT THE SLOTS, SEE IF WE CAN WIN A FEW BUCKS?
SURE, WHY NOT?
SO DID YOU TELL REED WHAT HAPPENED?
YEAH. TOLD HIM AFTER THE GAMMA BOMB, AND THEN YOU GOING NOVA, AND THE HULK STILL STANDING THERE, THAT MAYBE THERE WASN'T ANYTHING COULD KILL THE GUY.
THEN I MADE A LITTLE JOKE, AND SAID MAYBE THE ONLY WAY TO REALLY PROTECT THE WORLD FROM THE HULK IF HE EVER GOES REALLY NUTS IS TA STICK HIM IN A ROCKET AND SHOOT HIM OUT INTO SPACE--LET HIM BE SOMEBODY ELSE'S PROBLEM.
AND DID HE LAUGH?
ODDLY ENOUGH... NO.
HUH....

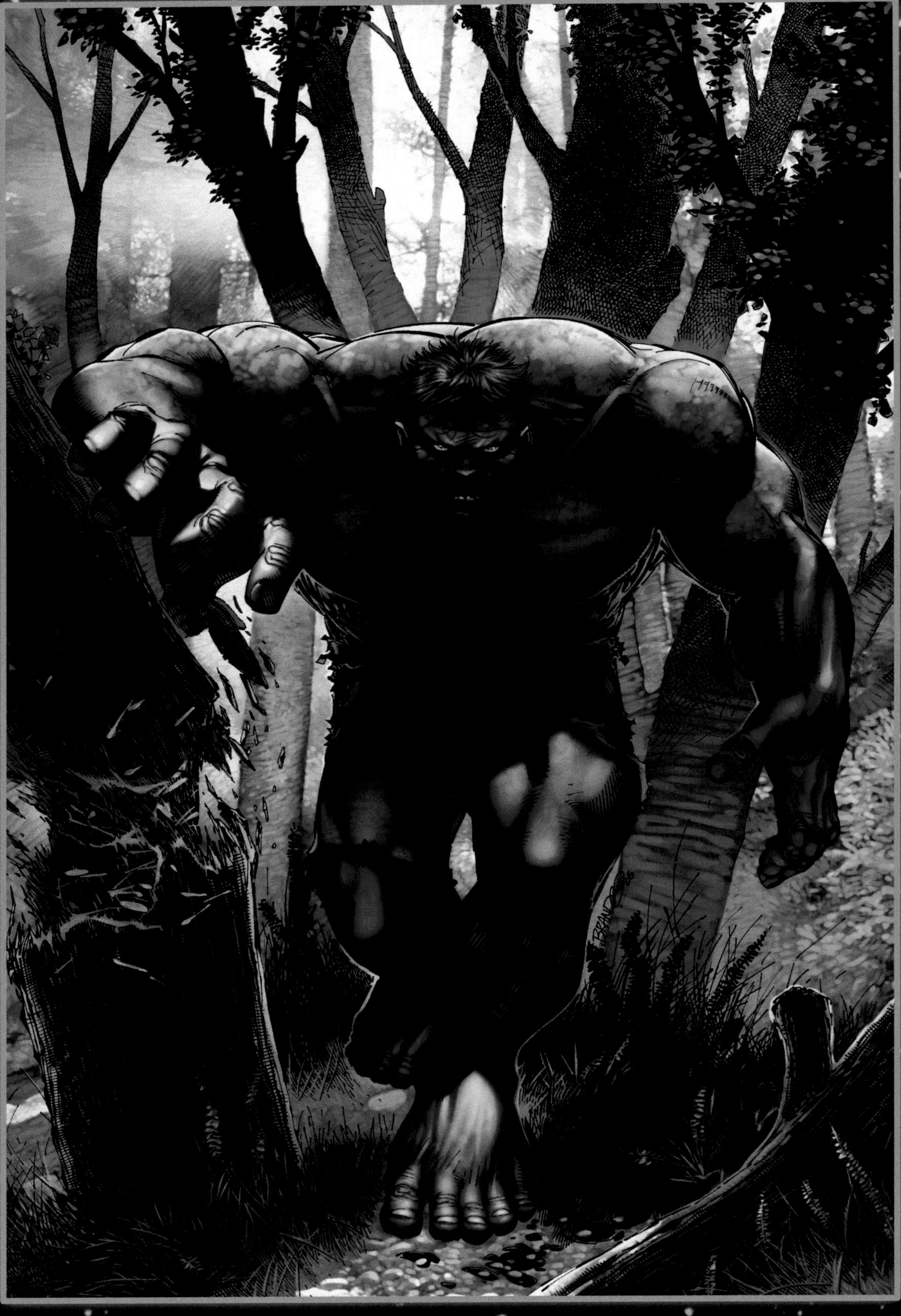

INCREDIBLE HULK #88

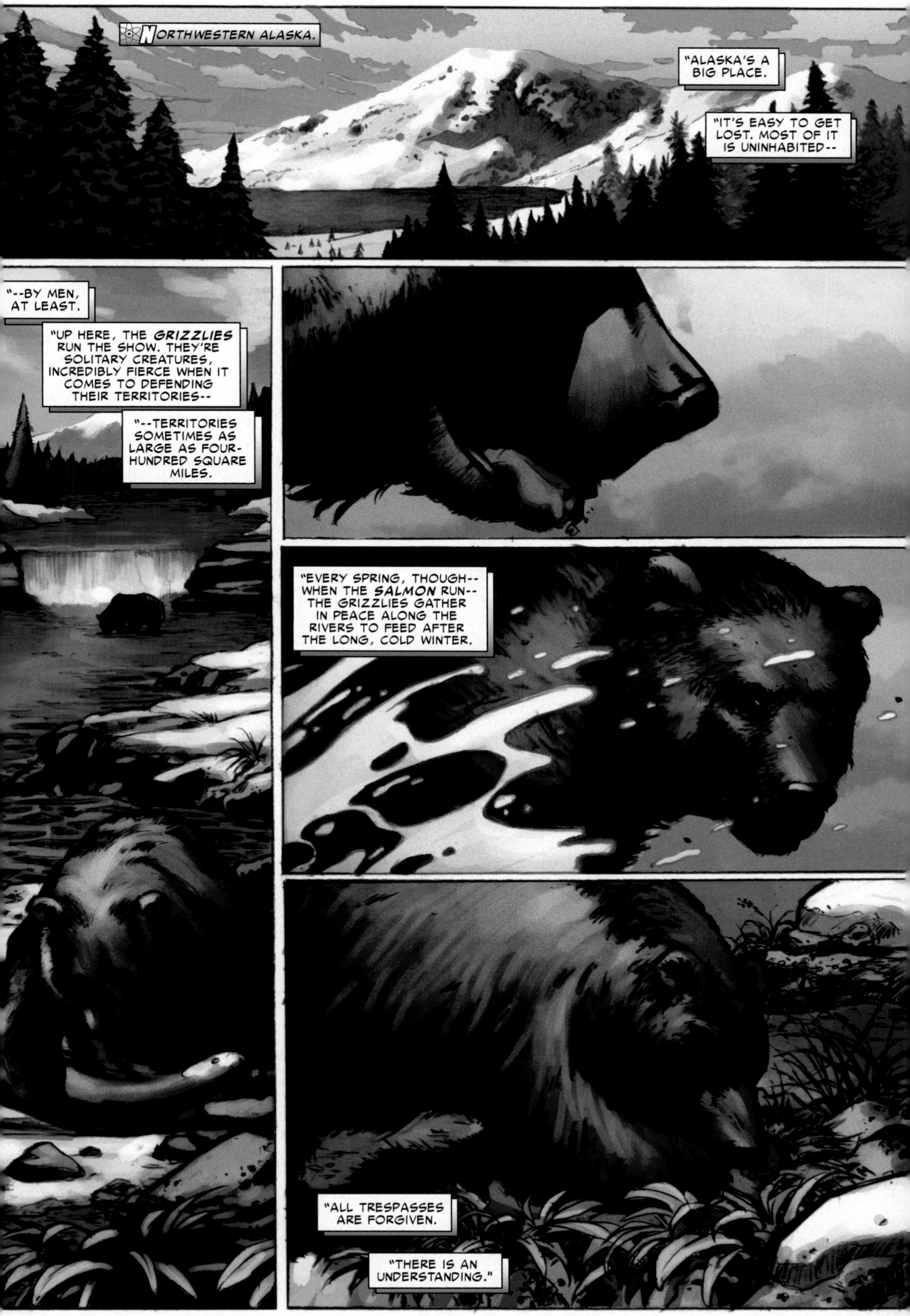
NORTHWESTERN ALASKA.
"ALASKA'S A BIG PLACE.
"IT'S EASY TO GET LOST. MOST OF IT IS UNINHABITED--
"--BY MEN, AT LEAST.
"UP HERE, THE GRIZZLIES RUN THE SHOW. THEY'RE SOLITARY CREATURES, INCREDIBLY FIERCE WHEN IT COMES TO DEFENDING THEIR TERRITORIES--
"--TERRITORIES SOMETIMES AS LARGE AS FOUR-HUNDRED SQUARE MILES.
"EVERY SPRING, THOUGH--WHEN THE SALMON RUN--THE GRIZZLIES GATHER IN PEACE ALONG THE RIVERS TO FEED AFTER THE LONG, COLD WINTER.
"ALL TRESPASSES ARE FORGIVEN.
"THERE IS AN UNDERSTANDING."

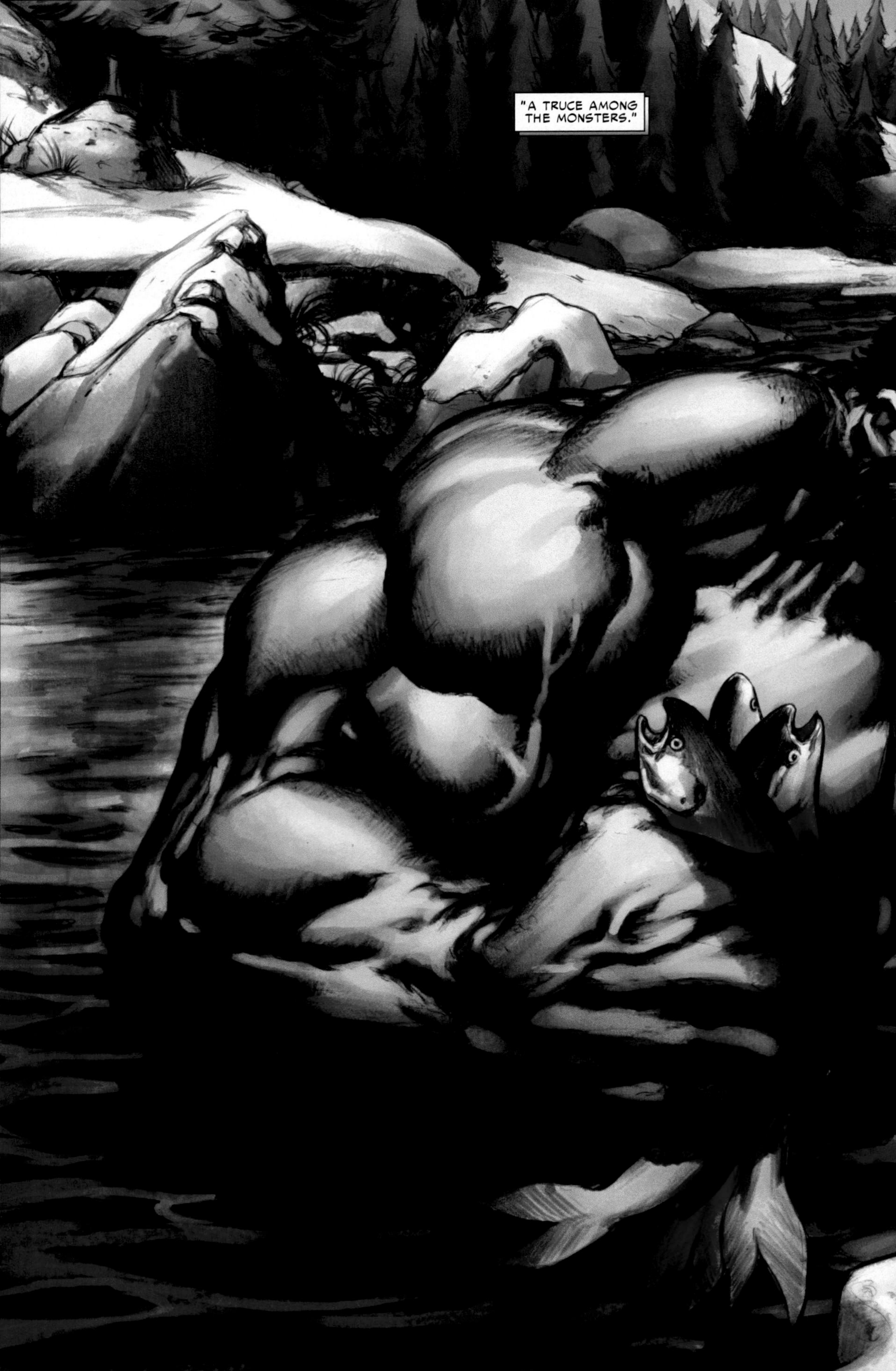
"A TRUCE AMONG THE MONSTERS."

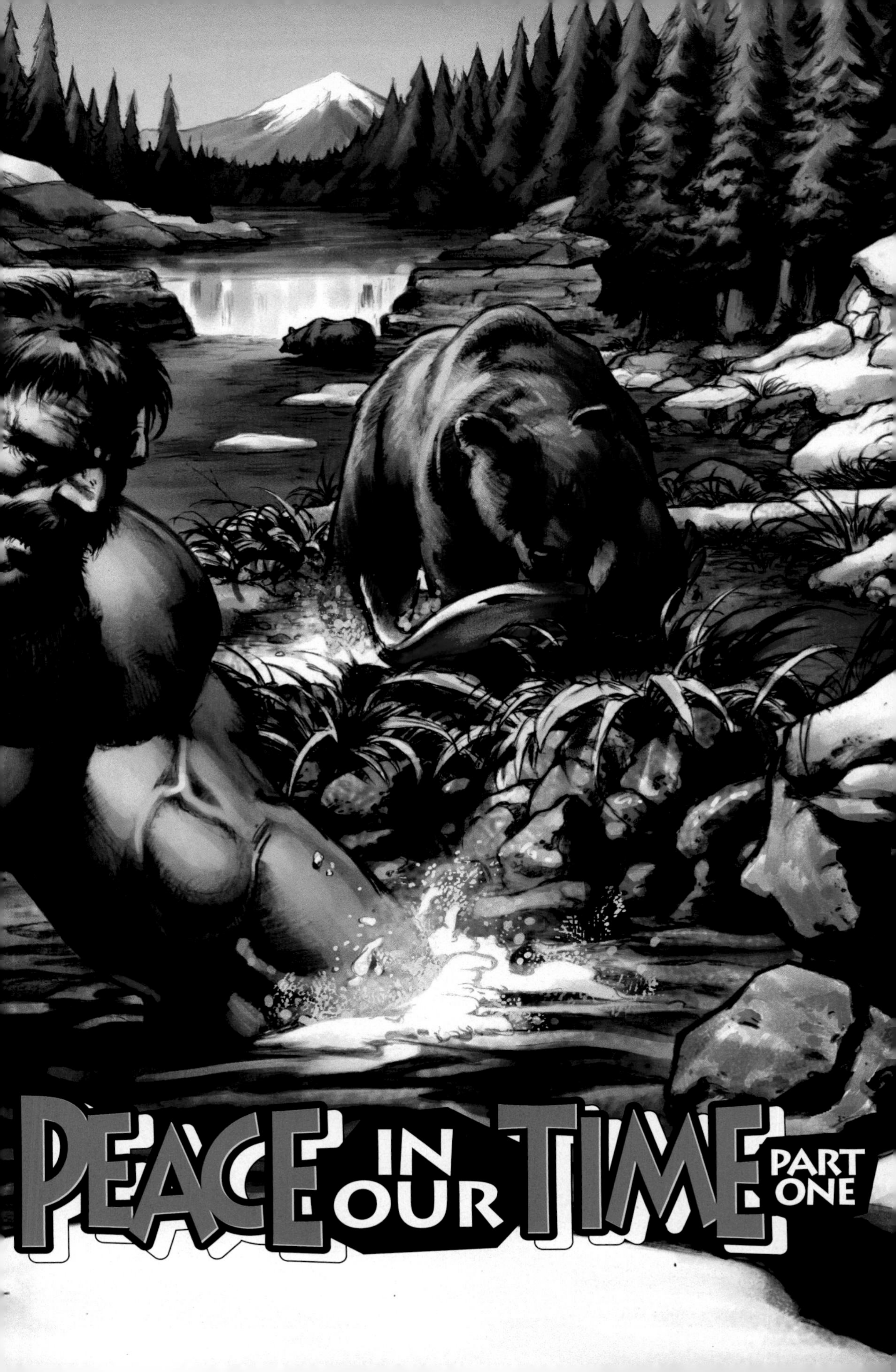
PEACE IN OUR TIME PART ONE

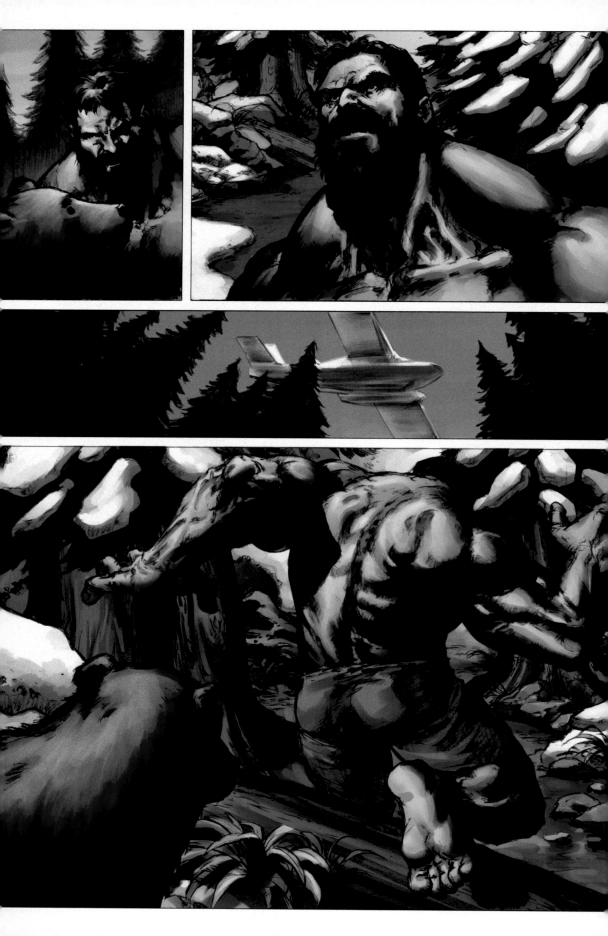

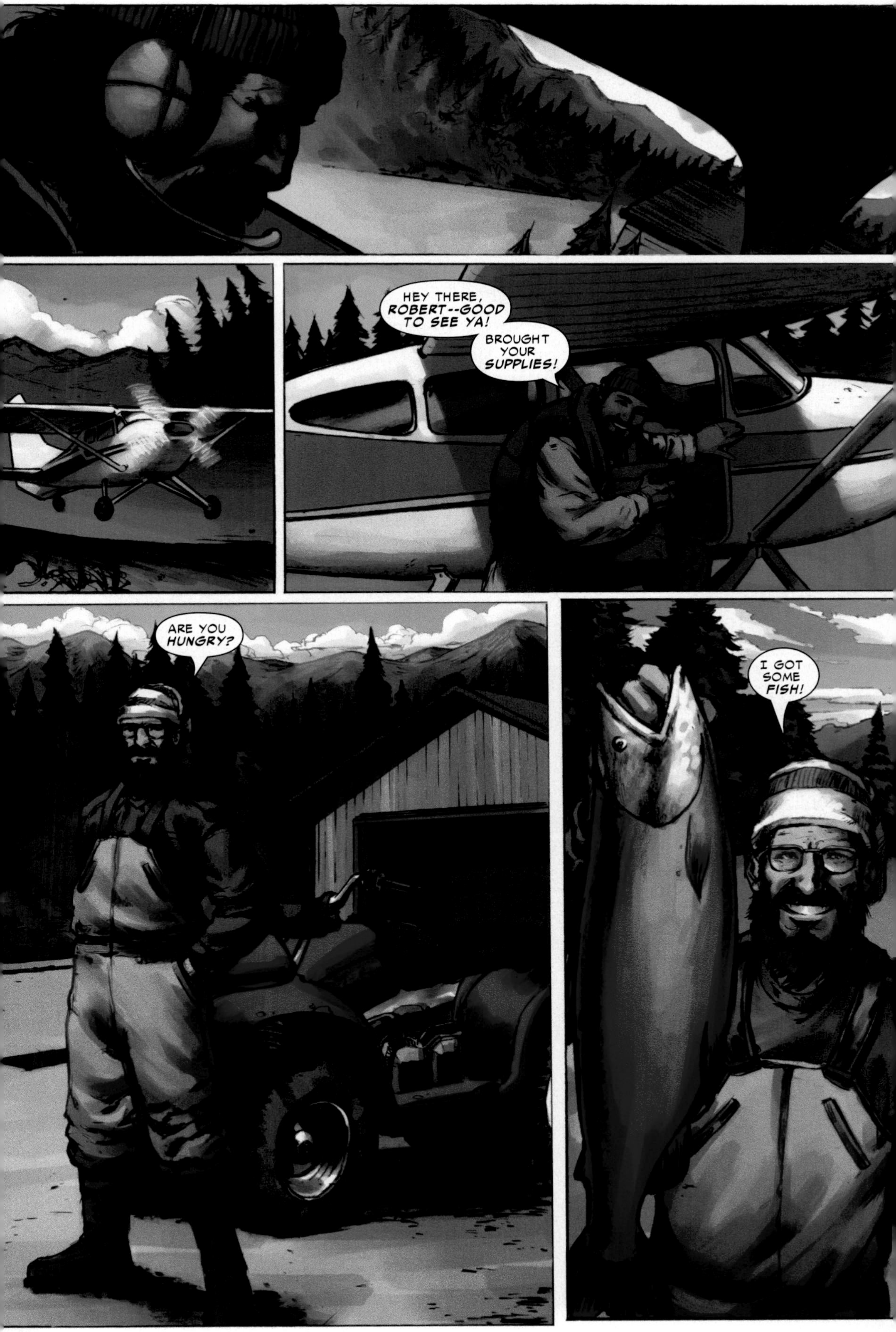
HEY THERE, ROBERT--GOOD TO SEE YA!
BROUGHT YOUR SUPPLIES!
ARE YOU HUNGRY?
I GOT SOME FISH!

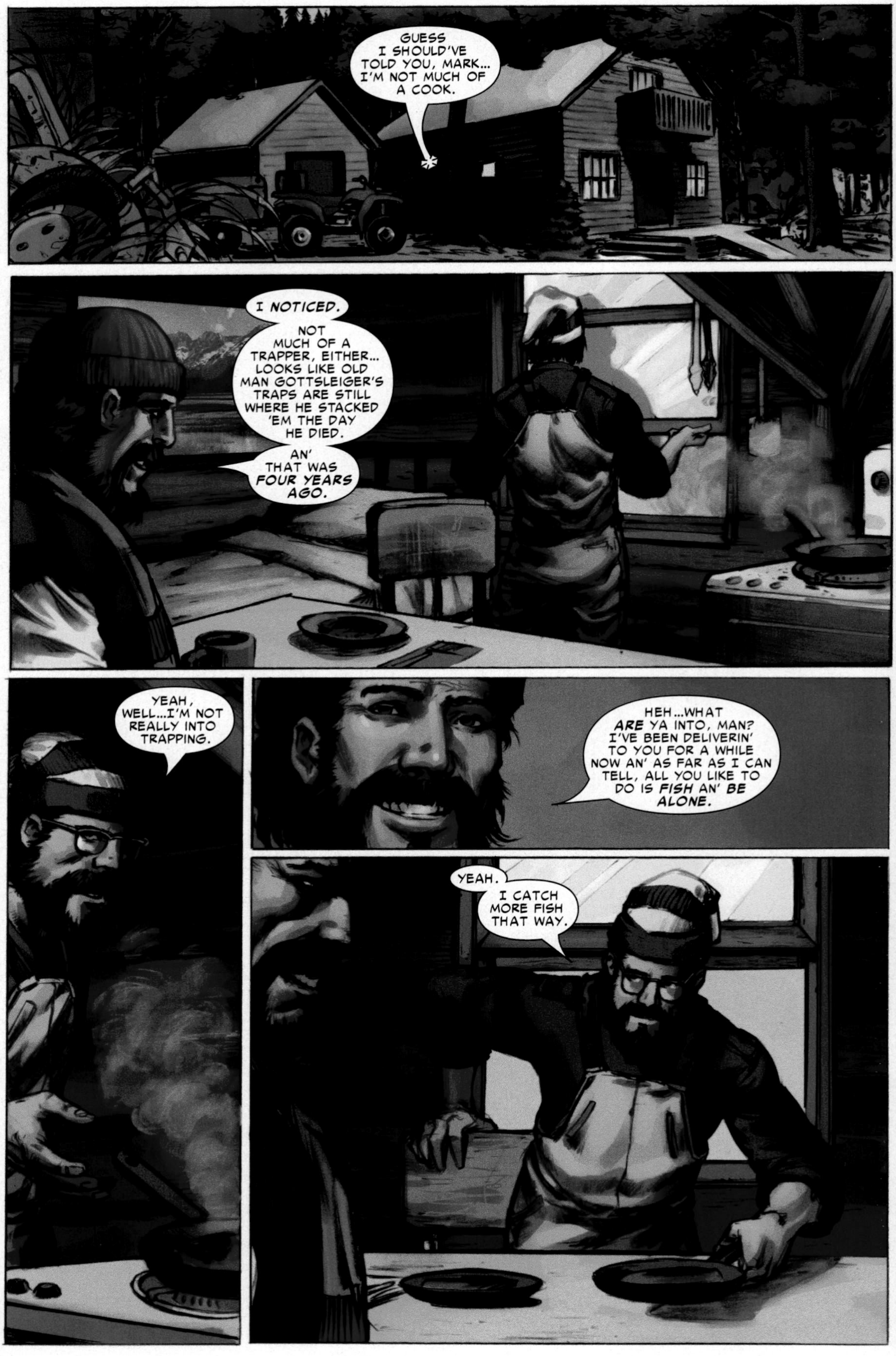
GUESS I SHOULD'VE TOLD YOU, MARK... I'M NOT MUCH OF A COOK.
I NOTICED.
NOT MUCH OF A TRAPPER, EITHER... LOOKS LIKE OLD MAN GOTTSLEIGER'S TRAPS ARE STILL WHERE HE STACKED 'EM THE DAY HE DIED.
AN' THAT WAS FOUR YEARS AGO.
YEAH, WELL...I'M NOT REALLY INTO TRAPPING.
HEH...WHAT ARE YA INTO, MAN? I'VE BEEN DELIVERIN' TO YOU FOR A WHILE NOW AN' AS FAR AS I CAN TELL, ALL YOU LIKE TO DO IS FISH AN' BE ALONE.
YEAH.
I CATCH MORE FISH THAT WAY.

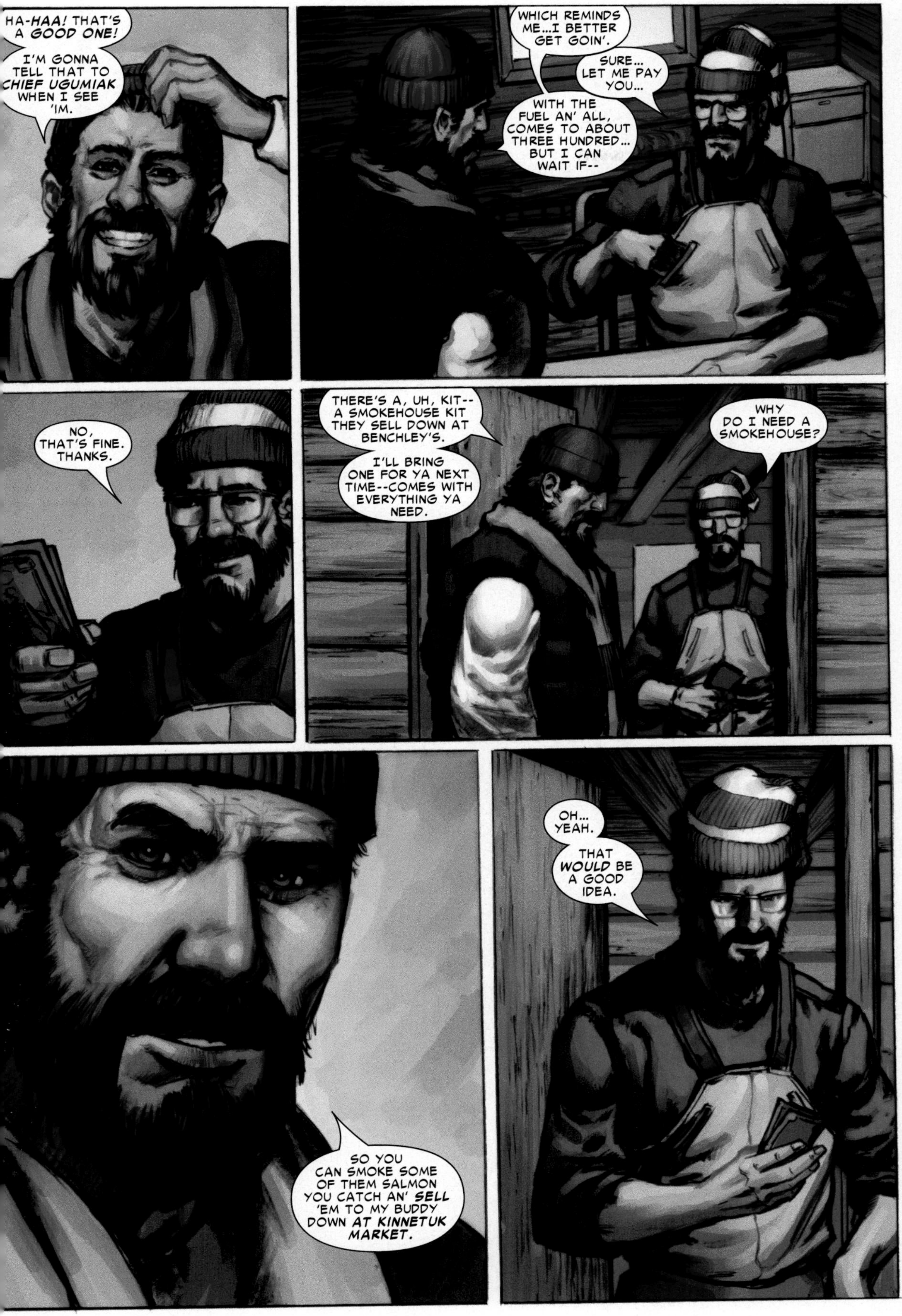
HA-HAA! THAT'S A GOOD ONE!
I'M GONNA TELL THAT TO CHIEF UGUMIAK WHEN I SEE 'IM.
WHICH REMINDS ME...I BETTER GET GOIN'.
SURE... LET ME PAY YOU...
WITH THE FUEL AN' ALL, COMES TO ABOUT THREE HUNDRED... BUT I CAN WAIT IF--
NO, THAT'S FINE. THANKS.
THERE'S A, UH, KIT-- A SMOKEHOUSE KIT THEY SELL DOWN AT BENCHLEY'S.
I'LL BRING ONE FOR YA NEXT TIME--COMES WITH EVERYTHING YA NEED.
WHY DO I NEED A SMOKEHOUSE?
SO YOU CAN SMOKE SOME OF THEM SALMON YOU CATCH AN' SELL 'EM TO MY BUDDY DOWN AT KINNETUK MARKET.
OH... YEAH.
THAT WOULD BE A GOOD IDEA.

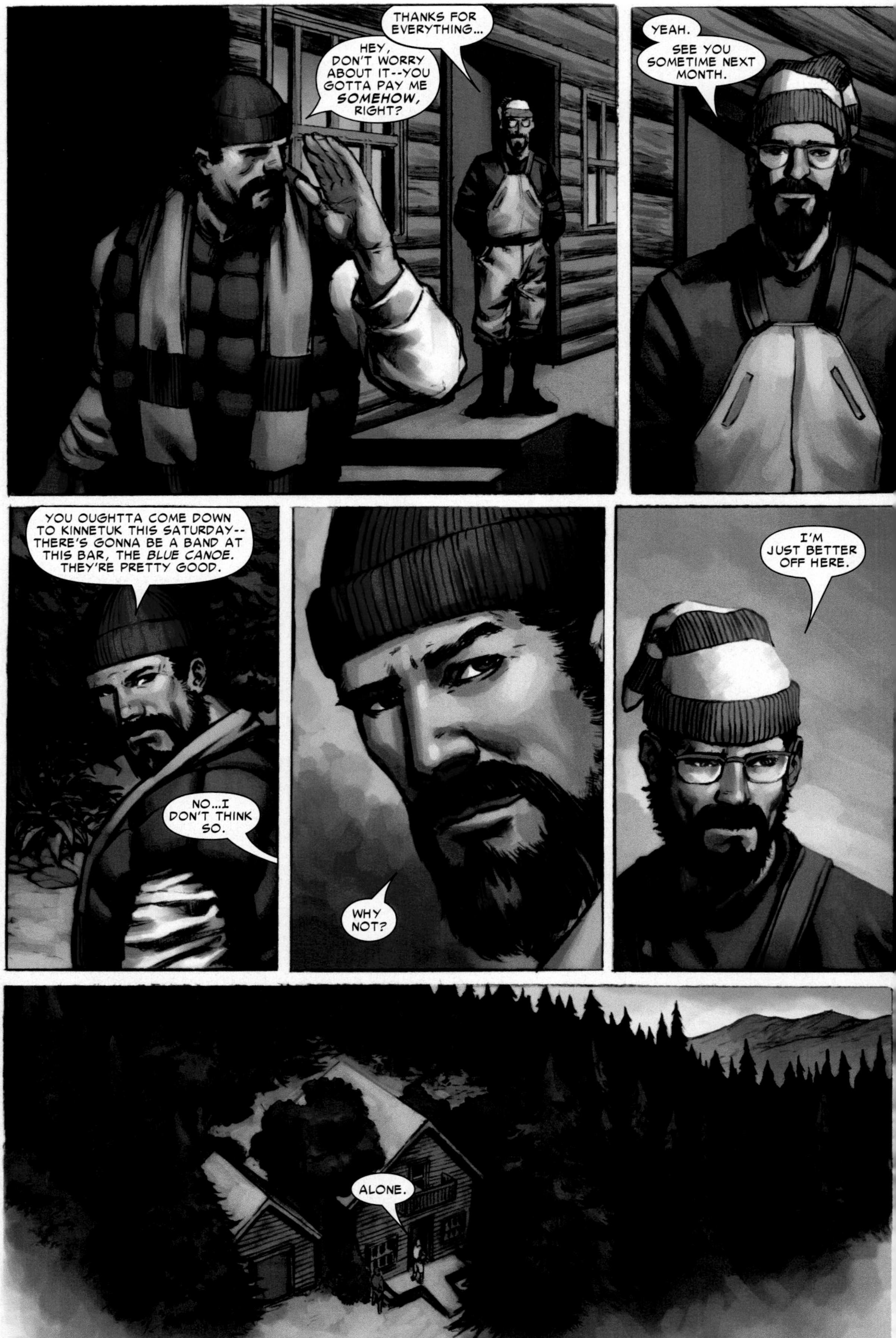
THANKS FOR EVERYTHING...
HEY, DON'T WORRY ABOUT IT--YOU GOTTA PAY ME *SOMEHOW*, RIGHT?
YEAH.
SEE YOU SOMETIME NEXT MONTH.
YOU OUGHTTA COME DOWN TO KINNETUK THIS SATURDAY-- THERE'S GONNA BE A BAND AT THIS BAR, THE *BLUE CANOE*. THEY'RE PRETTY GOOD.
NO...I DON'T THINK SO.
WHY NOT?
I'M JUST BETTER OFF HERE.
ALONE.

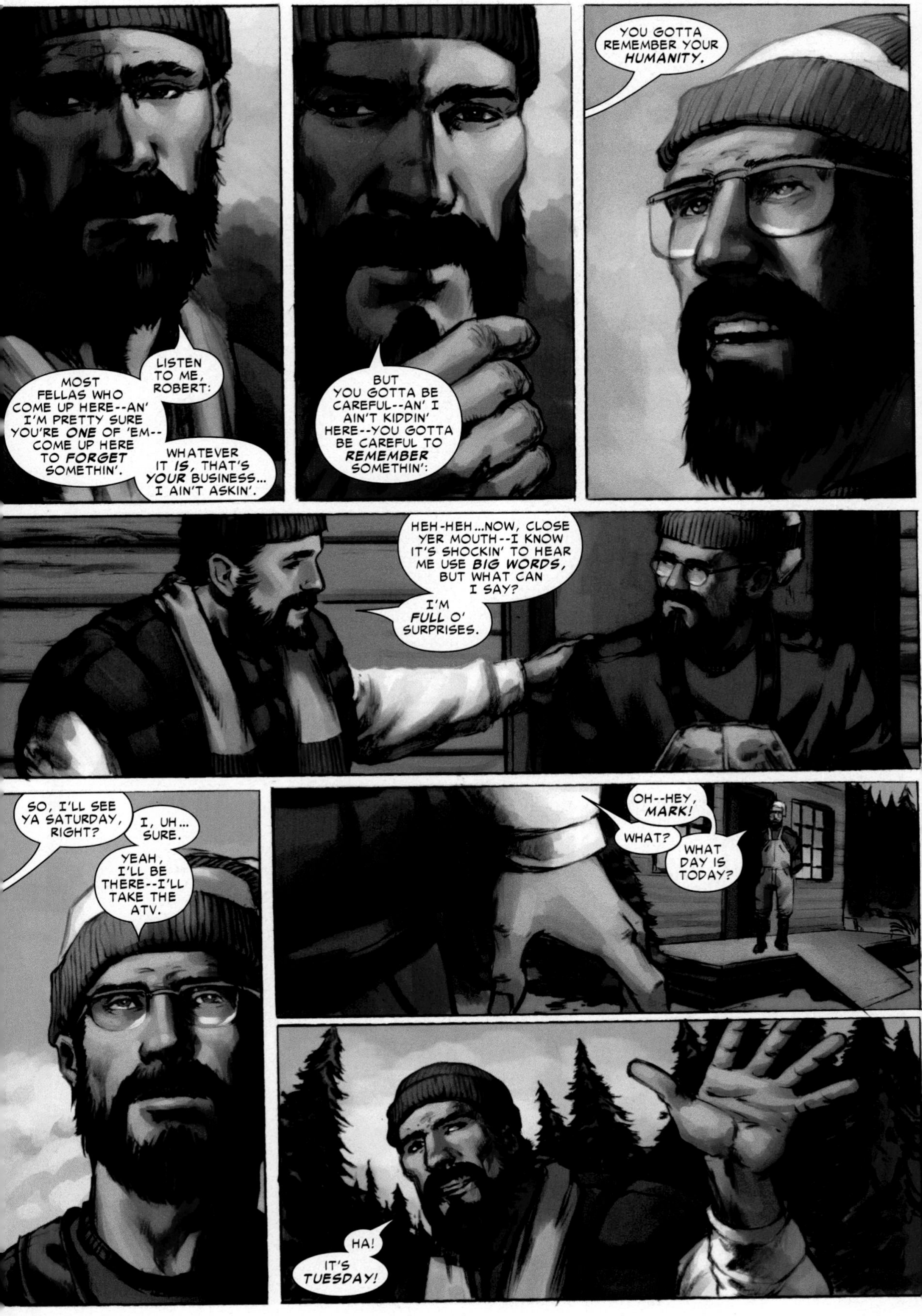
LISTEN TO ME, ROBERT:
MOST FELLAS WHO COME UP HERE--AN' I'M PRETTY SURE YOU'RE ONE OF 'EM--COME UP HERE TO FORGET SOMETHIN'.
WHATEVER IT IS, THAT'S YOUR BUSINESS... I AIN'T ASKIN'.
BUT YOU GOTTA BE CAREFUL--AN' I AIN'T KIDDIN' HERE--YOU GOTTA BE CAREFUL TO REMEMBER SOMETHIN':
YOU GOTTA REMEMBER YOUR HUMANITY.
HEH-HEH...NOW, CLOSE YER MOUTH--I KNOW IT'S SHOCKIN' TO HEAR ME USE BIG WORDS, BUT WHAT CAN I SAY?
I'M FULL O' SURPRISES.
SO, I'LL SEE YA SATURDAY, RIGHT?
I, UH... SURE.
YEAH, I'LL BE THERE--I'LL TAKE THE ATV.
OH--HEY, MARK!
WHAT?
WHAT DAY IS TODAY?
HA! IT'S TUESDAY!

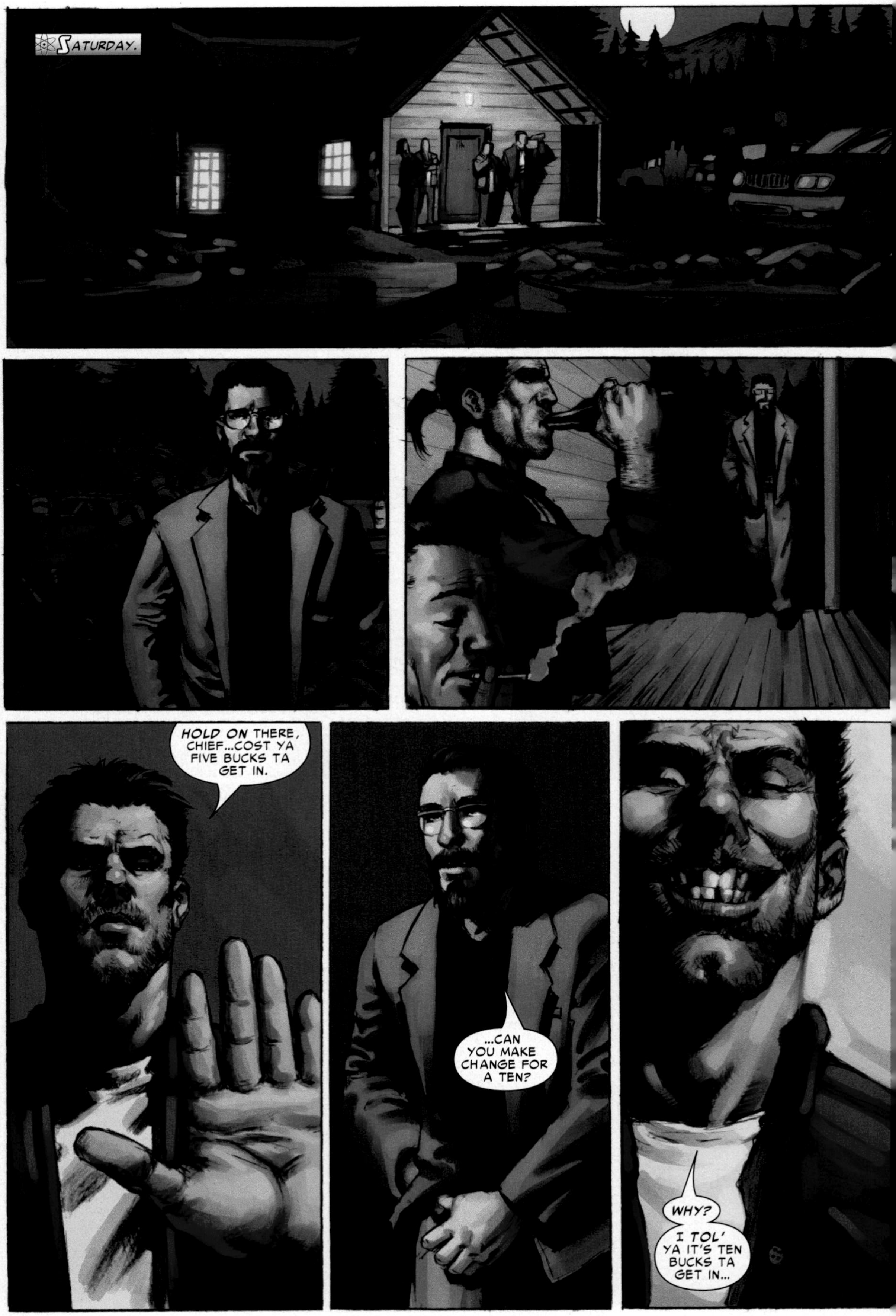
SATURDAY.
HOLD ON THERE, CHIEF...COST YA FIVE BUCKS TA GET IN.
...CAN YOU MAKE CHANGE FOR A TEN?
WHY?
I TOL' YA IT'S TEN BUCKS TA GET IN...

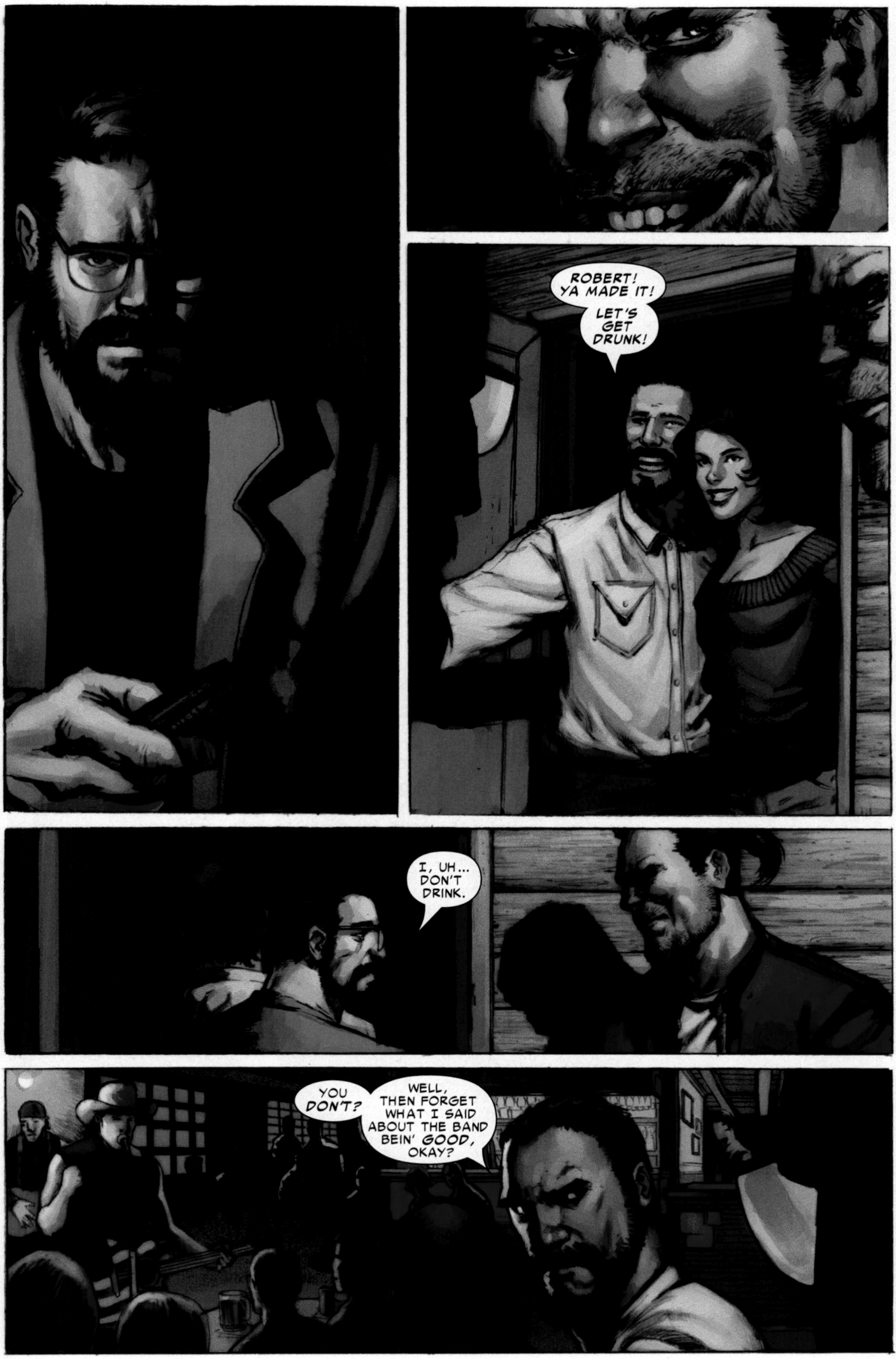
ROBERT! YA MADE IT!
LET'S GET DRUNK!
I, UH... DON'T DRINK.
YOU DON'T?
WELL, THEN FORGET WHAT I SAID ABOUT THE BAND BEIN' GOOD, OKAY?

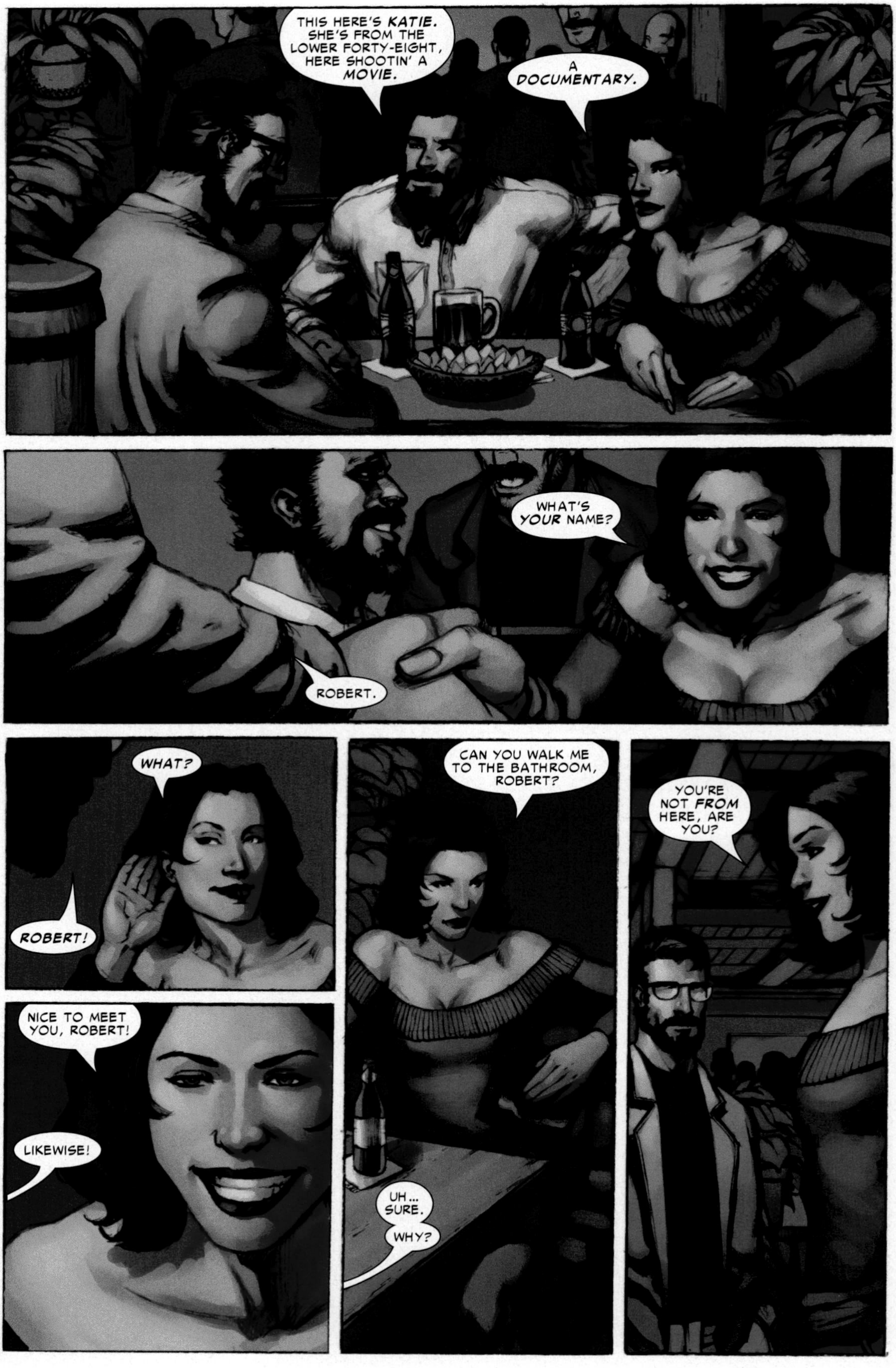
THIS HERE'S KATIE. SHE'S FROM THE LOWER FORTY-EIGHT, HERE SHOOTIN' A MOVIE.
A DOCUMENTARY.
WHAT'S YOUR NAME?
ROBERT.
WHAT?
ROBERT!
NICE TO MEET YOU, ROBERT!
LIKEWISE!
CAN YOU WALK ME TO THE BATHROOM, ROBERT?
UH... SURE.
WHY?
YOU'RE NOT FROM HERE, ARE YOU?

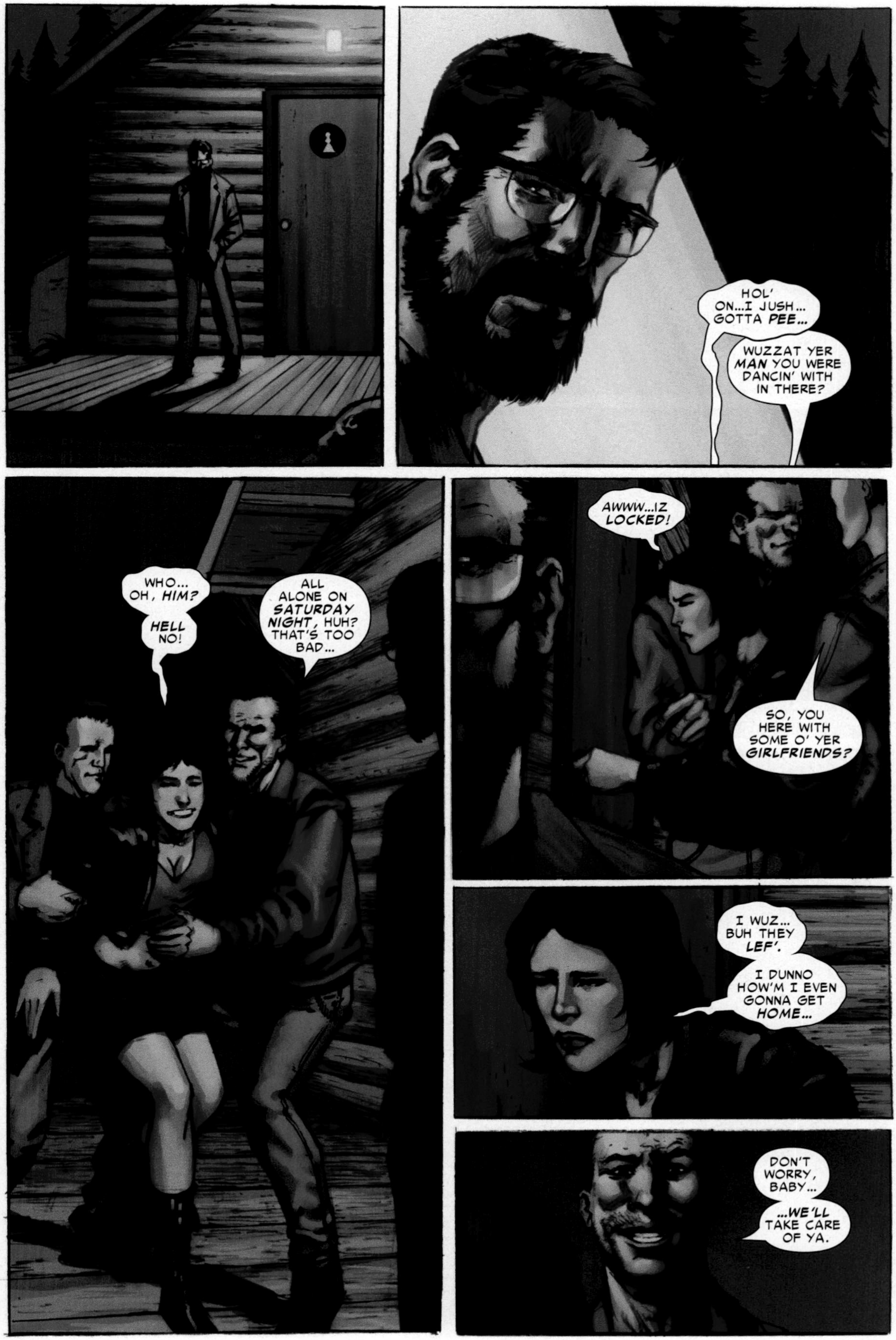
HOL' ON...I JUSH... GOTTA PEE...
WUZZAT YER MAN YOU WERE DANCIN' WITH IN THERE?
WHO... OH, HIM?
HELL NO!
ALL ALONE ON SATURDAY NIGHT, HUH? THAT'S TOO BAD...
AWWW...IZ LOCKED!
SO, YOU HERE WITH SOME O' YER GIRLFRIENDS?
I WUZ... BUH THEY LEF'.
I DUNNO HOW'M I EVEN GONNA GET HOME...
DON'T WORRY, BABY...
...WE'LL TAKE CARE OF YA.

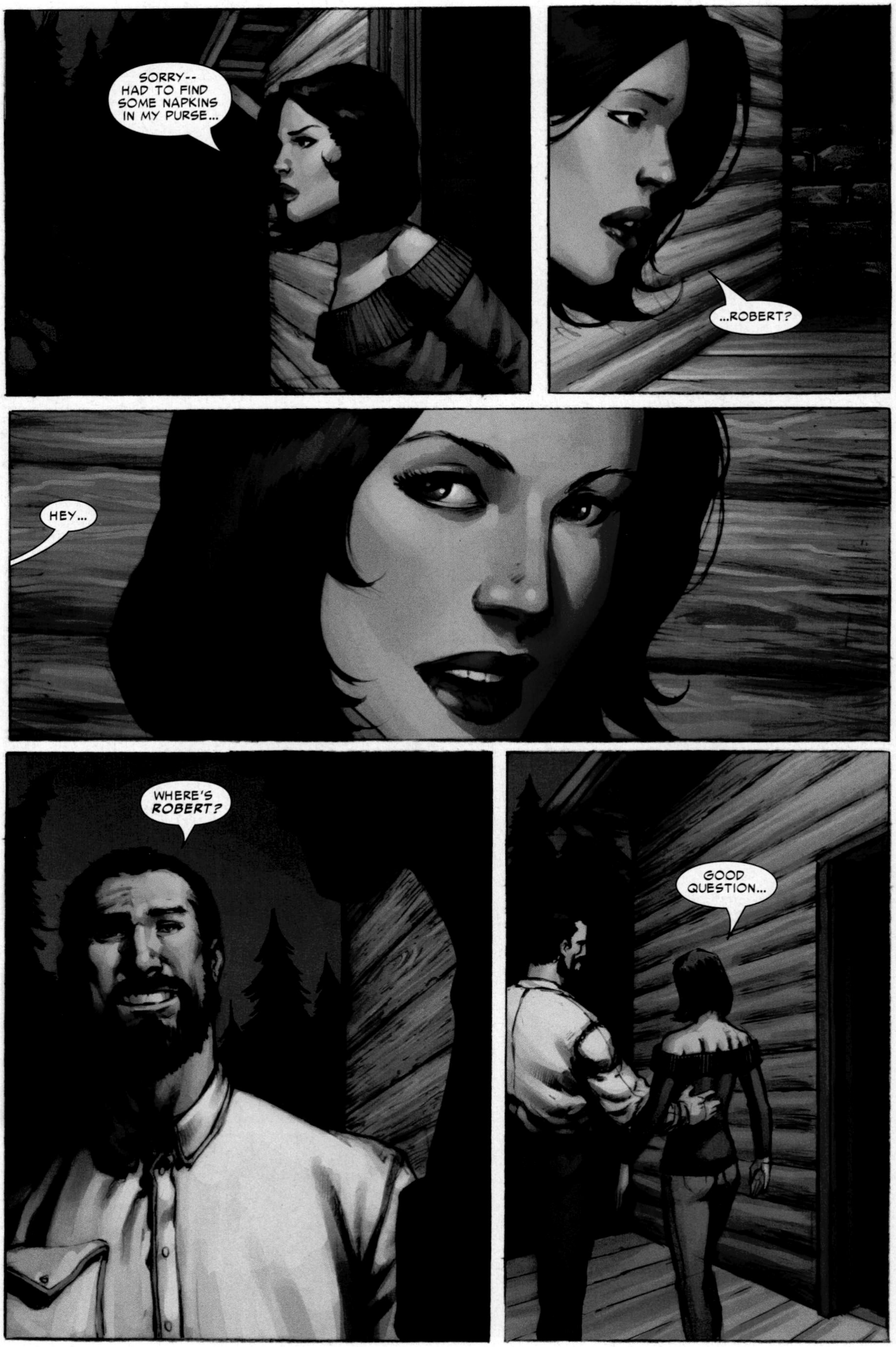
SORRY-- HAD TO FIND SOME NAPKINS IN MY PURSE...
...ROBERT?
HEY...
WHERE'S ROBERT?
GOOD QUESTION...

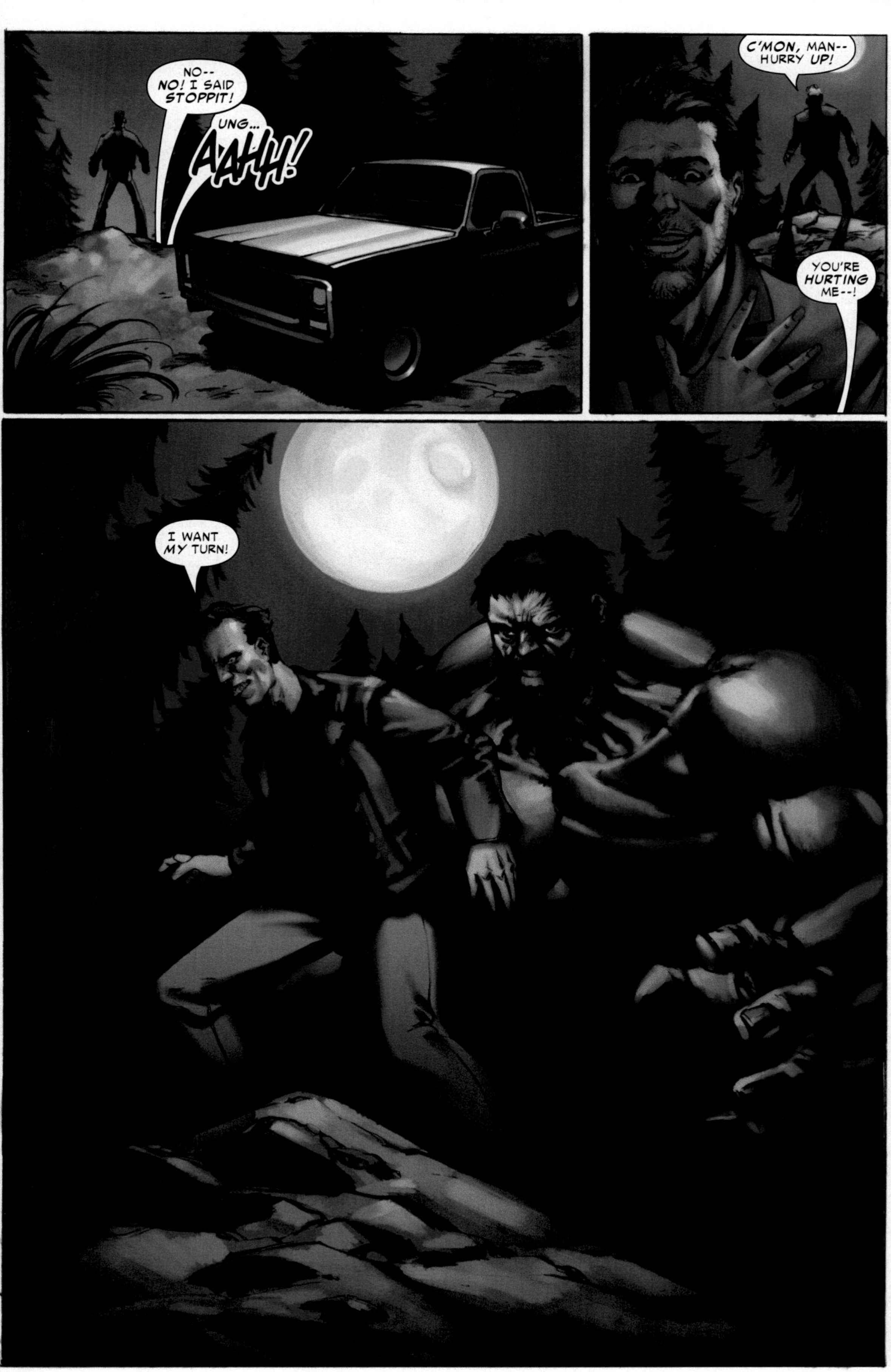
NO-- NO! I SAID STOPPIT!
UNG... AAHH!
C'MON, MAN-- HURRY UP!
YOU'RE HURTING ME--!
I WANT MY TURN!

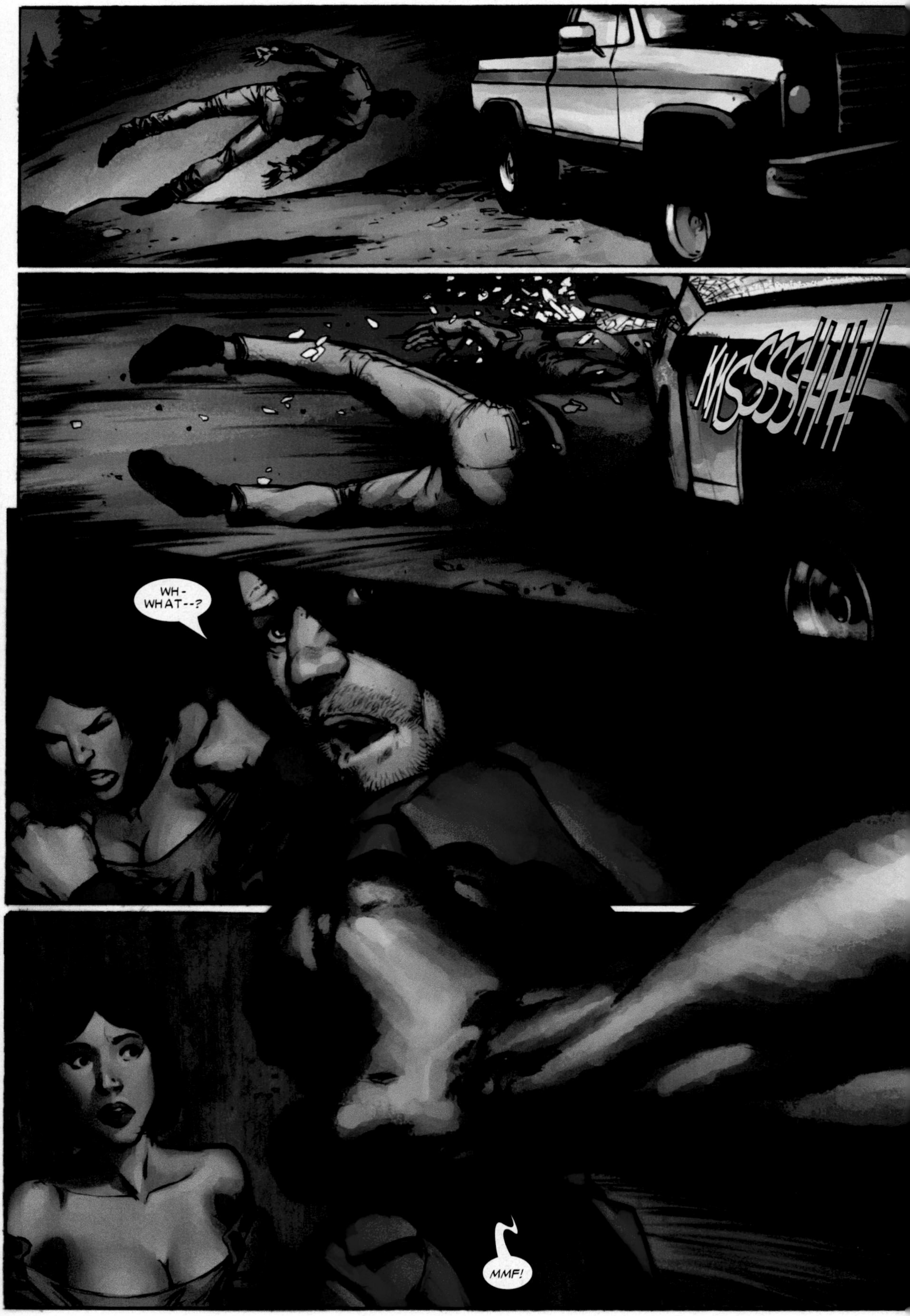
KKSSSSHHHH!
WH-
WHAT--?
MMF!

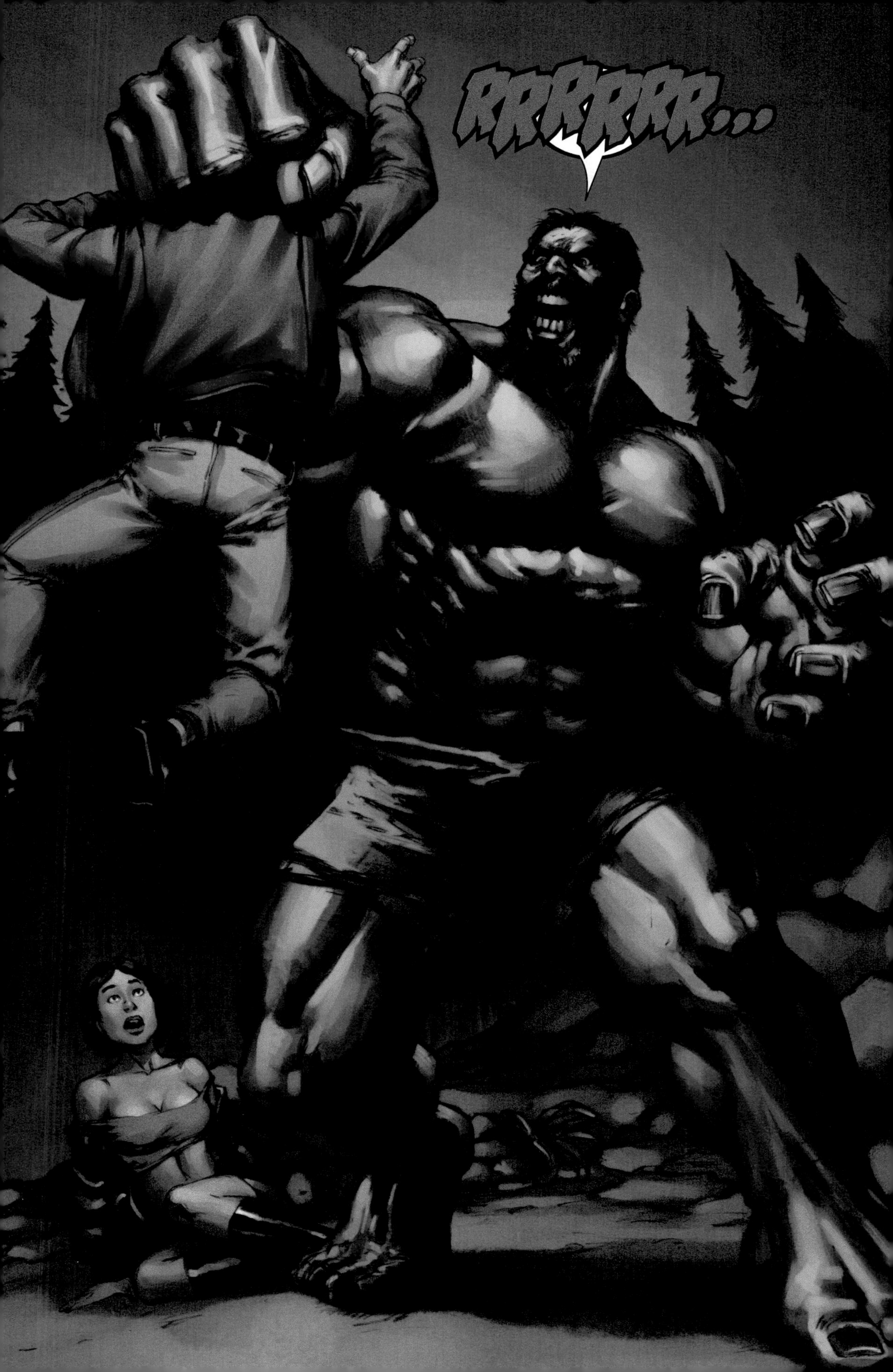
RRRRRR...

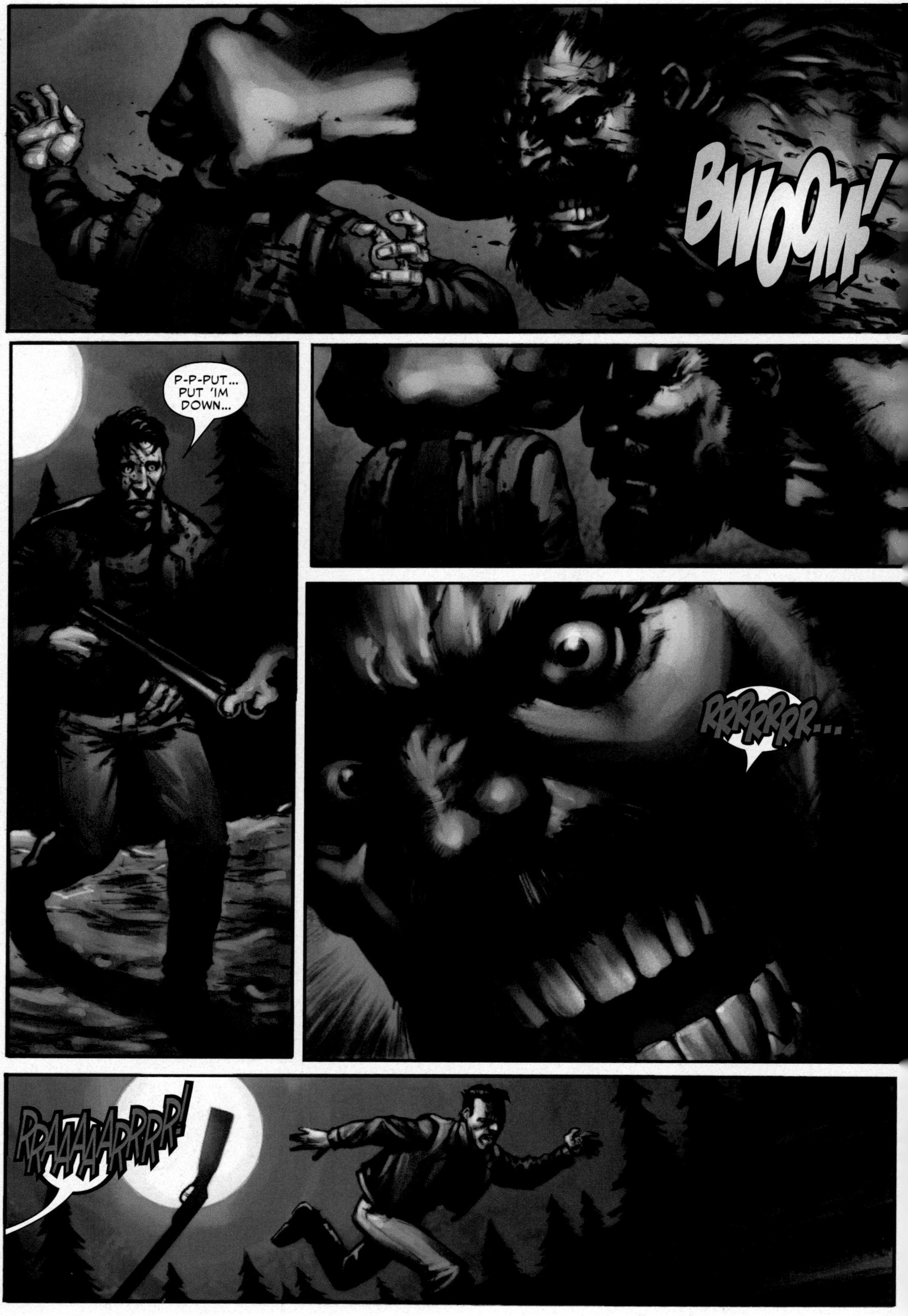
BWOOM!
P-P-PUT... PUT 'IM DOWN...
RRRRRRR...
RRAAAAAARRRR!

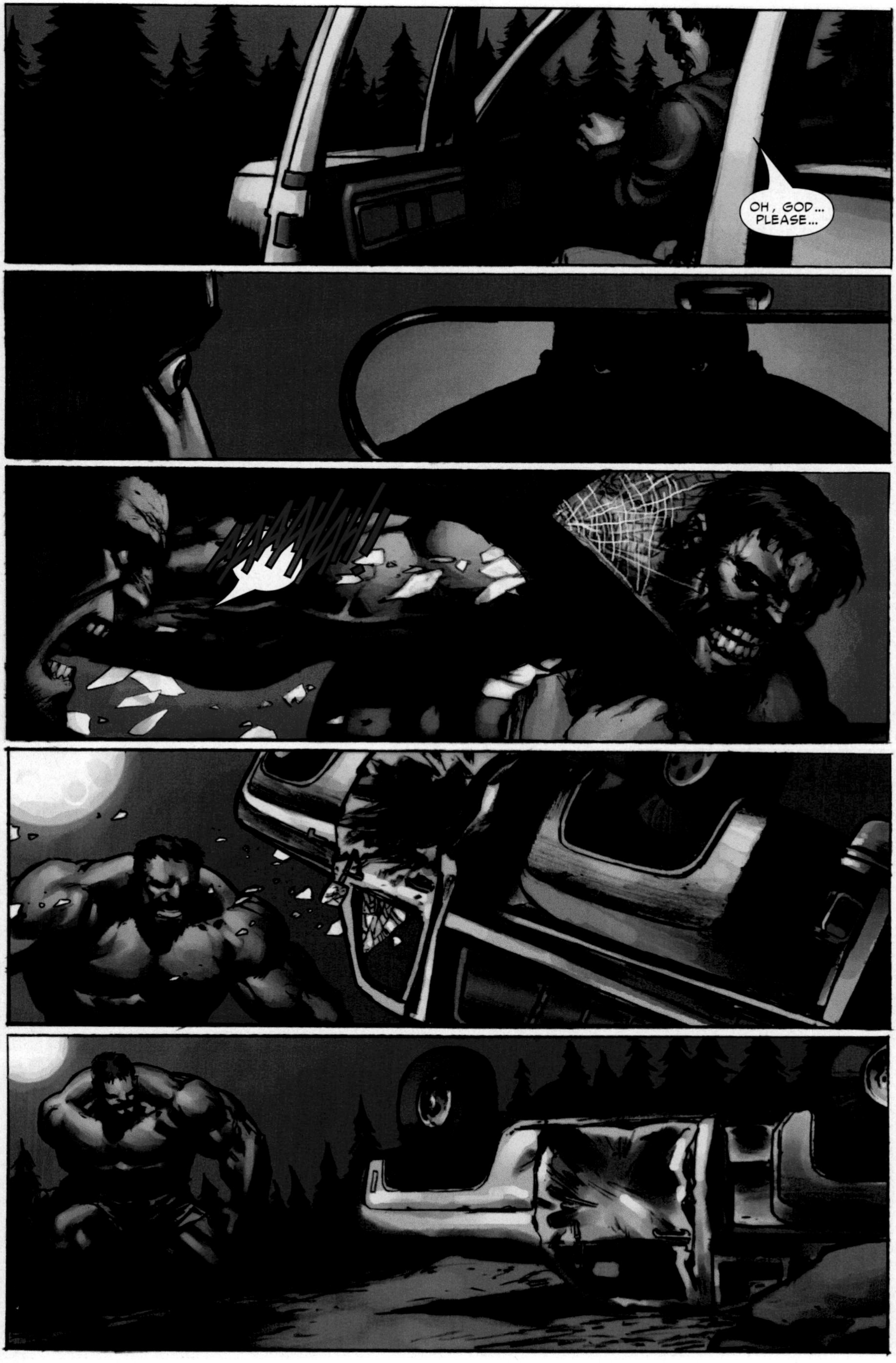

OH, GOD... PLEASE...
AAAAAHH!!

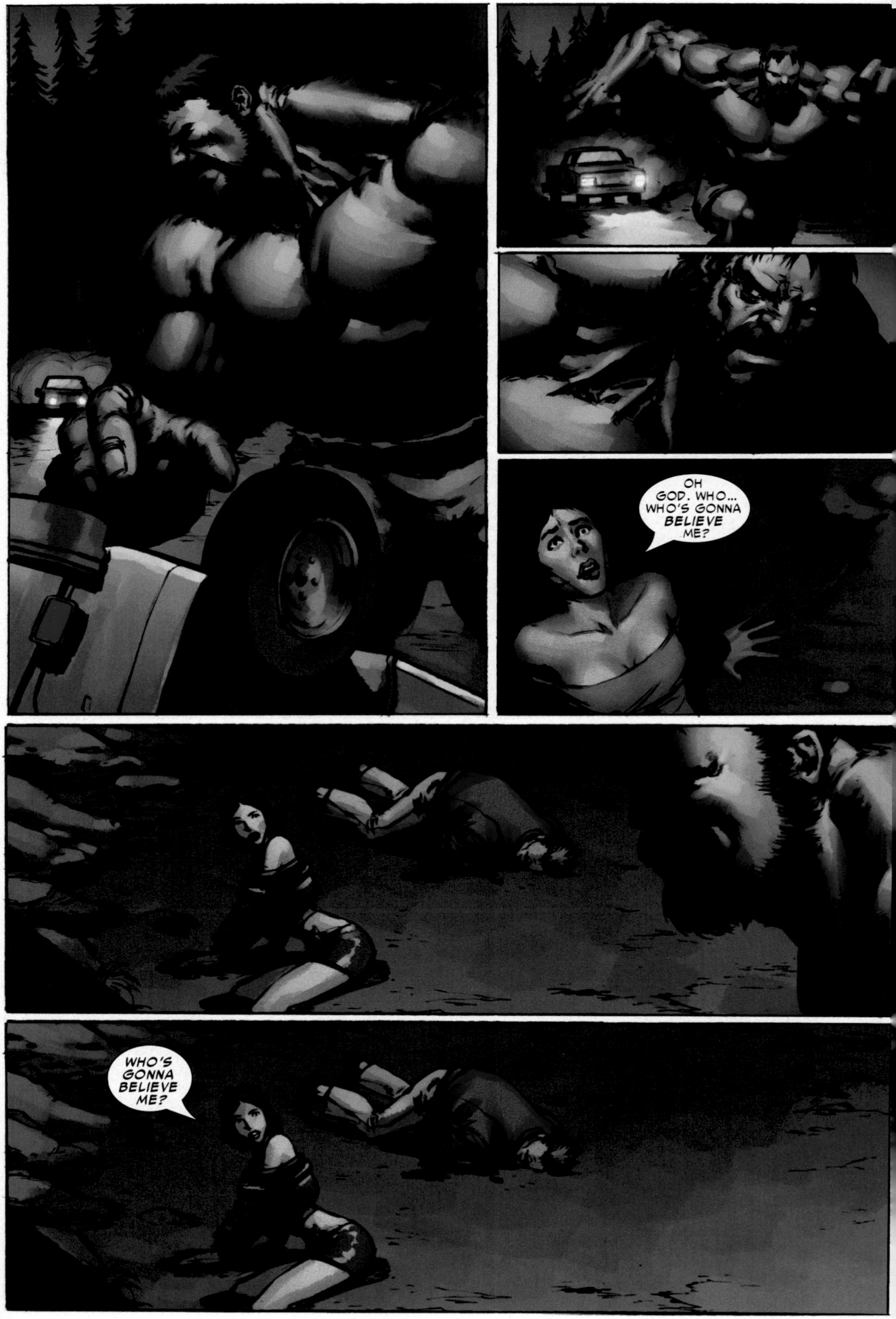
OH GOD. WHO... WHO'S GONNA BELIEVE ME?
WHO'S GONNA BELIEVE ME?

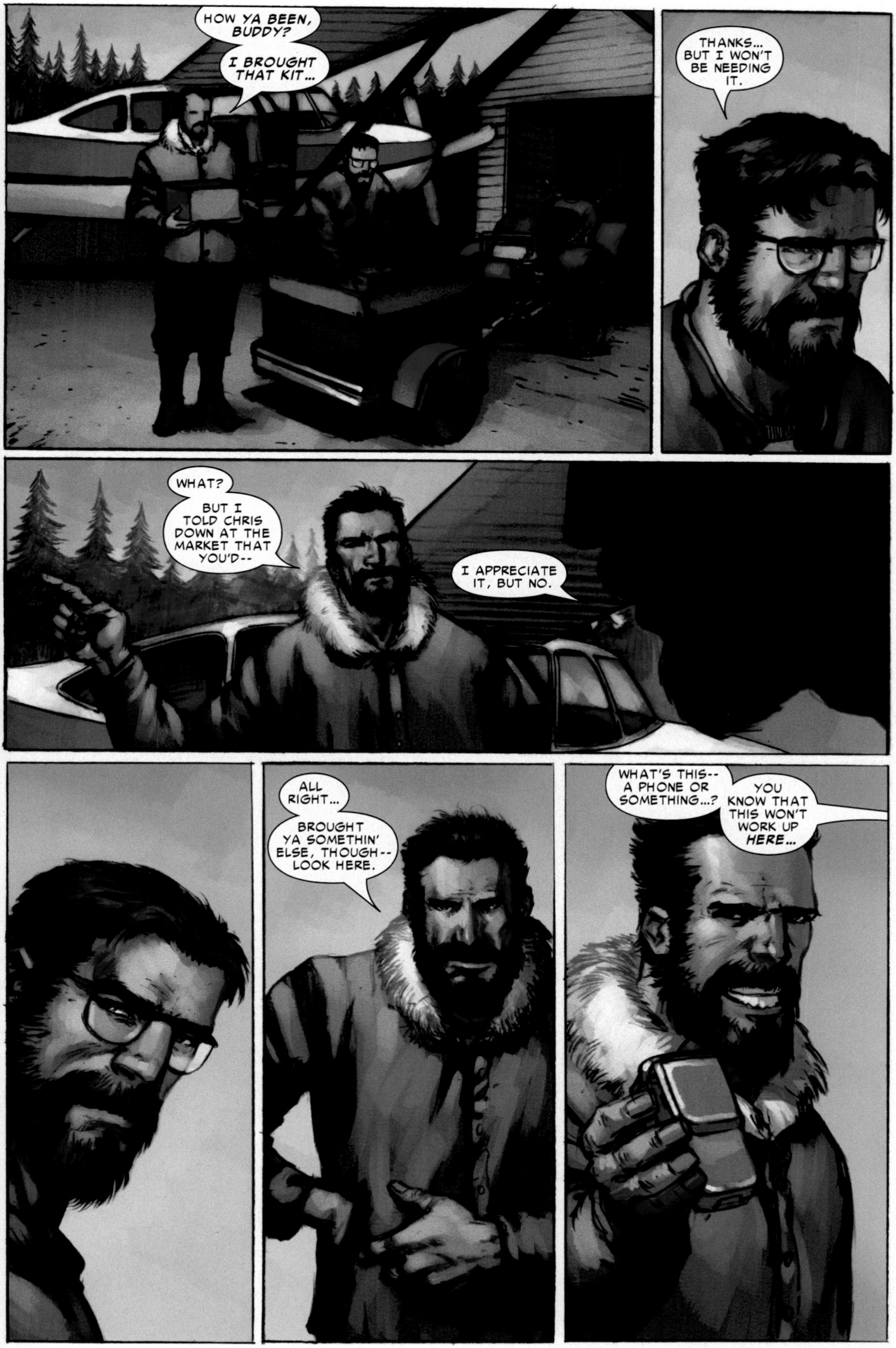
HOW YA BEEN, BUDDY?
I BROUGHT THAT KIT...
THANKS... BUT I WON'T BE NEEDING IT.
WHAT?
BUT I TOLD CHRIS DOWN AT THE MARKET THAT YOU'D--
I APPRECIATE IT, BUT NO.
ALL RIGHT...
BROUGHT YA SOMETHIN' ELSE, THOUGH-- LOOK HERE.
WHAT'S THIS-- A PHONE OR SOMETHING...?
YOU KNOW THAT THIS WON'T WORK UP HERE...

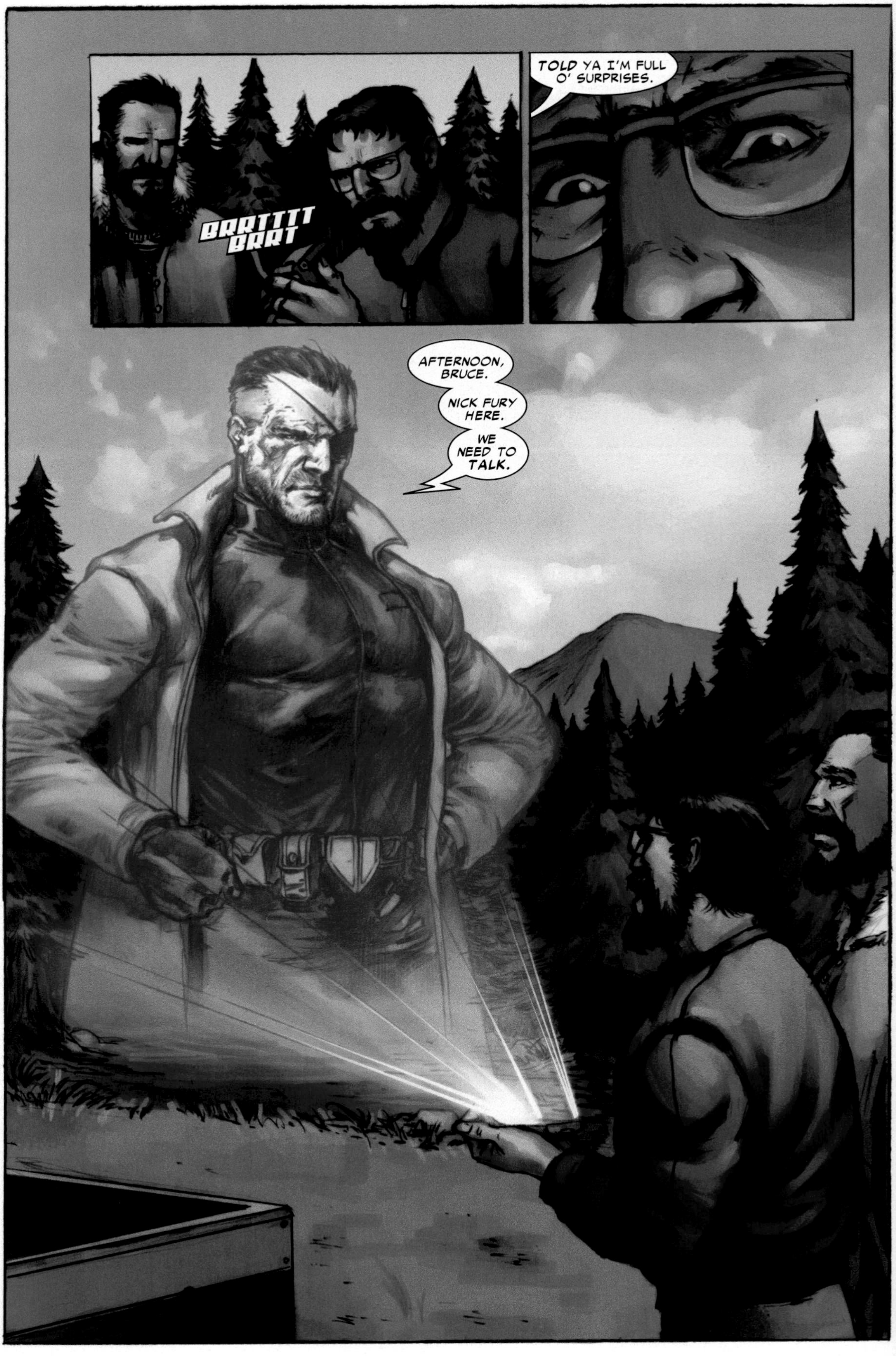
BRRTTTT BRRT
TOLD YA I'M FULL O' SURPRISES.
AFTERNOON, BRUCE.
NICK FURY HERE.
WE NEED TO TALK.

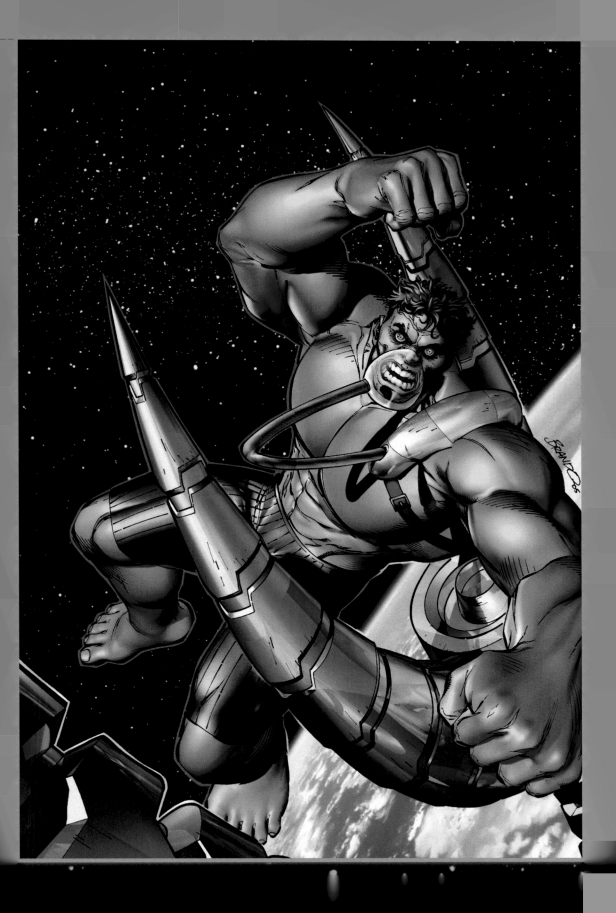

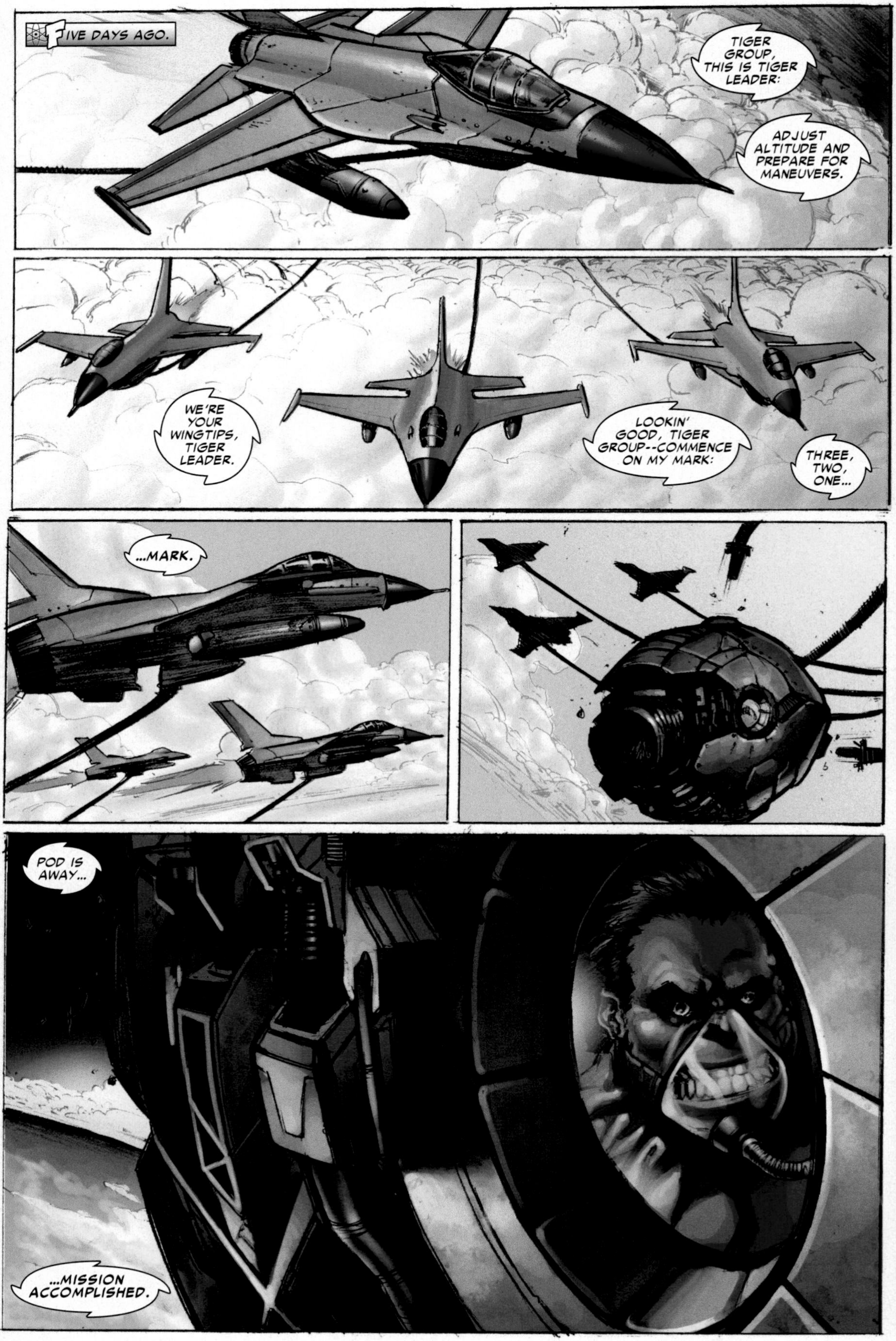
FIVE DAYS AGO.
TIGER GROUP, THIS IS TIGER LEADER:
ADJUST ALTITUDE AND PREPARE FOR MANEUVERS.
WE'RE YOUR WINGTIPS, TIGER LEADER.
LOOKIN' GOOD, TIGER GROUP--COMMENCE ON MY MARK:
THREE, TWO, ONE...
...MARK.
POD IS AWAY...
...MISSION ACCOMPLISHED.

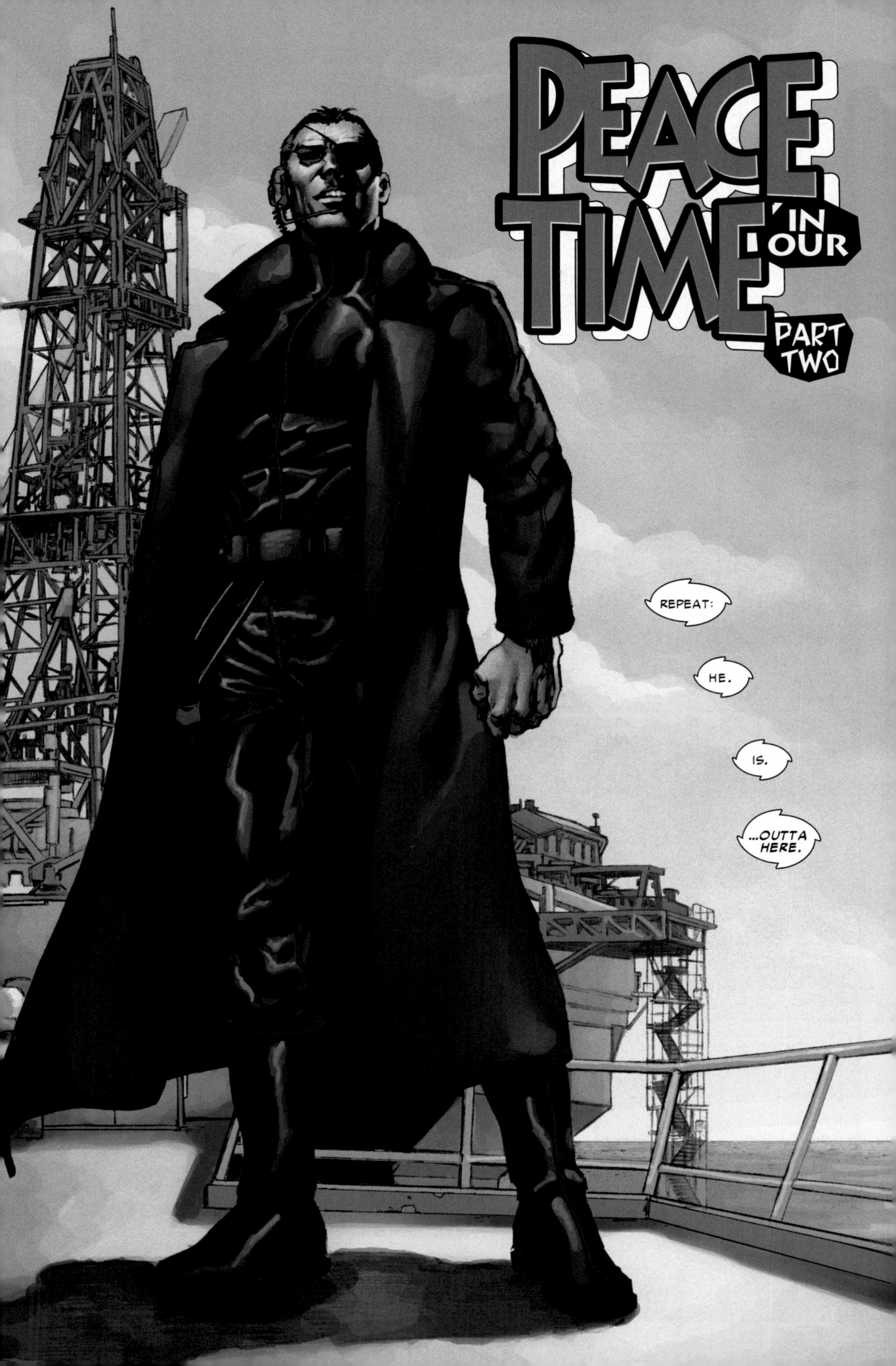
PEACE IN OUR TIME
PART TWO
REPEAT:
HE.
IS.
...OUTTA HERE.

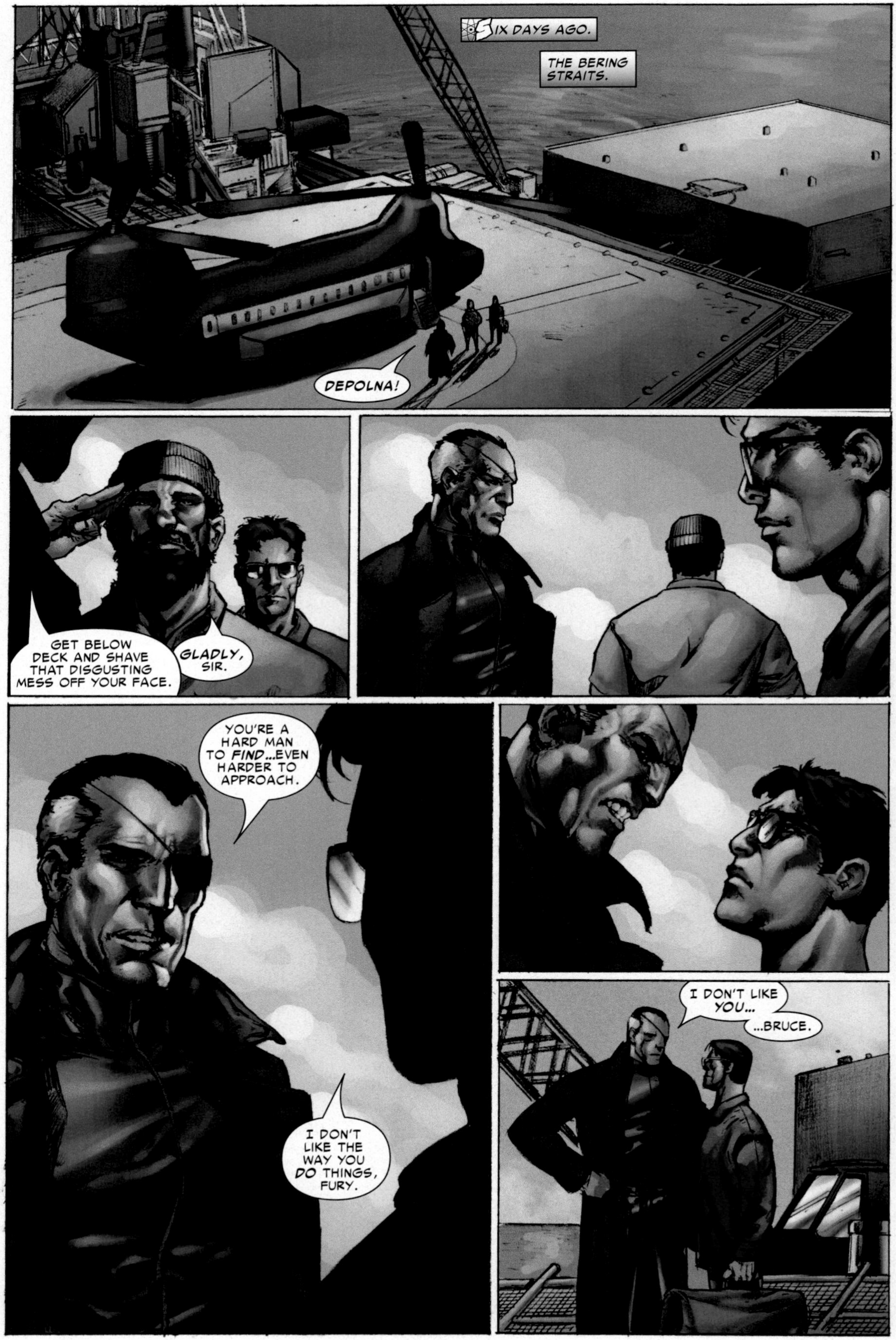
SIX DAYS AGO.
THE BERING STRAITS.
DEPOLNA!
GET BELOW DECK AND SHAVE THAT DISGUSTING MESS OFF YOUR FACE.
GLADLY, SIR.
YOU'RE A HARD MAN TO FIND...EVEN HARDER TO APPROACH.
I DON'T LIKE THE WAY YOU DO THINGS, FURY.
I DON'T LIKE YOU...
...BRUCE.

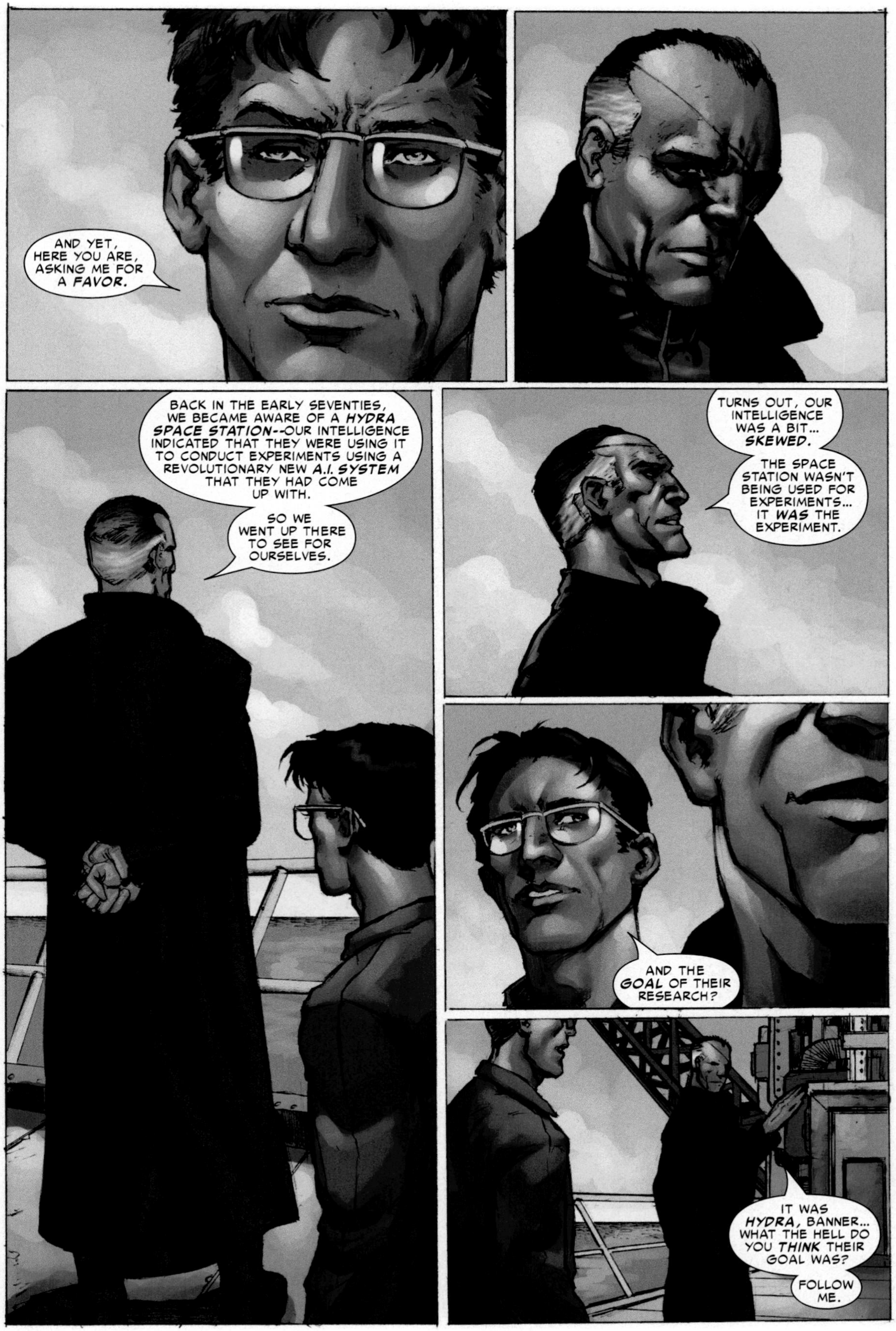
AND YET, HERE YOU ARE, ASKING ME FOR A *FAVOR*.
BACK IN THE EARLY SEVENTIES, WE BECAME AWARE OF A *HYDRA SPACE STATION*--OUR INTELLIGENCE INDICATED THAT THEY WERE USING IT TO CONDUCT EXPERIMENTS USING A REVOLUTIONARY NEW *A.I. SYSTEM* THAT THEY HAD COME UP WITH.
SO WE WENT UP THERE TO SEE FOR OURSELVES.
TURNS OUT, OUR INTELLIGENCE WAS A BIT... ***SKEWED.***
THE SPACE STATION WASN'T BEING USED FOR EXPERIMENTS... IT *WAS* THE EXPERIMENT.
AND THE *GOAL* OF THEIR RESEARCH?
IT WAS *HYDRA*, BANNER... WHAT THE HELL DO YOU *THINK* THEIR GOAL WAS?
FOLLOW ME.

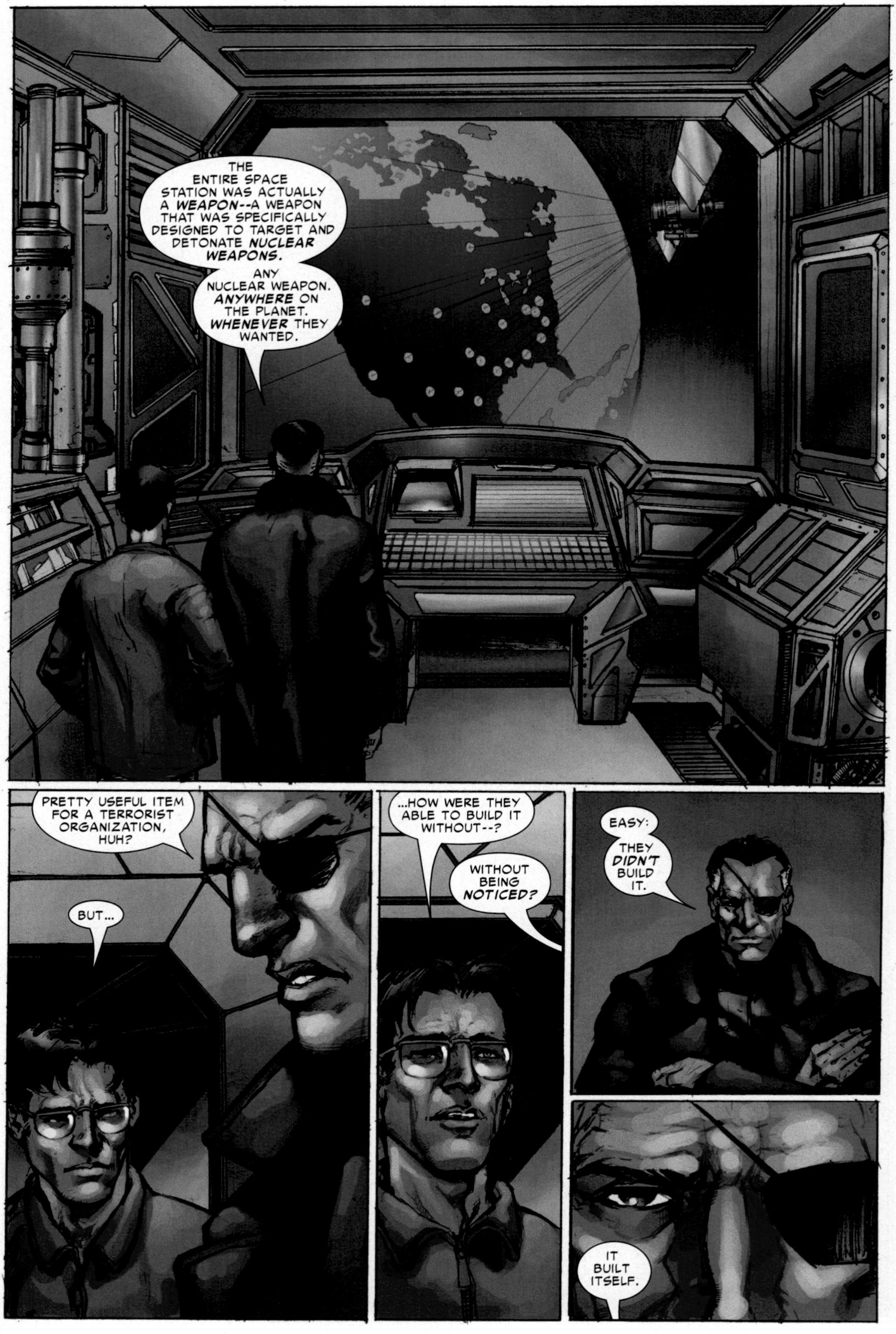
THE ENTIRE SPACE STATION WAS ACTUALLY A WEAPON--A WEAPON THAT WAS SPECIFICALLY DESIGNED TO TARGET AND DETONATE NUCLEAR WEAPONS.
ANY NUCLEAR WEAPON. ANYWHERE ON THE PLANET. WHENEVER THEY WANTED.
PRETTY USEFUL ITEM FOR A TERRORIST ORGANIZATION, HUH?
BUT...
...HOW WERE THEY ABLE TO BUILD IT WITHOUT--?
WITHOUT BEING NOTICED?
EASY:
THEY DIDN'T BUILD IT.
IT BUILT ITSELF.

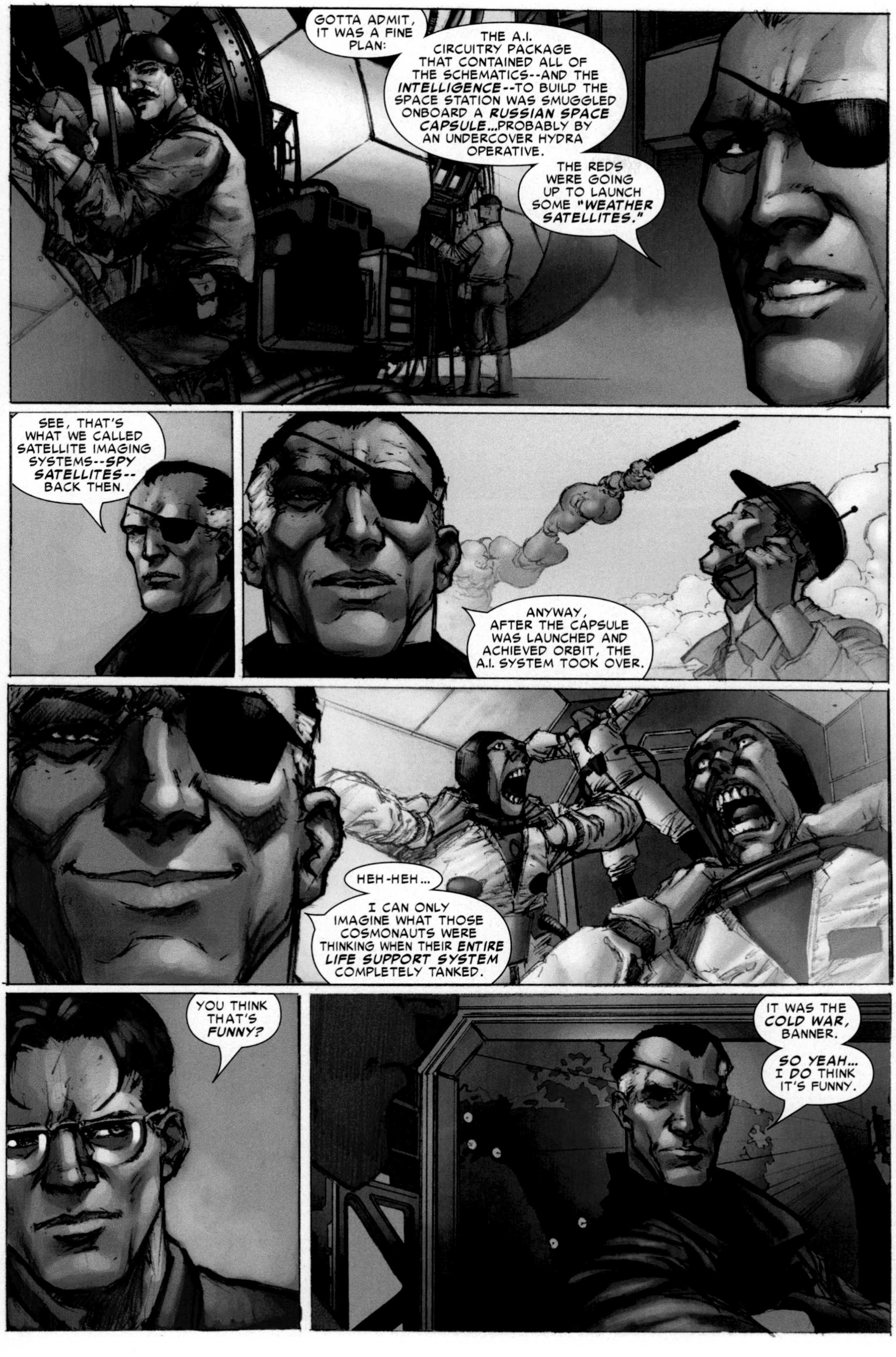
GOTTA ADMIT, IT WAS A FINE PLAN:
THE A.I. CIRCUITRY PACKAGE THAT CONTAINED ALL OF THE SCHEMATICS--AND THE INTELLIGENCE--TO BUILD THE SPACE STATION WAS SMUGGLED ONBOARD A RUSSIAN SPACE CAPSULE...PROBABLY BY AN UNDERCOVER HYDRA OPERATIVE.
THE REDS WERE GOING UP TO LAUNCH SOME "WEATHER SATELLITES."
SEE, THAT'S WHAT WE CALLED SATELLITE IMAGING SYSTEMS--SPY SATELLITES--BACK THEN.
ANYWAY, AFTER THE CAPSULE WAS LAUNCHED AND ACHIEVED ORBIT, THE A.I. SYSTEM TOOK OVER.
HEH-HEH...
I CAN ONLY IMAGINE WHAT THOSE COSMONAUTS WERE THINKING WHEN THEIR ENTIRE LIFE SUPPORT SYSTEM COMPLETELY TANKED.
YOU THINK THAT'S FUNNY?
IT WAS THE COLD WAR, BANNER.
SO YEAH... I DO THINK IT'S FUNNY.

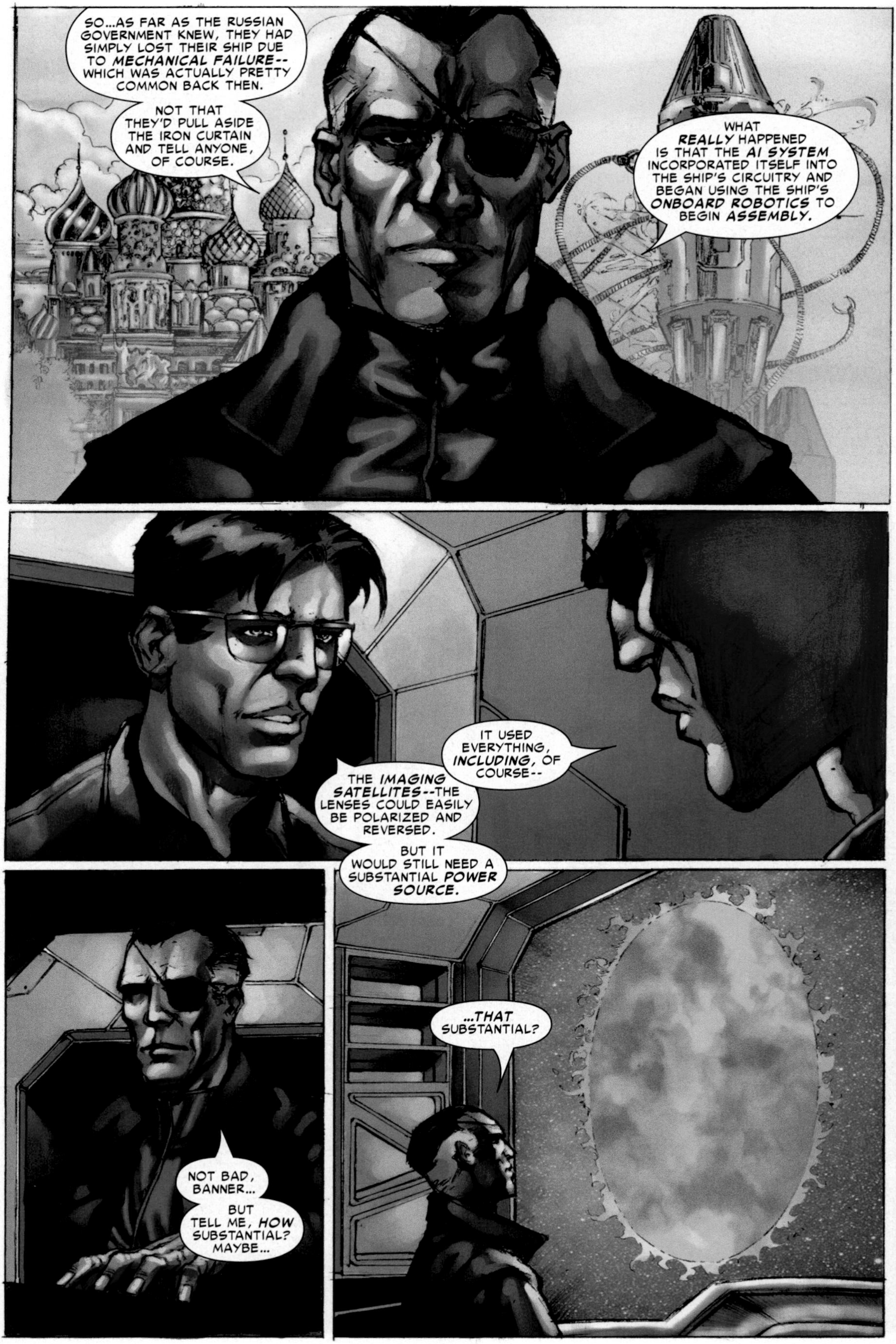
SO...AS FAR AS THE RUSSIAN GOVERNMENT KNEW, THEY HAD SIMPLY LOST THEIR SHIP DUE TO MECHANICAL FAILURE-- WHICH WAS ACTUALLY PRETTY COMMON BACK THEN.
NOT THAT THEY'D PULL ASIDE THE IRON CURTAIN AND TELL ANYONE, OF COURSE.
WHAT REALLY HAPPENED IS THAT THE AI SYSTEM INCORPORATED ITSELF INTO THE SHIP'S CIRCUITRY AND BEGAN USING THE SHIP'S ONBOARD ROBOTICS TO BEGIN ASSEMBLY.
IT USED EVERYTHING, INCLUDING, OF COURSE--
THE IMAGING SATELLITES--THE LENSES COULD EASILY BE POLARIZED AND REVERSED.
BUT IT WOULD STILL NEED A SUBSTANTIAL POWER SOURCE.
NOT BAD, BANNER...
BUT TELL ME, HOW SUBSTANTIAL? MAYBE...
...THAT SUBSTANTIAL?

YES...IT'S POSSIBLE: GIVEN ENOUGH TIME, THE SOLAR PANELS FROM THE SATELLITES--AND FROM THE SPACE CAPSULE, ALSO-- COULD GATHER A SUFFICIENT AMOUNT OF ENERGY...BUT IT WOULD NEED AN ALMOST *INFINITE* AMOUNT OF STORAGE SPACE TO HOLD IT.

WHERE--?

HOLD ON-- I HAD TO HAVE THIS EXPLAINED TO ME, TOO:

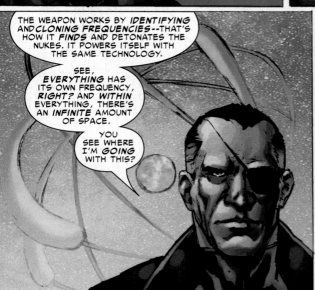

THE WEAPON WORKS BY *IDENTIFYING* AND *CLONING FREQUENCIES*--THAT'S HOW IT *FINDS* AND DETONATES THE NUKES. IT POWERS ITSELF WITH THE SAME TECHNOLOGY.

SEE, *EVERYTHING* HAS ITS OWN FREQUENCY, *RIGHT?* AND *WITHIN* EVERYTHING, THERE'S AN *INFINITE* AMOUNT OF SPACE.

YOU SEE WHERE I'M *GOING* WITH THIS?

SO...

YOU'RE SAYING THAT THIS--THIS *THING*-- IS ABLE TO CONVERT *SOLAR* ENERGY INTO *ATOMIC* ENERGY...AND THEN *STORE* IT AT A *SUB-ATOMIC* LEVEL?

IF THIS IS *TRUE*... THIS COULD CHANGE THE WORLD.

OH, IT'S TRUE...BUT IT AIN'T GONNA CHANGE THE WORLD.

IT'S JUST GONNA *BLOW IT UP.*

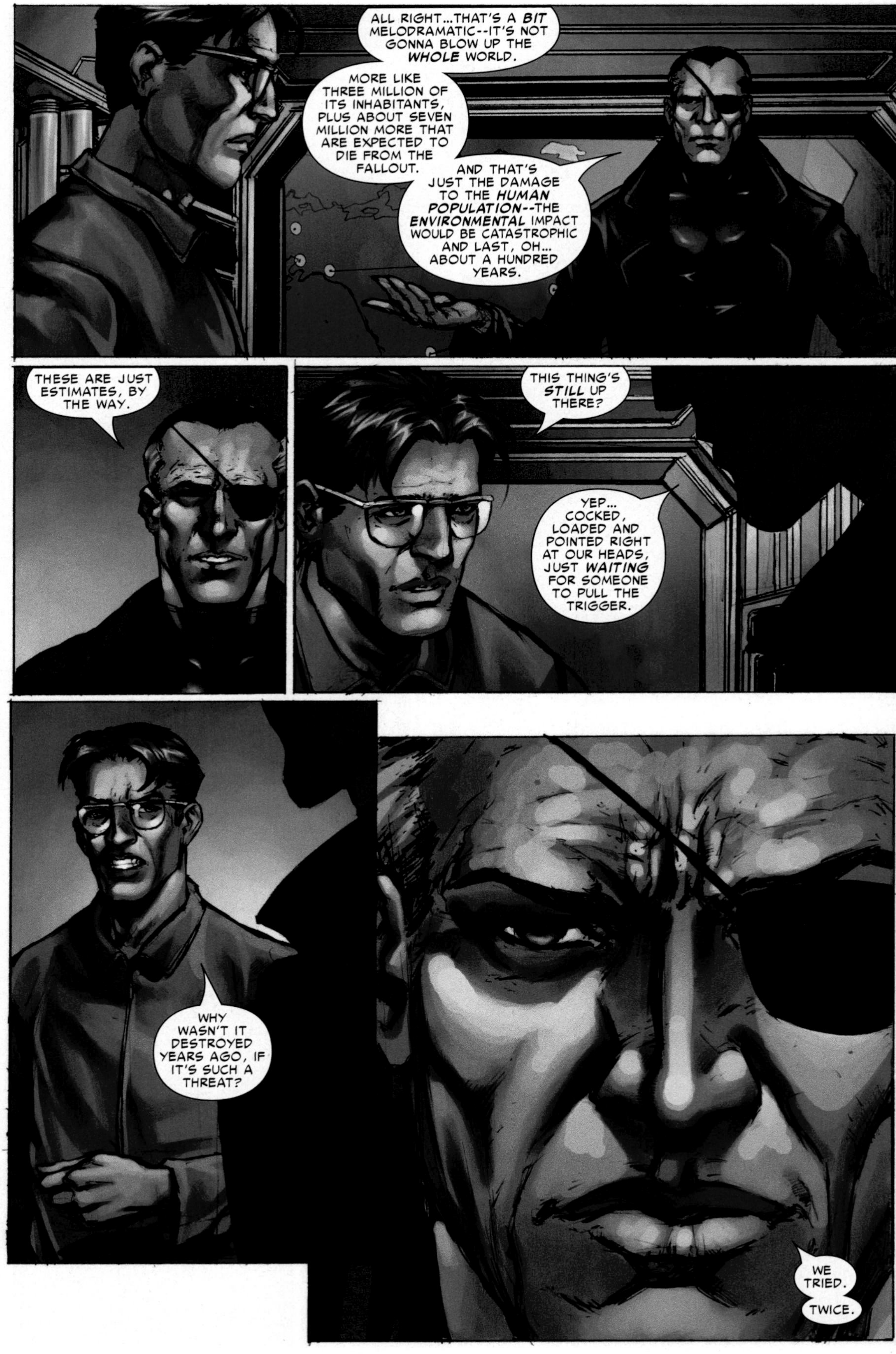
ALL RIGHT...THAT'S A BIT MELODRAMATIC--IT'S NOT GONNA BLOW UP THE WHOLE WORLD.
MORE LIKE THREE MILLION OF ITS INHABITANTS, PLUS ABOUT SEVEN MILLION MORE THAT ARE EXPECTED TO DIE FROM THE FALLOUT.
AND THAT'S JUST THE DAMAGE TO THE HUMAN POPULATION--THE ENVIRONMENTAL IMPACT WOULD BE CATASTROPHIC AND LAST, OH... ABOUT A HUNDRED YEARS.
THESE ARE JUST ESTIMATES, BY THE WAY.
THIS THING'S STILL UP THERE?
YEP... COCKED, LOADED AND POINTED RIGHT AT OUR HEADS, JUST WAITING FOR SOMEONE TO PULL THE TRIGGER.
WHY WASN'T IT DESTROYED YEARS AGO, IF IT'S SUCH A THREAT?
WE TRIED.
TWICE.

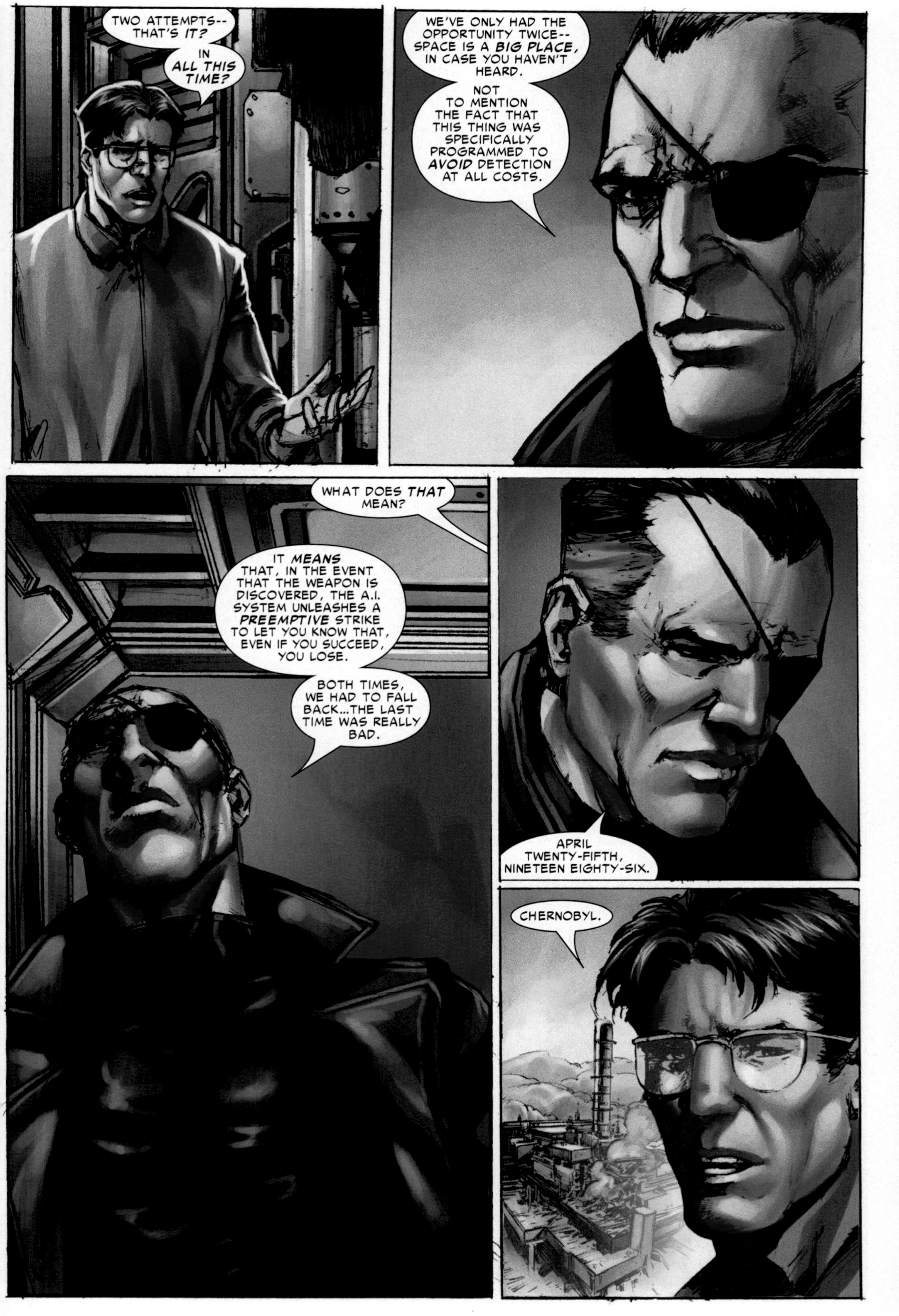
TWO ATTEMPTS-- THAT'S IT?
IN ALL THIS TIME?
WE'VE ONLY HAD THE OPPORTUNITY TWICE-- SPACE IS A BIG PLACE, IN CASE YOU HAVEN'T HEARD.
NOT TO MENTION THE FACT THAT THIS THING WAS SPECIFICALLY PROGRAMMED TO AVOID DETECTION AT ALL COSTS.
WHAT DOES THAT MEAN?
IT MEANS THAT, IN THE EVENT THAT THE WEAPON IS DISCOVERED, THE A.I. SYSTEM UNLEASHES A PREEMPTIVE STRIKE TO LET YOU KNOW THAT, EVEN IF YOU SUCCEED, YOU LOSE.
BOTH TIMES, WE HAD TO FALL BACK...THE LAST TIME WAS REALLY BAD.
APRIL TWENTY-FIFTH, NINETEEN EIGHTY-SIX.
CHERNOBYL.

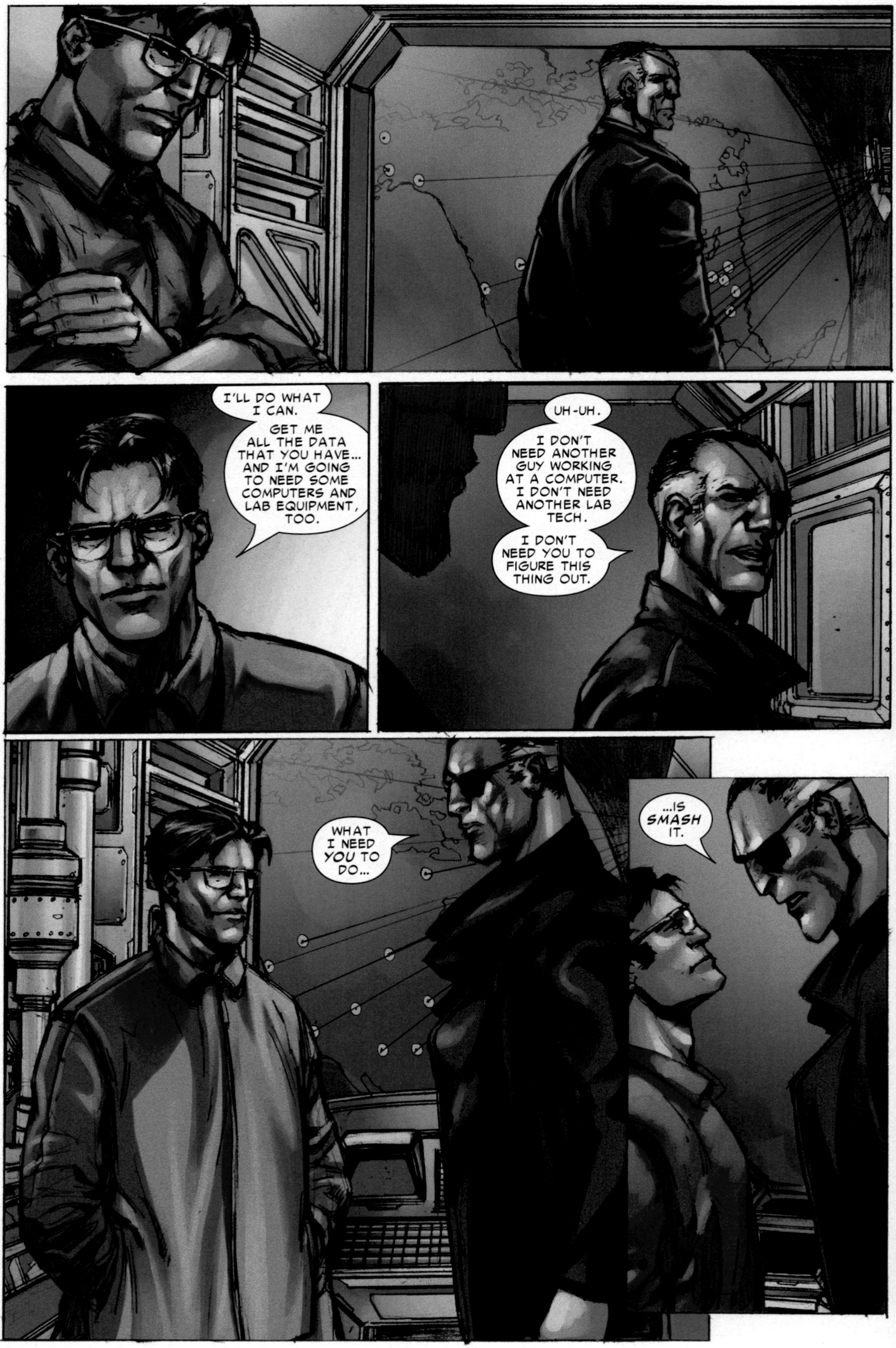
I'LL DO WHAT I CAN.
GET ME ALL THE DATA THAT YOU HAVE... AND I'M GOING TO NEED SOME COMPUTERS AND LAB EQUIPMENT, TOO.
UH-UH.
I DON'T NEED ANOTHER GUY WORKING AT A COMPUTER. I DON'T NEED ANOTHER LAB TECH.
I DON'T NEED YOU TO FIGURE THIS THING OUT.
WHAT I NEED *YOU* TO DO...
...IS *SMASH* IT.

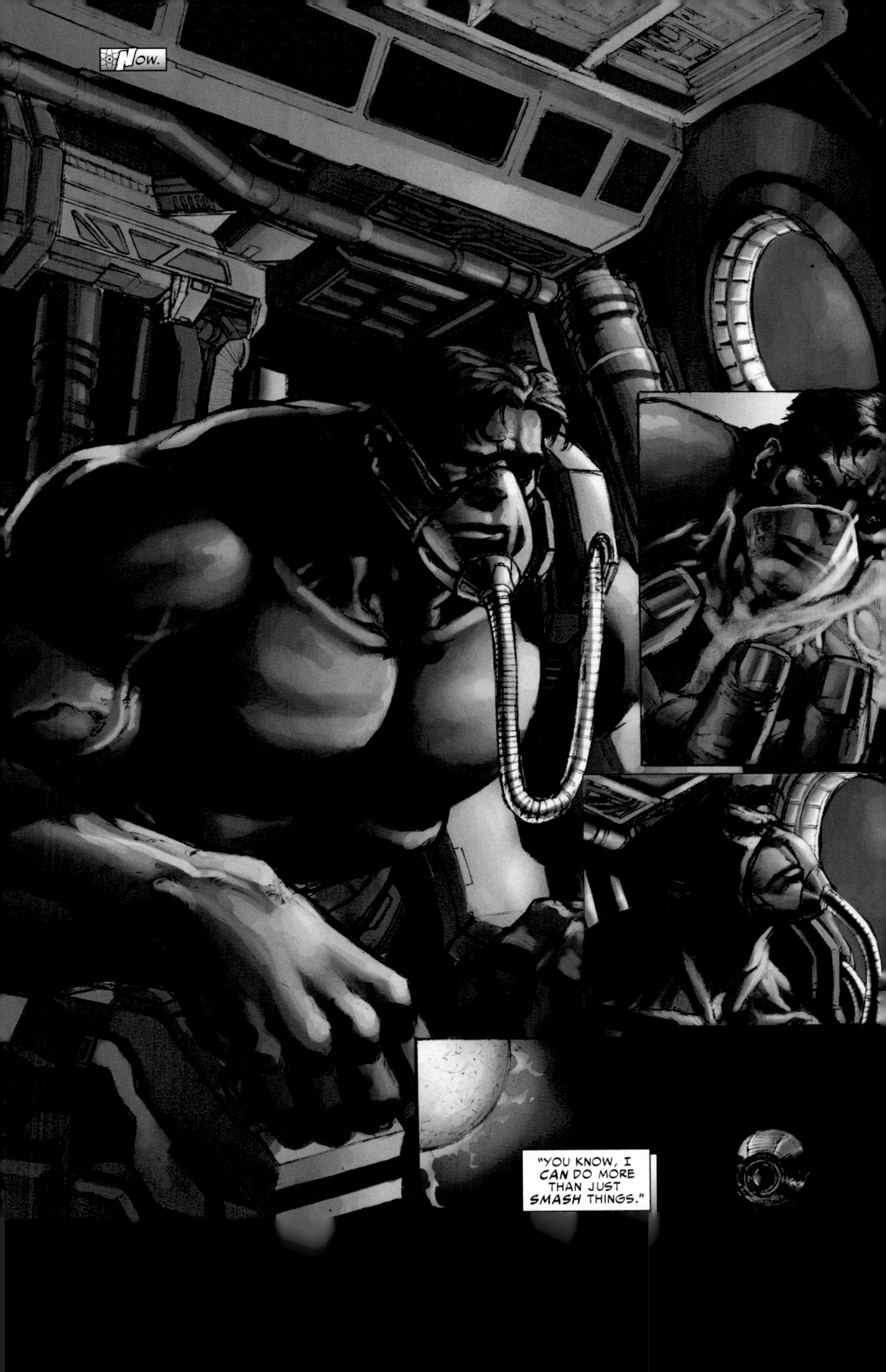
NOW.
"YOU KNOW, I CAN DO MORE THAN JUST SMASH THINGS."

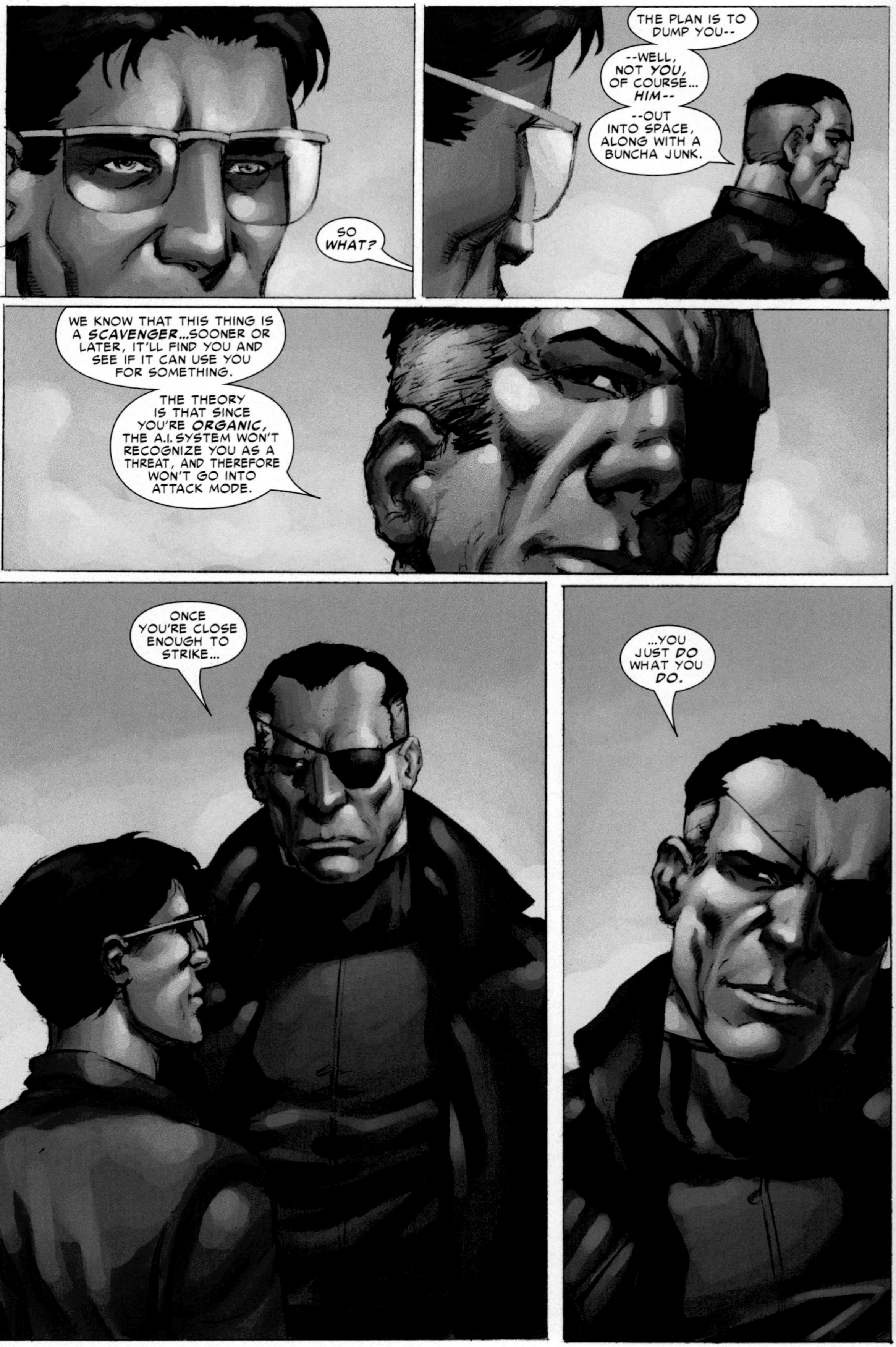
SO WHAT?
THE PLAN IS TO DUMP YOU--
--WELL, NOT YOU, OF COURSE... HIM--
--OUT INTO SPACE, ALONG WITH A BUNCHA JUNK.
WE KNOW THAT THIS THING IS A SCAVENGER...SOONER OR LATER, IT'LL FIND YOU AND SEE IF IT CAN USE YOU FOR SOMETHING.
THE THEORY IS THAT SINCE YOU'RE ORGANIC, THE A.I. SYSTEM WON'T RECOGNIZE YOU AS A THREAT, AND THEREFORE WON'T GO INTO ATTACK MODE.
ONCE YOU'RE CLOSE ENOUGH TO STRIKE...
...YOU JUST DO WHAT YOU DO.

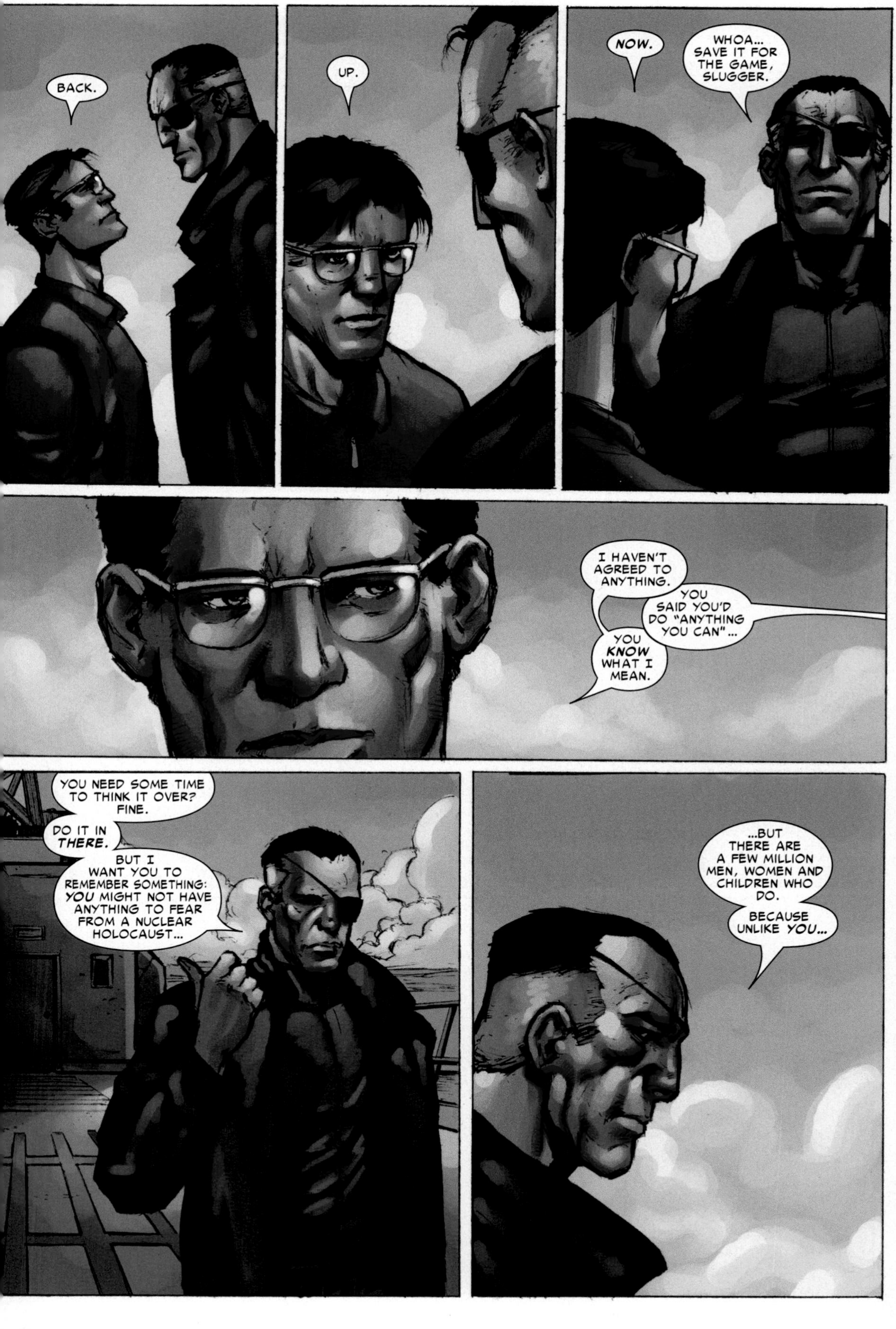
BACK.
UP.
NOW.
WHOA... SAVE IT FOR THE GAME, SLUGGER.
I HAVEN'T AGREED TO ANYTHING.
YOU SAID YOU'D DO "ANYTHING YOU CAN"...
YOU KNOW WHAT I MEAN.
YOU NEED SOME TIME TO THINK IT OVER? FINE.
DO IT IN THERE.
BUT I WANT YOU TO REMEMBER SOMETHING: YOU MIGHT NOT HAVE ANYTHING TO FEAR FROM A NUCLEAR HOLOCAUST...
...BUT THERE ARE A FEW MILLION MEN, WOMEN AND CHILDREN WHO DO.
BECAUSE UNLIKE YOU...

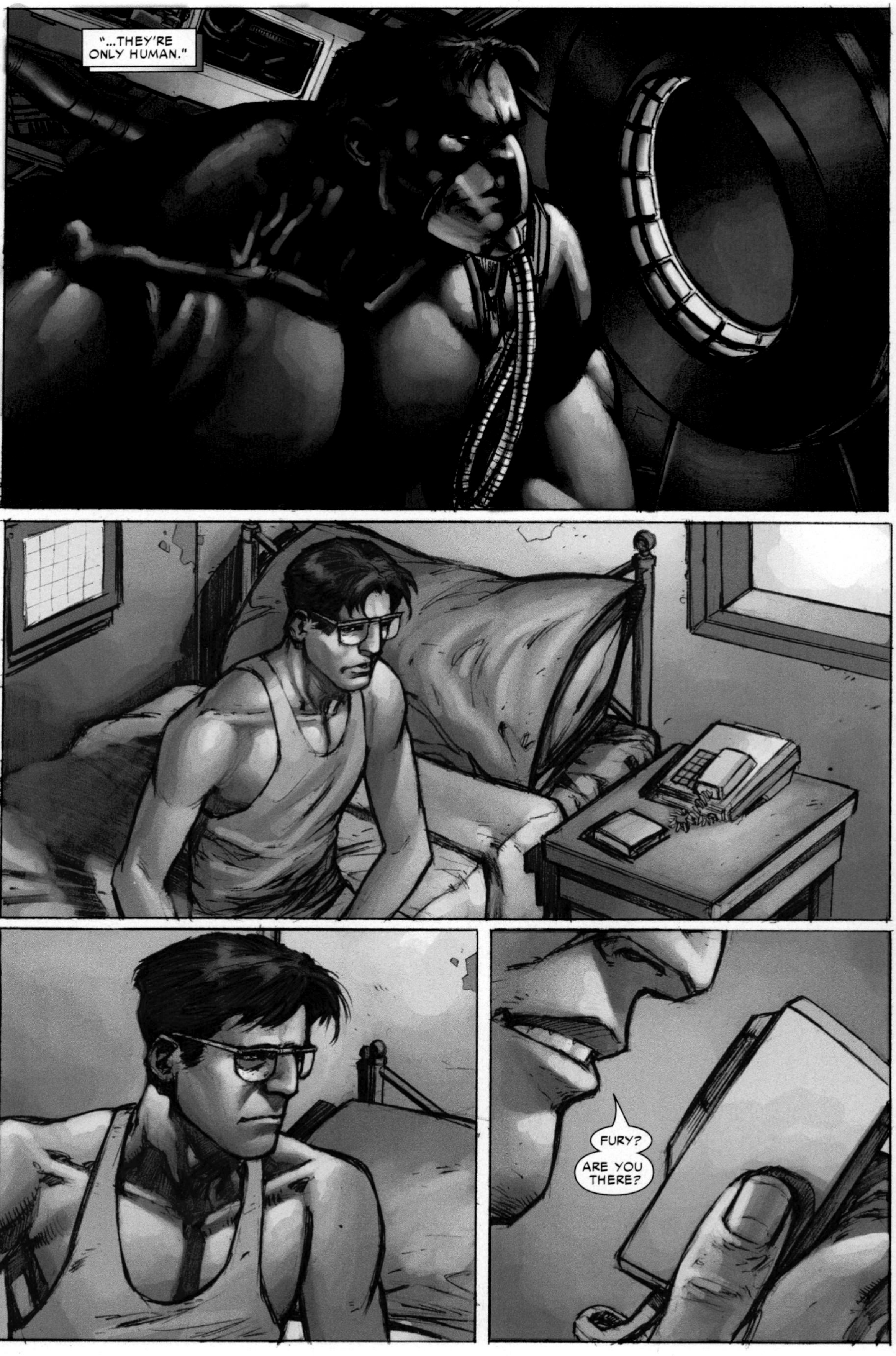
"...THEY'RE ONLY HUMAN."
FURY?
ARE YOU THERE?

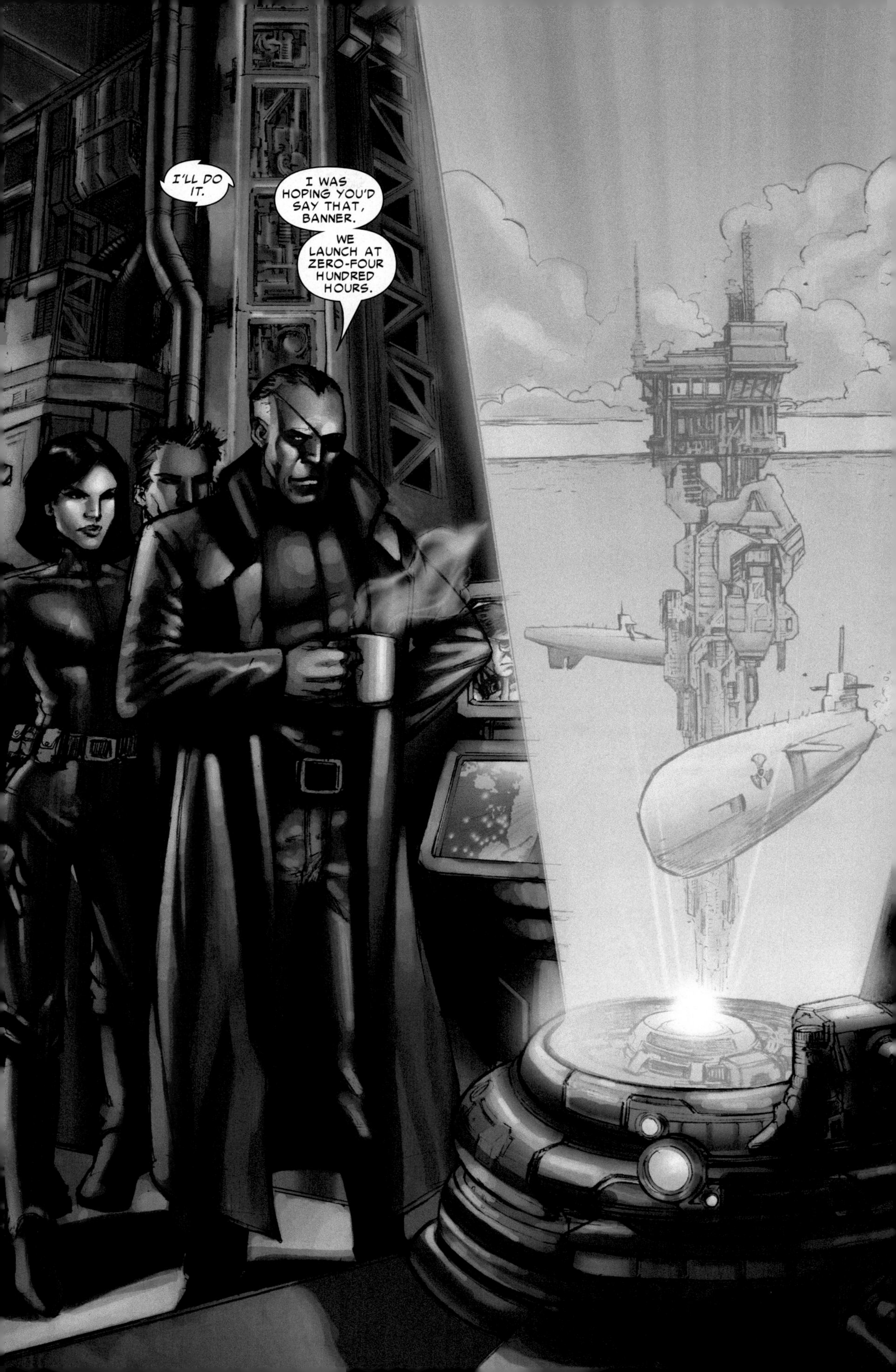
I'LL DO IT.
I WAS HOPING YOU'D SAY THAT, BANNER.
WE LAUNCH AT ZERO-FOUR HUNDRED HOURS.

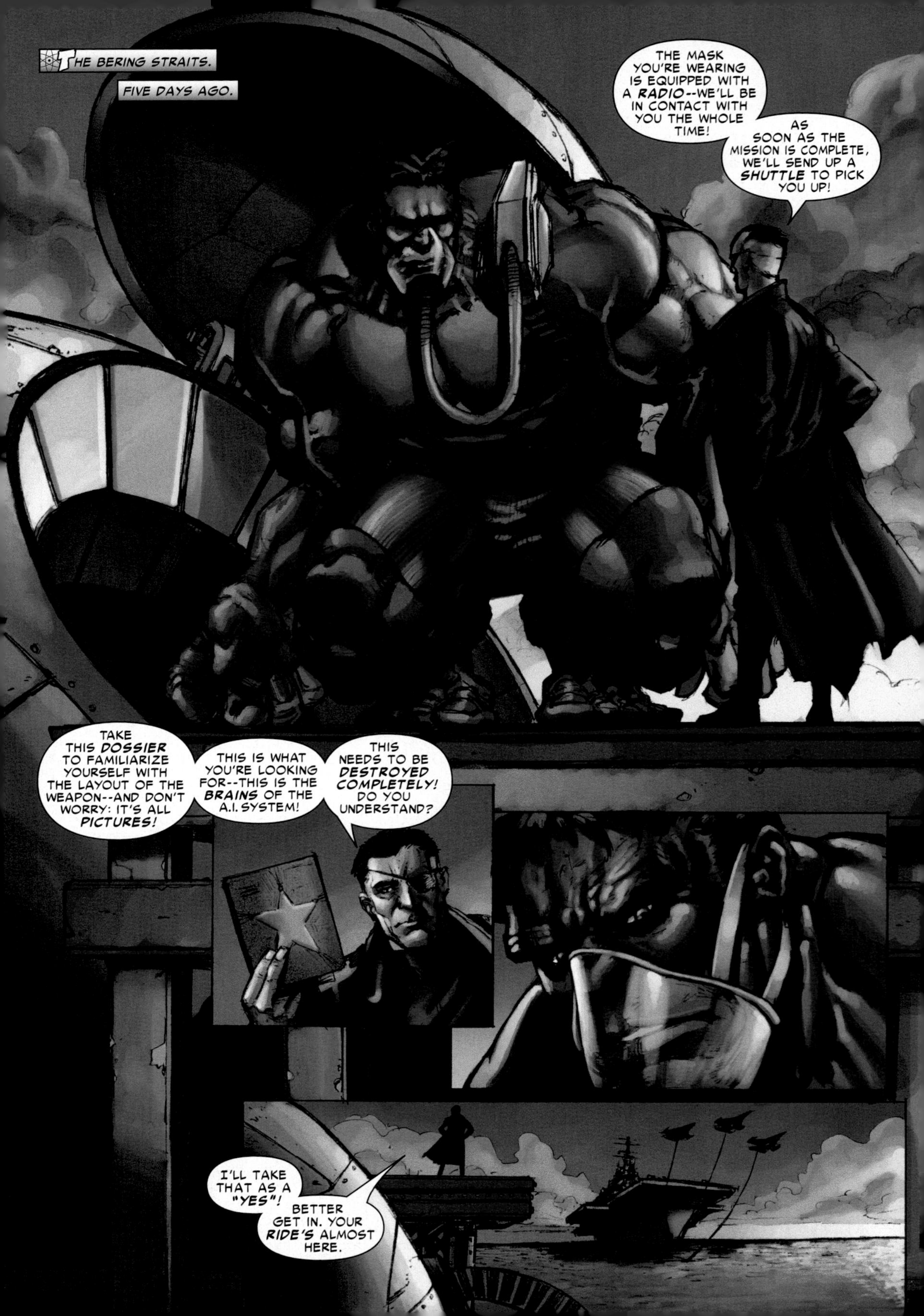

THE BERING STRAITS.
FIVE DAYS AGO.
THE MASK YOU'RE WEARING IS EQUIPPED WITH A RADIO--WE'LL BE IN CONTACT WITH YOU THE WHOLE TIME!
AS SOON AS THE MISSION IS COMPLETE, WE'LL SEND UP A SHUTTLE TO PICK YOU UP!
TAKE THIS DOSSIER TO FAMILIARIZE YOURSELF WITH THE LAYOUT OF THE WEAPON--AND DON'T WORRY: IT'S ALL PICTURES!
THIS IS WHAT YOU'RE LOOKING FOR--THIS IS THE BRAINS OF THE A.I. SYSTEM!
THIS NEEDS TO BE DESTROYED COMPLETELY! DO YOU UNDERSTAND?
I'LL TAKE THAT AS A "YES"!
BETTER GET IN. YOUR RIDE'S ALMOST HERE.

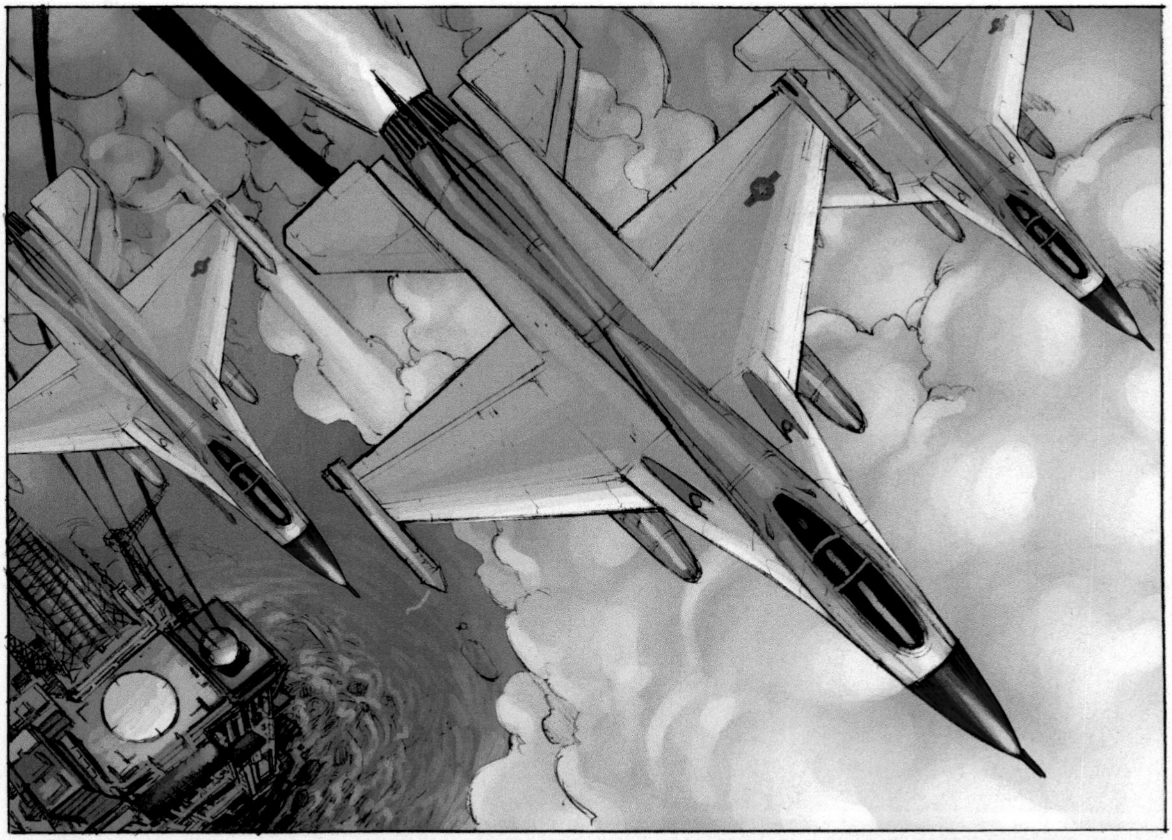

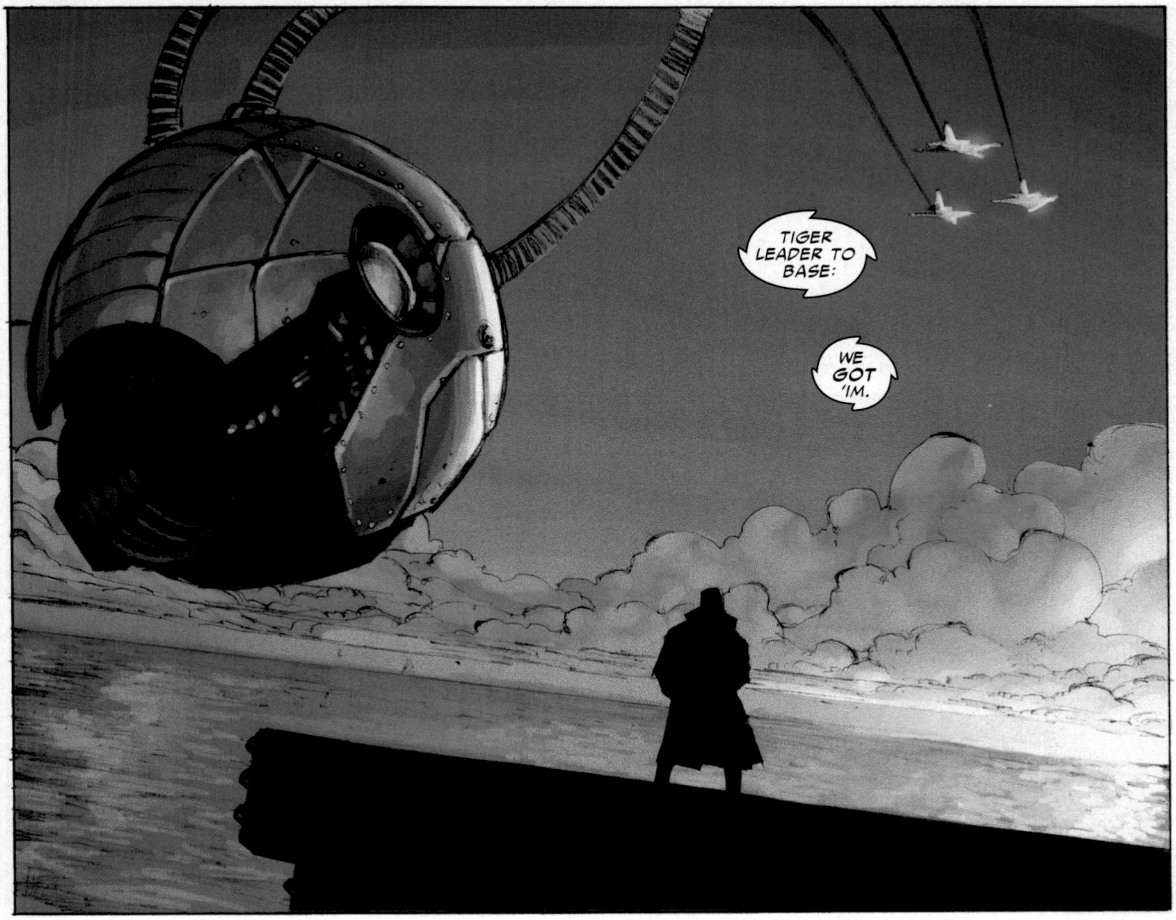
TIGER LEADER TO BASE:
WE GOT 'IM.

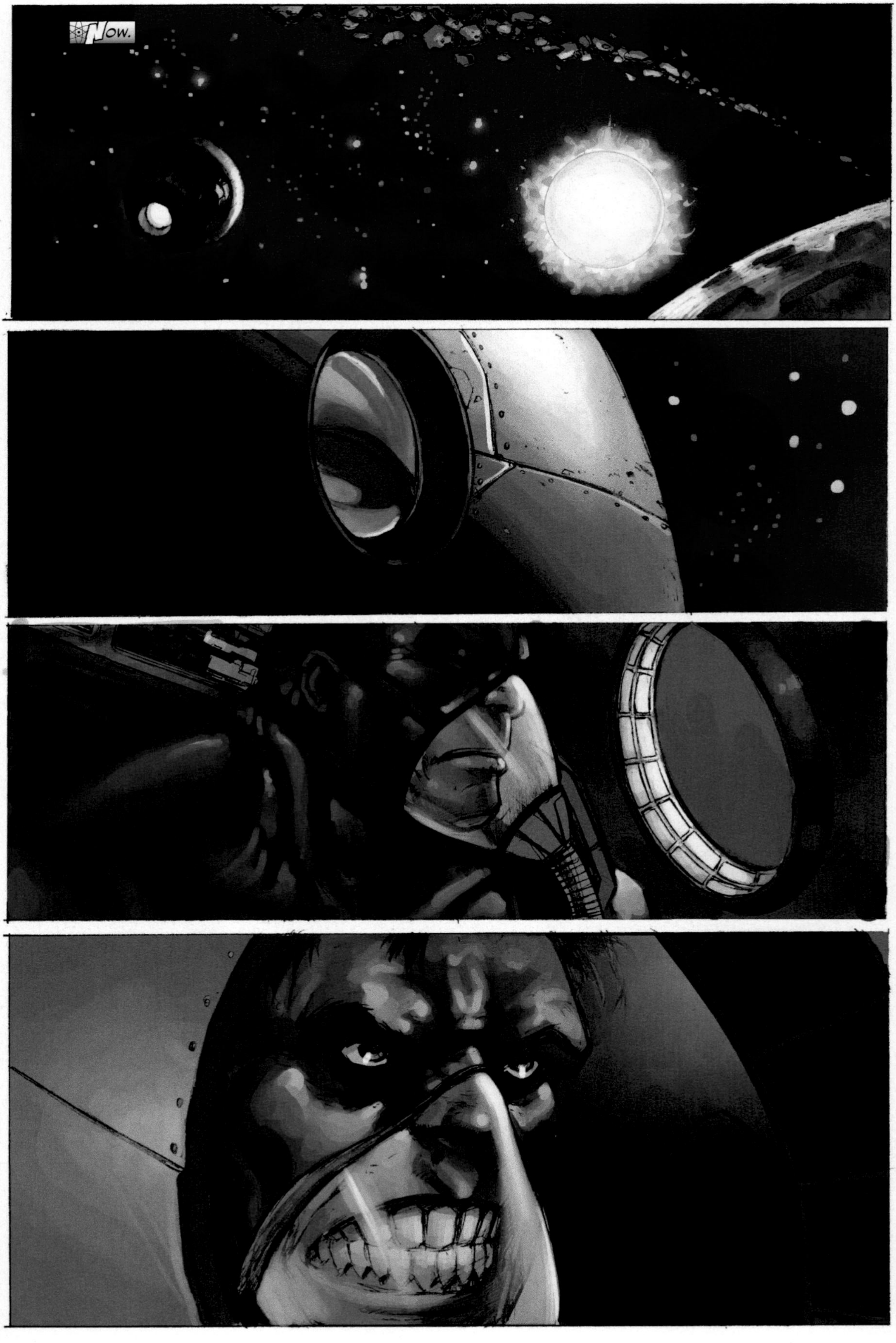
Now.

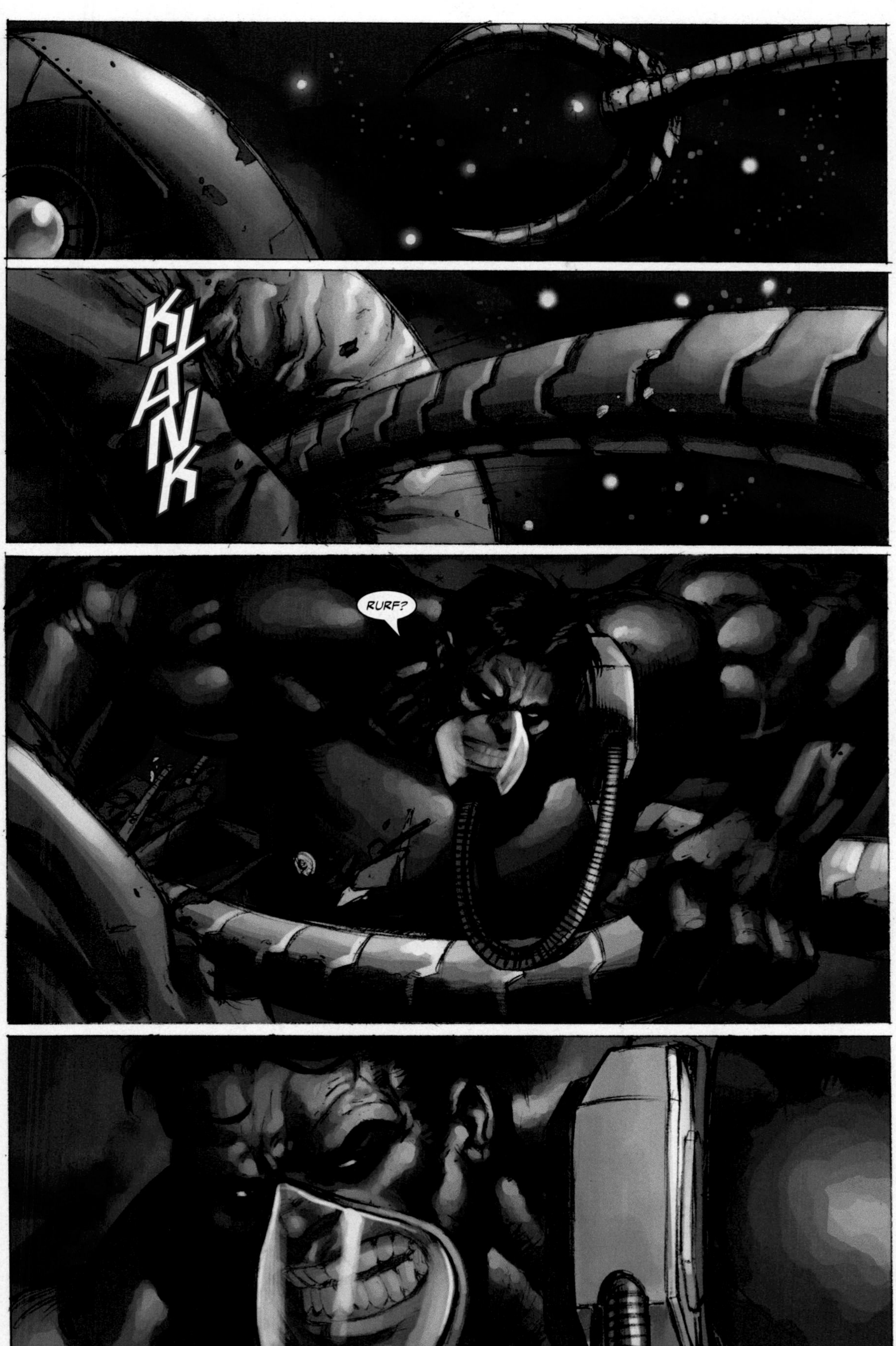
KLANK
RURF?

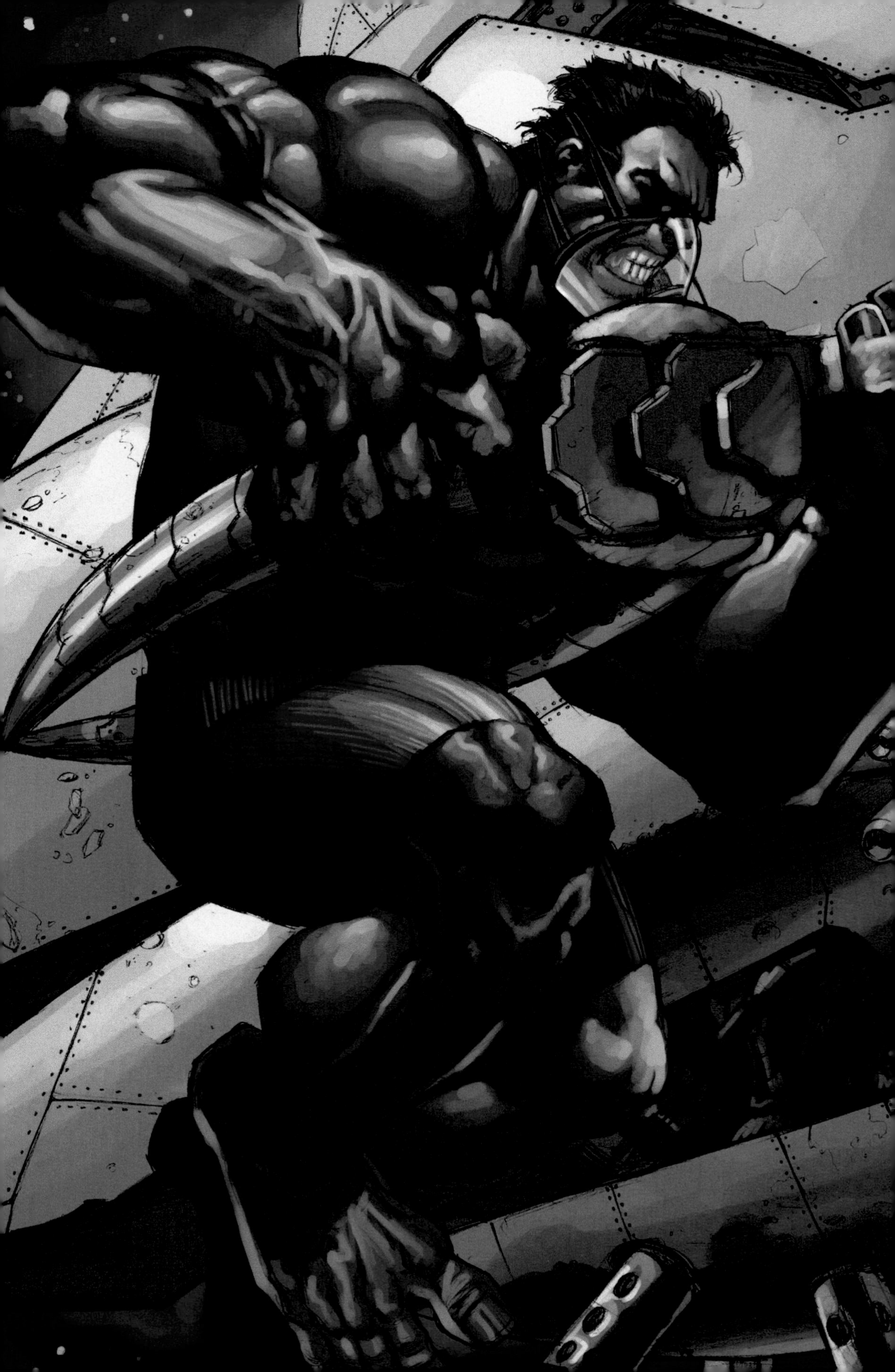

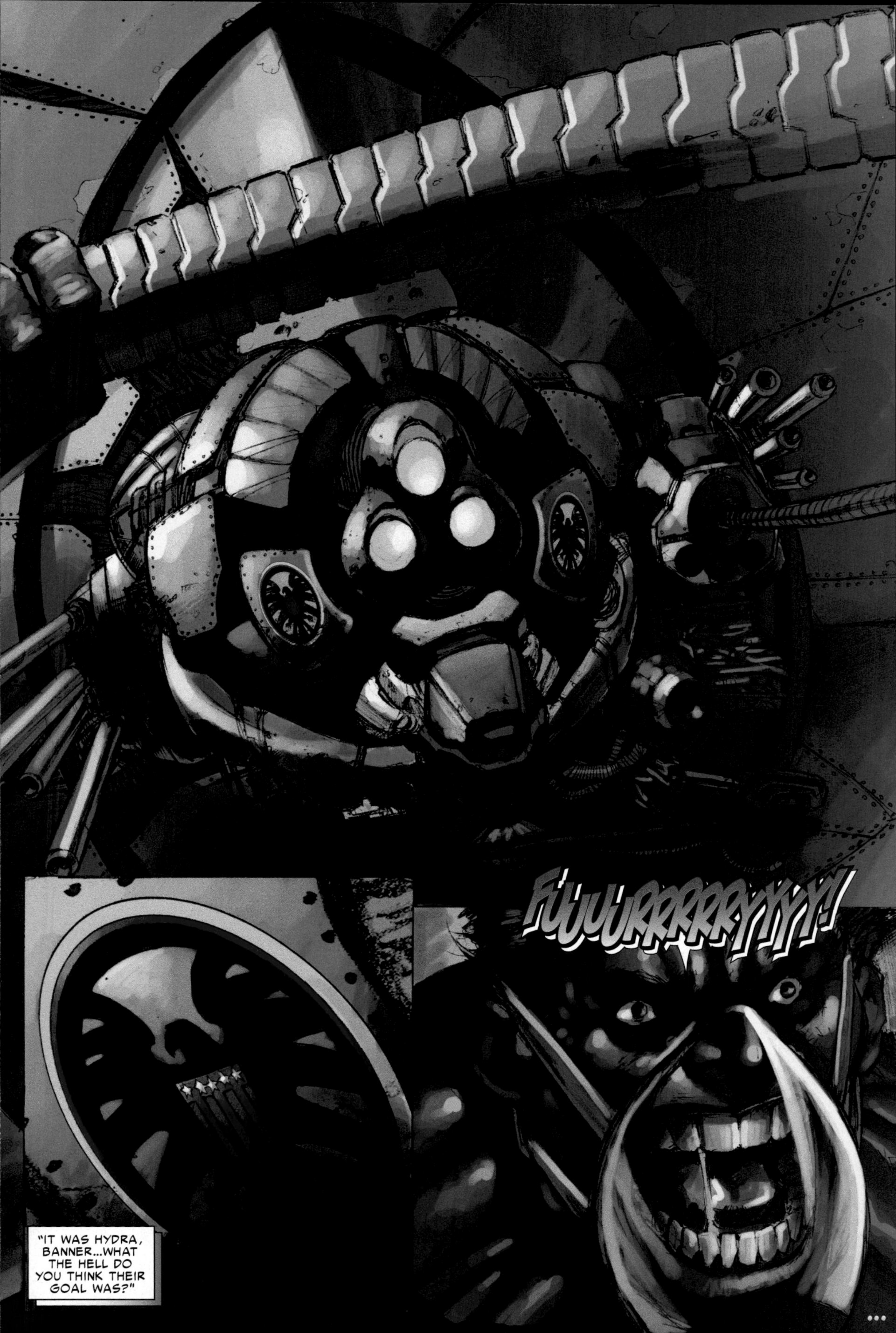
FUUUURRRRRYYYY!
"IT WAS HYDRA, BANNER...WHAT THE HELL DO YOU THINK THEIR GOAL WAS?"

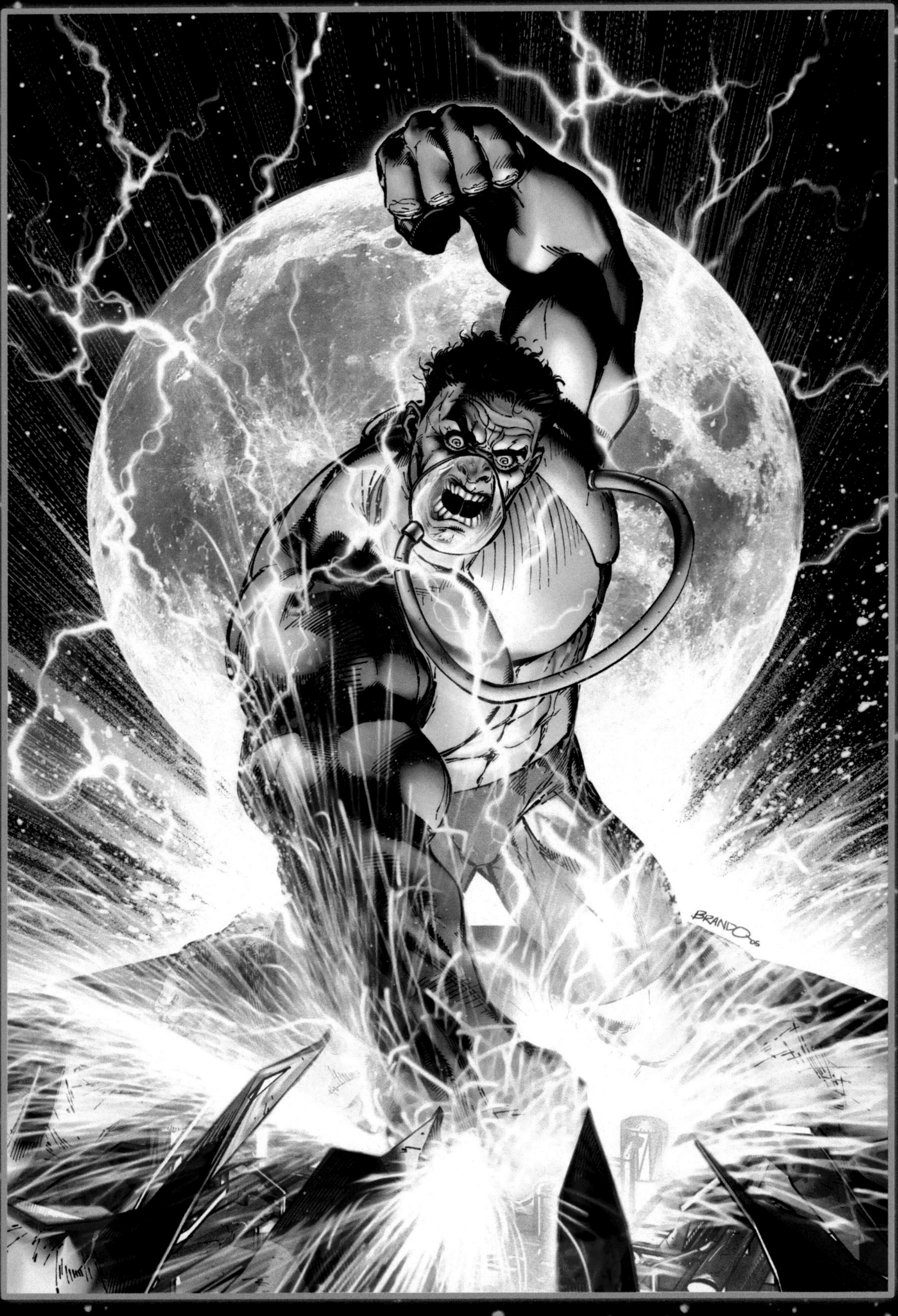
BRANDO '06

INCREDIBLE HULK #90

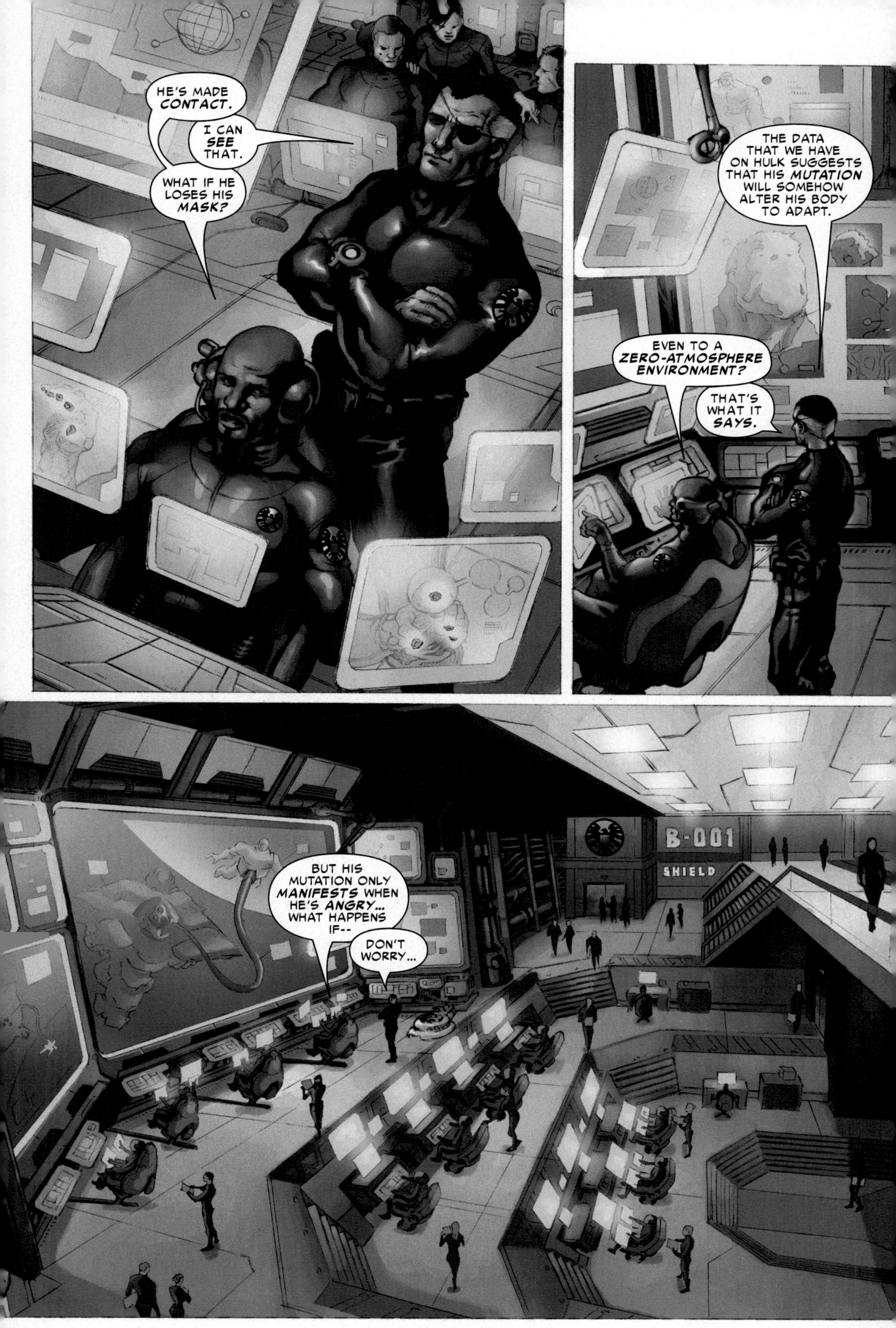
HE'S MADE CONTACT.
I CAN SEE THAT.
WHAT IF HE LOSES HIS MASK?
THE DATA THAT WE HAVE ON HULK SUGGESTS THAT HIS MUTATION WILL SOMEHOW ALTER HIS BODY TO ADAPT.
EVEN TO A ZERO-ATMOSPHERE ENVIRONMENT?
THAT'S WHAT IT SAYS.
B-001
SHIELD
BUT HIS MUTATION ONLY MANIFESTS WHEN HE'S ANGRY... WHAT HAPPENS IF--
DON'T WORRY...

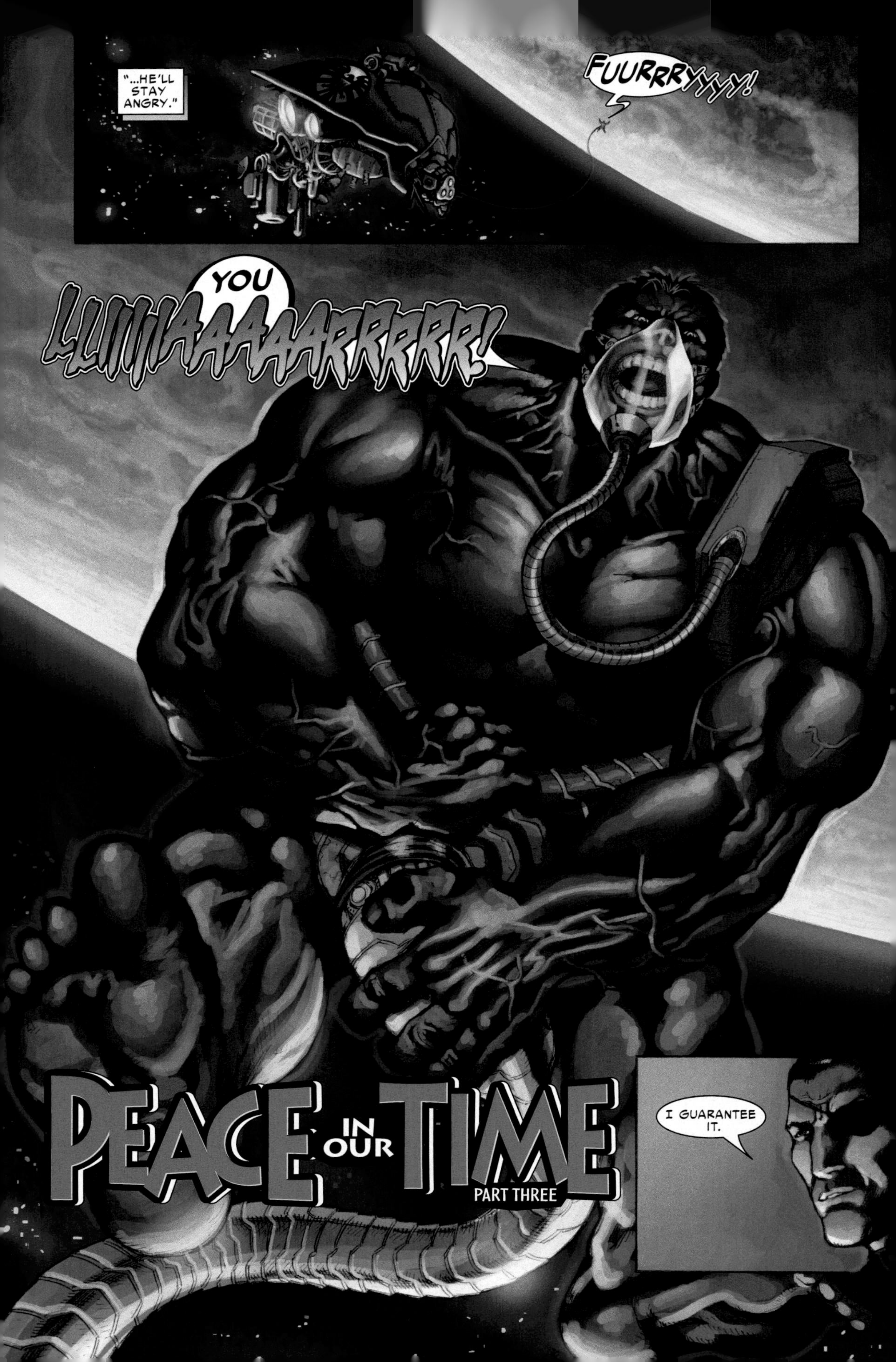
"...HE'LL STAY ANGRY."
FUURRRYYYYY!
YOU LLIIIIAAAAARRRRR!
PEACE IN OUR TIME
PART THREE
I GUARANTEE IT.

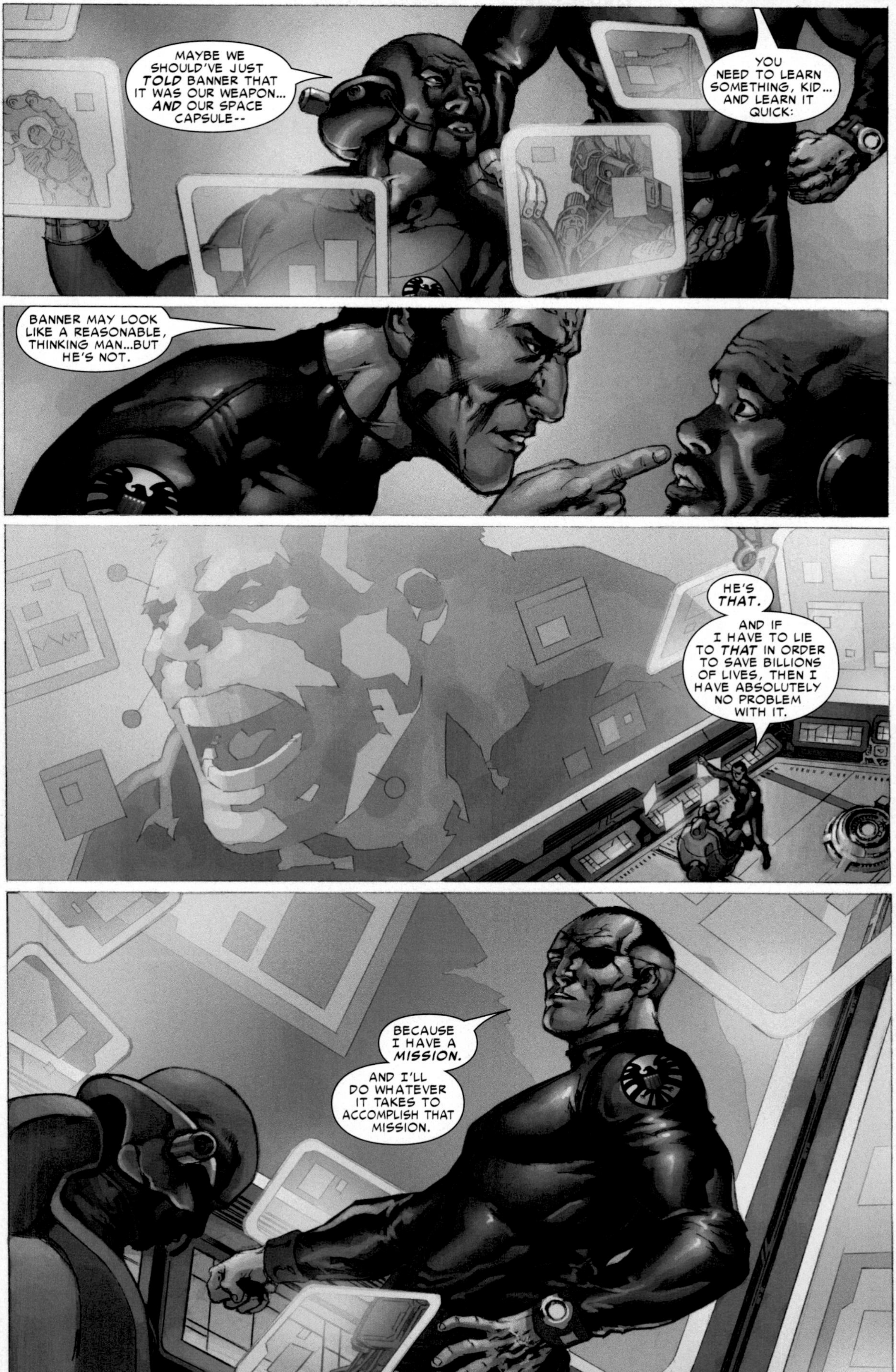
MAYBE WE SHOULD'VE JUST TOLD BANNER THAT IT WAS OUR WEAPON... AND OUR SPACE CAPSULE--
YOU NEED TO LEARN SOMETHING, KID... AND LEARN IT QUICK:
BANNER MAY LOOK LIKE A REASONABLE, THINKING MAN...BUT HE'S NOT.
HE'S THAT.
AND IF I HAVE TO LIE TO THAT IN ORDER TO SAVE BILLIONS OF LIVES, THEN I HAVE ABSOLUTELY NO PROBLEM WITH IT.
BECAUSE I HAVE A MISSION.
AND I'LL DO WHATEVER IT TAKES TO ACCOMPLISH THAT MISSION.

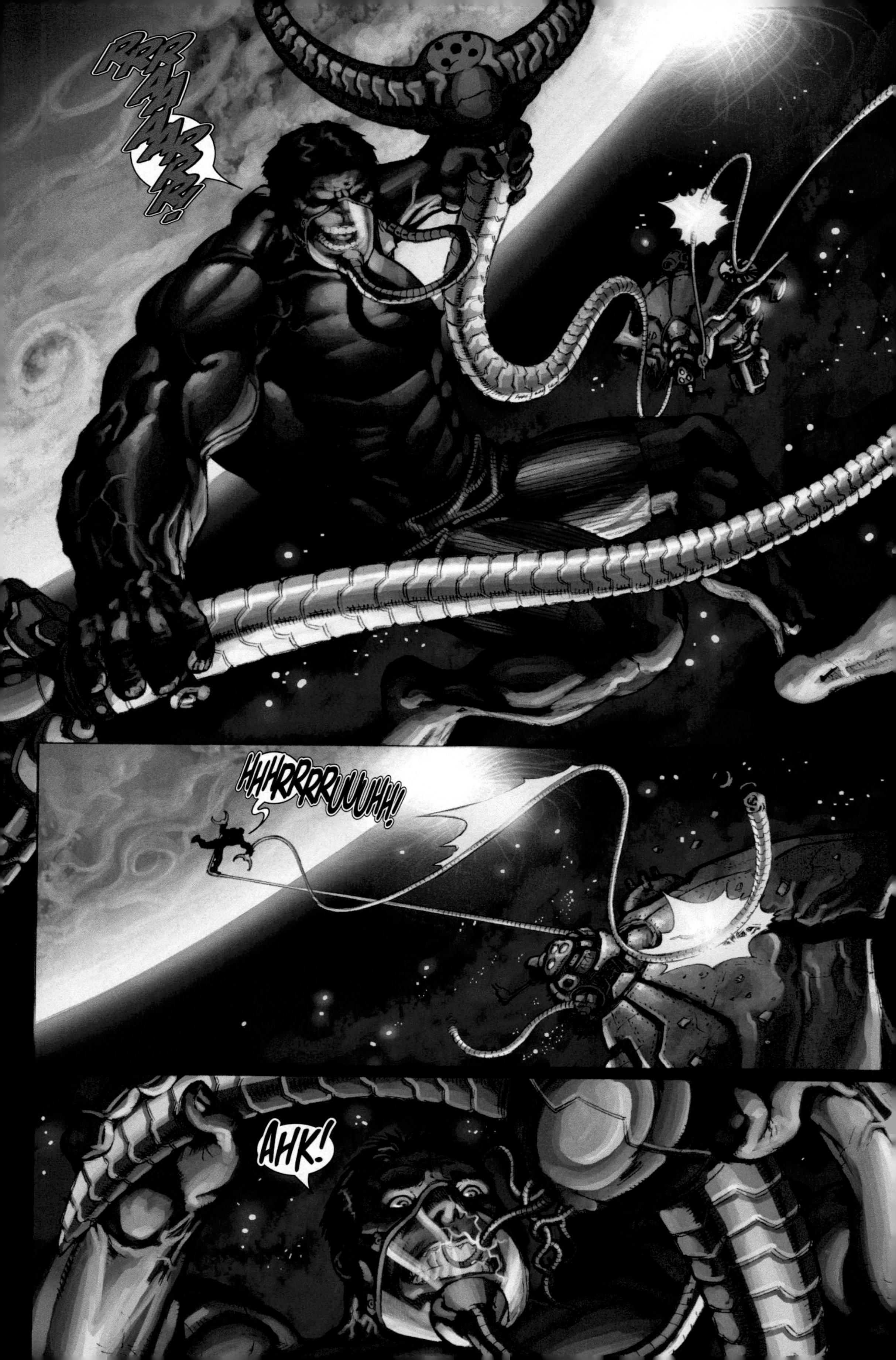
RRRAAAARRGH!
HHHRRRRUUUHH!
AHK!

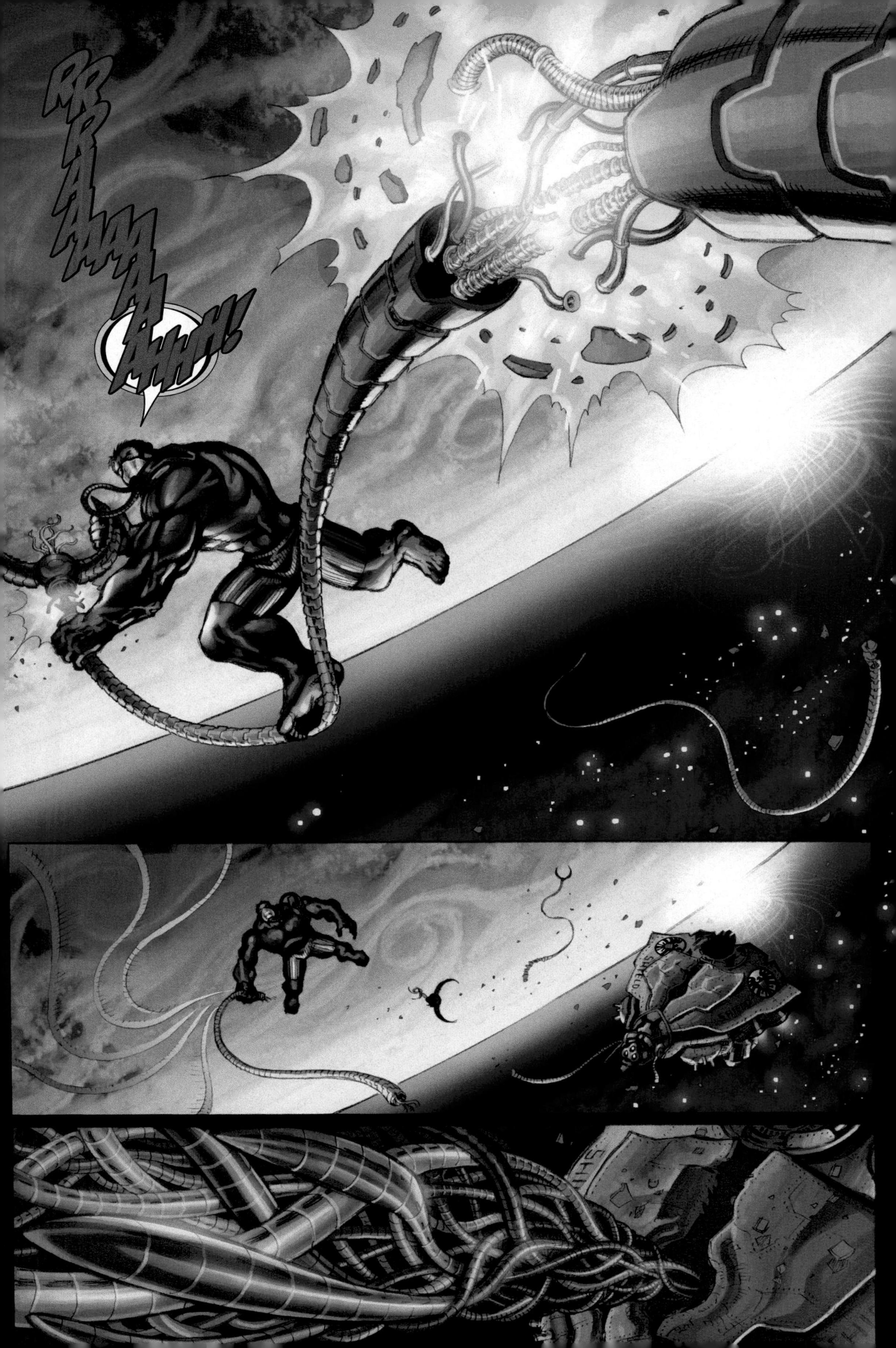
RRRAAAAAAAHHH!

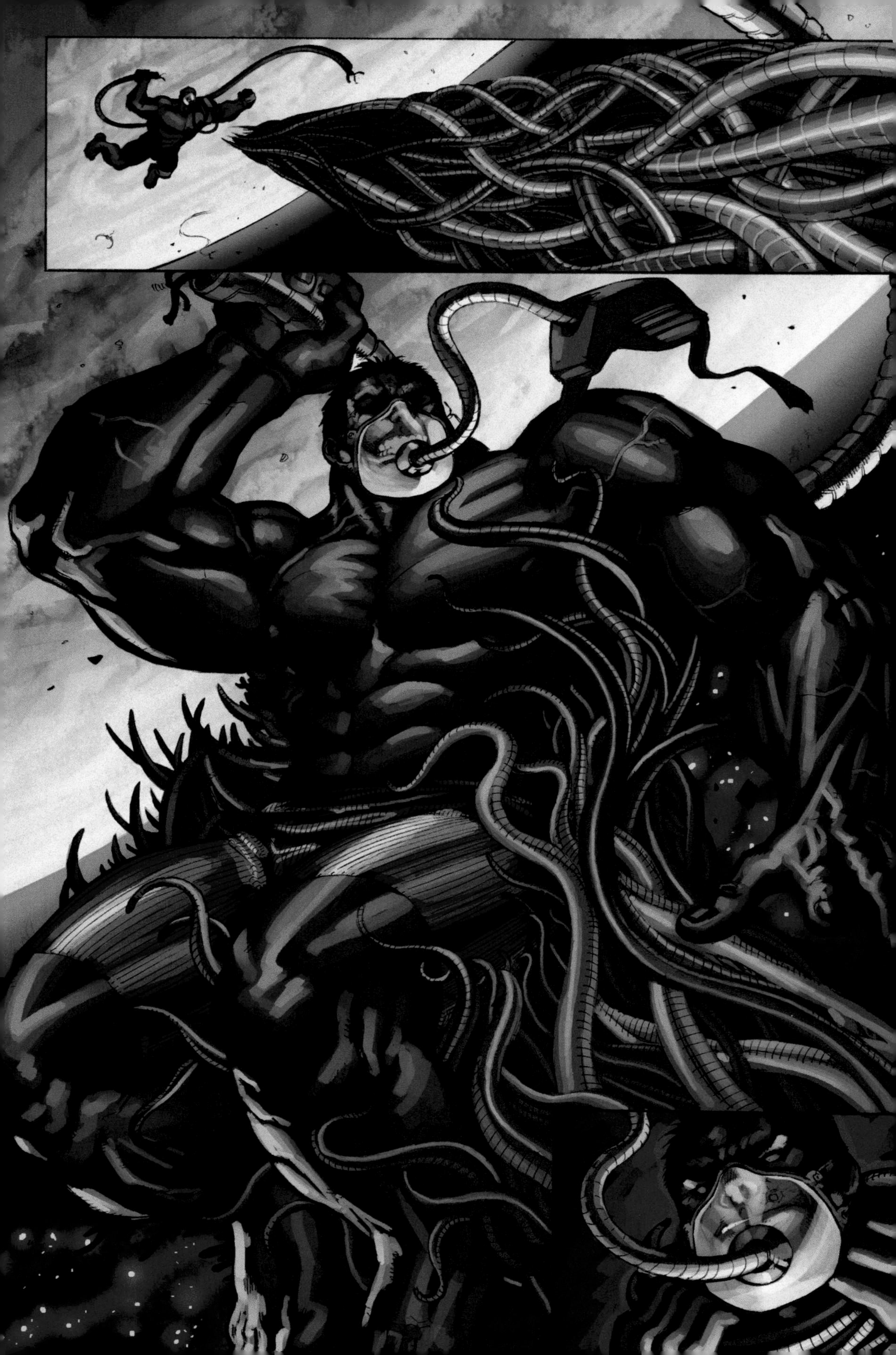

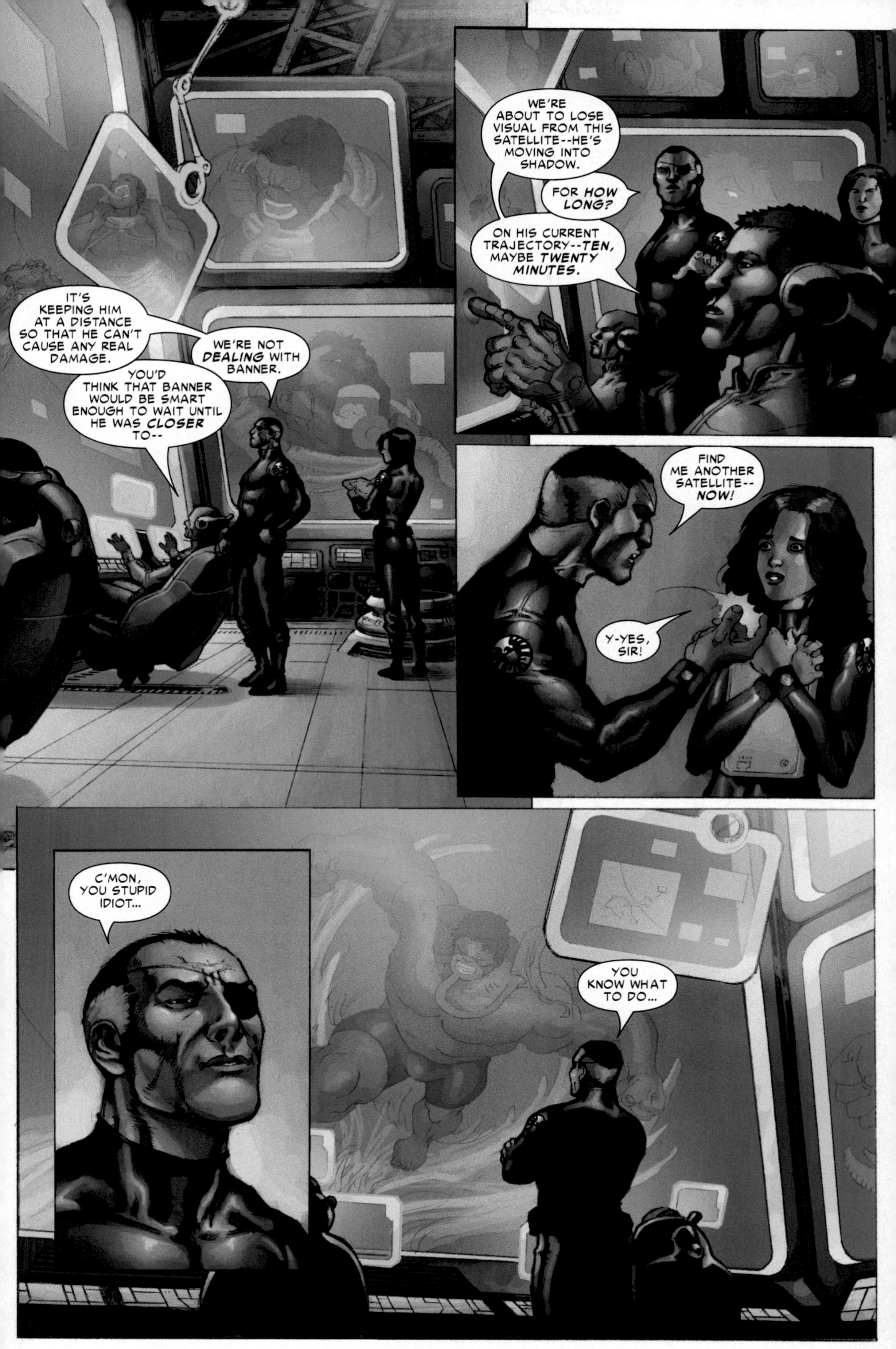
IT'S KEEPING HIM AT A DISTANCE SO THAT HE CAN'T CAUSE ANY REAL DAMAGE.
YOU'D THINK THAT BANNER WOULD BE SMART ENOUGH TO WAIT UNTIL HE WAS CLOSER TO--
WE'RE NOT DEALING WITH BANNER.
WE'RE ABOUT TO LOSE VISUAL FROM THIS SATELLITE--HE'S MOVING INTO SHADOW.
FOR HOW LONG?
ON HIS CURRENT TRAJECTORY--TEN, MAYBE TWENTY MINUTES.
FIND ME ANOTHER SATELLITE--NOW!
Y-YES, SIR!
C'MON, YOU STUPID IDIOT...
YOU KNOW WHAT TO DO...

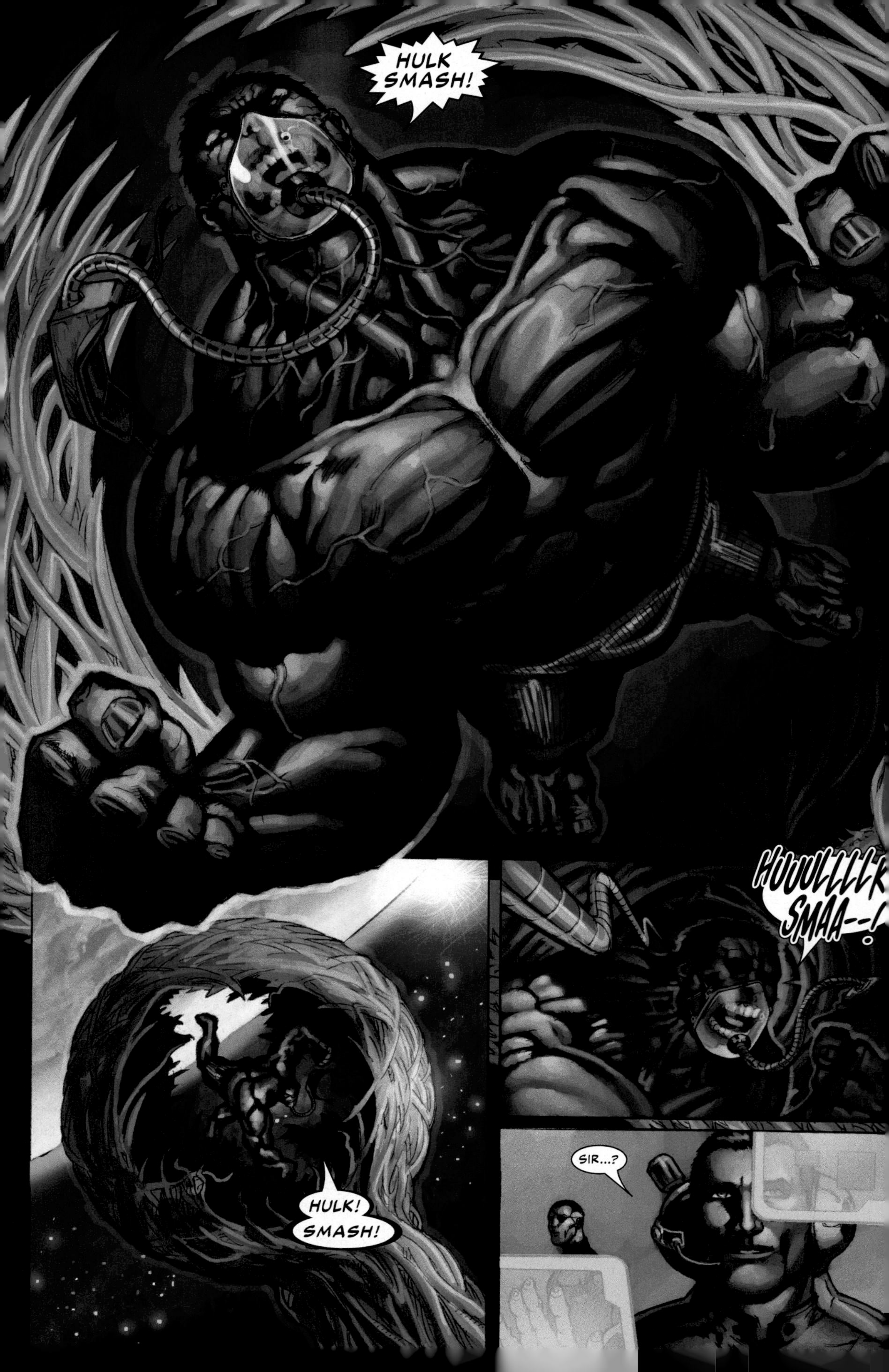
HULK SMASH!
HULK! SMASH!
HOUUULLLLK SMAA--!
SIR...?

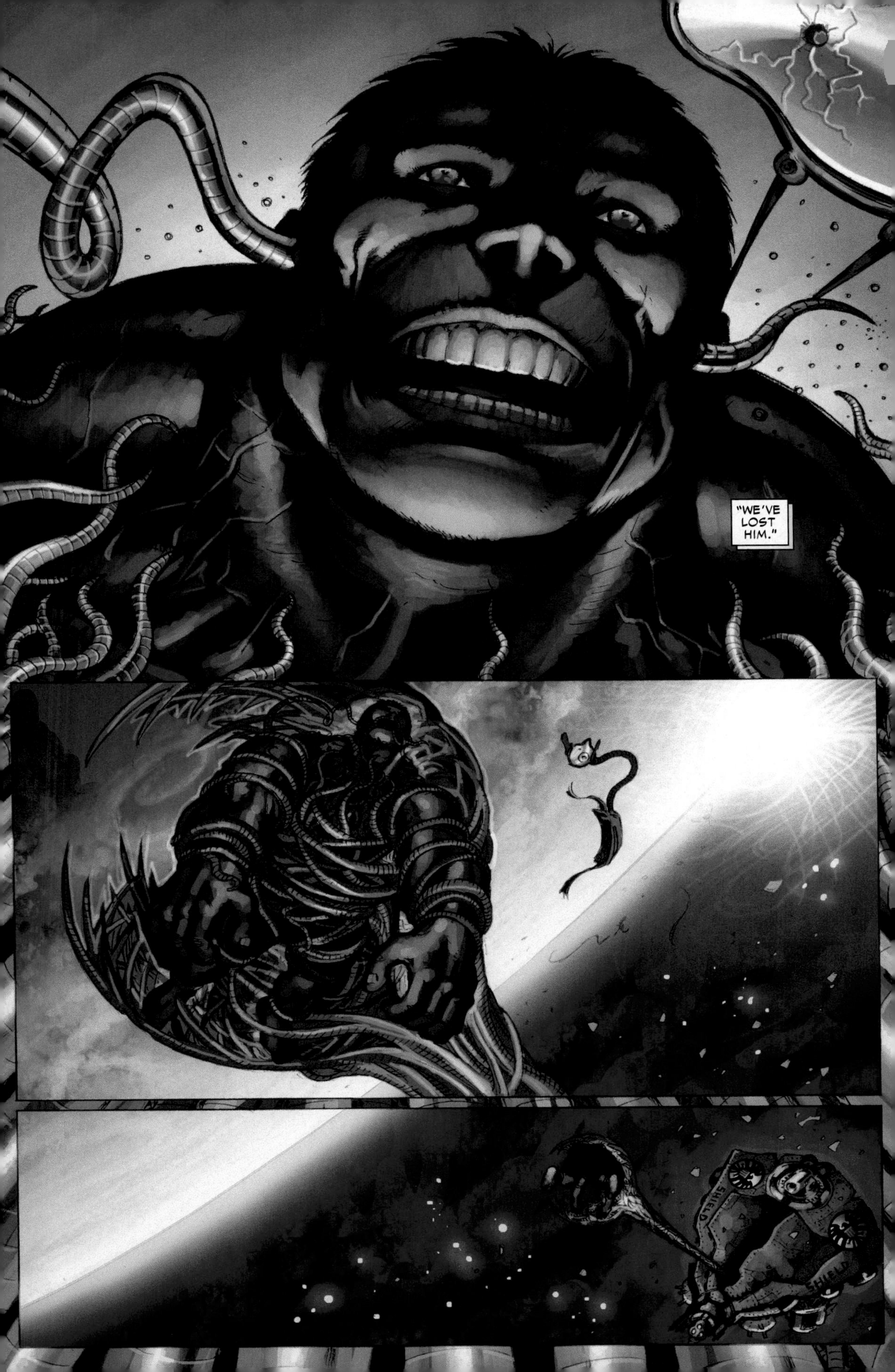
"WE'VE LOST HIM."
SHIELD
SHIELD

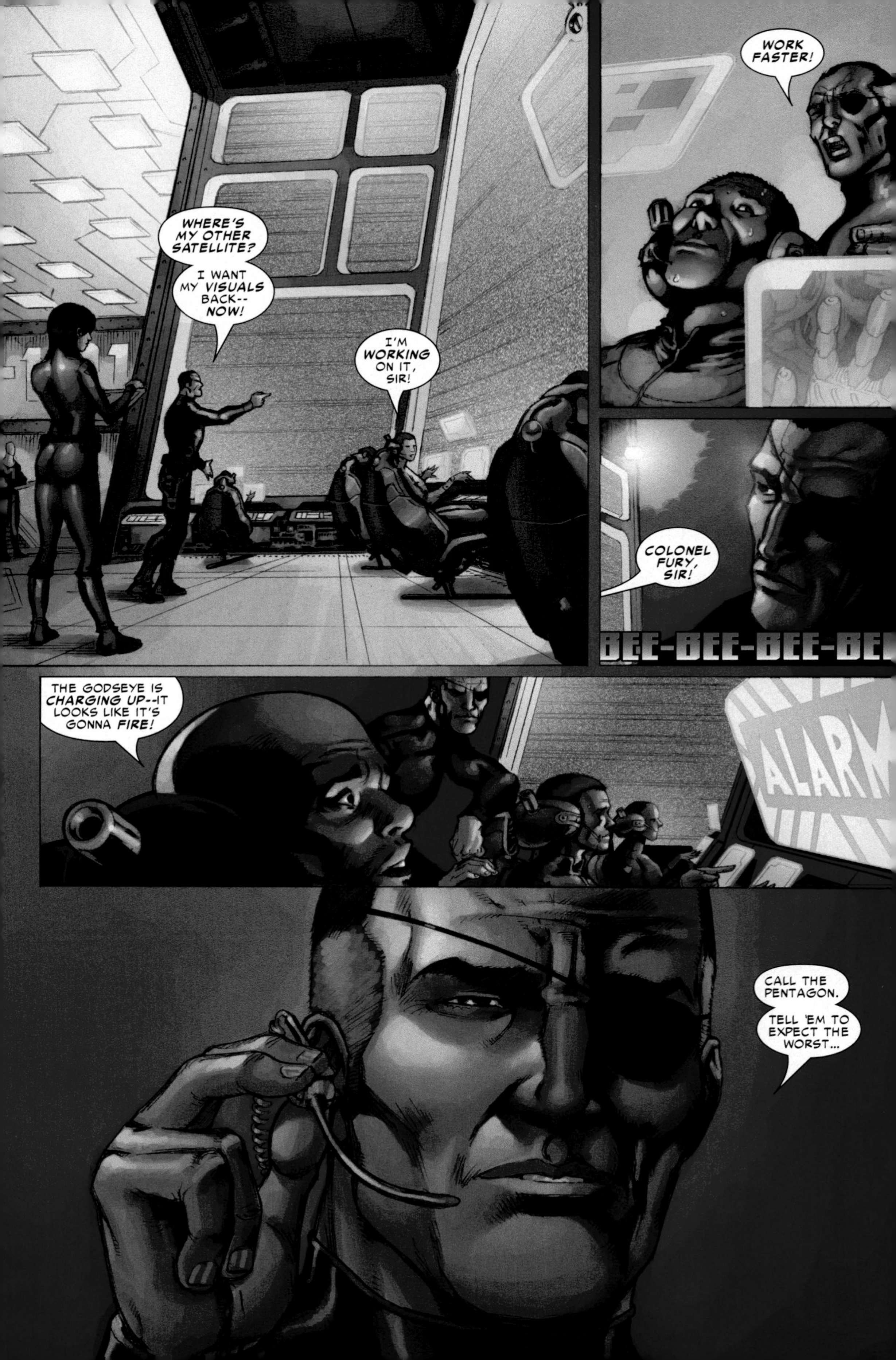
WHERE'S MY OTHER SATELLITE?
I WANT MY VISUALS BACK-- NOW!
I'M WORKING ON IT, SIR!
WORK FASTER!
COLONEL FURY, SIR!
BEE-BEE-BEE-BE
THE GODSEYE IS CHARGING UP--IT LOOKS LIKE IT'S GONNA FIRE!
ALARM
CALL THE PENTAGON.
TELL 'EM TO EXPECT THE WORST...

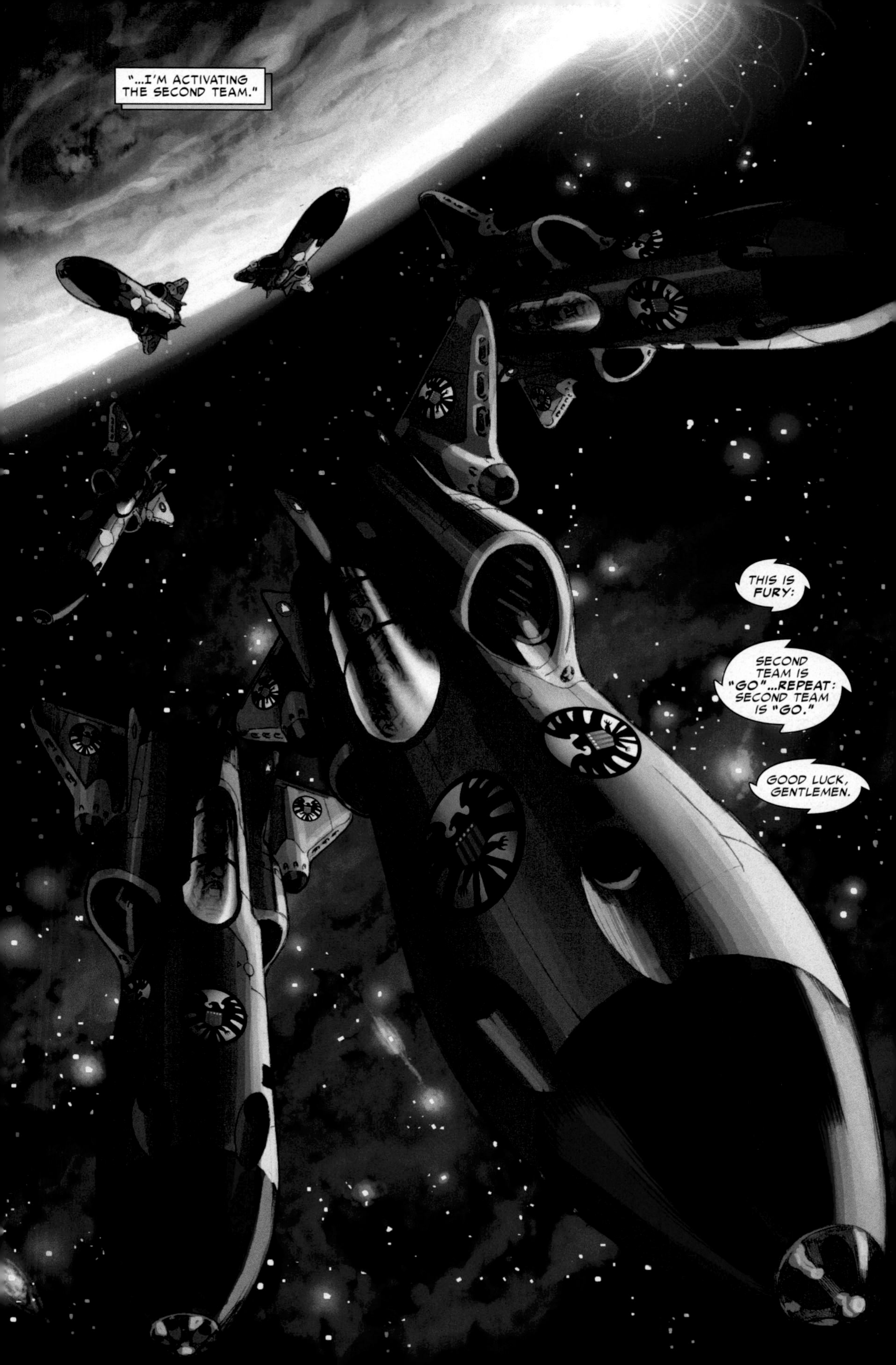
"...I'M ACTIVATING THE SECOND TEAM."
THIS IS FURY:
SECOND TEAM IS "GO"...REPEAT: SECOND TEAM IS "GO."
GOOD LUCK, GENTLEMEN.

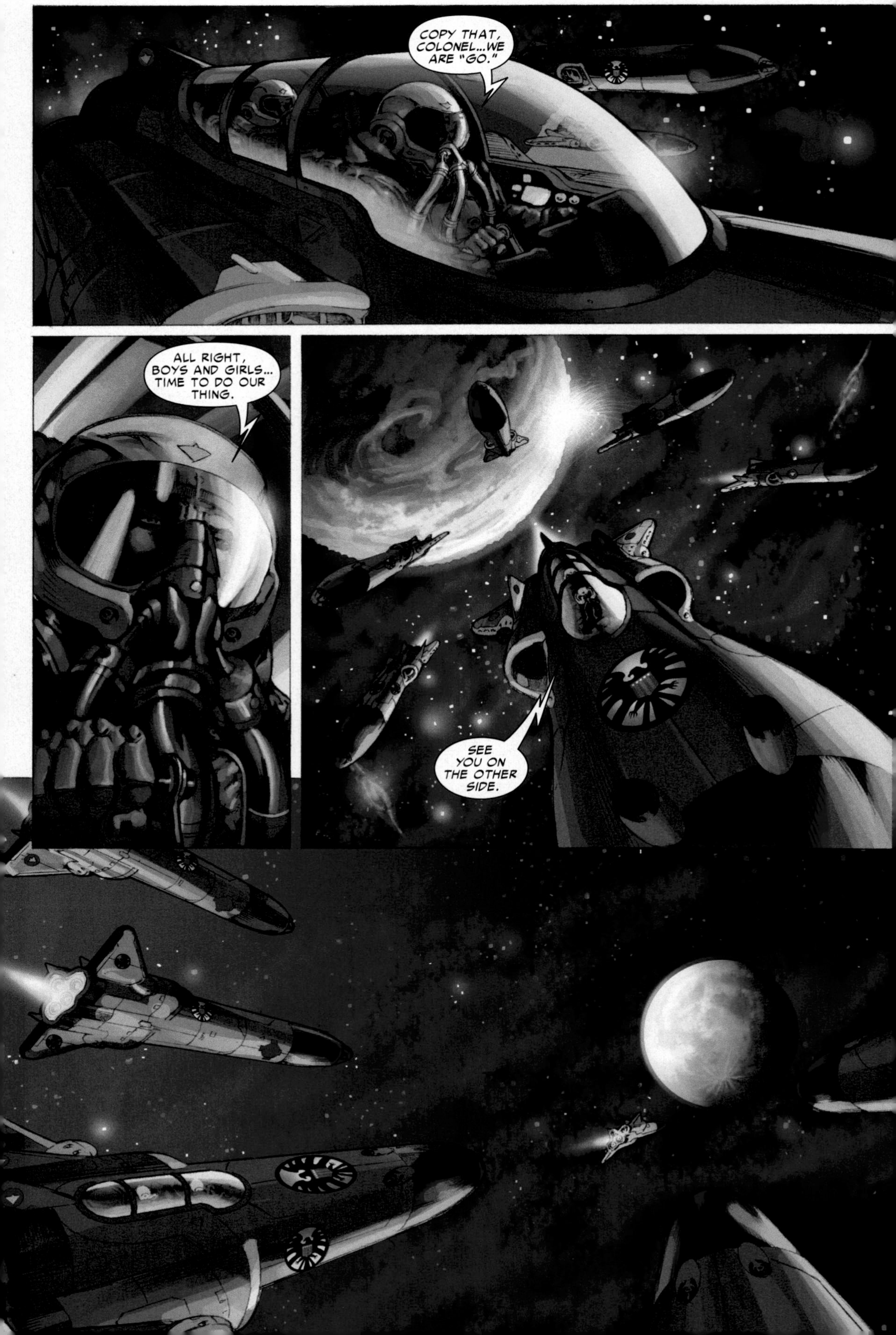
COPY THAT, COLONEL...WE ARE "GO."
ALL RIGHT, BOYS AND GIRLS... TIME TO DO OUR THING.
SEE YOU ON THE OTHER SIDE.

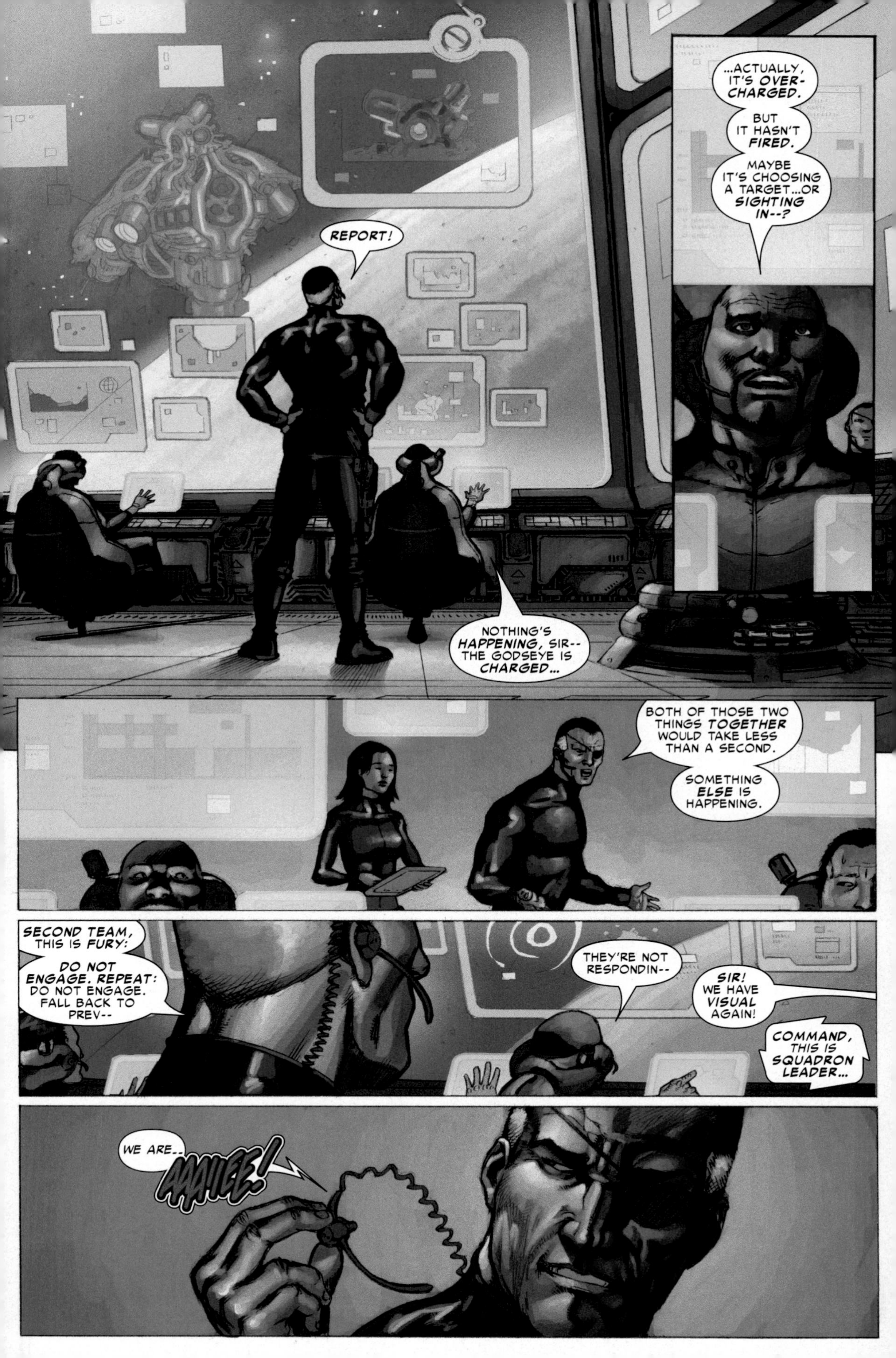
REPORT!
...ACTUALLY, IT'S OVER-CHARGED.
BUT IT HASN'T FIRED.
MAYBE IT'S CHOOSING A TARGET...OR SIGHTING IN--?
NOTHING'S HAPPENING, SIR-- THE GODSEYE IS CHARGED...
BOTH OF THOSE TWO THINGS TOGETHER WOULD TAKE LESS THAN A SECOND.
SOMETHING ELSE IS HAPPENING.
SECOND TEAM, THIS IS FURY:
DO NOT ENGAGE. REPEAT: DO NOT ENGAGE. FALL BACK TO PREV--
THEY'RE NOT RESPONDIN--
SIR! WE HAVE VISUAL AGAIN!
COMMAND, THIS IS SQUADRON LEADER...
WE ARE--
AAAIIEE!

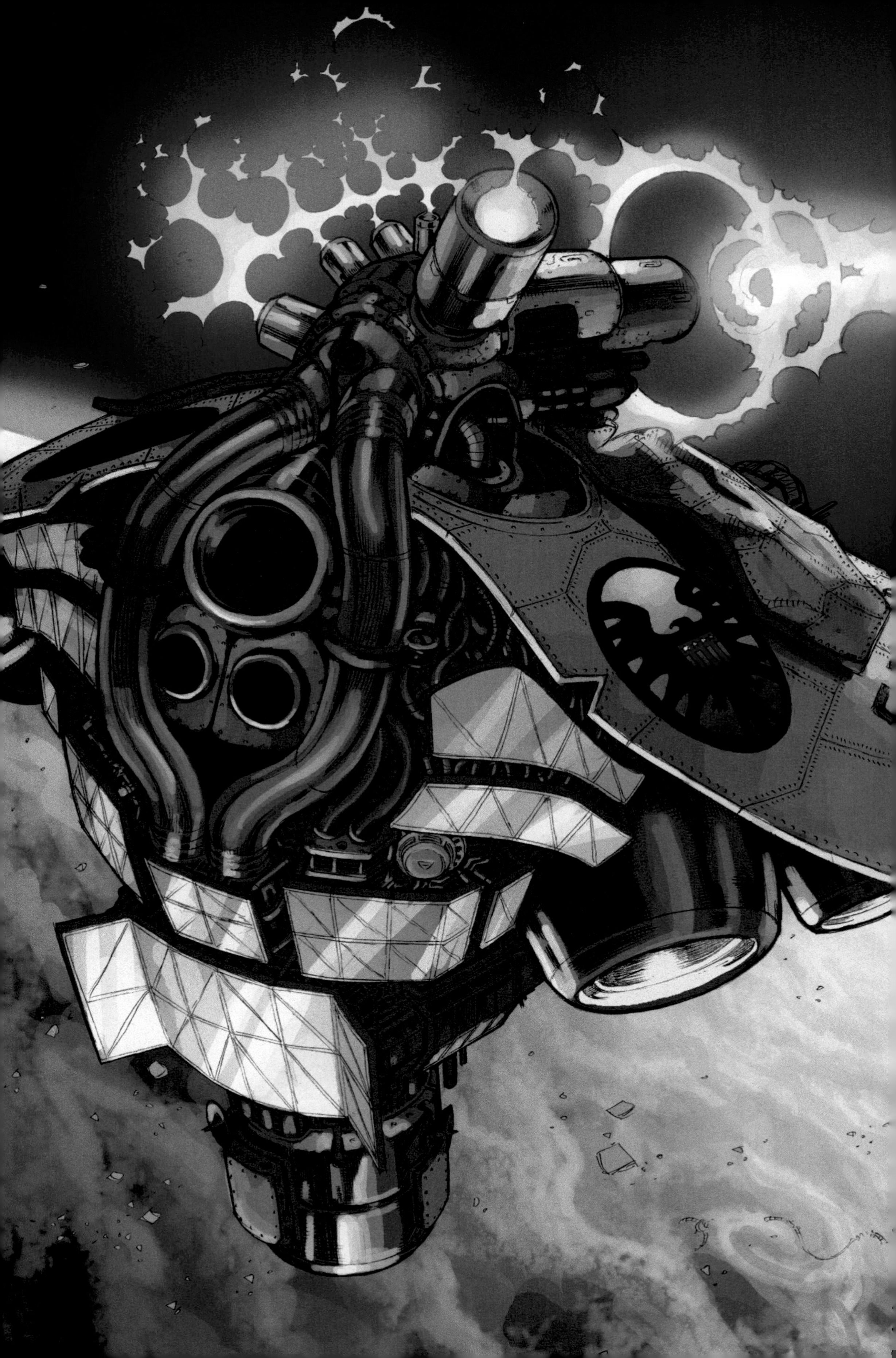

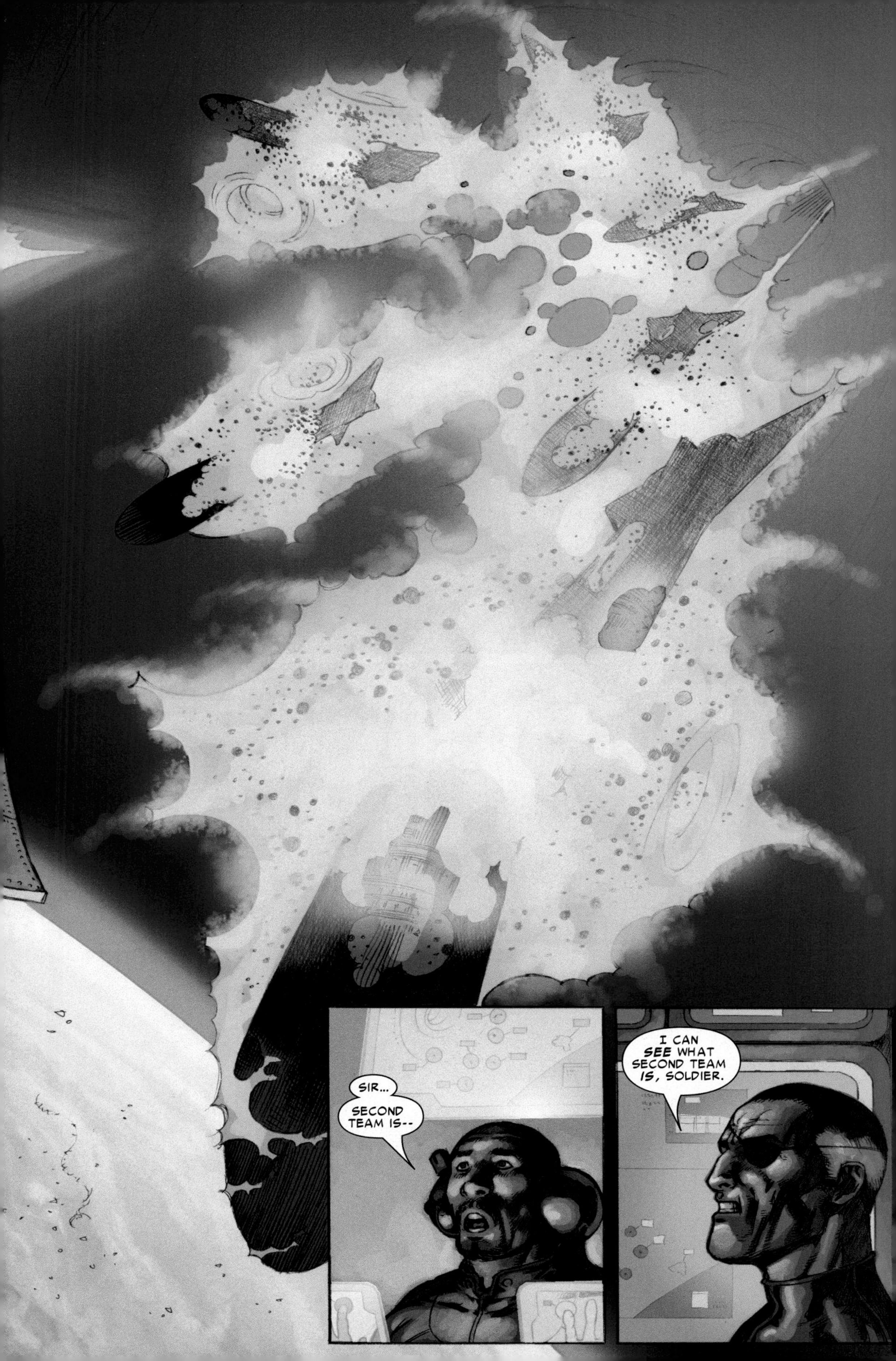
SIR... SECOND TEAM IS--
I CAN SEE WHAT SECOND TEAM IS, SOLDIER.

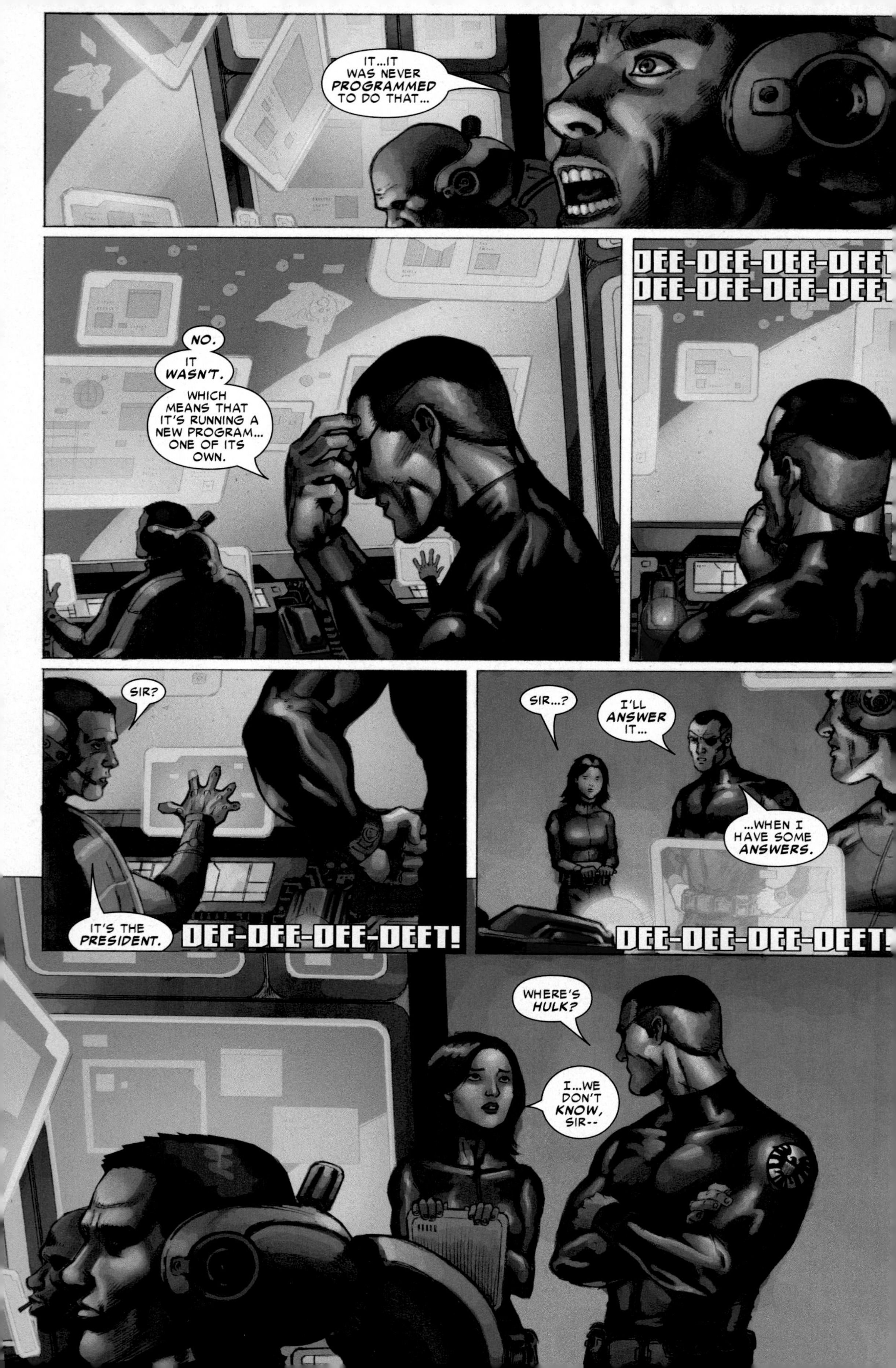
IT...IT WAS NEVER PROGRAMMED TO DO THAT...
NO.
IT WASN'T.
WHICH MEANS THAT IT'S RUNNING A NEW PROGRAM... ONE OF ITS OWN.
DEE-DEE-DEE-DEET
DEE-DEE-DEE-DEET
SIR?
IT'S THE PRESIDENT.
DEE-DEE-DEE-DEET!
SIR...?
I'LL ANSWER IT...
...WHEN I HAVE SOME ANSWERS.
DEE-DEE-DEE-DEET!
WHERE'S HULK?
I...WE DON'T KNOW, SIR--

"--HE'S DISAPPEARED."

HRNN...

NNNAAAH!

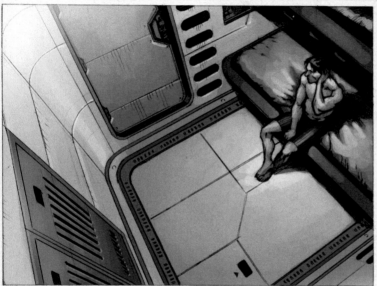

"SIR? WE HAVE ANOTHER PROBLEM."

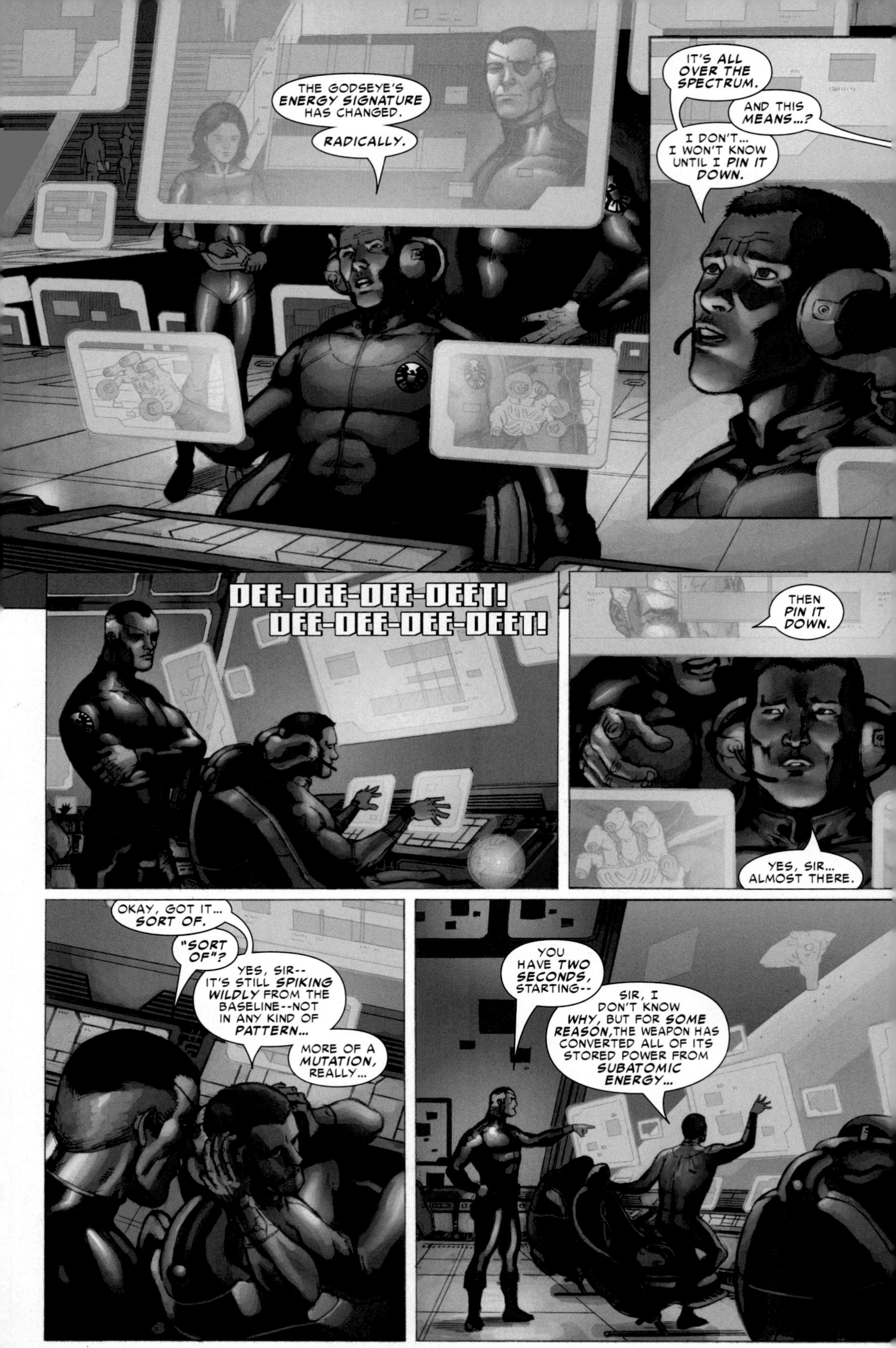
THE GODSEYE'S ENERGY SIGNATURE HAS CHANGED.
RADICALLY.
IT'S ALL OVER THE SPECTRUM.
AND THIS MEANS...?
I DON'T... I WON'T KNOW UNTIL I PIN IT DOWN.
DEE-DEE-DEE-DEET! DEE-DEE-DEE-DEET!
THEN PIN IT DOWN.
YES, SIR... ALMOST THERE.
OKAY, GOT IT... SORT OF.
"SORT OF"?
YES, SIR-- IT'S STILL SPIKING WILDLY FROM THE BASELINE--NOT IN ANY KIND OF PATTERN...
MORE OF A MUTATION, REALLY...
YOU HAVE TWO SECONDS, STARTING--
SIR, I DON'T KNOW WHY, BUT FOR SOME REASON, THE WEAPON HAS CONVERTED ALL OF ITS STORED POWER FROM SUBATOMIC ENERGY...

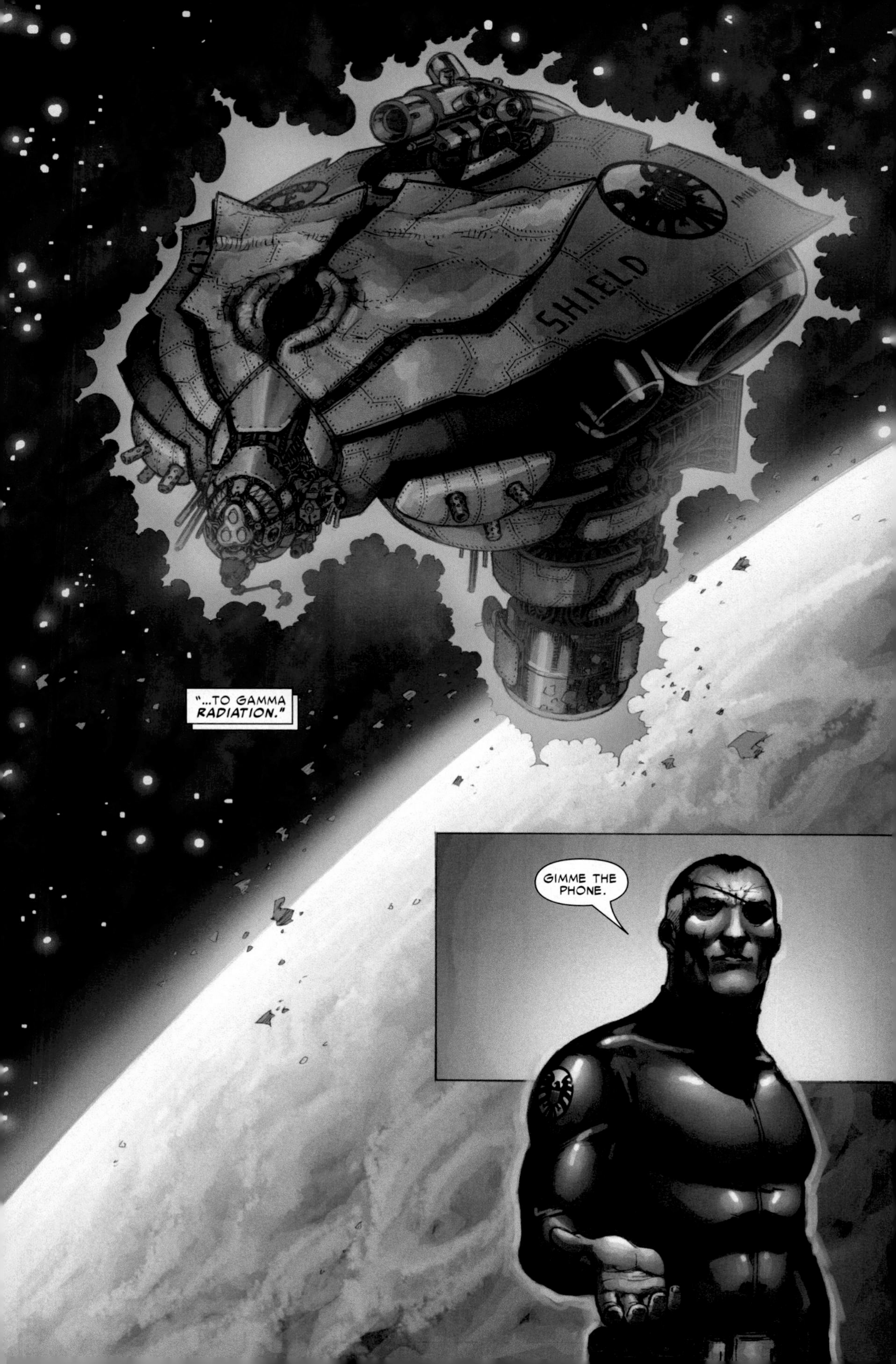
S.H.I.E.L.D
"...TO GAMMA RADIATION."
GIMME THE PHONE.

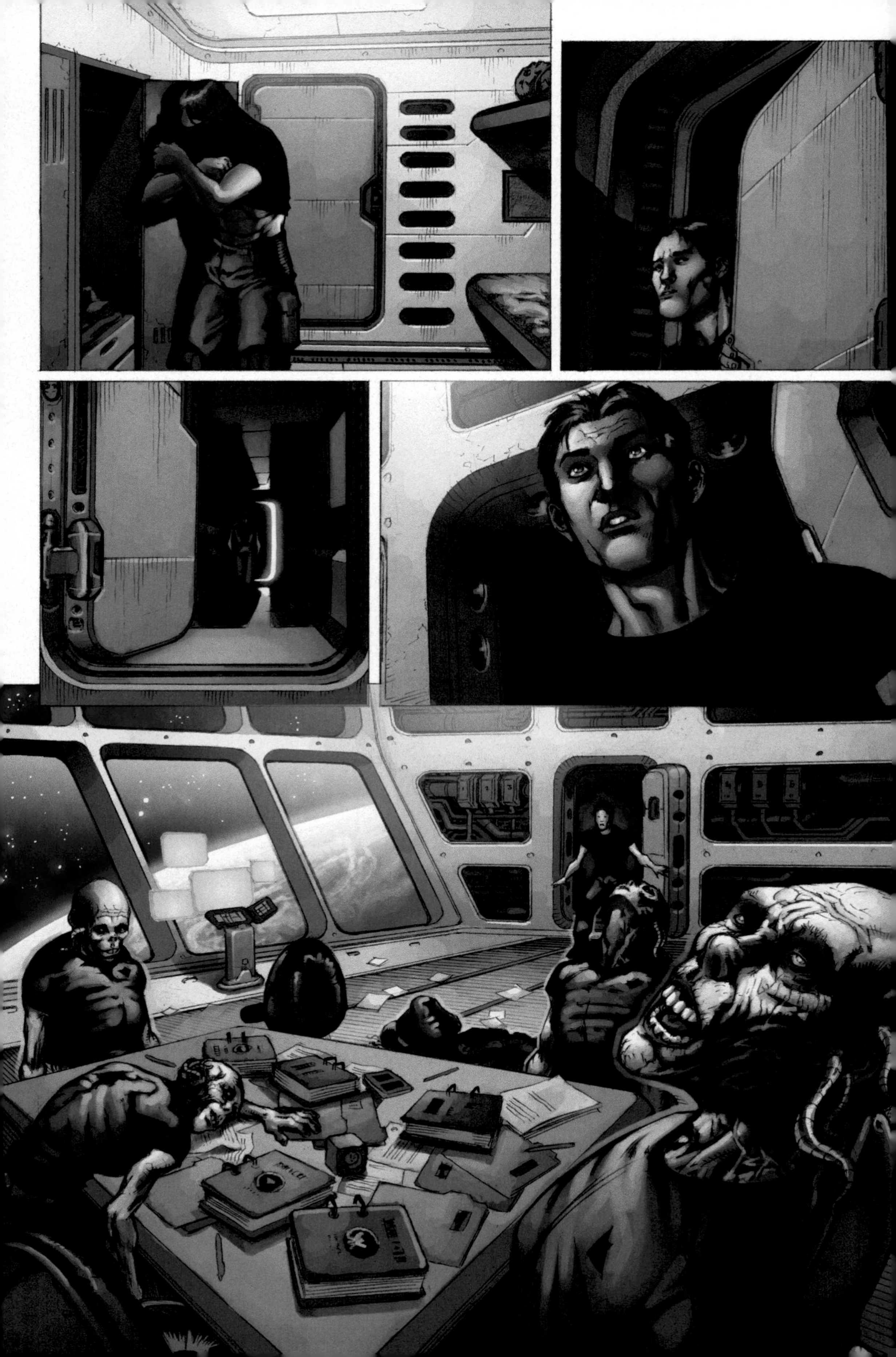

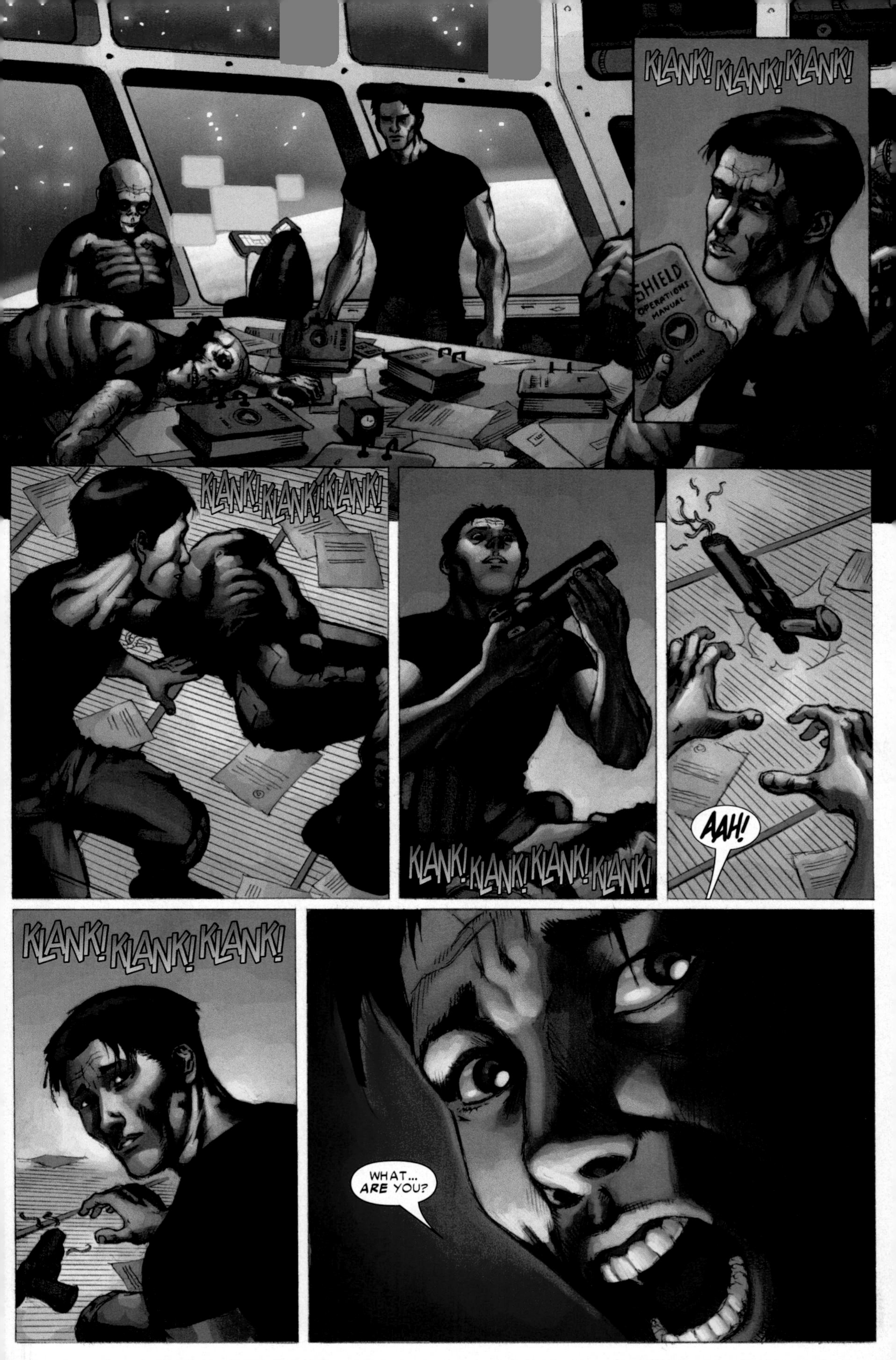
KLANK! KLANK! KLANK!
SHIELD OPERATIONS MANUAL
KLANK! KLANK! KLANK!
KLANK! KLANK! KLANK! KLANK!
AAH!
KLANK! KLANK! KLANK!
WHAT... ARE YOU?

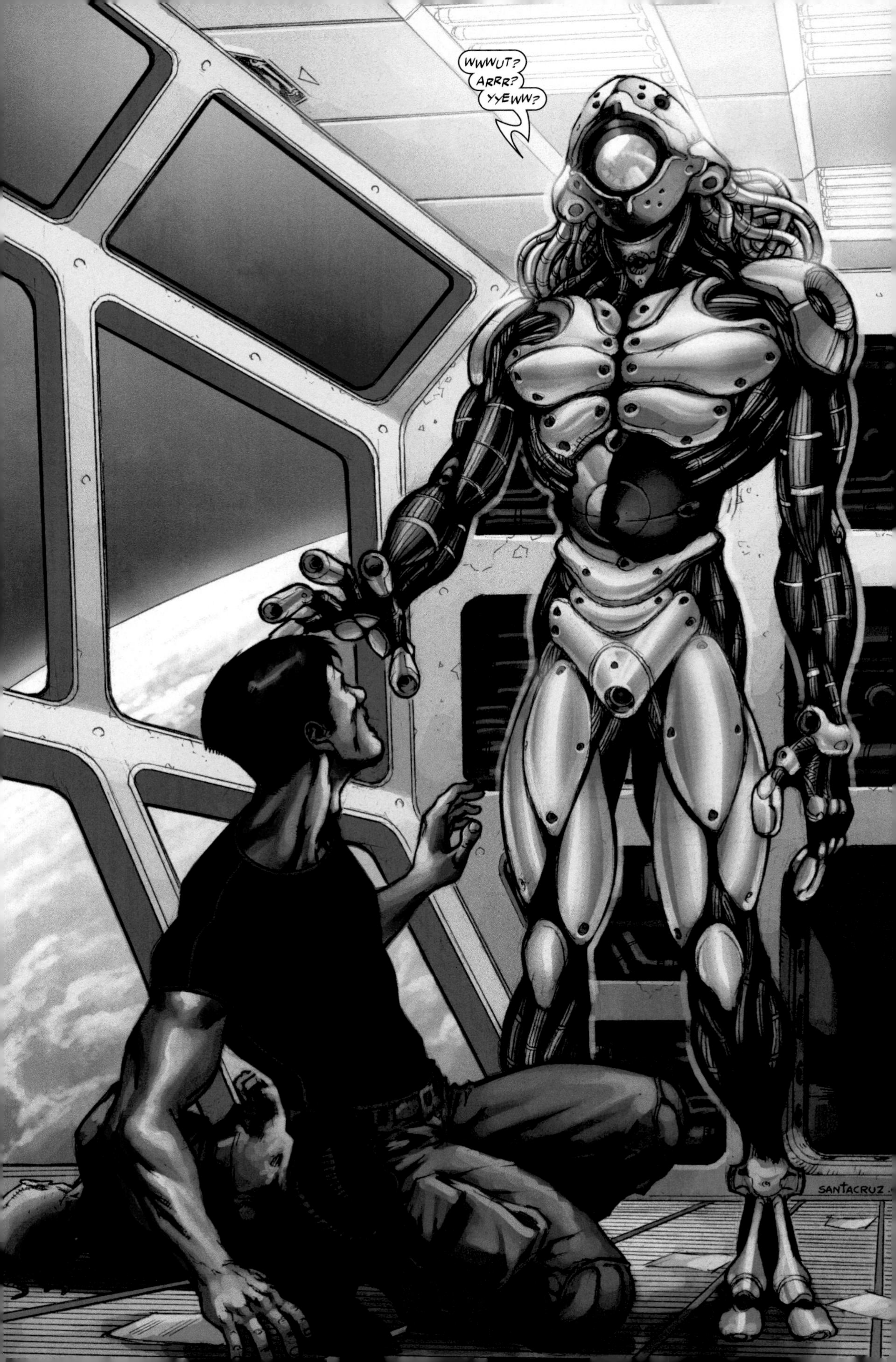
WWWUT? ARRR? YYEWW?
SANTACRUZ

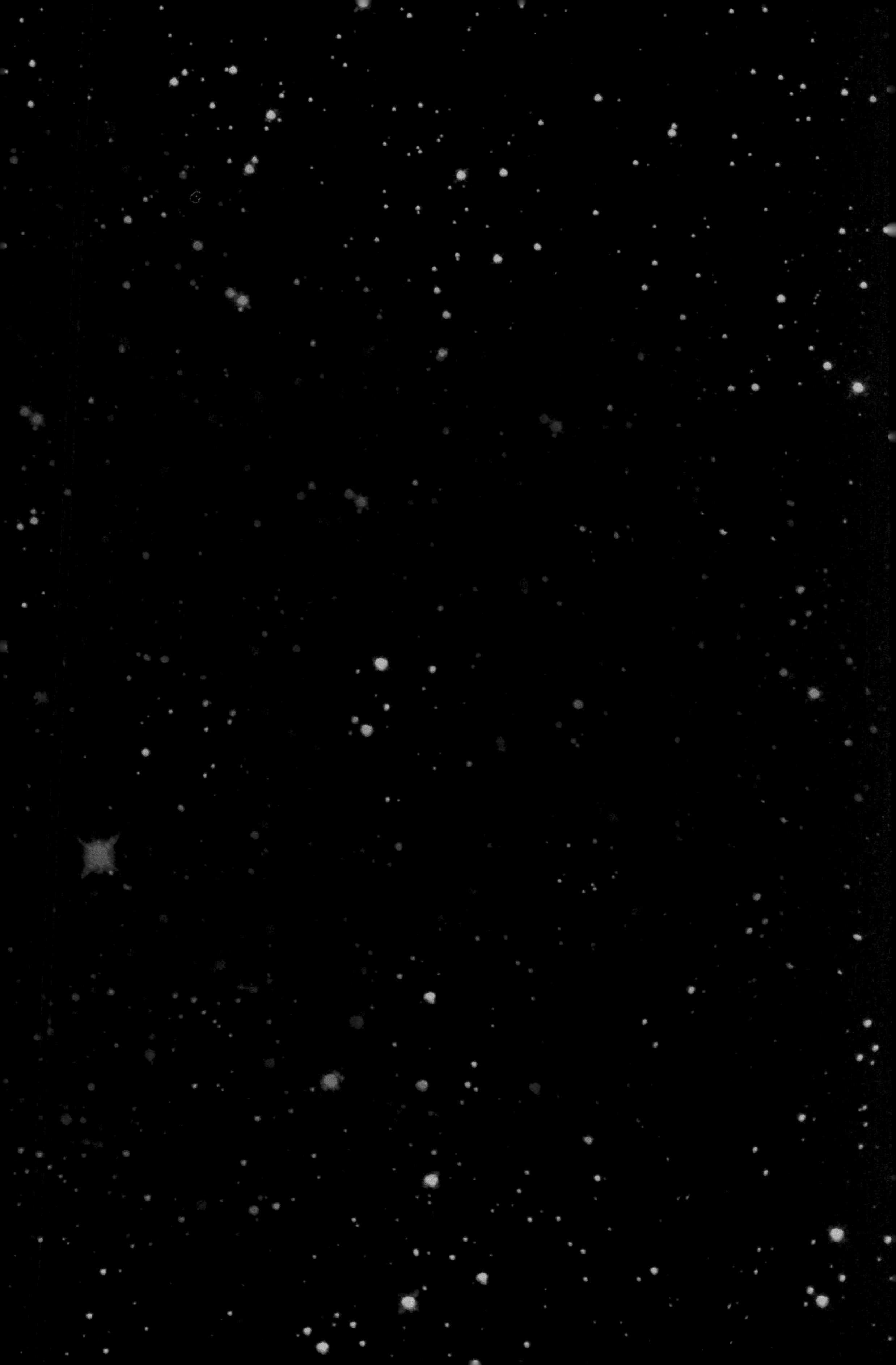

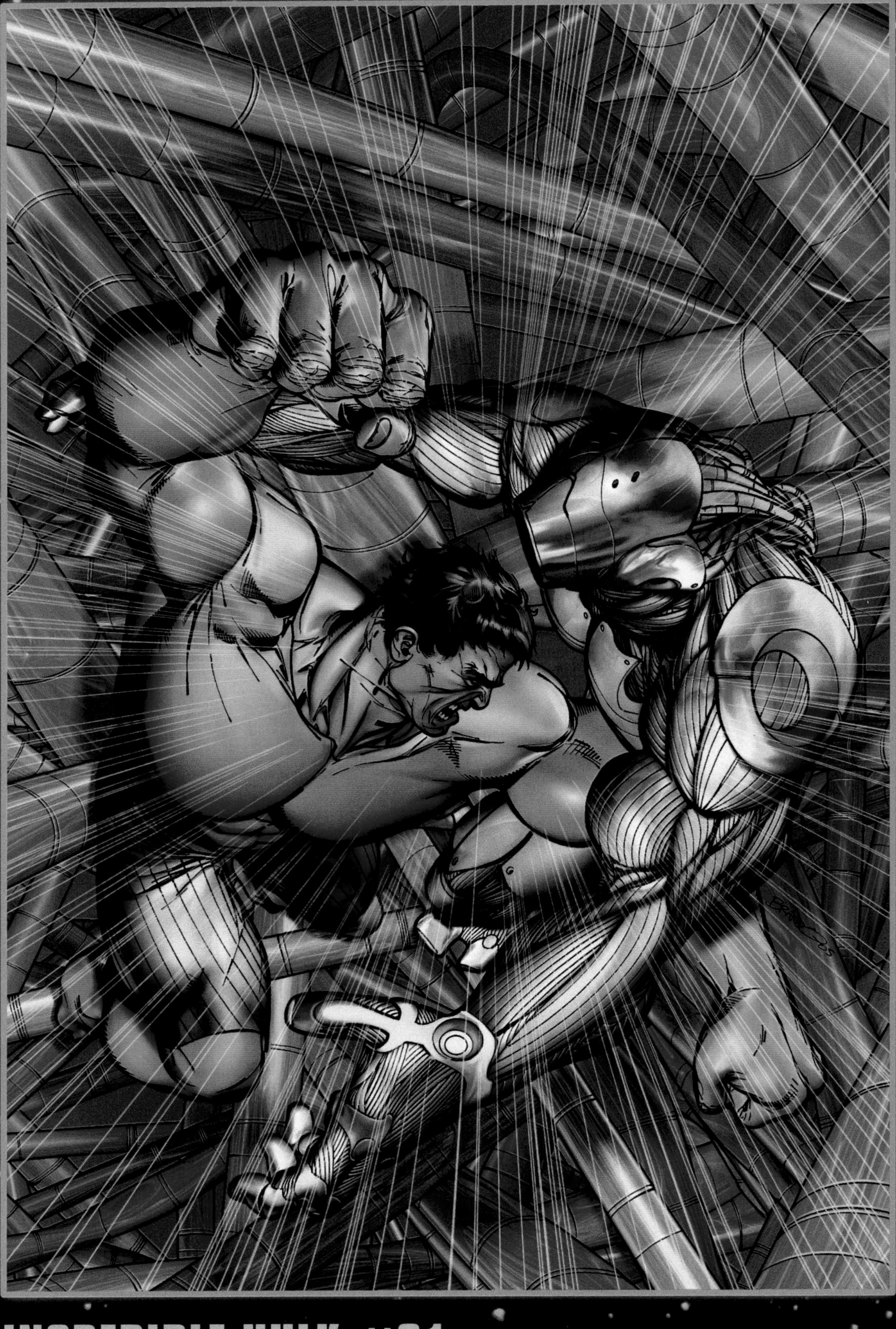

INCREDIBLE HULK #91

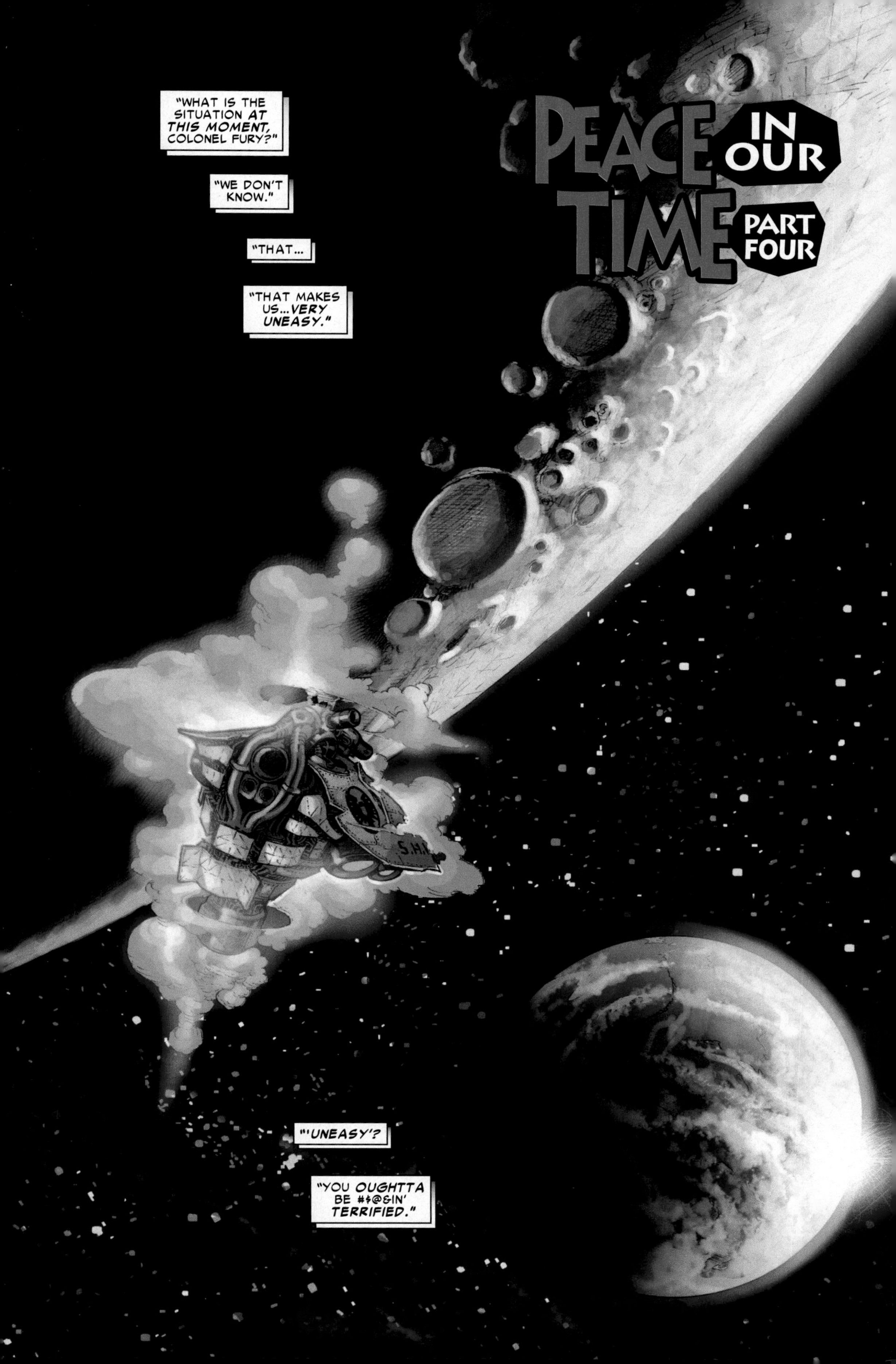
"WHAT IS THE SITUATION AT THIS MOMENT, COLONEL FURY?"
PEACE IN OUR TIME PART FOUR
"WE DON'T KNOW."
"THAT...
"THAT MAKES US...VERY UNEASY."
S.H.I.
"'UNEASY'?
"YOU OUGHTTA BE #$@&IN' TERRIFIED."

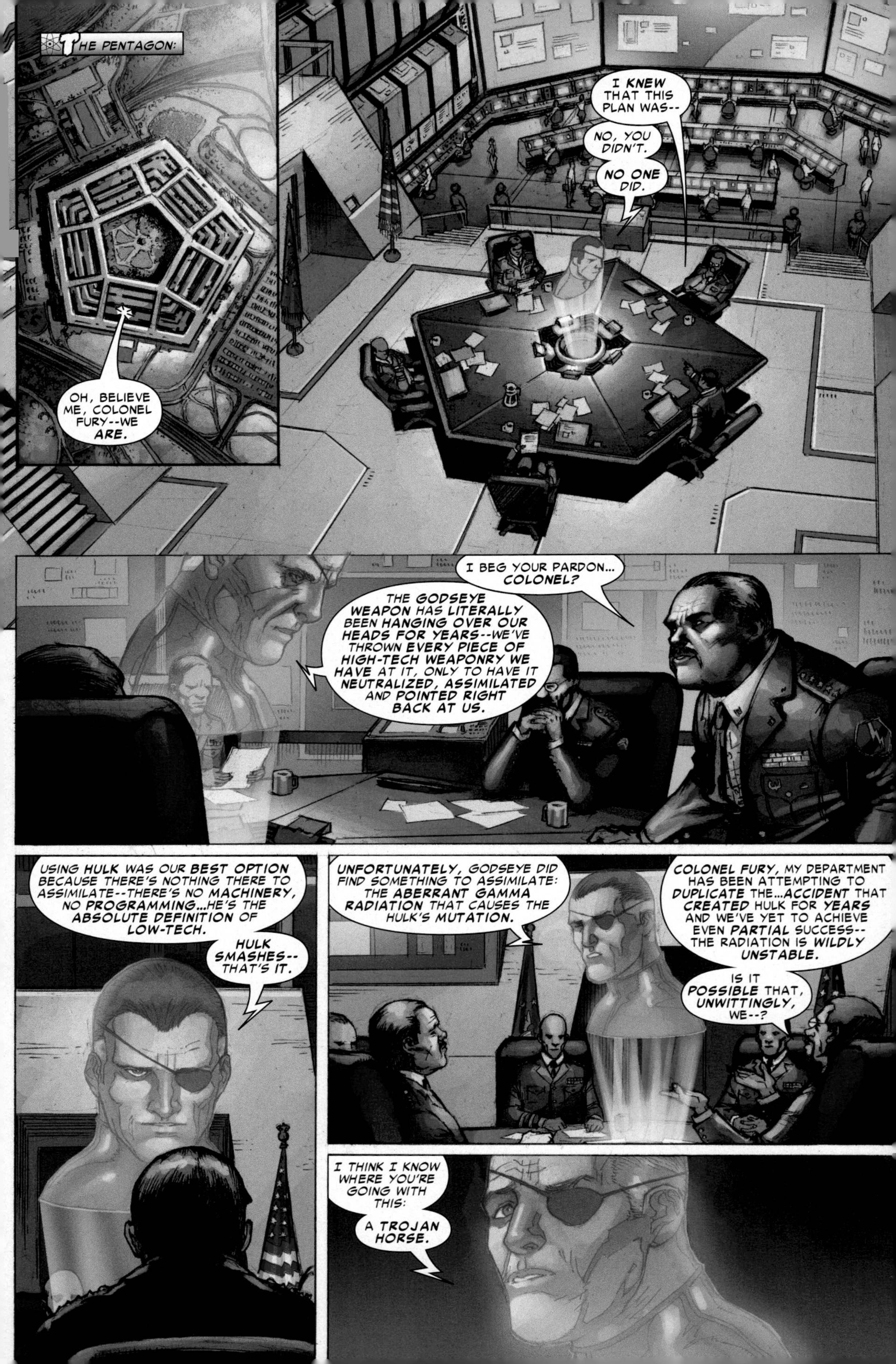
THE PENTAGON:
OH, BELIEVE ME, COLONEL FURY--WE ARE.
I KNEW THAT THIS PLAN WAS--
NO, YOU DIDN'T.
NO ONE DID.
I BEG YOUR PARDON... COLONEL?
THE GODSEYE WEAPON HAS LITERALLY BEEN HANGING OVER OUR HEADS FOR YEARS--WE'VE THROWN EVERY PIECE OF HIGH-TECH WEAPONRY WE HAVE AT IT, ONLY TO HAVE IT NEUTRALIZED, ASSIMILATED AND POINTED RIGHT BACK AT US.
USING HULK WAS OUR BEST OPTION BECAUSE THERE'S NOTHING THERE TO ASSIMILATE--THERE'S NO MACHINERY, NO PROGRAMMING...HE'S THE ABSOLUTE DEFINITION OF LOW-TECH.
HULK SMASHES--THAT'S IT.
UNFORTUNATELY, GODSEYE DID FIND SOMETHING TO ASSIMILATE: THE ABERRANT GAMMA RADIATION THAT CAUSES THE HULK'S MUTATION.
COLONEL FURY, MY DEPARTMENT HAS BEEN ATTEMPTING TO DUPLICATE THE...ACCIDENT THAT CREATED HULK FOR YEARS AND WE'VE YET TO ACHIEVE EVEN PARTIAL SUCCESS--THE RADIATION IS WILDLY UNSTABLE.
IS IT POSSIBLE THAT, UNWITTINGLY, WE--?
I THINK I KNOW WHERE YOU'RE GOING WITH THIS:
A TROJAN HORSE.

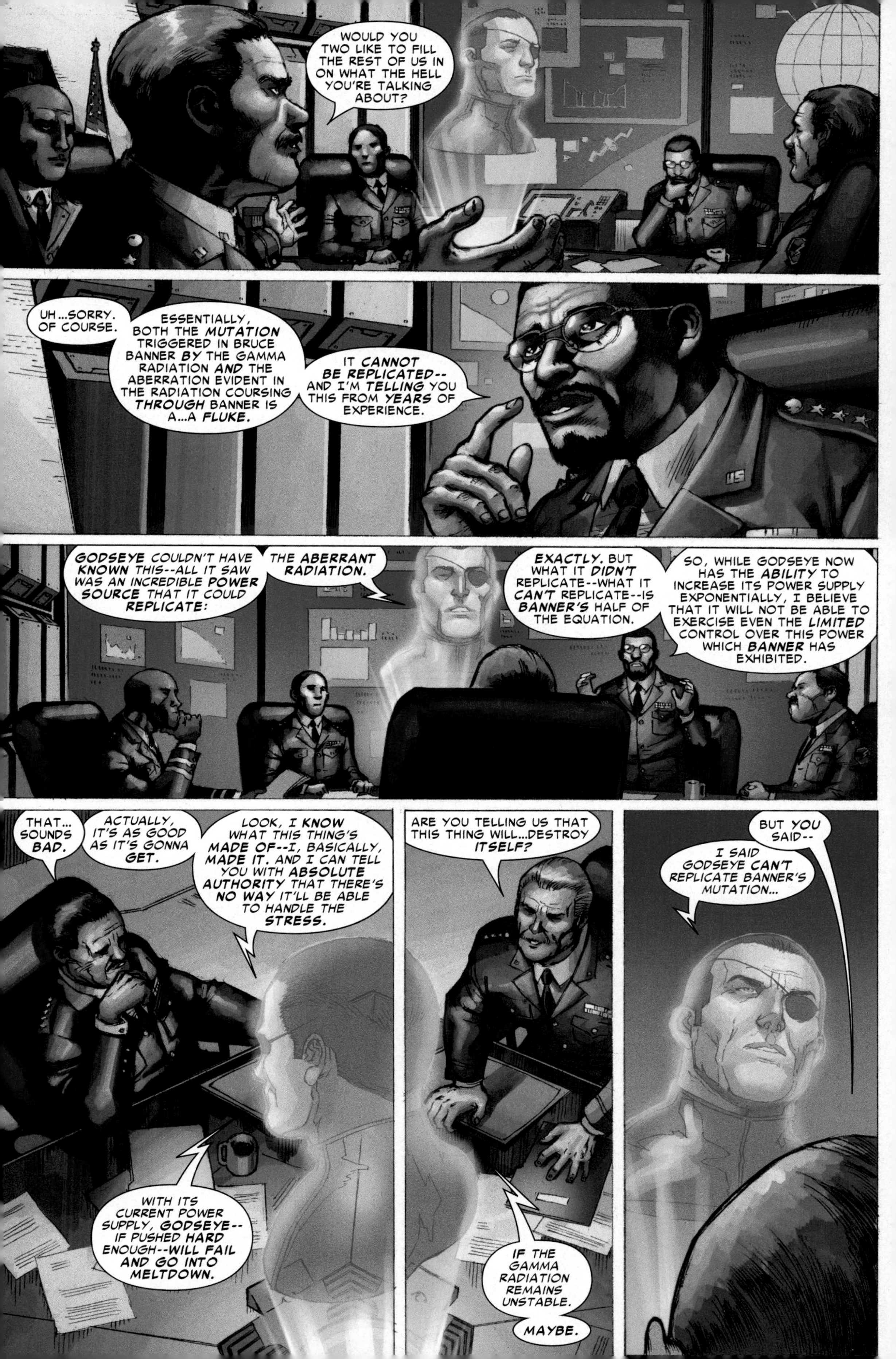
WOULD YOU TWO LIKE TO FILL THE REST OF US IN ON WHAT THE HELL YOU'RE TALKING ABOUT?
UH...SORRY. OF COURSE.
ESSENTIALLY, BOTH THE MUTATION TRIGGERED IN BRUCE BANNER BY THE GAMMA RADIATION AND THE ABERRATION EVIDENT IN THE RADIATION COURSING THROUGH BANNER IS A...A FLUKE.
IT CANNOT BE REPLICATED--AND I'M TELLING YOU THIS FROM YEARS OF EXPERIENCE.
GODSEYE COULDN'T HAVE KNOWN THIS--ALL IT SAW WAS AN INCREDIBLE POWER SOURCE THAT IT COULD REPLICATE:
THE ABERRANT RADIATION.
EXACTLY. BUT WHAT IT DIDN'T REPLICATE--WHAT IT CAN'T REPLICATE--IS BANNER'S HALF OF THE EQUATION.
SO, WHILE GODSEYE NOW HAS THE ABILITY TO INCREASE ITS POWER SUPPLY EXPONENTIALLY, I BELIEVE THAT IT WILL NOT BE ABLE TO EXERCISE EVEN THE LIMITED CONTROL OVER THIS POWER WHICH BANNER HAS EXHIBITED.
THAT... SOUNDS BAD.
ACTUALLY, IT'S AS GOOD AS IT'S GONNA GET.
LOOK, I KNOW WHAT THIS THING'S MADE OF--I, BASICALLY, MADE IT. AND I CAN TELL YOU WITH ABSOLUTE AUTHORITY THAT THERE'S NO WAY IT'LL BE ABLE TO HANDLE THE STRESS.
WITH ITS CURRENT POWER SUPPLY, GODSEYE--IF PUSHED HARD ENOUGH--WILL FAIL AND GO INTO MELTDOWN.
ARE YOU TELLING US THAT THIS THING WILL...DESTROY ITSELF?
IF THE GAMMA RADIATION REMAINS UNSTABLE.
MAYBE.
BUT YOU SAID--
I SAID GODSEYE CAN'T REPLICATE BANNER'S MUTATION...

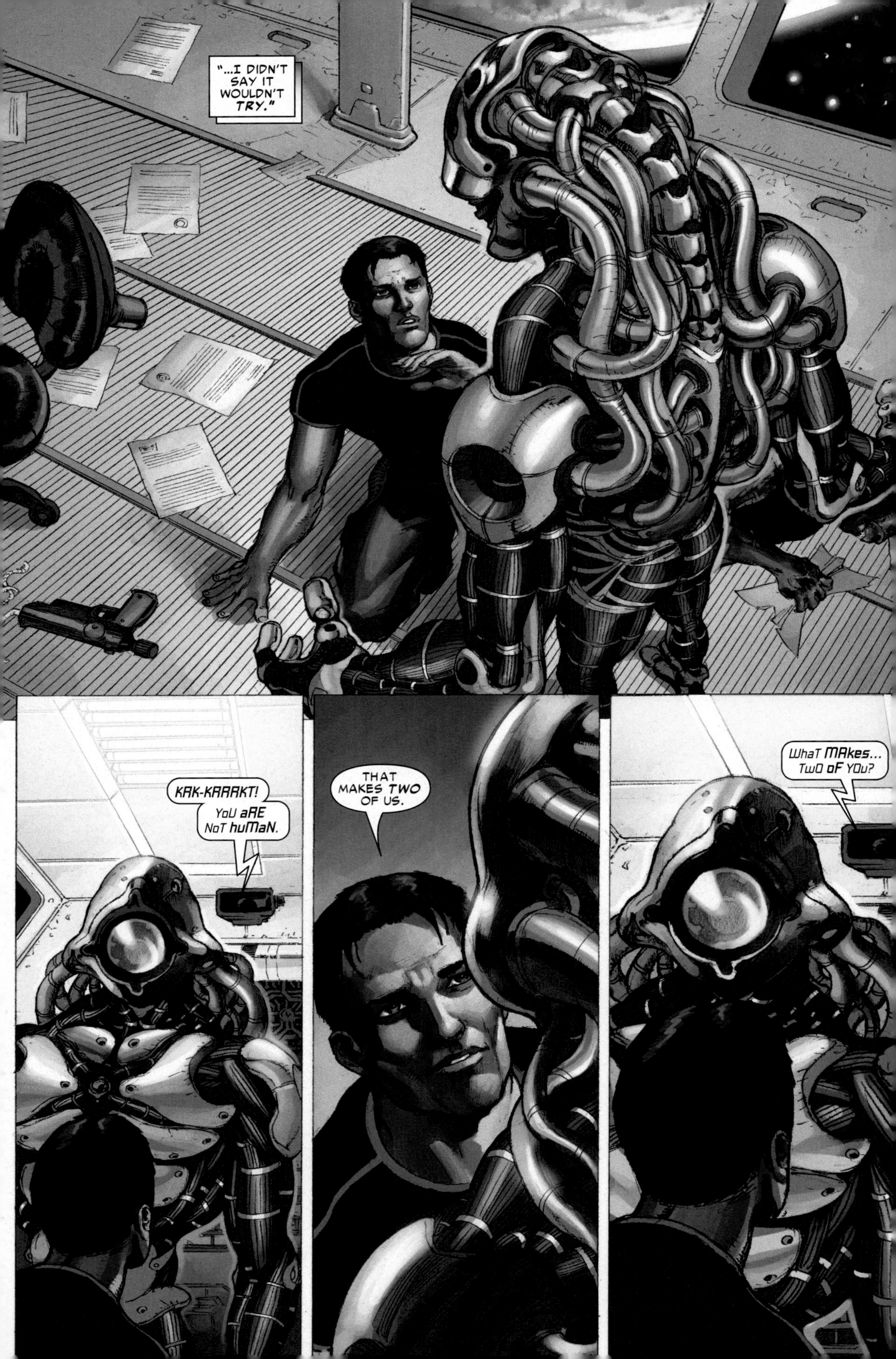
"...I DIDN'T SAY IT WOULDN'T TRY."
KRK-KRRRKT!
YoU aRE NoT huMaN.
THAT MAKES TWO OF US.
WhaT MAkes... TwO oF YOu?

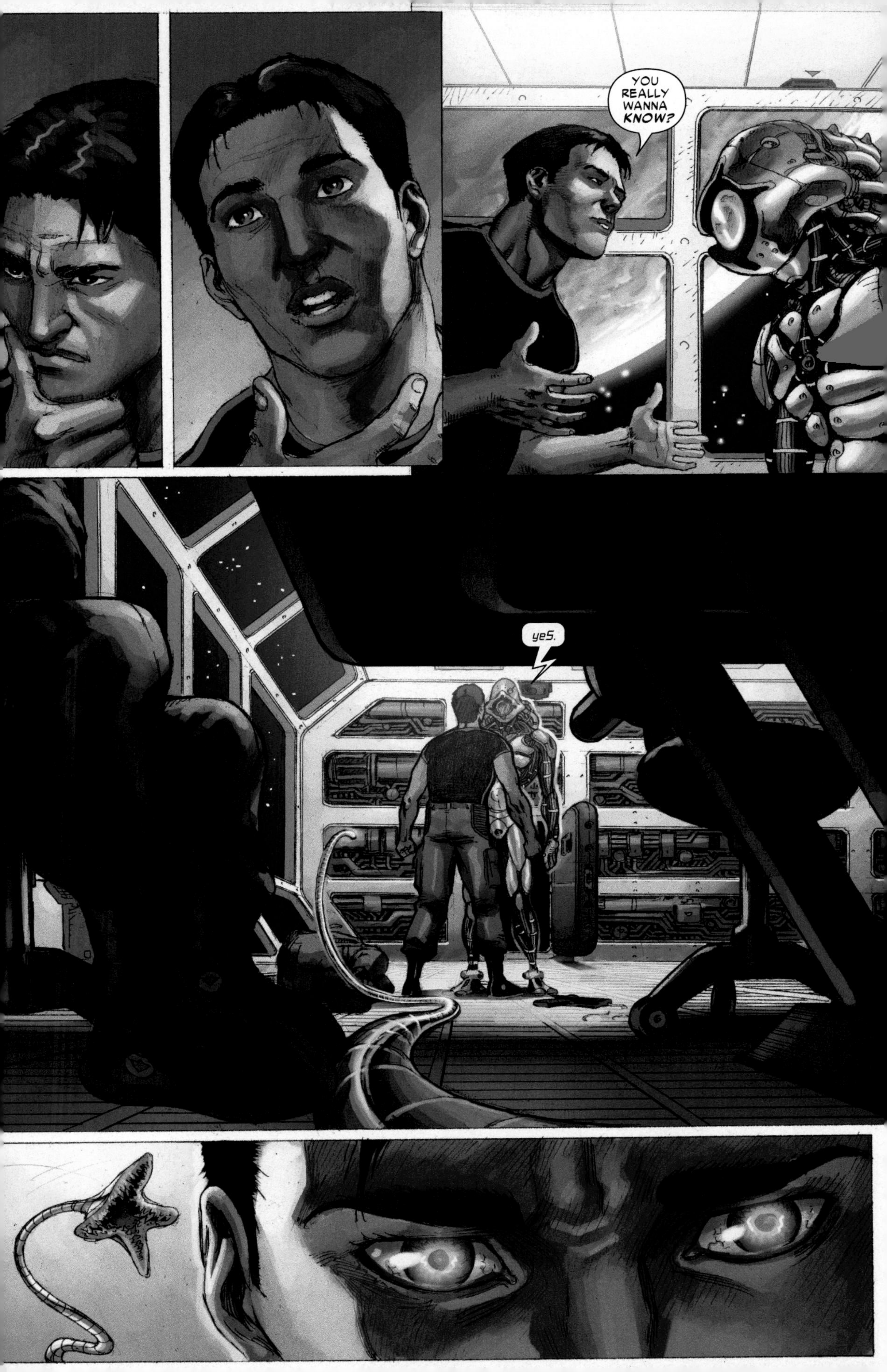
YOU REALLY WANNA KNOW?
yes.

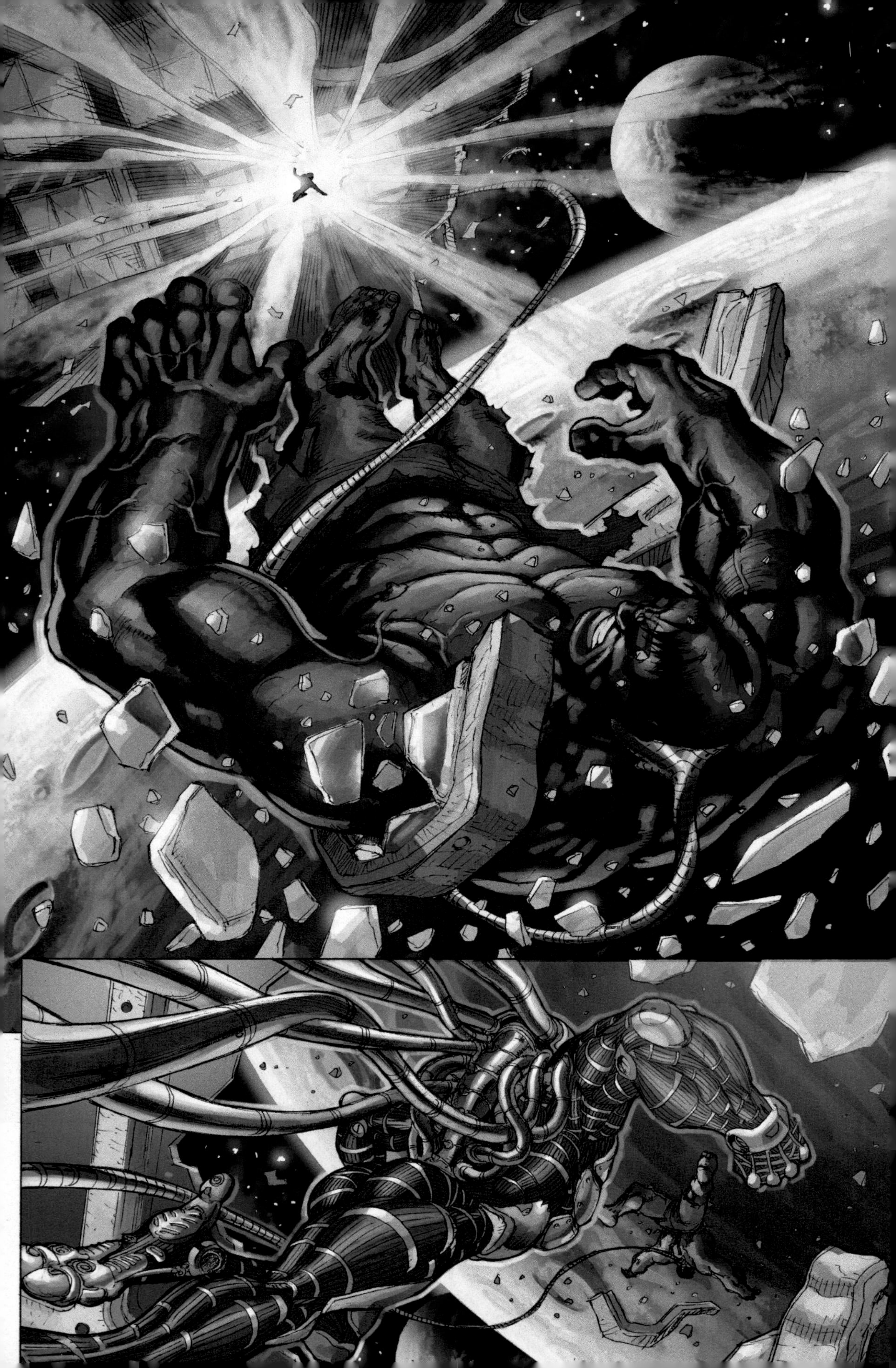

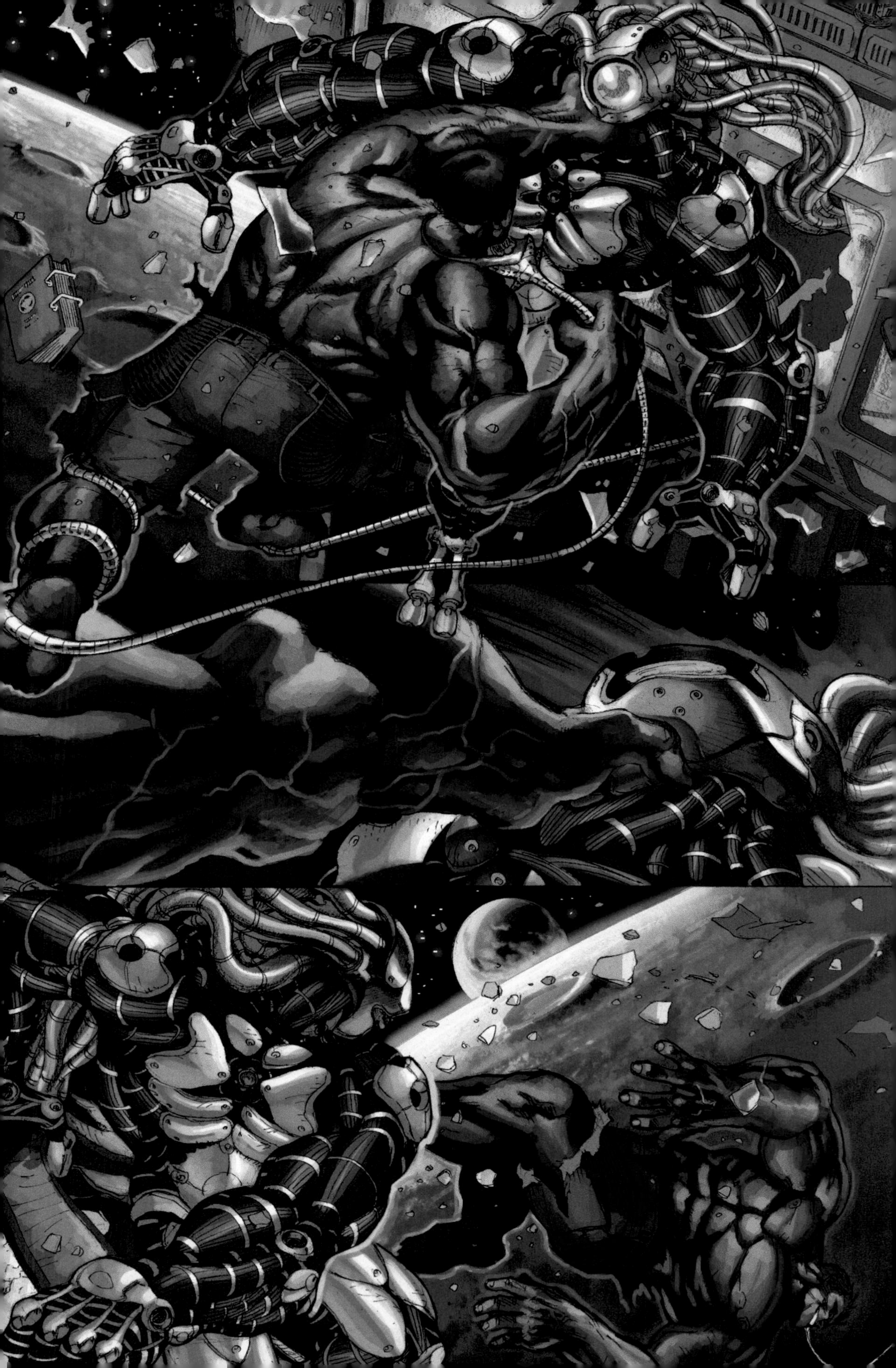

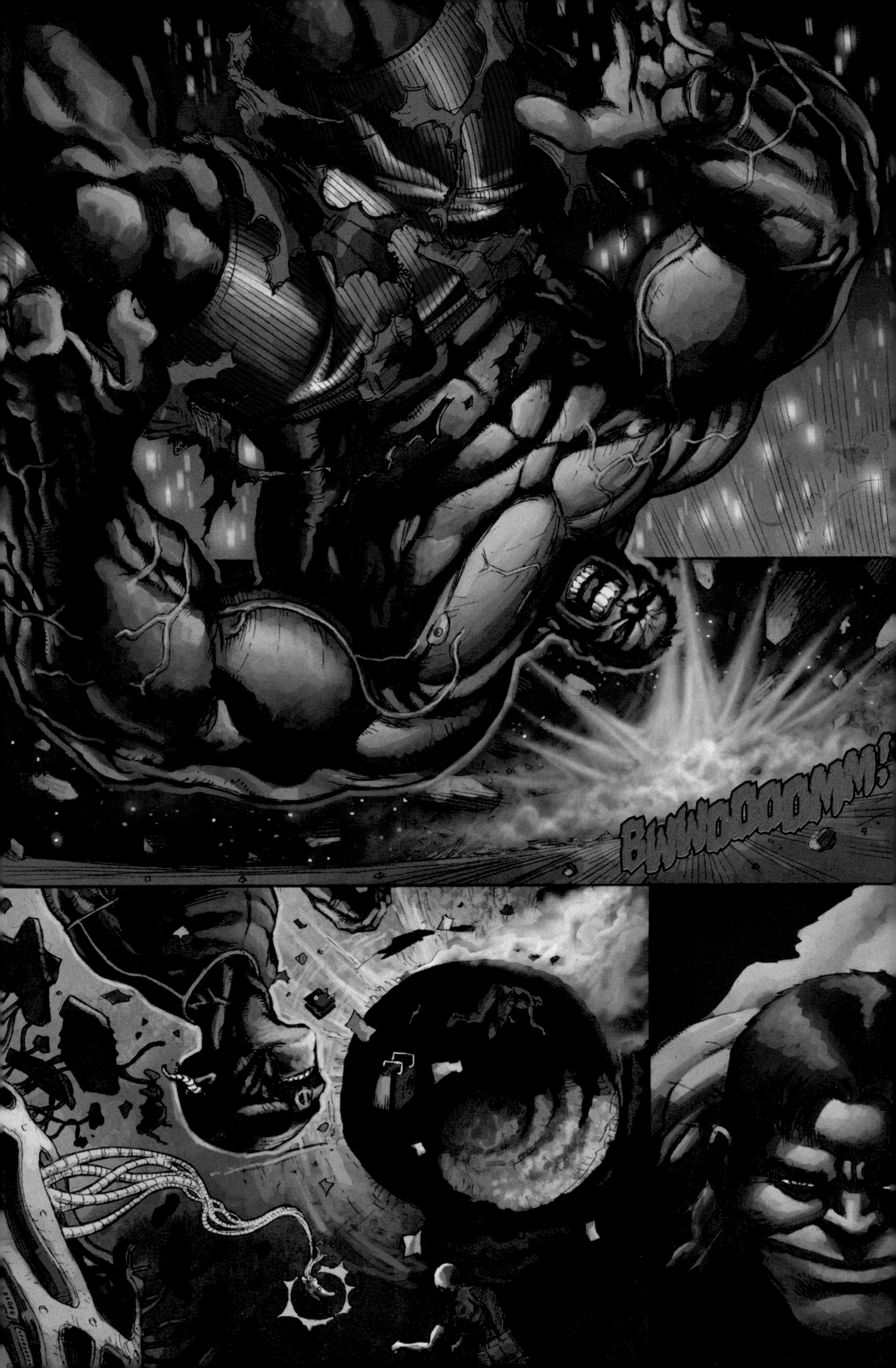
BWWOOOOMM!

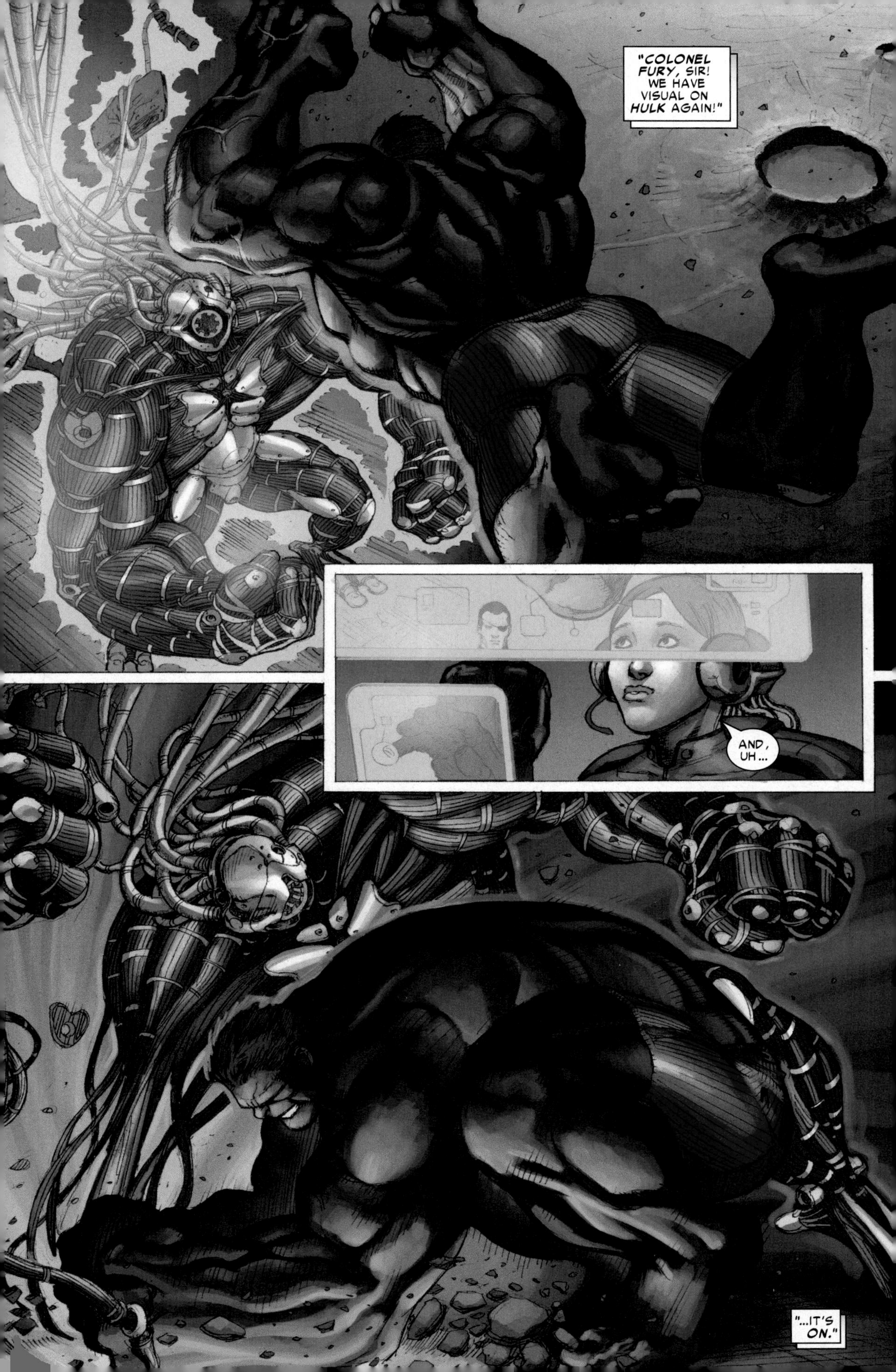
"COLONEL FURY, SIR! WE HAVE VISUAL ON HULK AGAIN!"
AND, UH...
"...IT'S ON."

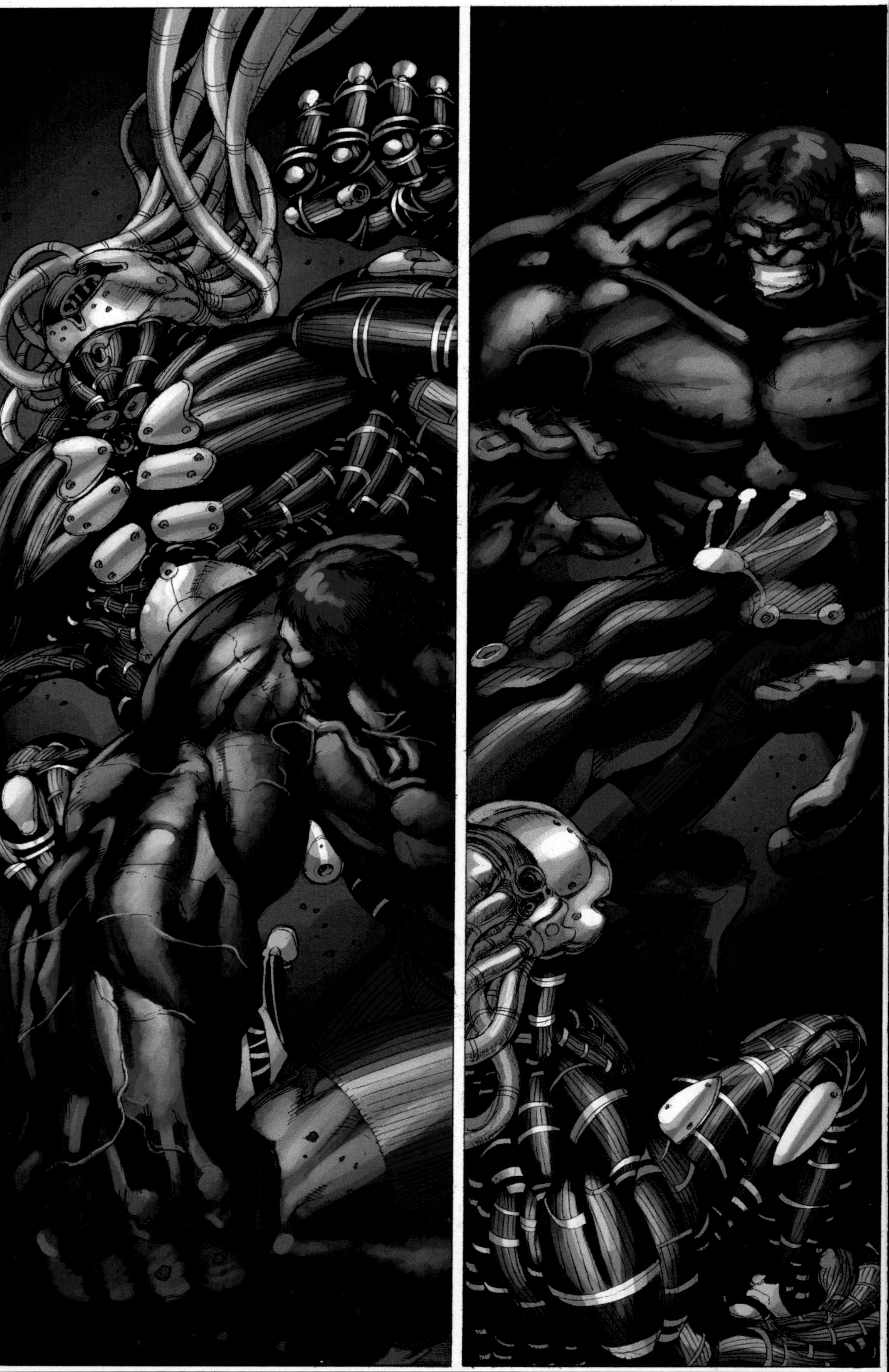

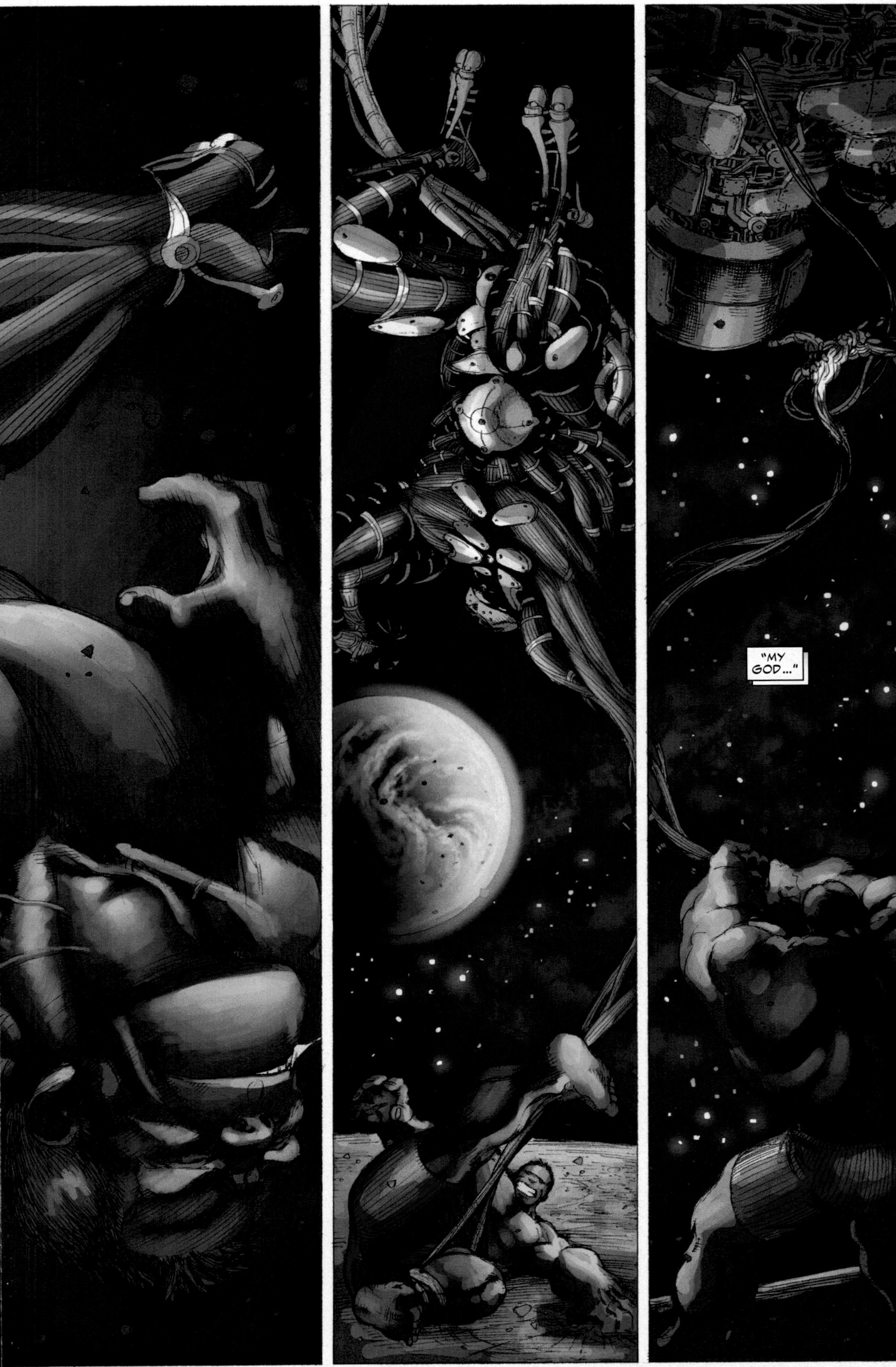
"MY GOD..."

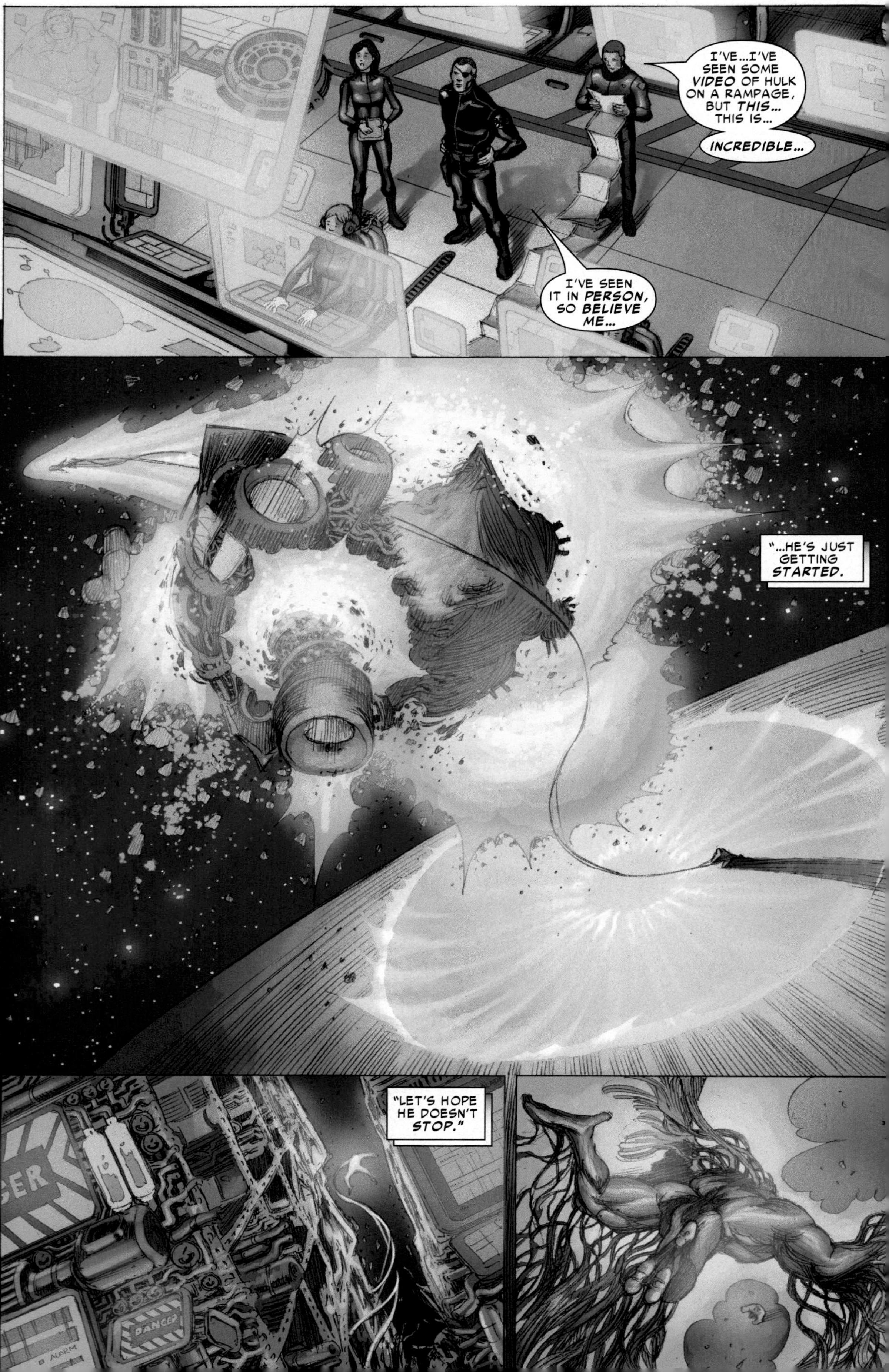
I'VE...I'VE SEEN SOME VIDEO OF HULK ON A RAMPAGE, BUT THIS... THIS IS...
INCREDIBLE...
I'VE SEEN IT IN PERSON, SO BELIEVE ME...
"...HE'S JUST GETTING STARTED.
"LET'S HOPE HE DOESN'T STOP."

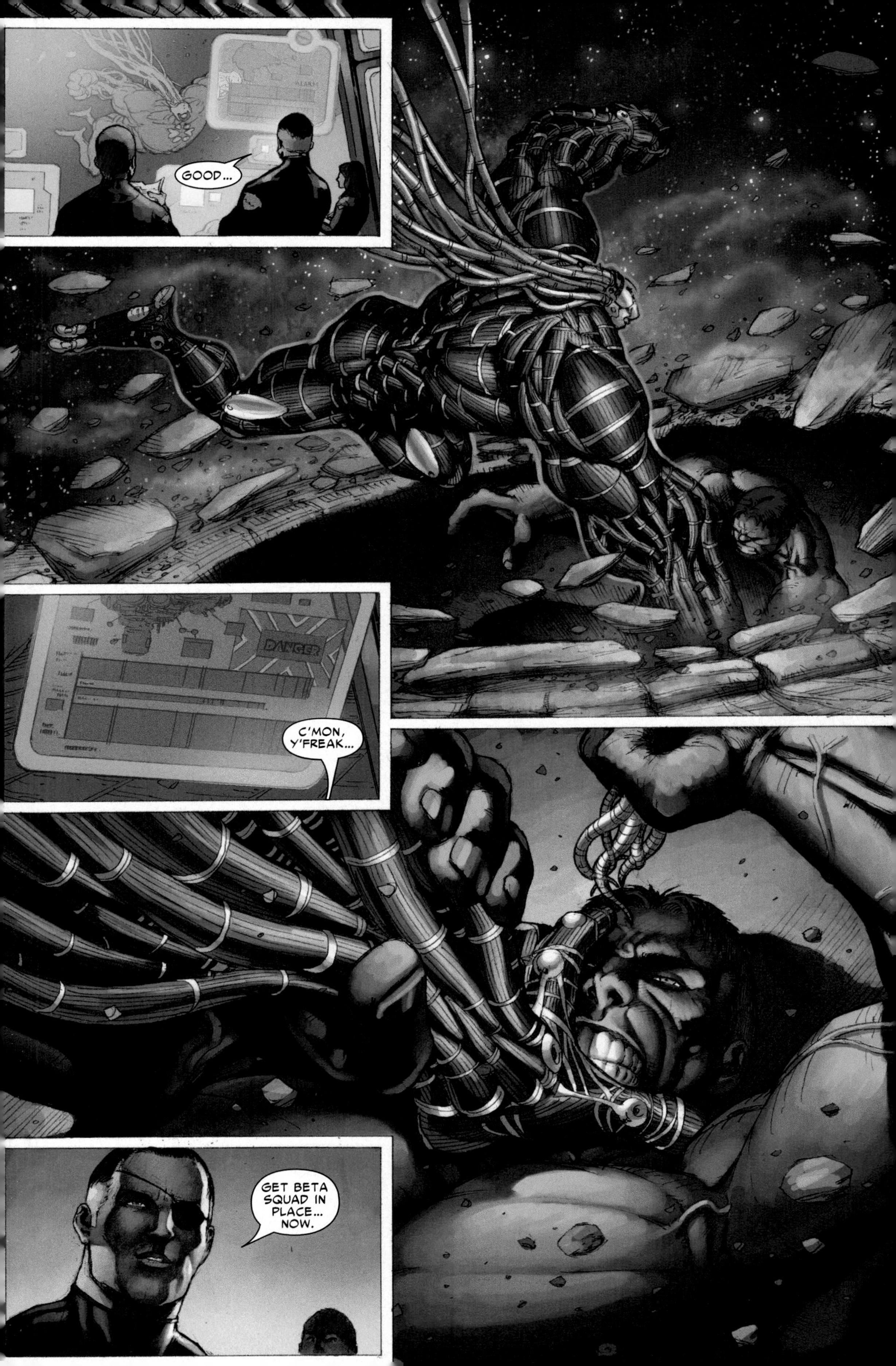

GOOD...
ALARM
DANGER
C'MON, Y'FREAK...
GET BETA SQUAD IN PLACE... NOW.

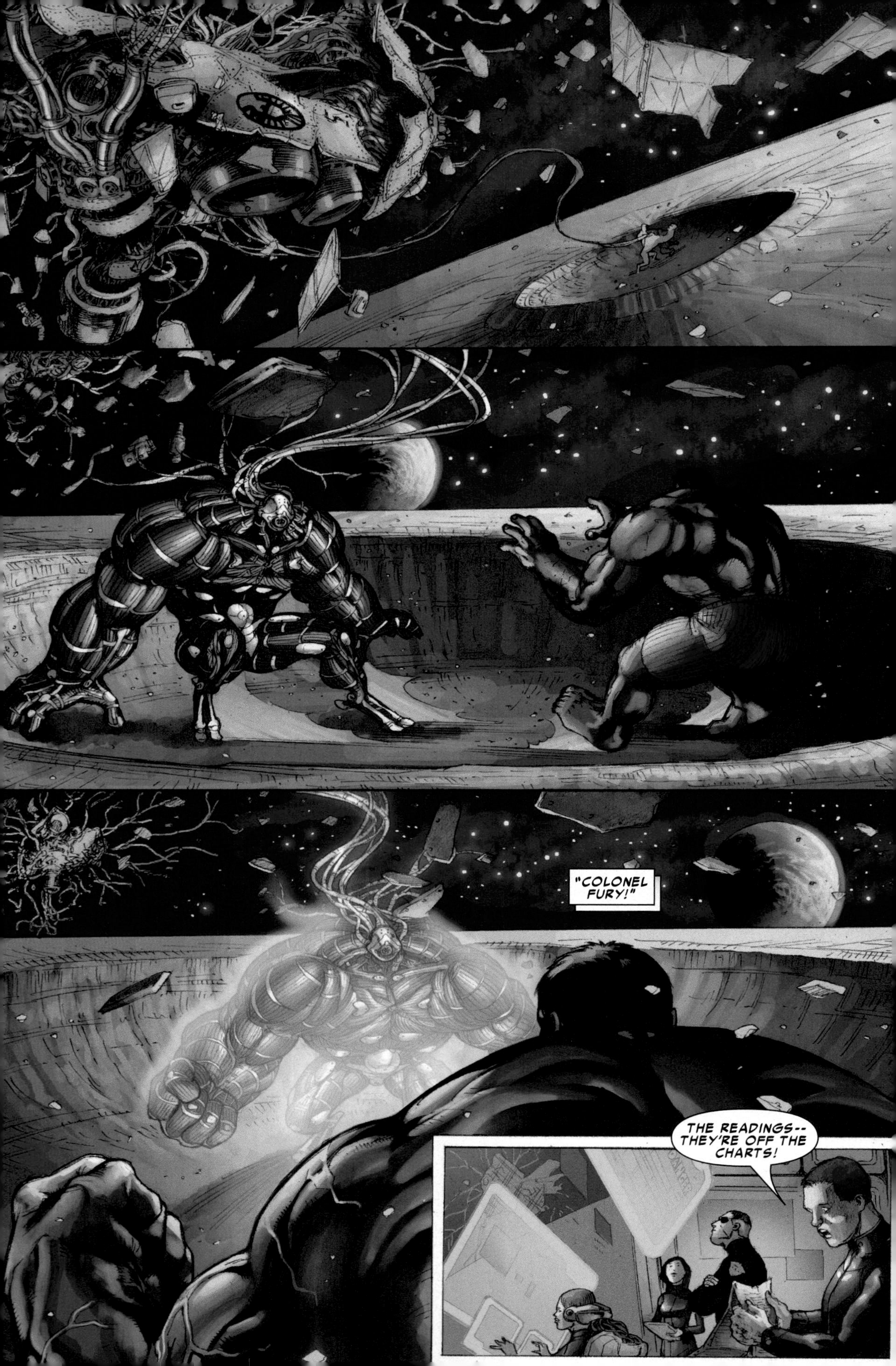
"COLONEL FURY!"
THE READINGS-- THEY'RE OFF THE CHARTS!

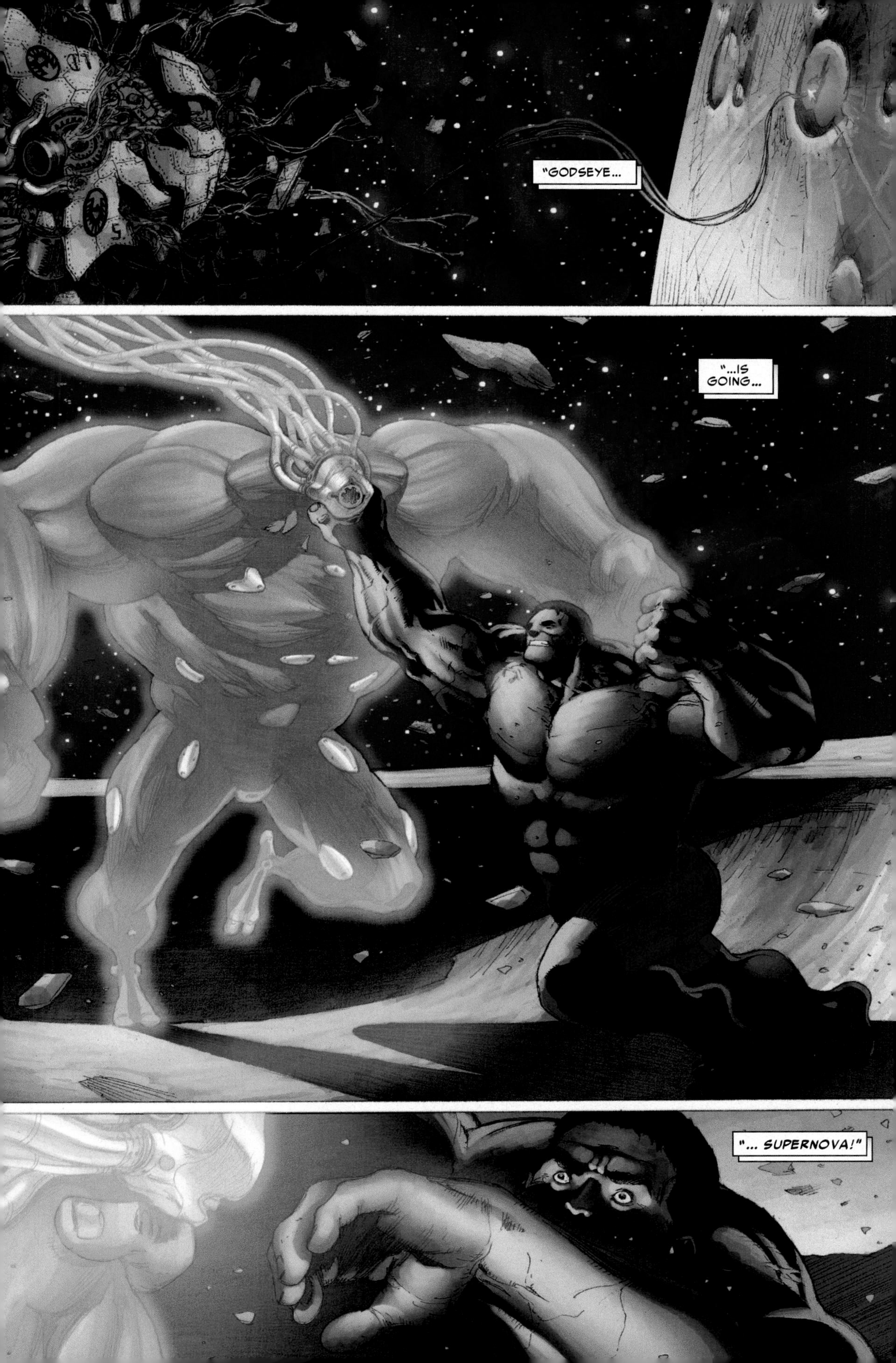
"GODSEYE...
"...IS GOING...
"... SUPERNOVA!"

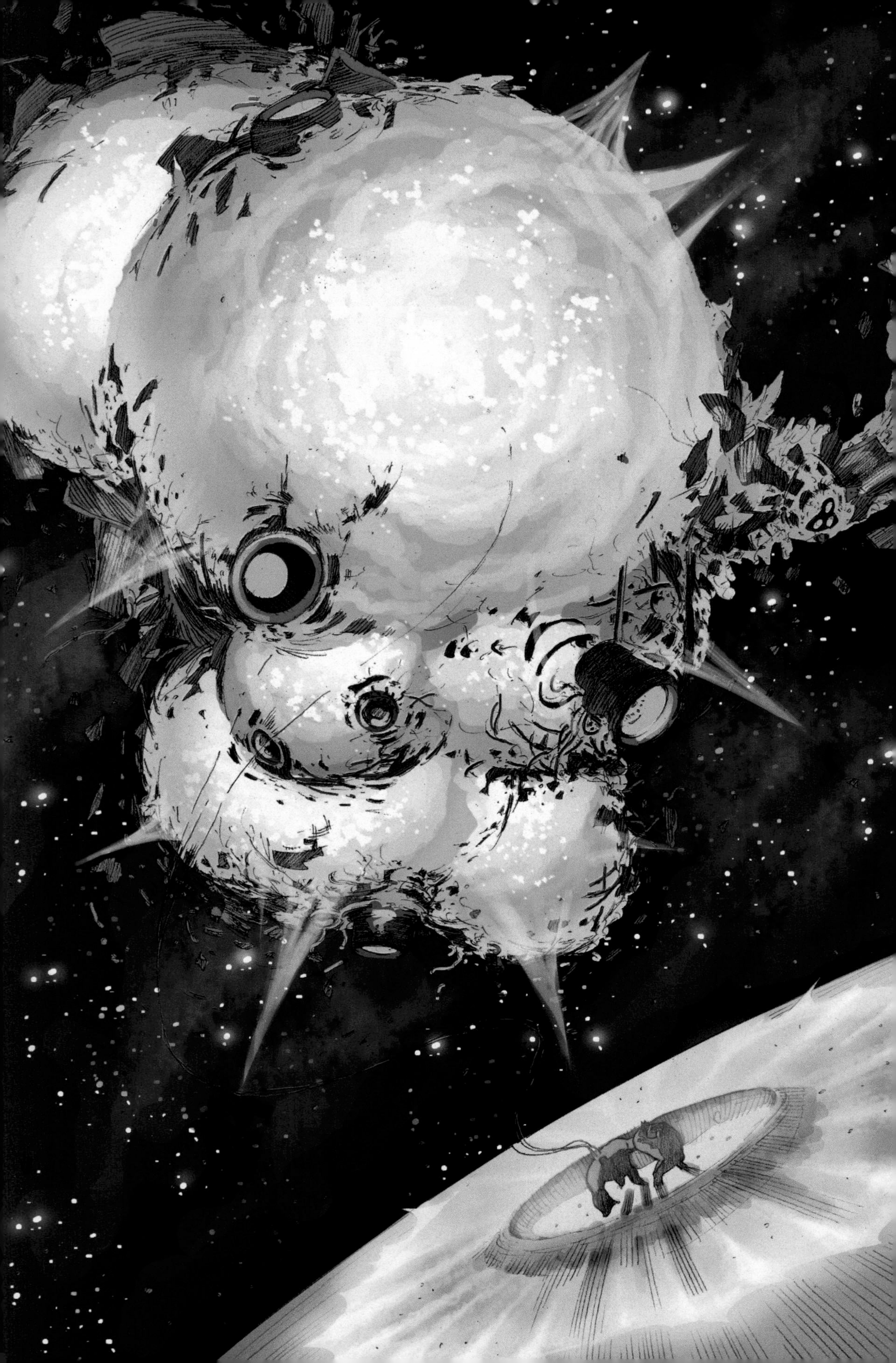

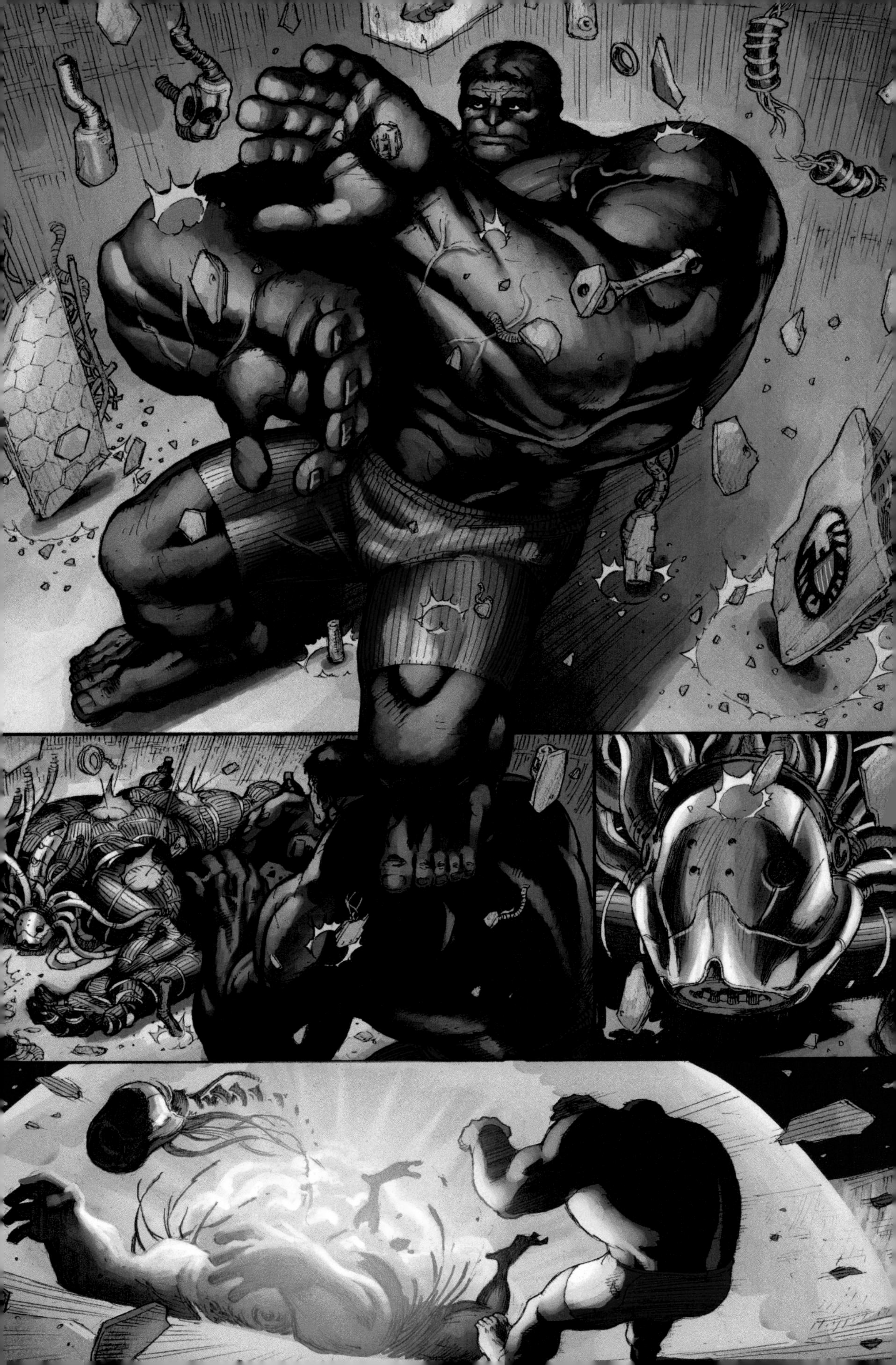

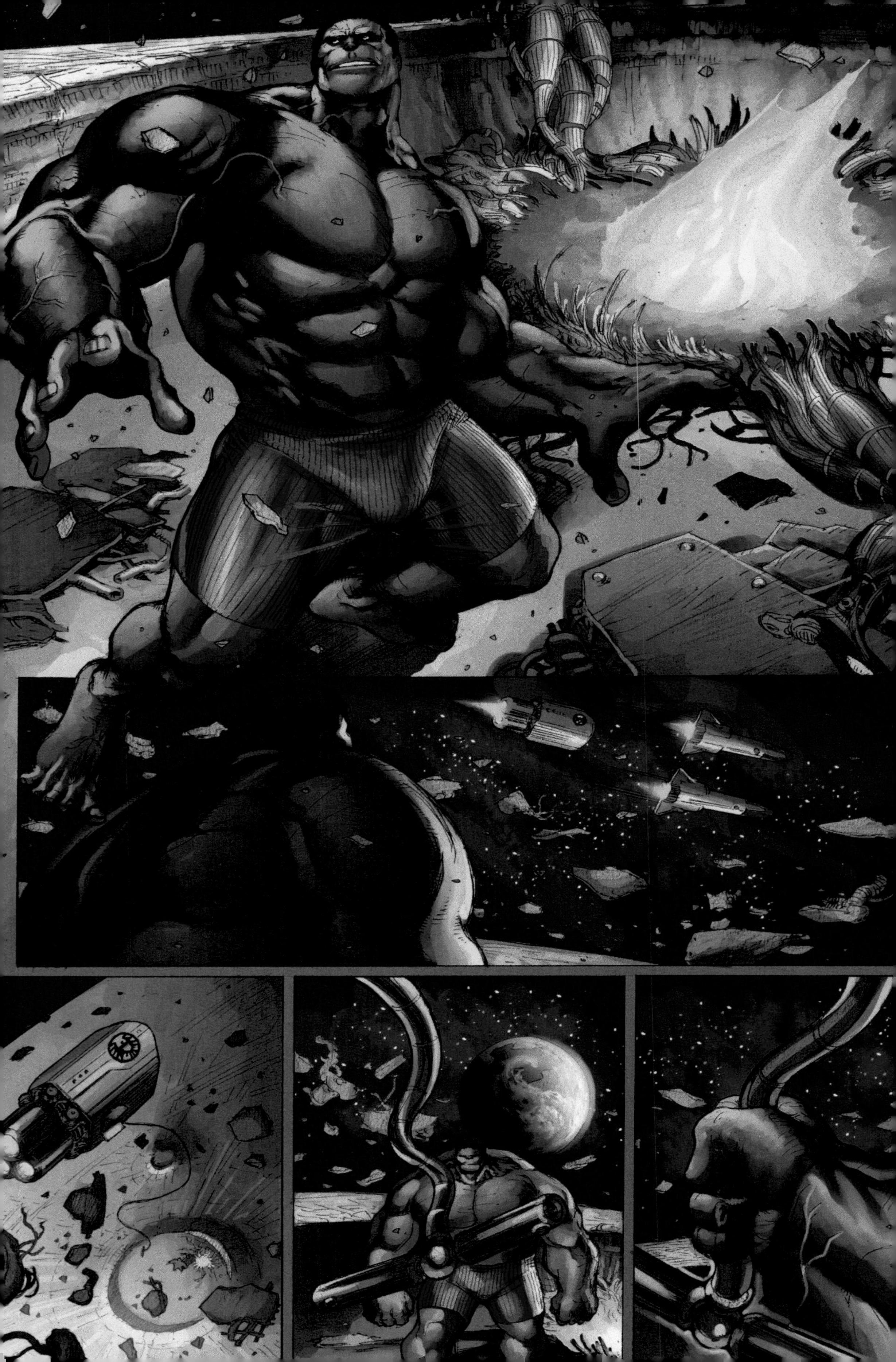

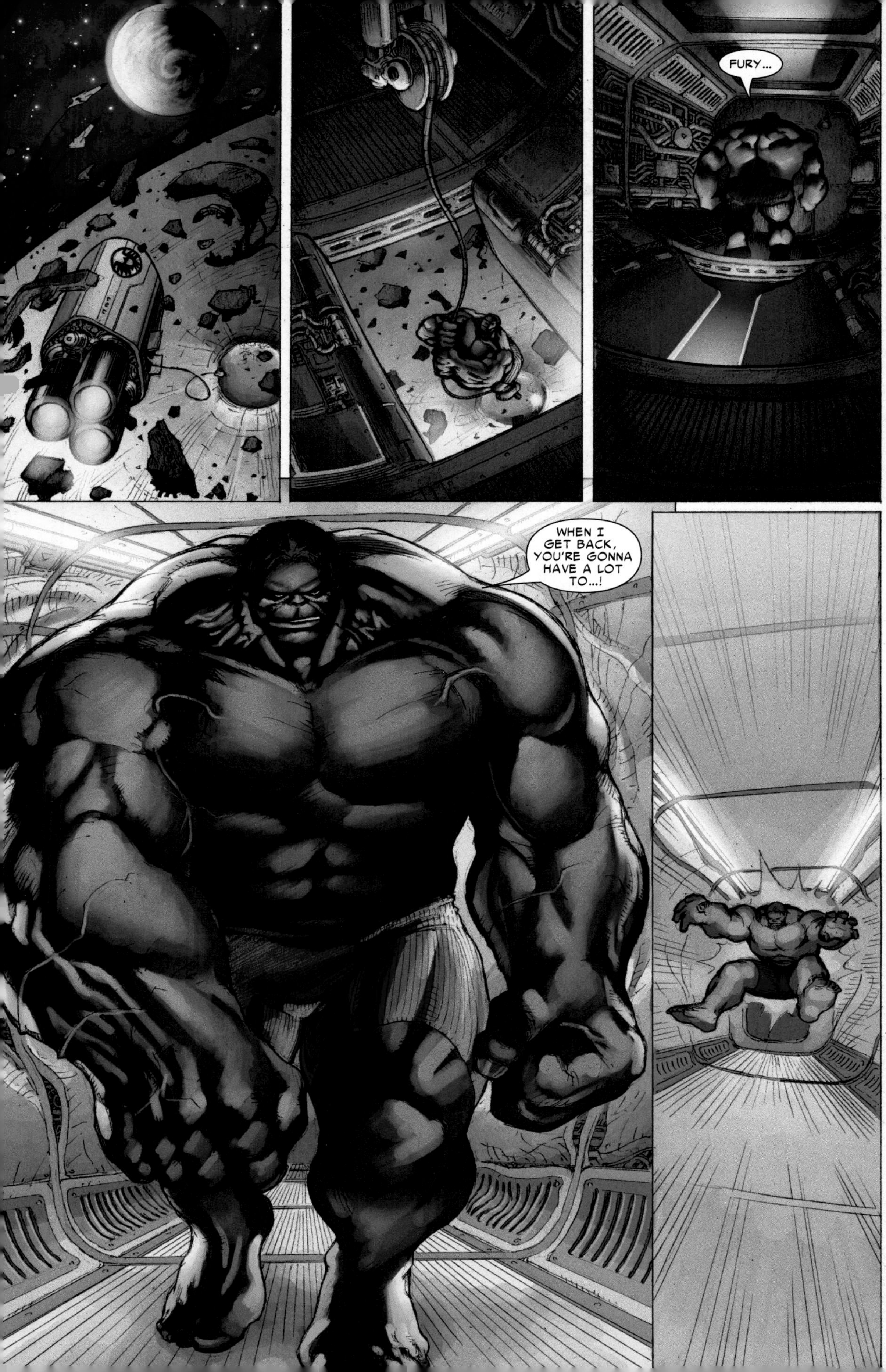
FURY...
WHEN I GET BACK, YOU'RE GONNA HAVE A LOT TO...!

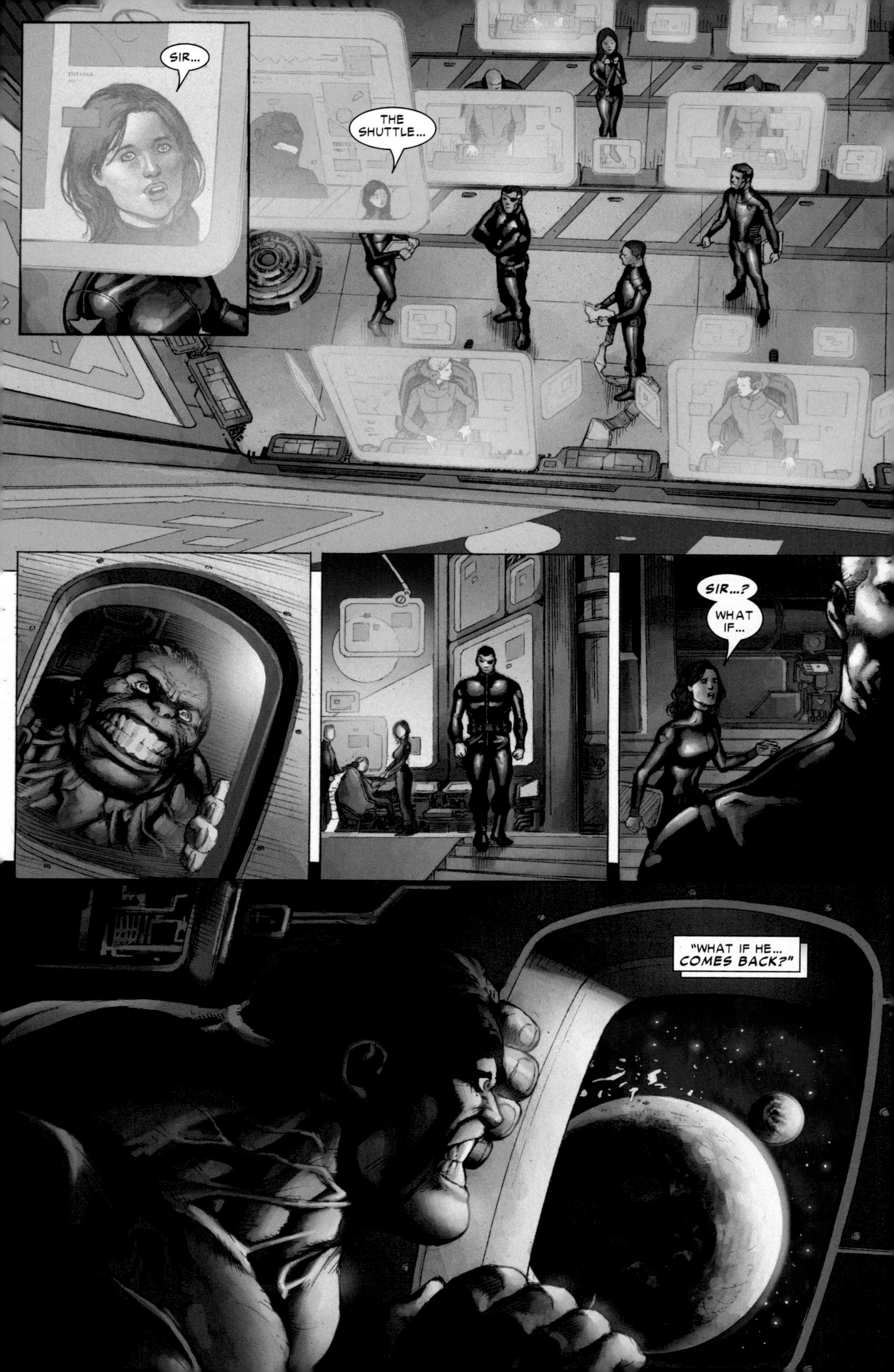

SIR...
THE SHUTTLE...
SIR...?
WHAT IF...
"WHAT IF HE... COMES BACK?"

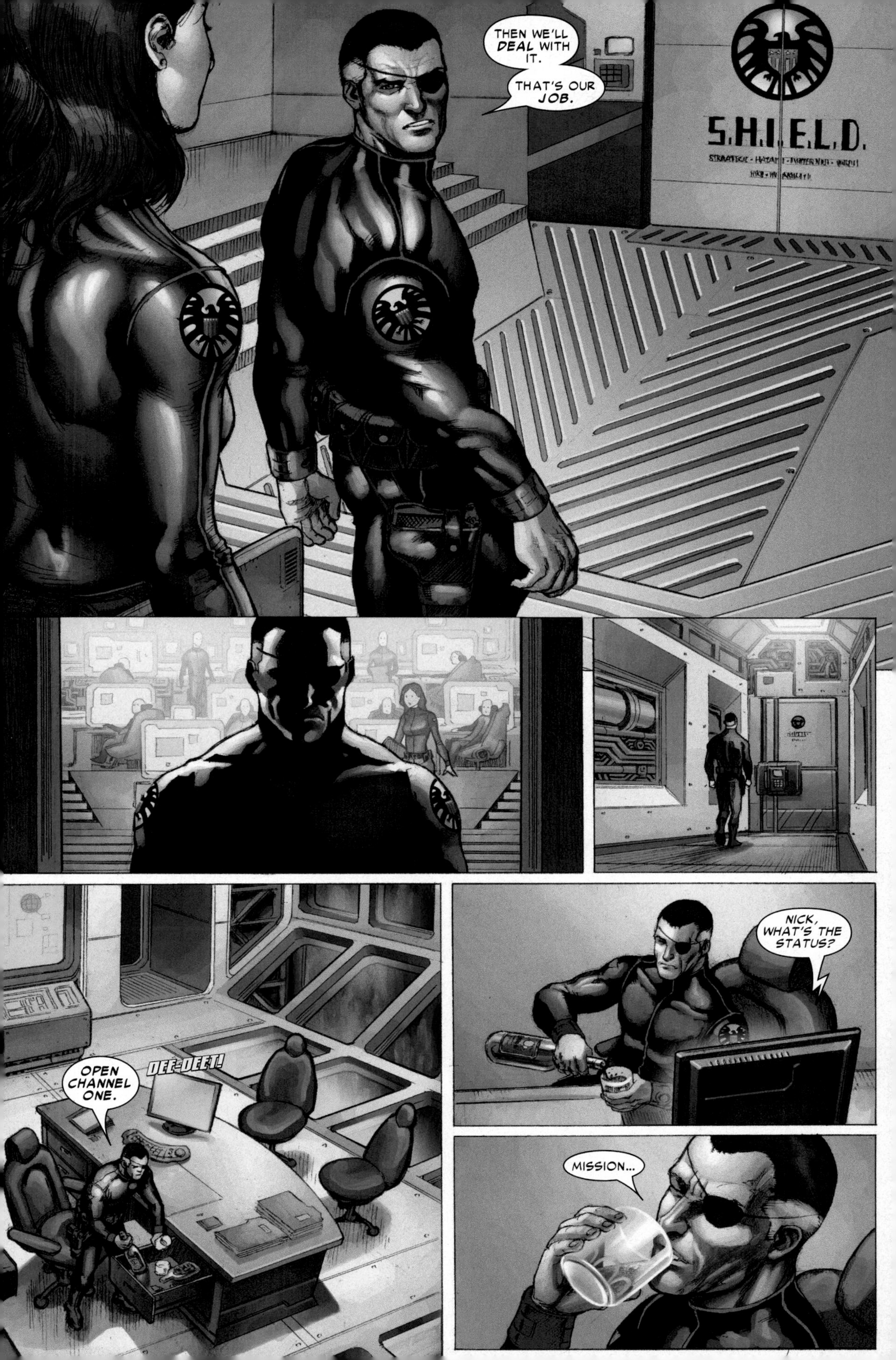
THEN WE'LL DEAL WITH IT.
THAT'S OUR JOB.
S.H.I.E.L.D.
OPEN CHANNEL ONE.
DEE-DEET!
NICK, WHAT'S THE STATUS?
MISSION...

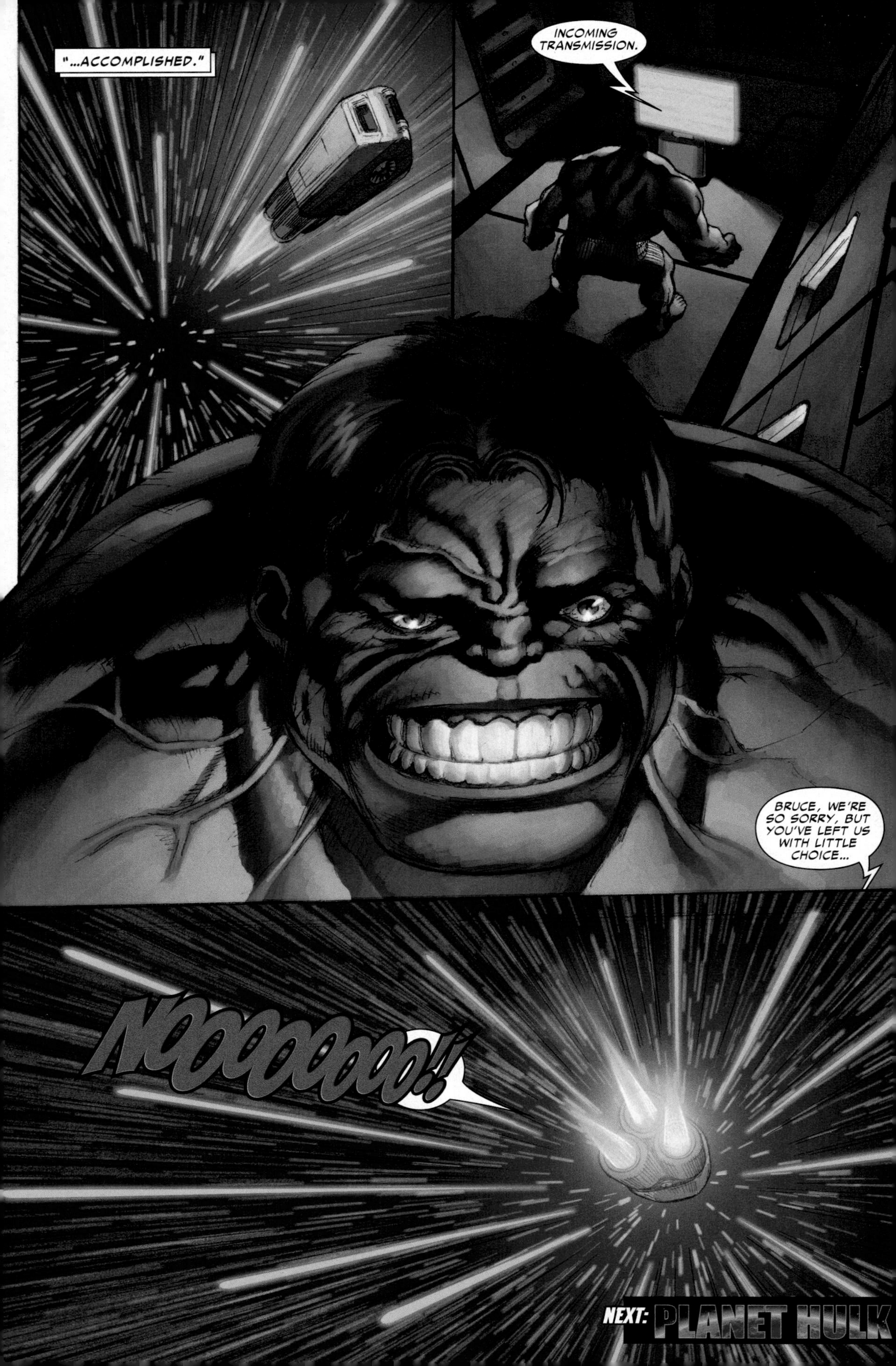
"...ACCOMPLISHED."
INCOMING TRANSMISSION.
BRUCE, WE'RE SO SORRY, BUT YOU'VE LEFT US WITH LITTLE CHOICE...
NOOOOOOO!!
NEXT: PLANET HULK